War
on
Privacy

War on Privacy

Edited by Lester A. Sobel

Contributing editors: Joseph Fickes, Mary Elizabeth Clifford,
Stephen Orlofsky, Gerry Satterwhite
Indexed by Grace M. Ferrara

FACTS ON FILE, INC. NEW YORK, N.Y.

War
on
Privacy

Library of Congress Catalog Card Number 75-43354
ISBN 0-87196-289-6

9 8 7 6 5 4 3 2 1
PRINTED IN
THE UNITED STATES OF AMERICA

Contents

Privacy Under Attack

THE HARD-WON AMERICAN RIGHT OF PRIVACY is again under attack. Federal, state and city investigators spend millions of hours each year keeping track of criminals, suspected revolutionaries, alleged tax cheats, possible spies and other persons believed to endanger society. But ordinary, non-criminal citizens are also subjected to surveillance or other data-seeking intrusion in thousands of instances every day, and these wholesale invasions of our privacy are performed by unofficial as well as government functionaries.

Department stores, seeking to prevent shop-lifting, have used one-way mirrors and closed-circuit television cameras to spy on customers as they tried on clothes. Many companies have used similar surveillance methods to prevent theft by their own personnel. Businessmen routinely tape-record conversations with customers, suppliers, employes and other associates. They hire private detectives to provide information about competitors, workers and their own partners. Shoppers seeking credit for normal purchases undergo at least cursory investigation through credit bureaus that, over the years, have built up computerized dossiers on millions of Americans. Such a dossier may contain detailed—and possibly incorrect—data on the subject's health, sex life, education, police record, juvenile misdeeds and associates as well as on his history of paying or failing to pay his debts. Job-hunters in private industry expect their prospective employers to make at least some effort to check into their backgrounds, and the federal government uses the FBI or other intelligence agencies to investigate job applicants and taxpayers as well as criminals and other public enemies. Files maintained on unoffending citizens are often filled with intimate, detrimental information that in at least some cases may turn out to be wildly erroneous and can result in serious injustice. In all but a very few cases, the subjects of the dossiers do not know what information appears in their files. They may be unaware that the files on them even exist.

Newsweek reported in its issue of July 27, 1970 that "over the past twenty years, the U.S. has become (partly of necessity and mostly for good reasons) one of the snoopiest and most data-conscious nations in the history of the world. Big merchants, little merchants, tax bureaus, police organizations, census takers, sociologists, banks, schools, medical groups, employers, federal agencies, newspapers, motor-vehicle bureaus, insurance companies, clubs, mail-order houses, credit bureaus, pollsters, advertisers, mortgage lenders, public utilities, the armed forces—every blessed one of them and scores of other organizations have been chasing down, storing and putting to use every scrap of information they can find about all 205 million Americans, singly and in groups."

The age of the computer has made this tremendous and growing mass of information—accurate or inaccurate, evaluated or unevaluated, legally obtained or illegally obtained—instantly available to the many people who know where to buy it or who can make the necessary arrangements for securing it through other means. Once such information is obtained—often without the knowledge, let alone the authority, of the person it purports to describe—it can be used to the detriment of the subject as easily as to his advantage.

Because of the importance of computers in collecting, organizing and disseminating information about people, the Institute of Computer Sciences & Technology of the National Bureau of Standards held two conferences on the subject of privacy and security in computer systems. Speaking to several hundred computer specialists and information users in the federal, state and private sectors, Dr. Ruth Davis, director of the institute, outlined the essential differences in the principles of privacy, confidentiality and security with respect to record-keeping and computers:

Privacy is a concept which applies to *individuals*. In essence, it defines the degree to which an individual wishes to interact with his social environment and manifests itself in the willingness with which an individual will share information about himself with others. This concept conflicts with the trend toward collecting and storing personal information in support of social programs of various importance. The government's role often makes the supplying of this information mandatory—thus, creating a direct and acute compromise of the individual's privacy. Under this circumstance, the burden of protecting personal data is all the more important.

Confidentiality is a concept that applies to data. It describes the status accorded to data and the degree of protection that must be provided for it. It is the protection of data confidentiality that is one of the objects of *security*. Data confidentiality applies not only to data about individuals but to any proprietary or sensitive data that must be treated in confidence.

Security is the realization of protection for the data, the mechanisms and resources used in processing data, and the security mechanism(s) themselves. *Data security* is the protection of data against accidental or unauthorized destruction, modification or disclosure using both physical security measures and controlled accessibility techniques. *Physical security* is the protection of all computer facilities against all physical threats (*e.g.,* damage or loss from accident, theft, malicious action, fire and other environmental hazards). Physical security techniques involve the use of locks, badges (for personnel identification), guards, personnel security clearances and administrative measures to control the ability and means to approach, communicate with, or otherwise make use of, any material or component of a data processing system. *Controlled accessibility* is the term applied to the protection provided to data and computational resources by hardware and software mechanisms of the computer itself.

From these definitions, it is possible to see that there is no *direct* relationship between privacy (a desire by individuals, groups or organizations to control the collection, use or dissemination of information about them) and security (the realization of the protection of resources), although they are interrelated. . . .

In a June 16, 1975 discussion in the House of Representatives, Rep. Robert F. Drinan (D, Mass.) declared that "when the newspapers and the committees of Congress only a few years ago began to uncover the surveillance activities of the Executive Branch into the lives of our citizens and elected officials, few persons ever expected such revelations to reach the magnitude they have. The initial disclosures, such as the wiretaps of . . . 17 public officials and newspaper reporters in connection with alleged national security materials, were considered by many to be abberations by an overzealous Executive seeking, in good faith, to protect the nation against subversion. What followed, however, was a series of disclosures which widened the circle of persons who were considered proper subjects of surveillance by the investigatory units of the Executive Branch. We soon learned, for example, that during the '60s and the '70s, the U.S. Army, in cooperation with the FBI and other agencies, engaged in an extensive program of surveillance over the lawful activities of American citizens who were merely exercising their constitutional rights in protesting a terrible war in Southeast Asia and other social and political injustices. Civil rights groups, dissident organizations, splinter political parties, and others became the targets of extensive surveillance by federal and state investigators into permissible and protected conduct. These surveillance activities did not, to be sure, stop at the organizational level. Not only did government agents consider members of these groups as fair game for their intrusions into political beliefs, but they also spied on persons who had any connection with such groups or their members. A few years ago, a high school student in New Jersey wrote to an organization which was then the subject of government surveillance, apparently because someone in the Justice Department disagreed with its political viewpoint. The student had written for some information in connection with a course in political thought. Because the FBI then had a mail cover on the group, the student's name was acquired and an inquiry into her activities was undertaken. Of course, the investigation did not uncover any unlawful activity nor anything resembling illegality. But the data collected was used to open an FBI file on the unsuspecting student and retained by the FBI until the U.S. district court ordered it destroyed.''

Rep. Abner J. Mikva (D, Ill.), a participant in the discussion, said: ''There is a feeling extant in the country that if one has nothing to hide, if one has done nothing wrong, what difference does it make if somebody is following him around or if somebody is listening in on his telephone conversations? And indeed there is also a feeling that, after all, if a few thousand people or even 10,000 people are being watched and spied upon and their activities are being reviewed, in a country containing 213 million citizens this somehow is not a very serious problem. . . . I think, in addition to the violations of the rights of people who are being followed and who are being interdicted and their freedom threatened, that there is a much more serious problem, and that is the deterrent effect that this kind of activity has on the whole free society, because there is the danger that, through surveillance or even because of the popular belief that there is the existence of surveillance, we will discourage the kind of full, free, and unrestrained exchange of ideas and viewpoints on which democracy is based. When people and citizens and participants in political debate feel they must restrain their utterances, that they must watch their tongues, that they must have a care about which groups they join or which candidates they vote for and who they write letters to or who they receive letters from because somebody might be watching them, we are taking that first step—but it is a very long step—toward the very totalitarianism that these activities are proclaimed to prevent and deter; then we are in our way in America reaching toward the kind of closed society that the CIA, the FBI, and all the other intelligence-gathering agencies assure us in the defense of their actions they are trying to keep from happening.''

Rep. Edward G. Biester Jr. (R, Pa.), also speaking in the House discussion, said that "clearly the questions at stake in consideration of the whole issue of governmental surveillance go to the very core of the democratic process. This issue forces us to contend with perhaps the most basic question faced by a free society: where do we draw the line between the rights of the individual and the legitimate and necessary functions of society as embodied in the government? Such a question has never been easy to answer, and it is particularly difficult in this complex and technically sophisticated age. The introduction of national security considerations further complicates the issue. . . . Government surveillance—divorced from suspected criminality and unrestrained by any check—imperils our constitutional system, and thus undermines the very national security it is ostensibly designed to protect."

A similar concern with this aspect of the issue was expressed by Supreme Court Justice Lewis F. Powell. Speaking for a unanimous court (in *United States v. United States District Court for the Eastern District of Michigan*), Powell held June 19, 1972 that "[o]fficial surveillance, whether its purpose be criminal investigation or ongoing intelligence gathering, risks infringement of constitutionally protected privacy of speech. Security surveillances are especially sensitive because of the inherent vagueness of the domestic security concept, the necessarily broad and continuing nature of intelligence gathering, and the temptation to utilize such surveillances to oversee political dissent. We recognize, as we have before, the constitutional basis of the President's domestic security role, but we think it must be exercised in a manner compatible with the Fourth Amendment. . . ."

The increase in invasions of privacy, made possible in recent decades by modern technology and made profitable by business, government and political requirements, has resulted in both a surge of concern over the issue and a fear that invasion of privacy was becoming commonplace enough to be accepted by many people as normal. Ashley Montague's article "The Annihilation of Privacy," in the March 31, 1965 issue of *Saturday Review,* noted "an increasing callousness" toward "the violations of our privacy." He warned that "the harder it [these violations of privacy] grows, the more hardened do we become to it."

U.S. News & World Report, in its May 16, 1966 issue, cited Dr. Roger Revelle, director of Harvard's Center for Population Studies, as alarmed about "what happens to the citizen when his identity and every detail of his life are coded and classified in the government's computing system. . . . Not only does it become impossible to cheat even in a piddling sort of way on your income tax, it becomes impossible to do almost anything without the government knowing about it, and knowledge is liable to lead inevitably to control."

A possible illustration of such control was given by Michael Harrington Dec. 15, 1970, in a lecture in the "Privacy and the Law" series at the University of Illinois College of Law. Harrington said that "many poor people get their incomes from welfare, and, as a price of getting welfare, they make an enormous surrender of their right to privacy. In a sense they have to pay [by surrendering privacy] for welfare. . . . [However], not all poor people are on welfare . . . so when I talk about the problem of poverty, privacy and welfare, I am talking only about one-third of the poor. Indeed, I suggest that the invasion of privacy which accompanies welfare is designed to keep these people off welfare. The welfare system hounds the poor in such a way that those who are unwilling to surrender their privacy will not apply for welfare."

The psychiatrist Bruno Bettelheim wrote (in the July 27, 1968 issue of *The Saturday Evening Post*) that, "historically, privacy has always been a luxury few could afford. One need not go far back to a time when whole families lived together in one room. Nobody had privacy then." According to Bettelheim: "It appears that as long as the bodily functions, including sex and elimination, were more or less public, no great shame was attached to them. Only as they became more and more relegated to a private room . . . did we learn to feel shame at our bodies and bodily functions. The tragedy is that alienation from one's own body leads to alienation from others. And once we no longer feel comfortable with others, we crave still more privacy. This wish for privacy is closely connected with the increased value placed on private property. . . . The more class-structured a society becomes, the more privacy do its privileged members demand. How understandable, then, that a society which tries to do away with class structure should also try to do away with privacy, and demand that ever-larger areas of life should be public. What is harder to realize is that as long as everyone knows everything about everyone else, there is no need for informers, for elaborate spy systems, for bugging, in order to know what people do, say and think. . . ."

The problem of securing the right—or luxury—of privacy was a major anxiety of the founders of the American republic. Sen. Sam J. Ervin Jr. (D, N.C.) noted June 28, 1973, in a discussion on "Computers and Privacy" at Miami University in Hamilton, Ohio, that five of the first ten amendments to the Constitution, the Bill of

Rights, were created to safeguard specific rights of privacy. Ervin said: "The First Amendment was designed to protect the sanctity of the individual's private thoughts and beliefs. It protects the rights to speak and remain silent, to receive and impart information and ideas, and to associate in private and in public with others of like mind. After all, it is only by protecting this inner privacy that freedom of speech, religion, assembly and many other individual liberties can be protected. The Third Amendment's prohibition of quartering soldiers in private homes protects the privacy of the individual's living space. This aspect of privacy is also protected by the Fourth Amendment's guarantee of 'the right of the people to be secure in their persons, houses, papers, and effects, against unreasonable searches and seizures.' In addition to the privacy of the individual's home and personal effects, the privacy of his person (or bodily integrity) and even his private telephone conversations are protected by the Fourth Amendment from unwarranted governmental intrusion. The Fifth Amendment guarantees that an individual accused of a crime shall not be forced to divulge private information which might incriminate him. This privilege against self-incrimination focuses directly on the sanctity of the individual human personality and the right of each individual to keep private information which might place his life and freedom in jeopardy. The Fifth Amendment also guarantees that no person shall be 'deprived of life, liberty, or property without due process of law.' This right to due process protects individual privacy by preventing unwarranted governmental interference with the individual's person, personality and property. The Ninth Amendment's reservation that 'the enumeration in the Constitution, of certain rights, shall not be construed to deny or disparage others retained by the people' clearly shows that the Founding Fathers contemplated that certain basic individual rights not specifically mentioned in the Constitution—such as privacy—should nevertheless be safe from governmental interference. Just recently, in *Roe v. Wade,* the Supreme Court has located the right of privacy in the Fourteenth Amendment's guarantee that no state shall 'deprive any person of life, liberty, or property without due process of law.' Rights to give and receive information, to family life and child-rearing according to one's conscience, to marriage, to procreation, to contraception, and to abortion are all aspects of individual privacy which the courts have similarly held to be constitutionally protected."

Even before the adoption of the Constitution, colonial legislatures had sought to protect citizens against such invasions of privacy as unlawful searches and seizures by government officials. The Pennsylvania Declaration of Rights of 1776 provided in article X: "That the people have a right to hold themselves, their houses, papers, and possessions free from search and seizure, and therefore warrants without orders or affirmation first made, affording a sufficient foundation for them, and whereby any officer or messenger may be commanded or required to search suspected places, or to seize any person or persons, his or their property, not particularly described, are contrary to that right, and ought not to be granted." Similar provisions were found in the Virginia Declaration of Rights of 1776, the Delaware Declaration of Rights of 1776, the Maryland Declaration of Rights of 1776, the Massachusetts Declaration of Rights of 1780, the New Hampshire Bill of Rights of 1783 and the Vermont Declaration of Rights of 1787.

The late Supreme Court Justice Louis D. Brandeis, in a 1928 case (*Olmstead v. United States*), characterized the right of privacy—"the right to be let alone"—as "the most comprehensive of rights and the right most valued by civilized men." "To protect that right," Brandeis said, "every unjustifiable intrusion by the government upon the privacy of the individual, whatever the means employed must be deemed a violation of the Fourth Amendment." (Yet Brandeis was a dissenter in this decision, and the court majority upheld the legality of the wiretapping of a bootlegger on the grounds that the electronic eavesdropping was performed without the seizure of "tangible" property or the physical invasion of property.)

As Sen. Gaylord Nelson (D, Wis.) pointed out to the Senate June 18, 1973, "the history of individual liberty, and particularly the right of privacy, has been a history of resistance to governmental encroachments and an insistence upon fair procedural protections. Where liberty has prevailed, the rights of man have been translated into action; where liberty has lost, only silence has followed the soft echo of declarations of freedom." Tracing some of the major developments in establishing the American rights of privacy, Nelson recalled the struggle for such rights in England:

Unannounced entry into private homes was denounced in English common law as early as 1603. In Semayne's Case, 5 Cook 91, 11 ERC 629, 77 Eng. Reprint 194, the principle was firmly enunciated: 'In all cases where the King is party, the sheriff (if the doors be not open) may break in the party's house, either to arrest him, or to do other execution of the K(ing)'s process, if otherwise he cannot enter. But before he breaks it, he ought to signify the cause of his coming, and to make request to open doors. . .'

One hundred and sixty-three years later in 1766, the sanctity of the individual's right of privacy in his home and the importance of protecting against unlawful invasion of privacy by the government were again argued with magnificent eloquence. The British were having difficulty collecting an excise tax . . . upon cider. To solve their problem, it was proposed that the tax collectors be given the authority to enforce their cider tax by entering a man's house without knocking. When this proposal was debated in the House of Lords, William Pitt closed his argument in opposition to this government invasion of privacy by stating: 'The poorest man may, in his cottage, bid defiance to all the forces of the Crown. It may be frail. Its roof may shake. The wind may blow through it. The storm may enter. The rain may enter. But the King of England cannot enter. All his force dares not cross the threshold of that ruined tenement.'

The word "privacy," however, does not even appear in the Constitution. This was pointed out again in a 1974 study, entitled "Federal Data Banks and Constitution Rights," that was prepared by the staff of the Constitutional Rights Subcommittee of the Senate Judiciary Committee. Actually, no discussion of a right to privacy appears "in any of the documents left by the framers of the Constitution and the Bill of Rights. Privacy is, rather, one of those rights reserved to the people, which are implicit in the entire scheme of constitutional government limited to the exercise of only those powers expressly conferred upon it by the people through the Constitution." In the context of the subcommittee staff study, "privacy refers to the capacity of the individual to determine what information about that individual will be collected and disseminated to others. Privacy also involves a subjective sense of self-determination and control over personal information. It is bound up with fundamental concepts of individualism and pluralism which are basic to our society and institutions." According to the study:

As a legal concept, an independent right of privacy was first prominently discussed by the renowned Judge Cooley in his *Treatise on the Law of Torts,* originally published in 1879. In discoursing on 'The Right of Privacy,' Judge Cooley asserted that 'The right to one's person may be said to be a right to complete immunity: to be let alone.' Then, in 1890, Samuel D. Warren and Louis D. Brandeis published an article, 'The Right to Privacy,' that was to become a classic—and generated an interest that has burgeoned ever since. The authors were inspired by personal outrage over frequent abuses by a then novel breed of snooper—the photographer, professional and amateur. Warren and Brandeis were concerned about non-governmental invasions of privacy and the right of an aggrieved individual to sue for damages another person who invaded his privacy.

At the end of the nineteenth century, government data collection was apparently not yet perceived as sufficiently intrusive to arouse protest. Considering the government's relatively minimal ability to store, interrelate and disseminate what information it did collect, this lack of interest in governmental invasions of privacy is not surprising. Moreover, the existence of the frontier meant that individuals who wanted to get away from the government and its data collection, for whatever reason, could go West and leave the past behind.

It took the scientific and technological revolutions of this century, together with the trend toward centralizing more and more power in government, to bring the privacy issue to the fore. In other words, it was the greatly increased governmental capacity to create massive federal data banks containing intimate details about the personal lives of individuals, which raised the issue of the impact of these data banks on constitutional rights as a major social and political concern.

The rapid development of information-gathering and communications technologies in the latter half of the nineteenth century set the stage for the privacy controversy which followed over a hundred years later. Photography processes and equipment became easier, less expensive and more mobile. Wiretaps were invented with the telegraph in the 1860s. Telephones and telephone-line taps followed, as well as microphones and various sound-recording devices. By the early 1900s, electronic surveillance was an established method of investigation on the part of both police and private detectives.

Early in this century, some Members of Congress and aggrieved parties in the courts protested against invasions of privacy; but the issue of surveillance—by camera, wiretap, sound-recording, etc.—remained unresolved during the first half of the twentieth century. In congressional debate on these issues, the propriety of surveillance frequently became entangled with law enforcement and national security issues. . . .

Also in the early decades of the twentieth century, new technologies of recording and assessing individual personality became available. Polygraphs and personality tests began to be used to record and to measure the most intimate recesses of the human personality. Polygraphs (so-called 'lie-detectors') were developed as a police tool in the late 1920s. Personality tests, based on the then newly created sciences of psychology and psychoanalysis, gained respectability through their extensive use by the military during World Wars I and II. Such techniques did not arouse much public antagonism in these years of limited application.

At the same time, communications technologies—from the typewriter to new printing processes, to radio and swifter mail service based on faster means of transportation—brought more and more current information into the hands of more and more people. The technologies of information dissemination were themselves developing concurrently with the development of new methods of collecting information. The public response was generally enthusiastic.

By mid-century (1945–1965), the United States was characterized by even more rapid technological advances and increased reliance on 'scientific' methods. Electronic surveillance devices became more powerful, more versatile, smaller and cheaper. Polygraphs became an increasingly popular personnel tool among both private and public employers. Personality tests were embraced by many groups and accepted as a routine procedure in schools, industry and government. Communications technologies developed apace. Most important, computers became an integral part of the nation's record-keeping activities.

At about the same time, there was a growing demand for both administrative personal data and statistical information about individuals. The social service responsibilities of the federal government greatly expanded during the 'New Deal' era; and these new mandates stimulated the need for facts on which to base planning, programming and budgeting decisions. In the many cases where the allocation of federal grants was made to depend on the population characteristics of a given area, the collection of highly detailed information about such population groups by the federal and state governments became essential. Added emphasis in the private sector on social and biomedical research began to involve the gathering of much personal data, sometimes shared with a financially supporting federal agency. In the private sector, business concerns began to collect detailed information about many aspects of their operations, particularly for tax and marketing purposes. During this period, too, a mobile population discovered the convenience of credit cards. . . .

As Americans began to relinquish more and more personal information in response to numerous governmental and private sector requirements, fears of losing privacy and freedom began to be articulated. Labor, in particular, voiced its opposition to the use of lie detectors in business, and in the early 1960s both Congress and the executive branch began to investigate the use and propriety of polygraphs. Personality tests roused the ire of conservative groups alarmed at their potential for producing conformity among schoolchildren. As their use became pervasive, however, diverse groups began to object to these tests as being unreliable, unscientific, and an infringement of individual rights. In the mid-1960s several best sellers, including *The Organization Man* (1965), *The Brain Watchers* (1962), *The Naked Society* (1964), and *The Privacy Invaders* (1964), aroused public opinion by focusing on growing trends toward depersonalization and loss of individual privacy.

About this same time, computers began to produce noticeable effects on American society. Congressional hearings noted the growing use of automatic data processing by the federal government, and its impact on established patterns of data collection and interagency information sharing. Soon after the Internal Revenue Service adopted computer procedures in 1963, citizens became obliged to indicate their Social Security number on tax forms. By the mid-1960s, too, growing numbers of state and local law enforcement agencies began to automate various aspects of their operations, such as fingerprint identification, analysis of crime characteristics, and retrieval of criminal histories. The computerization of consumer reports by the credit industry made 'credit checks' on individuals feasible within seconds. The trend towards centralizing and manipulating information, especially personal information, in computerized data banks began to be viewed with apprehension by a growing number of both politicians and private citizens.

The anxieties generated by these privacy concerns were galvanized in the mid-1960s by discussion in the Executive Branch of proposals for a computerized federal statistical center, a 'National Data Center.' This plan was labeled in the press, and before Congress, as a giant step towards centralization of power, depersonalization and realization of the totalitarian society George Orwell portrayed in his novel *1984*. Proponents of the 'National Data Center' idea defended the concept at committee hearings during the 89th and 90th Congresses as a means to improve the efficiency of government functions and private research efforts. However, when Congress and the public expressed unqualified objection to this national data bank proposal, which would have had profound effects on personal privacy and individual freedom from government control, the proposal was abandoned. . . .

. . . Of the many legislative proposals pertaining to these privacy issues which were introduced in the 89th through 92nd Congresses, only two major public laws were enacted which directly address the problem: the 'Omnibus Crime Control and Safe Streets Act of 1968' (P.L. 90–351) contains provisions that limit the legal use of wiretaps to police-related activity under specified conditions; the 'Fair Credit Reporting Act' (P.L. 91–508), approved three years later, in 1971, gives credit customers the right to receive notification of consumer agency reports that result in negative actions taken against them, to know the content of their files, and to challenge disputed data.

During the past decade, faced with public and Congressional outrage over invasions of privacy, several executive agencies have expressed concern over the effects of statistical and behavioral research on individual privacy. In 1966, the Bureau of the Budget issued the report of the 'Task Force on the Storage of and Access to Government Statistics,' which briefly considered the questions regarding privacy and confidentiality raised by the National Data Center proposal. The task force recommended that Congress define statutory standards governing the disclosure of personal information collected by the government, and that these standards be enforced by the Director of the Federal Statistical System. One year later, the Office of Science and Technology issued a paper on 'Privacy and Behavioral Research' that discussed the ethical responsibilities of social scientists engaged in studies of human behavior, especially research sponsored by the federal government. In 1971, an evaluation of federal statistical systems was published by a special presidential commission as a two-volume report on *Federal Statistics* containing several chapters on privacy considerations. The commission recommended that public confidence in federal data gathering be increased by strengthening legal safeguards and by establishing an independent advisory board to handle public grievances.

In July 1973 an advisory committee appointed by the Secretary of Health, Education and Welfare issued a report on *Records, Computers, and the Rights of Citizens*. This HEW advisory committee examined the potential privacy hazards of computer-based record-keeping and the trend towards using the Social Security number as an all-purpose identifier. The HEW advisory committee concluded that excessive use of the Social Security number should be curtailed, in part to allay public fears of governmental intrusion and surveillance. The HEW advisory committee also recommended that citizens be informed as to the nature of information concerning them in government files, and be given meaningful rights to access, control, and correct such data.

The response of America's private sector to privacy issues from 1965 to 1972 has included [many law review and journal articles, newspaper and magazine articles, computer industry speeches and publications and studies by private research organizations]. . . . This period was also marked by the appearance of many books, sensational and scholarly, on the subject of privacy rights in a technological age. . . . Among these texts, a comprehensive treatment is provided by Alan Westin's *Privacy and Freedom* (1967) and by Arthur Miller's *The Assault on Privacy* (1971).

Beginning in 1970, concern turned to the impact of computer technology on society. . . .

In 1972 the National Academy of Sciences published *Databanks in a Free Society*, an important empirical study which summarizes the results of a three-year project challenging some widely held assumptions about the effects of computerization on large scale personal .information systems. Based partly on fifty-five detailed on-site visits, the authors, Alan Westin and Michael Baker, assessed the impact of automatic data processing on the practices and policies of many organizations. Their analysis featured these two conclusions: (1) The new capacity of the computer to store, consolidate, and share confidential information has not led, inevitably, to greater collection and manipulation of such data. (2) In computerizing files on individuals, organizations have generally adhered to their traditional administrative policies regarding the collection and sharing of data. The most sensitive personal information is still maintained in manual files. The report recognizes, however, that computers have brought about a dramatic and increasing expansion of information networks with attendant impact on individual privacy. Proper legal restraints on data-sharing have become imperative. Other policy suggestions include publication of 'A Citizen's Guide to Files,' new limits on the collection of personal information, development of effective technological safeguards, limits on the use of the Social Security number, and the establishment of 'information-trust agencies' to hold particularly sensitive bodies of personal data. . . .

THIS BOOK IS DESIGNED TO SERVE as a record of the assaults on the right of privacy in the United States—and of the defense against such attacks—as they developed during the first half of the 1970s. The material that follows consists largely of the account compiled by FACTS ON FILE in its weekly coverage of world events. As in all FACTS ON FILE works, there was a conscientious effort to keep this volume free of bias and to make it an accurate and useful reference tool.

LESTER A. SOBEL

New York, N.Y.
August, 1976

Electronic Surveillance

Wiretaps Curbed

Wiretapping and other electronic eavesdropping methods became major investigative tools during the first half of the twentieth century despite complaints that such invasions of privacy were violations of the Fourth Amendment's guarantee against "unreasonable searches and seizures." In 1928 the Supreme Court held (in the case of Olmstead v. United States) that the Fourth Amendment's protection did not extend to electronic searches. But six years later the Federal Communications Act of 1934 provided that "no person not being authorized by the sender shall intercept any communication and divulge ... the existence, contents, substance, purport, effect, or meaning of such intercepted communication to any person." The Supreme Court then ruled in 1937 (in the case of Nardone v. United States) that the act's prohibition covered wiretapping. More than three decades later the Omnibus Crime Control & Safe Streets Act of 1968 authorized electronic eavesdropping by federal, state and local officials in national security and many other cases. But this provision was ruled unconstitutional, a violation of the Fourth Amendment, by the Supreme Court in 1972.

Mitchell on Policy. John N. Mitchell was nominated by Richard M. Nixon as the first attorney general of the Nixon Administration. At Mitchell's confirmation hearings, Mitchell said Jan. 14, 1969 that the wiretapping authority of the 1968 Omnibus Crime Control Act "should be used, carefully and effectively, not only in national security cases [as under the Johnson Administration] but against organized crime and other major crimes."

Mitchell disclosed July 14, 1969 that since he assumed office Jan. 22 the government had reduced its use of wiretaps and monitoring devices. He said that a great number of "national security" taps had been discontinued because they were "non-productive" and that the number of authorized wiretaps was less than the 54 acknowledged by FBI Director J. Edgar Hoover in April.

Mitchell also denied allegations made the previous week by Sens. Ralph W. Yarborough (D, Tex.) and Carl T. Curtis (R, Neb.) that many Congressional phones were tapped by the Justice Department. Mitchell said: "It would be inconceivable beyond any consideration to place a tap to a member of Congress or on anyone else in government."

The Justice Department had said June 13 that it had Constitutional authority to eavesdrop, without prior court approval, on organizations it believed threatened the internal security of the nation.

The agency, in papers filed in Federal District Court in Chicago, asked that the court expand the legal usage of government electronic surveillance. Attorney General Mitchell said further that recorded conversations involving domestic groups need not be disclosed to them. The government revealed it had used monitoring equipment to eavesdrop on several antiwar activists who were indicted for inciting riots during the 1968 Democratic National Convention.

The Justice Department contended it had the legal authority to monitor domestic groups it believed were seeking to "attack and subvert the government by unlawful means."

(District Court Judge Julius J. Hoffman had rejected April 11 the claim of the defendants that the Federal Bureau of Investigation had acted illegally when it monitored a meeting between the demonstrators and their attorneys.)

Thirteen law professors asked Mitchell June 25 to drop his proposal. "To grant such a claim would gravely threaten some of our most fundamental liberties as well as the rule of the law itself," the professors wrote to Mitchell. They took no position on the government's right to unfettered eavesdropping in "foreign intelligence" investigations under the President's foreign affairs powers.

The American Civil Liberties Union (ACLU) filed suit in Washington D.C. District Court June 27 to block Mitchell's attempt to obtain expanded eavesdropping rights. The ACLU suit named Mitchell and FBI Director J. Edgar Hoover as defendants and asked for criminal prosecution of the two officials.

Definition of Key Terms

1. *wiretapping:* interception of communication transmitted over wire from phone *without* consent of participant.

2. *bugging:* interception of communication transmitted orally *without* consent of participant.

3. *recording:* electronic recording of wire or oral communication *with* the consent of a participant.

4. *transmitting:* radio transmission of oral communication *with* the consent of a participant.

5. *electronic surveillance:* generic term loosely used to cover all of the above, but often confined to "wiretapping" or "bugging."

6. *national security:* generic term loosely used to refer to wiretapping or bugging aimed at either "foreign" or "domestic" threats to the national security.

a. *foreign security:* usually meant to cover "wiretapping" or "bugging" to obtain coverage of foreign diplomats, spies, and their American contacts; also directed at Communist party and Communist front activities in the United States; sometimes used to obtain coverage of those involved in foreign intrigue, e.g., gun running to Latin American countries, etc.; primarily useful to prevent damage (theft of documents, etc.), not "solve crimes."

b. *domestic security:* usually meant to cover "wiretapping" or "bugging" to obtain coverage of extremist groups in the United States, e.g., the Black Panthers, groups within the K.K.K., and La Cosa Nostra; sometimes used to determine the influence of extremist groups in other legitimate organizations (civil rights or peace); primarily useful to prevent damage (assaults, bombings, kidnapping, homicides, riots, etc.).

Note that the "foreign" and "domestic" security distinction is sharper in theory than in practice. Often it is difficult without "wiretapping" or "bugging" to determine the "foreign" or "domestic" character of the threat.

Note, too, that since the emphasis is on the prevention of harmful activity rather than the punishment of those who have already caused harm, police action in these areas tends to cover more people for longer periods of time under less precise standards than conventional criminal investigations.

Caveat: Newspaper reporters, in particular, but all of us sometimes use "wiretapping," "bugging" and "national security" to refer to some or all of these techniques or areas of activity without carefully discriminating between them. This fact alone leads to most of the controversy; people often are not talking about the same things, even though they are using the same words.

From April 30, 1971 memo by Chief Counsel G. Robert Blakey of Senate Subcommittee on Criminal Laws & Procedures

Wiretaps Curbed. A series of federal court decisions beginning in January 1971 culminated June 19, 1972 in a Supreme Court ruling against the government's practice of warrantless wiretapping and electronic surveillance.

In the first decision, U.S. District Court Judge Warren J. Ferguson ruled in Los Angeles Jan. 11, 1971 that the government could not conduct wiretaps without warrants in domestic cases, even if national security was involved. The ruling came in the case of Melvin Carl Smith, 41, a Black Panther convicted in October 1969 on charges of being a felon and possessing firearms.

The government had long claimed the right to eavesdrop without a warrant in national security cases involving foreign subversives.

Ferguson said the U.S. Constitution protected domestic political activity, but "the government seems to approach these dissident domestic organizations in the same fashion as it deals with unfriendly foreign powers." He said: "The government cannot act in this manner when only domestic political organizations are involved, even if those organizations espouse views which are inconsistent with our present form of government. To do so is to ride roughshod over numerous political freedoms which have long received constitutional protection."

In a similar decision, U.S. District Court Judge Damon J. Keith ruled in Detroit Jan. 25, 1971 that the government could not conduct warrantless wiretaps in domestic cases on the ground that the national security was involved.

Keith said transcripts of the illegal wiretaps on Lawrence R. (Pun) Plamondon, 25, accused of conspiracy in the Sept. 29, 1968 bombing of a Central Inligence Agency building in Ann Arbor, Mich., must be given to the defense.

The Detroit judge said: "An idea which seems to permeate much of the government's argument is that a dissident domestic organization is akin to an unfriendly foreign power that must be dealt with in the same fashion."

He said this argument "strikes at the very constitutional privileges and immunities that are inherent in United States citizenship." Keith challenged the government's right to "determine unilaterally what comes within its own definition of national security." He said that "attempts of domestic organizations to attack and subvert the existing structure of government" were criminal "only where it can be shown that such activity was accomplished through unlawful means."

Plamondon was one of three members of the Ann Arbor-based White Panther party charged in the bomb plot. The other defendants were John A. Sinclair, 29, who was serving a 10-year sentence for possession of marijuana, and John W. Forrest, 21.

Deputy Attorney General Richard G. Kleindienst, in a United Press International interview published Feb. 22, defended the government's claim of the right to conduct wiretaps without court approval in domestic national security cases.

Kleindienst said: "It would be silly to say that an American citizen, because he is an American, could subvert the government by actions of violence and revolution and be immune from, first, identification, and second, prosecution." He said, "The whole question of internal security is not a divisible subject matter. . . . You can't divide subversion into two parts—domestic and foreign."

The 6th U.S. Circuit Court of Appeals, ruling in Cincinnati April 8, rejected the Justice Department's contention that the government had a right to conduct wiretaps in "domestic subversion" cases without court warrants. The court's 2-1 ruling upheld Judge Keith's ruling that the government must disclose information obtained through an illegal wiretap or drop its case against Plamondon.

In the first federal appellate court ruling on Attorney General John N. Mitchell's assertion that the government could conduct unwarranted taps in domestic security cases, Judge George C. Edwards Jr. said there was not "one written phrase" in the Constitution to justify the attorney general's claim. Commenting on the government's statement that "the awesome power sought by the attorney general will be used with discretion," Edwards said "obviously, even in very recent days, this has not always been the case." Edwards was joined in his ruling by Judge Harry Phillips.

In a dissent, Judge Paul C. Weick said the President had the sworn duty "to protect and defend the nation from attempts of domestic subversives, as well

FDR Authorized Wiretaps

National-security wiretaps conducted by the U.S. government from 1940 through the early 1970s were based on the following wartime memo issued by President Franklin D. Roosevelt to the attorney general:

CONFIDENTIAL MEMORANDUM FOR THE
ATTORNEY GENERAL

THE WHITE HOUSE,
Washington, D.C., May 21, 1940.

I have agreed with the broad purpose of the Supreme Court decision relating to wiretapping in investigations. The Court is undoubtedly sound both in regard to the use of evidence secured over tapped wires in the prosecution of citizens in criminal cases; and is also right in its opinion that under ordinary and normal circumstances wiretapping by Government agents should not be carried on for the excellent reason that it is almost bound to lead to abuse of civil rights.

However, I am convinced that the Supreme Court never intended any dictum in the particular case which it decided to apply to grave matters involving the defense of the nation.

It is, of course, well known that certain other nations have been engaged in the organization of propaganda of so-called "fifth columns" in other countries and in preparation for sabotage, as well as in actual sabotage.

It is too late to do anything about it after sabotage, assassinations and "fifth column" activities are completed.

You are, therefore, authorized and directed in such cases as you may approve, after investigation of the need in each case, to authorize the necessary investigation agents that they are at liberty to secure information by listening devices direct to the conversation or other communications of persons suspected of subversive activities against the Government of the United States, including suspected spies. You are requested furthermore to limit these investigations so conducted to a minimum and to limit them insofar as possible to aliens.

(s) F. D. R.

as foreign enemies, to destroy it by force and violence."

Speaking before the Virginia Bar Association June 11, Mitchell defended the government stand. He argued that "the threat to our society from so-called 'domestic' subversion is as serious as any threat from abroad" and that if it were possible to separate them, "history has shown greater danger from the domestic variety."

Mitchell said, "never in our history has this country been confronted with so many revolutionary elements determined to destroy by force the government and the society it stands for." He said radicals being tapped "are idealogically and in many instances directly connected with foreign interests."

Making a distinction between wiretaps for "intelligence" purposes or for prosecution, Mitchell asserted that the Administration and not the courts was in a better position to know if taps should be installed for intelligence. Mitchell said: "The Constitution of the United States cannot possibly be construed as containing provisions inconsistent with its own survival. It is the charter for a viable government system, not a suicide pact."

Mitchell resigned as attorney general Feb. 15, 1972 to head President Nixon's reelection campaign, and Nixon nominated Kleindienst to be attorney general. During Kleindienst's confirmation hearing Feb. 3, he upheld the continued limited use of national security wiretaps without court order as, primarily, "intelligence gathering." "A lot of it is done without the thought of prosecuting," he said.

(In 1973, the Watergate scandal caused Kleindienst's resignation. A later successor, Sen. William B. Saxbe [R, Ohio], was confirmed by the Senate after affirming at his confirmation hearing Dec. 12, 1973 that he considered wiretapping "abhorrent" but a necessary law-enforcement "tool.")

Wiretap law held unconstitutional—For the first time in a U.S. court, a judge in Philadelphia ruled June 1, 1972 that the 1968 act authorizing law-enforcement agencies to wiretap phones under certain circumstances was unconstitutional.

In more than a dozen other cases, federal judges had upheld the law.

But Judge Joseph S. Lord 3rd found the law "unconstitutional on its face" because it violated the Constitution's Fourth Amendment protecting citizens against "unreasonable searches and seizures."

At issue in the case was a motion sought by seven defendants in a gambling case to suppress evidence gathered by electronic surveillance.

In granting the defendants' request, Lord wrote: "The privacy of every citizen is in jeopardy if we become a nation which sanctions the indiscriminate use of secret electronic searches by the government."

In a related development, newly-confirmed Attorney General Richard G. Kleindienst said in a speech to members of the legal profession June 9 that wiretapping "is a legitimate, constitutional means to root out organized crime," asserting that the Administration would continue using it.

Speaking to the Philadelphia chapter of the Federal Bar Association, Kleindienst foresaw a continued use of the wiretaps. "This will be done while this President [Nixon] is President and while I am attorney general."

High Court curbs wiretaps—The Supreme Court June 19, 1972 declared unconstitutional the federal government's use of wiretapping and electronic surveillance to monitor domestic radicals without first obtaining court warrants.

Three of President Nixon's four appointees to the bench—Chief Justice Warren Burger, Harry A. Blackmun and Lewis F. Powell Jr.—joined the other justices in an 8-0 decision rejecting the Administration claim that warrants for taps in such cases were unnecessary. The Justice Department had argued that the President's authority to protect the country from internal subversion gave the government the constitutional authority to use wiretaps on "dangerous" radicals without court approval.

The fourth Nixon appointee, Justice William H. Rehnquist, had helped shape that argument while he was a Justice

Department official. He did not participate in the ruling.

The court's decision was a major legal setback for the Nixon Administration, which had argued strenuously for its position.

But the court held in an opinion by Powell that "Fourth Amendment freedoms cannot properly be guaranteed if domestic surveillances may be conducted solely within the discretion of the executive branch."

While the court did not rule on wiretapping without court warrants of agents of foreign nations, the justices held that "national security" wiretapping of domestic radicals who had no foreign ties can be done only with the type of warrants now in use by police investigating organized crime.

In writing the court's opinion, Powell relied heavily upon the threat to free speech he saw in unchecked wiretapping of dissenters by the government.

"History abundantly documents the tendency of government—however benevolent and benign its motives—to view with suspicion those who most fervently dispute its policies."

Powell held that in cases involving domestic radicals as well as in ordinary criminal investigations, the Fourth Amendment protections against unreasonable searches and seizures required court approval for wiretapping.

"Unreviewed executive discretion may yield too readily to pressures to obtain incriminating evidence and overlook potential invasions of privacy and speech."

Free speech, Powell wrote, was at the heart of the matter. He added:

"The price of lawful public dissent must not be a dread of subjection to an unchecked surveillance power. Nor must the fear of unauthorized official eavesdropping deter vigorous citizen dissent and discussion of government action in private conversation."

Aside from the immediate effect of having the government stop its warrantless wiretapping of domestic radicals, the court's decision meant that any defendant in a federal prosecution had the right to see complete transcripts of any conversations monitored through warrantless taps in a domestic case so that his attorney could make certain that no illegally obtained information was being used in the prosecution.

Since 1968, the Justice Department had used wiretaps without warrants in a number of prominent cases, including the prosecution of the Chicago Seven riot-conspiracy defendants and the kidnaping and conspiracy case against the Rev. Philip F. Berrigan and other antiwar activists.

The court's decision came in a case involving the government's wiretapping of three members of the radical White Panther party who had been accused of plotting to blow up a government building in Detroit.

Chief Justice Warren E. Burger noted that he concurred only in the court's result. Also concurring in a separate opinion was Justice Byron R. White.

Kleindienst issues order—After learning of the decision, Attorney General Richard G. Kleindienst said June 19 he had "directed the termination of all electronic surveillance in cases involving security that conflict with the court's opinion."

Kleindienst added that henceforth surveillance would be done "only under procedures that comply" with the court's ruling.

Curb set on wiretap evidence—Over the dissent of the four Nixon-appointed justices, the court June 26 held 5-4 that grand jury witnesses had the right to refuse to answer questions gleaned from information overheard on illegal listening devices.

The court's decision sustained the challenge brought by Sister Jogues Egan and Anne Walsh, a former nun, against their convictions for refusing to testify about an alleged plot to kidnap Presidential adviser Henry A. Kissinger.

The government had argued that a ruling in the plaintiffs' favor would slow down the work of grand juries by requiring tedious searching through wiretap

transcripts before questioning could begin.

Disclosure Ordered. U.S. District Court Judge Aubrey E. Robinson Jr. ruled in Washington Jan. 11, 1974 that the Justice Department must reveal the nature and extent of wiretaps and other surveillance of antiwar activists in 1968–69.

The ruling came in a civil suit filed in 1969 under the Omnibus Crime Act of 1968 providing compensation for victims of illegal wiretapping. The suit had been delayed during criminal trials of some of the plaintiffs, including the "Chicago Seven." Among other plaintiffs involved in the suit were the War Resisters League the Catholic Priests Fellowship, the Southern Conference Education Fund and the Black Panther Party.

Judge Robinson rejected Justice Department contentions that the wire taps should be kept secret for national security reasons and refused as "highly irregular" a government request that he examine the information privately.

Wiretaps Under Mitchell Invalid. The Supreme Court ruled unanimously May 13, 1974 that former Attorney General John N. Mitchell had failed to meet the requirements of the Organized Crime Control Act of 1968 when he allowed his executive assistant to approve wiretap applications, rather than doing it himself or designating a specific assistant attorney general to act in his place, as required by law.

In ruling that the wiretap requests approved by Mitchell's executive assistant Sol Lindenbaum were illegal, the court upheld the dismissal of a narcotics indictment againt Dominic N. Giordano of Baltimore. The ruling was expected to have the same effect in 60 other narcotics and gambling cases involving 626 defendants.

While the full court agreed that evidence from the wiretaps authorized by Lindenbaum was inadmissable, the four Nixon appointees to the court—Chief Justice Warren E. Burger and Justices Harry A. Blackmun, Lewis F. Powell Jr. and William H. Rehnquist—argued in a separate dissent that court-ordered extensions of the Lindenbaum-authorized taps were not improper.

Writing for the court in its unanimous ruling, Justice Byron R. White brushed aside government arguments that the defective procedures were merely technicalities. White said he had traced the history of the provision and found that Congress had included it to make "doubly sure that statutory authority [would] be used with restraint."

In a parallel case, the court upheld by a 5-4 margin the validity of another set of wiretaps affecting 99 cases and 807 defendants. Here, wiretap applications had been authorized by Mitchell but signed by former Assistant Attorney General Will R. Wilson, who had not actually played any part in their preparation. The court majority said it did not "condone" Mitchell's practices, but attributed defects in these wiretap requests to poor bookkeeping practices. Arguing in dissent that the Wilson-signed tap authorizations resulted in tainted evidence were Justices William O. Douglas, William J. Brennan Jr., Potter Stewart and Thurgood Marshall.

Use of Wiretaps

FBI Wiretap Activity. An agent of the Federal Bureau of Investigation disclosed June 4, 1969 that the FBI had maintained telephone surveillance on the Rev. Dr. Martin Luther King Jr. until his death in April 1968.

During a special hearing ordered for Cassius Clay in Houston, Tex., the agent, Robert Nicols, gave details of the King wiretapping. Clay, former world heavyweight boxing champion, had accused the government of using "tainted" evidence to convict him for failing to accept induction into the Army. Clay's attorneys argued that he was denied conscientious objector (CO) status for "political reasons." (Clay had been sentenced to a five-year prison term.)

The Houston hearing, conducted by Appeals Court Judge Joe Ingraham, was ordered by the Supreme Court after the Justice Department disclosed that the FBI had tapped phone conversations involving Clay. The court ordered the hearing to determine if illegal wiretap evidence had contributed to Clay's conviction. Ingraham ruled July 14 that the government had not used wiretap evidence to convict Cassius Clay for draft evasion. Ingraham ruled that the wiretaps on the telephone of the former heavyweight boxing champion had been "lawful surveillance."

Nicols testified that King's phone had been monitored at a time when King had criticized the FBI for assigning Southern rather than Northern agents to protect civil rights workers.

The FBI disclosed June 5 that it had also monitored telephone calls of Black Muslim leader Elijah Muhammad through 1966. The disclosure was linked to the fact that Clay's application for CO status was based on the claim that he was a Black Muslim minister.

Testimony at the hearing June 6 indicated the FBI had continued to maintain telephone surveillance on King and Muhammad after former President Lyndon Johnson had ordered an end to all wiretaps except those authorized by the attorney general for national security purposes.

FBI agent Nicols testified he had supervised the wiretap of King's phone until May 1965, and said he believed the bureau maintained the tap until King's death in April 1968.

Clyde Tolson, associate director of the FBI, told the Washington Star June 19 that the telephone surveillance on King had been authorized in writing by Robert F. Kennedy when he was attorney general. Tolson said the wiretapping did not violate President Johnson's order restricting such surveillance to national security investigations. (The Star June 15 had published an article by syndicated columnist Carl Rowan accusing FBI Director J. Edgar Hoover of illegal eavesdropping.)

Tolson defended Hoover asserting that the wiretap was "within the provisions laid down by the then President of the United States." Tolson said that the wiretap was related to internal security and therefore was legal.

Hoover told the Star June 19 that the wiretap on King's phone had been proposed by Robert F. Kennedy in June 1963. He said Kennedy had authorized it in writing in October 1963. Hoover said Kennedy first proposed the wiretap after expressing concern at the activities of King's followers.

Former Attorney General Nicolas deB. Katzenbach June 19 confirmed Hoover's statement that Kennedy had authorized the King wiretap, but denied Hoover's claim that the attorney general had initiated the idea.

Ramsey Clark, attorney general for former President Johnson, said June 20 that Hoover had repeatedly asked him to authorize a tap on King's phone. Clark said he refused the director's requests. He also suggested Hoover should retire now " . . . in the interests of the FBI, which has been a great investigative agency."

Clark said Hoover had asked him for permission to resume the King wiretap two days before the civil rights leader was slain. Clark said he denied the request.

President Nixon said June 19 he had personally investigated the wiretap controversy and found the FBI did not violate any government restrictions when it monitored King's phone. Speaking at a press conference, the President said Kennedy had authorized the King wiretap: "I found that the wiretapping had always been approved by the attorney general."

He said the use of court-approved investigative wiretapping against organized crime was up 100% over the previous year, when there were 33 eavesdropping instances. He said greater use of wiretapping by narcotics and anti-racketeering forces accounted for the increase and that wiretapping for national security purposes had remained constant.

Wiretaps Increase. By mid-1970, the Justice Department reported that the use of investigative wiretaps had doubled in a year. The disclosure was made by John N

Mitchell, then attorney general, at a press conference July 14, 1970.

Mitchell reiterated in a talk to the nation's police chiefs Oct. 5 that the government was stepping up its use of wiretapping against suspected criminals. In a speech before the annual meeting of the International Association of Chiefs of Police in Atlantic City, N.J., Mitchell called electronic surveillance the most effective weapon to fight organized crime.

The attorney general disclosed that the Justice Department had used 133 court-approved wiretaps during the first seven months of 1970, compared with the 33 deployed in 1969. Mitchell said the 133 taps had resulted in 419 arrests and 325 indictments. He said that about 80% of the calls intercepted by federal agents were incriminating. This, he asserted, proved that the government was not using the taps for "fishing expeditions."

Mitchell said most of the 133 taps were used in cases involving gambling, narcotics and extortion. Justice department officials said later that taps were also deployed in cases involving loan sharking, interstate transportation of stolen goods, counterfeiting, kidnaping and obstruction of justice.

Mitchell chided the Johnson Administration for refusing to use the wiretapping power authorized by Congress in 1968 on grounds that it might make people fear government repression. He said those fears were "bogeys" and said one of his first acts in office was to order the use of court-approved wiretapping.

President Nixon said at a press conference May 1, 1971, however, that there were only half as many warrantless government wiretaps "today . . . as there were in 1961, '62 and '63, and 10 times as many news stories about them." Nixon said the "hysteria" and "political demagoguery" about the FBI tapping telephones "simply doesn't serve the public purpose." He considered as "justified" the taps approved by the attorney general in cases "dealing with those who would use violence or other means to overthrow the government." Such taps, he said, were currently limited to less than 50 at any one time.

"This is not a police state," Nixon declared, and his Administration was "against any kind of repression, any kind of action that infringes on the right of privacy." He was for "that kind of action that is necessary to protect this country from those who would imperil the peace that all the people are entitled to enjoy."

Wiretaps during 1970—Sen. John L. McClellan (D, Ark.) provided the Senate May 10, 1971 with a summary of an Administrative Office (of the U.S. Courts) report on electronic surveillance during 1970. The summary said that during 1970, "597 applications for orders were made to federal and state judges. Of these applications, 183 were signed by federal judges, and 414 were signed by state judges. Of the 414 state orders, 215, or 52% were issued in New York, while 132 or 32 percent were issued in New Jersey." The summary continued:

The 597 applications filed during the 12 months of 1970 compare with the 304 applications filed in 1969 and 174 filed in last 6 months of 1968. On the Federal level, the increase from 33 in 1969 to 183 in 1970 reflects the growth in the Department of Justice's drive against organized crime. . . .

On the Federal level, of 183 authorized intercepts, 180 were installed and 43 extensions were granted. The 183 authorizations were granted for an average length of 17 days; the extensions for an average of 9 days. . . .

In 1970, of the 583 applications that resulted in an intercept, 539 involved a telephone wiretap, 21 intercepts used a nonconsensual listening device, such as a microphone. In 23 requests, both a telephone wiretap and a microphone were used for the interception.

The report does not, of course, include data on either the so-called national security or domestic security use of wiretaps or listening devices. In the national security area the use of these techniques, I should like to emphasize, was first begun as a result of a May 21, 1940, memorandum of President Franklin D. Roosevelt to Attorney General Robert Jackson, later Mr. Justice Jackson. In the domestic security area, this practice was first begun as a result of a July 17, 1947, memorandum of President Harry S. Truman to Attorney General Tom Clark, later Mr. Justice Clark. In both areas, it has been continued in each administration and by each Attorney General thereafter. No reports in either of these two areas are required under the 1968 act, however, since the Congress in the 1968 act did not wish to limit in any fashion the constitutional power of the President as Commander in Chief of the Nation's Armed Forces to respond to either foreign powers or clear and present domestic threats to the survival of the Nation. . . .   Nevertheless, the President recently commented on the number of wiretaps, indicating that none are currently in operation, while the number running at any one time in recent years has not exceeded 50. In the early 1960's, the figure was 100. . . .

The offenses specified in the applications summarized in the 1970 report covered a wide range of criminal activities. Several broad categories of crime, however, predominated: Arson 13; bribery, 16; drugs, 127; extortion, 17; gambling, 326; homicide, 20; larceny, 31; and robbery, 13.

The locations of the interceptions authorized included 203 residences, 163 apartments, 39 multiple dwelling, 122 business locations, and 30 business and living quarters.

The character of the interceptions were also described in the reports. In 1969, the average intercept involved 116 persons and 641 intercepts, of which 252 or 39 percent were incriminating. In 1970, on the other hand, the average intercept involved 44 people and 655 intercepts, of which 295 or 45 percent were incriminating. With more experience, therefore, it seems apparent that the intercepts are becoming more discriminating, a development that works well both for privacy and justice.

In certain areas, however, the picture is even better. In 1970, for example, on the Federal level, the average intercept touched on 57 persons and embraced 821 intercepts, of which 571 or 69 percent were incriminating, while in New Jersey, in the interceptions conducted by the office of the attorney general, 42 persons were involved and 294 intercepts were made, of vhich 237 or 80 percent were incriminating.

The total costs of each intercept—manpower and equipment—ranged from a low of $14 to a high of $146,300, with the average national intercept running $5,524, and the average Federal intercept running $12,106. These figures alone should do a great deal to put into context people's fear of excessive use of these techniques. Most police agencies including the Federal, simply do not have the manpower and other resources to conduct widespread surveillance.

Most of the cases in which there were interceptions reported are, of course, still under investigation or are awaiting trial. Nevertheless, the reports indicate that a total of 1,874 arrests have been made as of December 31, 1970. This figure compares favorably with the 625 arrested in 1969. Supplementary court action reports dealing with intercepts first reported in 1969 were also filed for 53 percent of the 1969 intercepts. Others are coming in periodically. A total of 31 trials and 70 convictions have occurred. One motion to suppress has been granted, one withdrawn, 25 are pending, and 25 have been denied. These figures, too, say a great deal about the judgment of those who say that these techniques are not effective or that they will be subject to widespread abuse. As the experience is beginning to develop, it shows clearly how important convictions can be obtained without an undue invasion of privacy. . . .

Senator suspects phone taps. Sen. Joseph M. Montoya (D, N.M.) said March 19, 1971 that he and other senators believed the Justice Department had tapped private telephone lines of congressmen. Montoya did not reveal the basis for the belief. A Justice Department spokesman said March 20 the suspicion was "absolutely false."

In a speech at Colorado's Jefferson-Jackson Day Dinner in Denver, Montoya said the Nixon Administration had encouraged and actively participated in "frightening invasions of citizens' rights and privileges." He said that "even the United States Senate is not immune" and that several senators "have plainly

stated they believe their conversations have been monitored."

Montoya also said the Post Office had opened first-class mail without the knowledge of the recipients.

Hoover reports FBI phone taps. Federal Bureau of Investigation (FBI) Director J. Edgar Hoover, in House Appriations subcommittee testimony released June 8, 1971, said the FBI was using 33 telephone taps and four microphone bugging devices in national security cases. In testimony given March 17, Hoover also said the bureau was operating 14 court-approved wiretaps and two bugging devices in organized crime cases.

The Justice Department said June 8 that FBI surveillance had remained stable since Hoover's appearance before the committee. The FBI director had said then that Attorney General John N. Mitchell had authorized all the taps "in the security field" and that the FBI had requested two additional authorizations. He said courts had issued warrants for 12 additional organized crime taps and that the bureau was seeking warrants for 45 more.

Hoover insisted that newspaper reports of FBI wiretapping were "replete with distortions, inaccuracies and outright falsehoods." He cited Washington Post articles published Feb. 7 and 8 that quoted former Attorney General Ramsey Clark as saying that FBI taps were double the number Hoover reported to Congress and "one well-informed source" that the number of FBI taps was reduced just before Hoover was to testify before a Congressional committee and resumed afterwards. Hoover also declared, "we have never tapped a telephone of any congressman or any senator since I have been director of the bureau."

Hoover said Jan. 6, 1972 that wiretaps had contributed to what he described as an increase in the conviction of gangsters involved with organized crime.

Hoover said "these devices have been increasingly valuable in penetrating these complex, tightly knit conspiracies involving intricate security precautions, and most of the 1,200 arrests under the Organized Crime Control Act were made possible by them."

According to Hoover, more than 650 persons linked to organized crime were convicted in 1971, a rise of almost 200 from 1970. He said that much of the gain "should go to court-approved electronic surveillance devices provided for in recent legislation.

Wiretaps of newsmen charged. Time magazine charged in its March 5, 1973 issue that over a period of more than two years, the White House had ordered the FBI to tap the phones of "six or seven" newsmen and a number of White House aides in order to pinpoint a news leak in the executive staff. Time attributed the story to "four different sources in the government." It declined, however, to name the sources or the newsmen involved. The magazine said the late J. Edgar Hoover at first had balked at using such wiretaps but was ordered by Attorney General John Mitchell to do as the White House directed.

Time said the wiretapping actually kept Hoover in office. Mitchell's deputy Richard Kleindienst had wanted Hoover to retire but had dropped the issue when Hoover threatened to expose the wiretaps to Congress. Time said the taps failed to uncover any leaks.

Kleindienst issued a statement Feb. 26 denying the Time magazine charges with regard to both himself and Mitchell.

Eavesdropping Cases

Hoffa Conviction Upheld. In a special hearing in Chicago, Federal District Court Judge Richard B. Austin refused July 14, 1969 to reverse the conviction of Teamster Union President James R. Hoffa. The case had been ordered back to the lower courts after Hoffa charged that the government had used illegal wiretap evidence in 1964 to convict him of conspiring to divert money from the union's welfare funds. Hoffa had petitioned for reversal and a new trial on the basis of recent Supreme Court decisions limiting the legal use of wiretaps.

Austin ruled that the government's wiretap evidence used in the union funds trial was irrelevant to the evidence on which Hoffa was convicted. (Hoffa, in U.S. District Court in Chattanooga, Tenn., was denied a new trial on charges of jury tampering, it was reported Jan. 5, 1970. Judge Frank W. Wilston said that hearings ordered by the Supreme Court to determine whether illegal wiretap evidence had been used to convict Hoffa "clearly established that the government conducted no unlawful surveillance.")

Panther Charges Dropped. Black Panther chief of staff David Hilliard was cleared of a perjury charge by U.S. District Judge Alfonso J. Zirpoli in San Francisco June 3, 1972, when the Justice Department refused to disclose wiretap evidence requested by Zirpoli. Hilliard had been accused of filing a false declaration of poverty in 1971. He was serving a prison sentence for assaulting a policeman.

The Justice Department announced Sept. 27 that it was dropping contempt of court charges against Black Panther leader Bobby Seale. The charges had been lodged by U.S. District Court Judge Julius Hoffman during the "Chicago 7" trial in 1969.

The 7th U.S. Circuit Court of Appeals in Chicago had ordered the charges dropped unless the department turned over to Seale's attorney a transcript of electronically overheard conversations that had been introduced in Hoffman's chambers during the trial. The department had admitted that the conversations, overheard while Seale was in jail, were relevant to the contempt charges.

The conversations had been intercepted by a "national security" wiretap installed without court approval. U.S. Attorney James R. Thompson told the appeals court that disclosure of the transcripts "would be inimical to our national security interests."

Charges dropped against radicals also —In two separate cases, the Justice Department dropped charges July 28 against Yippie leader Abbie Hoffman in Washington and against Lawrence Plamondon and two other White Panther Party leaders in Detroit, rather than disclose transcripts of unauthorized national security wiretaps.

Hoffman had been charged with crossing state lines to participate in a riot, in connection with the 1971 Mayday demonstrations. The Plamondon charges accused Plamondon of participating in a 1968 bombing plot.

The department said Nov. 1 that it was dropping a bomb conspiracy charge against Leslie Bacon, rather than reveal the contents of surveillance material.

Miss Bacon, an antiwar activist, had been charged in connection with a 1970 plot to bomb a New York branch of First National City Bank. An earlier perjury charge, relating to testimony about a 1971 bomb blast in the Capitol in Washington, had also been dropped for similar reasons.

U.S. Judge Julius J. Hoffman Jan. 3, 1974 dismissed the 1970 indictment of 12 Weathermen charged with conspiring to incite the "days of rage" riots in Chicago in October 1969.

Dismissal had been requested by government attorneys, who said that Supreme Court restraints on wiretapping would have hampered prosecution of the case.

The accused were: William Ayers, Kathy Boudin, Judy Clark, Bernardine Dohrn, Linda Evans, John Jacobs, Jeffrey Jones, Howard Machtinger, Terry Robbins, Mark Rudd, Michael Spiegel and Lawrence Weiss.

Military Surveillance

Domestic Spying Revealed

Controversy was caused during the early 1970s by disclosures that the Army had conducted an intensive domestic program of surveillance and the collection of information on civilians.

ConusIntel disclosed. The first public report on the Army operation, Continental U.S. Intelligence (or ConusIntel), was made by ex-Capt. Christoper H. Pyle in the January 1970 issue of Washington Monthly magazine.

The reports of Pyle and newsmen revealed that ConusIntel had used 1,000 Army agents to keep track of American citizens who, it apparently was thought, might become involved in subversion or civil disturbances. ConusIntel was in operation from the summer of 1967 through the fall of 1969. During this period the program produced data files on 18,000 Americans ranging from students to politicians, pacifists, environmentalists and the Daughters of the American Revolution. During 1969 ConusIntel agents produced 1,200 spot reports a month on incidents from every part of the U.S.

Sen. Sam J. Ervin Jr. (D, N.C.), who headed Senate Constitutional Rights Sub-committee hearings into the Army program and other alleged government invasions of privacy, discussed some of the implications of the disclosures in an address in Atlantic City, N.J. May 20, 1971 before the Spring Joint Computer Conference of the Federation of Information Processing Societies. This address formed the basis of an article on the subject in the Columbia Human Rights Review (Vol. 4, No. 1, 1972). Ervin said:

Allegedly, for the purpose of predicting and preventing civil disturbances which might develop beyond the control of state and local officials, Army agents were sent throughout the country to keep surveillance over the way the civilian population expressed their sentiments about government policies. In churches, on campuses, in classrooms, in public meetings, they took notes, tape-recorded, and photographed people who dissented in thought, word or deed. This included clergymen, editors, public officials, and anyone who sympathized with the dissenters.

With very few, if any, directives to guide their activities, they monitored the membership and policies of peaceful organizations who were concerned with the war in Southeast Asia, the draft, racial and labor problems, and community welfare. Out of this surveillance the Army created blacklists of organizations and personalities which were circulated to many federal, state and local agencies, who were all requested to supplement the data provided. Not only descriptions of the contents of speeches and political comments were included, but irrelevant entries about personal finances, such as the fact that a militant leader's credit card was withdrawn. In some cases, a psychiatric diagnosis taken from Army or other medical records was included.

This information on individuals was programmed into at least four computers according to their political beliefs, or their memberships, or their geographic residence.

The Army did not just collect and share this information. Analysts were assigned the task of evaluating and labeling these people on the basis of reports on their attitudes, remarks and activities. They were then coded for entry into computers or microfilm data banks.

The Army attempts to justify its surveillance of civilians by asserting that it was collecting information to enable the President to predict when and where civilians might engage in domestic violence, and that the President was empowered to assign this task to it by the statutes conferring upon him the power to use the armed forces to suppress domestic violence. . . .

The Army's spying violated First Amendment freedoms of the civilians who became aware that they or the groups to which they belonged had been placed under surveillance. This is so because it undoubtedly stifled their willingness to exercise their freedom of speech, association and assembly.

If any proof were needed of the logic and truth of this statement, it can be drawn from such testimony as the Subcommittee received from Dr. Jerome Wiesner who commented:

"Many, many students are afraid to participate in political activities of various kinds which might attract them because of their concern about the consequences of having a record of such activites in a central file. They fear that at some future date, it might possibly cost them a job or at least make their clearance for a job more difficult to obtain."

The Subcommittee has heard no testimony yet that the Army's information program was useful to anyone. The only result of the testimony by the Defense Department was to confirm my belief that under the Constitution and under the laws, the Army had no business engaging in such data-gathering and that the scope and breadth of the surveillance was so broad as to be irrelevant to the purpose. . . .

The bulk of investigative activity by the Army's own personnel occurred at the field level. Agents collected information and filed "spot reports," "agents reports," and "summaries of investigation." Most of this data was forwarded up the chain of command but record copies were kept in data centers at every level of command. Manual files were maintained at every level. At least four and possibly more computer systems were employed to store, analyse and retrieve the information collected. Many files on lawful citizens were microfilmed and integrated with other files on persons who were suspected of violations of security and espionage laws. These computer systems were located in the headquarters of the Intelligence Command (Fort Holabird), the Continental Army (Fort Monroe), the Third Army Corps (Fort Hood), and in the Pentagon. More than one computer data bank was maintained in some of these locations. (Subcommittee investigation.)

Army to end civilian protest watch. Rep. Cornelius E. Gallagher (D, N.J.) said Feb. 26, 1970 that the Army would halt surveillance of peaceful civilian demonstrations and would no longer publish a list of civilians who "might be involved" in a riot. Gallagher, chairman of the House Invasion of Privacy Subcommittee, released a letter from Army general counsel Robert E. Jordon 3d saying that copies of its civil disturbance list "have been ordered withdrawn and destroyed." Jordon also said the Army had discontinued operation of a computer data bank that included "information about potential incidents and individuals involved in potential civil disturbance incidents."

The American Civil Liberties Union (ACLU), on behalf of a dozen individuals and peace groups, had filed suit in U.S. District Court in Washington Feb. 18 asking that the Army be banned from "collection, maintenance, storage and distribution of information about the lawful political activities" of dissenters. At that time Army spokesmen had said that a 100-man intelligence unit based at Fort Holabird, Md. conducted probes for "security clearance purposes" and since 1965 had collected data "concerning the potential for civil disorders in order to permit [the Army] to discharge its responsibilities under the Constitution."

Gallagher said Feb. 28 that the Army had promised to destroy computer data it had collected on seven million persons over the last three years. He said the data included information on subscribers to peace newspapers, antiwar demonstrators and some members of the ACLU and other liberal organizations. Gallagher said the "construction of such a data bank

. . . is tantamount to a domestic espionage apparatus."

Army charged with political spying.
Sen. Sam J. Ervin Jr. charged Dec. 16, 1970 that Army intelligence agents had conducted political surveillance operations in Illinois, spying on Sen. Adlai E. Stevenson 3d (D, Ill.), former Illinois Gov. Otto Kerner, Rep. Abner J. Mikva (D, Ill.) and some 800 other prominent civilians in the state.

Ervin, who said his information was supplied by a former Army intelligence agent involved in the alleged surveillance, charged that the "Army investigated these men during their campaigns for office and while they were in office."

Commenting on those allegedly chosen for Army surveillance, Ervin said, "It was enough that they opposed or did not actively support the government's policy in Vietnam or that they disagreed with domestic policies of the Administration, or that they were in contact or sympathetic to people with such views."

In a statement Dec. 17, Army Secretary Stanley R. Resor denied Ervin's report. Resor said, "On the basis of information I have received . . . I can state that neither Sen. Stevenson, Rep. Mikva, nor former Gov. Kerner are or ever have been the subject of military intelligence activities or investigation related to political activities. Allegations to the contrary are without foundation in fact." Resor's statement did not mention the 800 other civilians cited in Ervin's charge or Army activities outside Illinois.

White House Press Secretary Ronald L. Ziegler said Dec. 17 that President Nixon "totally, completely and unequivocally" opposed military surveillance of political figures. Ziegler said no such spying was going on "in any way at this time" and that the President would not tolerate it during his Administration.

John M. O'Brien, 26, a former Army intelligence agent who had been revealed as Ervin's informant, said in a press conference Dec. 18 that he had written to Ervin because "I was trying to make unknowing people aware of a menace that existed, and might still exist." He said

he thought domestic intelligence operations "violated the civil liberties of everyone in this room." O'Brien, a former staff sergeant, had been honorably discharged from the Army in June 1970.

Rep. Ogden R. Reid (R, N.Y.) Feb. 17, 1971 released a letter in which Army Secretary Resor admitted that "some reports" filed by Army intelligence agents "could have contained the names" of Stevenson, Mikva, Kerner and other Illinois political figures. But Resor said these names would be in the form of newspaper clippings or reports of speeches rather than representing an effort to develop detailed dossiers on political figures.

With Army permission, Reid also disclosed Feb. 17 part of a May 2, 1968 intelligence collection plan that led to the surveillance of persons active in the civil rights and antiwar movements. Reid said the plan had been distributed to 319 federal and state government officials, but that "no one had the sense or the courage to question what they were doing." Reid added, "To me, it's almost as disturbing that so many remained silent as that this [plan] was conceived in the first place."

Surveillance on campus described. A former Army lieutenant, in an interview reported by the New York Times, said Dec. 23, 1970 that he had spied on campus political groups and, at one point, on welfare mothers demonstrating in New York City. Joseph Levan, 27, said he had been assigned to spy on student activities between July 1967 and February 1969, when he was attached to the Manhattan field office of the 108th Military Intelligence Group.

Levan said his unit had paid tuition fees for a black member to enter New York University's black studies program.

Levan said his own instructions were to go to Fordam University and City College "to pick up any propaganda that was distributed in my territory and report on any student activities." He added, "The Army thought this was well within the scope of its mission to protect itself, but most of us thought it was a little out of line."

The Times, in its report Dec. 23, also quoted Ralph M. Stein, a former Army intelligence sergeant, who said he had helped organize a "left-wing desk" at the Pentagon. He said hundreds of people were put under surveillance, including actress Jane Fonda and the Rev. Ralph David Abernathy, president of the Southern Christian Leadership Conference, and his associate, the Rev. Jesse Jackson.

In a related development, nine House members from New York City signed a letter to Defense Secretary Melvin R. Laird Dec. 22 deploring the Army's alleged surveillance of student activities on city campuses.

(Oliver A. Pierce, a former Army agent stationed at Fort Carson, Col., said Jan. 4, 1971 that he had spied for six months on a Colorado Springs youth group. Pierce said the head of G2, the intelligence unit, feared that the leader of the group "would get GIs into his youth group and then would indoctrinate them with antiwar beliefs." Pierce said the Army's method of identifying targets for surveillance was decentralized. He said: "It depends on the attitude of the commanding officer or, in this case, the G2.")

Newsmen watched in Saigon? Four U.S. government probers were reported Jan. 8, 1970 to have infiltrated the Saigon press corps to spy on U.S. newsmen. The U.S. mission in Saigon Jan. 30 denied that the agents—two Americans and two South Vietnamese—had spied on the press. It said the men, fraudulently accredited as newsmen by the U.S. command, had been on a mission "completely unrelated to the local or foreign press corps or their activities." The mission's chief spokesman, Edward T. Savage, refused to divulge the exact purpose of the agents' work.

The four men were identified as U.S. Army Specialists 4 William T. Tucker and Howard B. Hethcox and Nguyen Van Vien and Nguyen Van Thien. They had been issued press cards Jan. 8 after presenting letters of introduction from the American University Press,

which later denied any connection with the men. Their credentials were withdrawn Jan. 27 after their identity became known.

The Defense Department in Washington Jan. 28 identified Tucker and Hethcox as agents of the U.S. Army's Criminal Investigation Division, but said their accreditation had been "inadvertent."

The U.S. command in Saigon announced Feb. 6 that an American officer "assigned to a military investigative agency" had made an "erroneous assumption of authority" in placing the four men in the Saigon press corps. He had been reprimanded and placed in a new job, the command said.

Action on Abuses

Laird orders intelligence shakeup. Defense Secretary Melvin R. Laird issued an order Dec. 23, 1970 in a move to put military intelligence operations under tighter civilian control.

Laird said: "I want to be certain that Department of Defense intelligence and counterintelligence activities are completely consistent with constitutional rights, all other legal provisions and national security needs. These activities must be conducted in a manner which recognizes and preserves individual human rights."

He said actions had been taken to "eliminate some past abuses . . . but further corrective actions are necessary as a matter of urgent priority." Officials said that among past corrective actions was a June 9 order to the Army to destroy all "inappropriate" files kept on civilians.

Laird declared Dec. 28 that probes of civilians in connection with urban rioting "could more properly be performed by the Justice Department" rather than intelligence agents under Army control. Laird said that in some cases involving national security, military personnel had engaged in wiretapping and electronic eavesdropping "under terms prescribed" by Congress and the attorney general.

Army spokesmen said Jan. 28, 1971 that Brig. Gen. Jack B. Matthews, 52, commanding officer of the U.S. Army Intelligence Command, would be transferred Feb. 1 and would be replaced by Brig. Gen. Orlando C. Epp, 50, currently stationed in Hawaii. Matthews was to be reassigned from Ft. Holabird in Baltimore, where he was responsible for all Army security investigations of personnel, to Ft. Lewis, Wash.

ACLU suit dismissed. Judge Richard B. Austin of the U.S. District Court in Chicago June 5, 1971 dismissed a suit brought by the American Civil Liberties Union, which sought an injunction to halt Army domestic surveillance operations and an order to destroy files collected during the alleged spying. After nearly two weeks of hearings, Austin dismissed the Army intelligence activity as "typical Washington bureaucratic boondoggling."

The suit had been brought on behalf of Jay Miller, head of the Chicago ACLU chapter; the Rev. Jesse Jackson, a civil rights leader; and Gordon B. Sherman, who had organized Business Executives Move for Peace in Vietnam. The chief witness for the plaintiffs was John M. O'Brien, whose information about Army surveillance of political figures in Illinois had led to charges by Sen. Sam J. Ervin Jr. (D, N.C.) that the Army was conducting illegal spying operations.

Referring to testimony that much of the Army activity was in clipping and filing newspaper stories about their "targets," Austin said "the chief beneficiary of Army intelligence has been newspaper circulation. The only detriment... appears to have been an increase in air pollution from burning the newspapers after they were read." Although he referred to the intelligence unit that was the subject of the hearings as an "assemblage of Keystone Cops," Austin said the federal government was "well within its rights" to use any available facilities to prepare for civil disturbance emergencies.

Civilian panel to check Army probes. Defense Secretary Melvin Laird Feb. 18, 1971 announced the formation of a civilian-dominated board to directly control military intelligence investigations in the U.S. He said tighter civilian control "protects the national security interest while insuring the constitutional, civil and private rights" of individuals and organizations.

Laird established a five-man Defense Investigative Review Council, to be headed by Assistant Secretary of Defense Robert F. Froehlke. Three other civilian members were Undersecretaries of the Army, Thaddeus R. Beal; Navy, John W. Warner; and Air Force, John L. McLucas. The only military man appointed was director of the Defense Intelligence Agency, Lt. Gen. Donald V. Bennett.

In his Dec. 23, 1970 move, Laird had ordered the Defense Intelligence Agency to direct all domestic and foreign military intelligence activity and to report directly to him rather than through the Joint Chiefs of Staff. Forehlke said that after study, Laird had decided the civilian-controlled board would be preferable for overseeing domestic intelligence.

At the Pentagon news conference to announce the new panel, Froehlke said he believed abuses by military domestic spy operations had occurred and that the blame belonged to both military and civilian leaders. He said the biggest "culprit" was the political climate that followed the riots in Detroit in 1967. These disorders had led to alarm about potential riots all over the country. Froehlke said he believed civilian officials ordered a "reluctant" military to conduct probes in specific areas. He said "the military over-reacted" once it became involved but added, "I have found no grand conspiracy."

■ In a protest against Army surveillance of peace groups, 11 members of SANE lurked outside the Bethesda, Md. home of Defense Secretary Laird Feb. 15. The demonstrators questioned bystanders, took notes and carried tape recorders, cameras and toy telescopes. Sanford Gottlieb, executive director of the Citizens Organization for a Sane World, said Ralph Stein, a former Army intelligence agent, had admitted putting himself on the organization's mailing list under an alias as part of surveillance activity.

Eastland gets files. The Associated Press reported July 8, 1971 that extensive private files of alleged Communists and subversives had been turned over in March to Sen. James O. Eastland (D, Miss.) by the Defense Department. The files had been compiled by Maj. Gen. Ralph H. Van Deman, a former Army chief of intelligence, between his retirement in 1929 and 1952, the year of his death.

J. Fred Buzhardt, Defense Department general counsel, told about the transfer of the Van Deman files to Eastland, chairman of the Senate Internal Security Subcommittee, in a June 10 letter to Sen. Sam J. Ervin Jr. (D, N.C.), which was made available to reporters. Buzhardt said July 8 that the current policy of the Defense Department prohibited keeping such files. He said giving them to the Eastland subcommittee "was as good a way to get rid of them as any."

The New York Times reported Sept. 7 that the files contained information on politicians, labor leaders, civil rights leaders and entertainers, all suspected by Van Deman of being subversives. Among those reportedly listed in the files were Rep. Emanuel Celler (D, N.Y.), author Pearl Buck, actresses Joan Crawford and Helen Hayes, former Rep. Adam Clayton Powell (D, N.Y.) and Nobel Prize chemist Linus Pauling.

The Times reported an Army memorandum written in 1970 after investigation of the files said, "There may be some embarrassment to the Army because of the information contained on labor and civil rights movements. The question of the Army's relationship to Van Deman could also be embarrassing." There was reportedly evidence of a give-and-take of information between Van Deman, with his network of volunteer agents, and Army and Navy intelligence, the Federal Bureau of Investigation and agencies in California, Van Deman's home state.

Revelations Continue

Ervin hearings: Army bars abuses. Testimony on the Army's surveillance of civilians was taken by the Senate Constitutional Rights Subcommittee under the chairmanship of Sen. Sam J. Ervin Jr.

John M. O'Brien, whose letter to Ervin in 1970 had been the basis of Ervin's Dec. 16, 1970 charge of Army spying on civilians, presented a statement to the subcommittee Feb. 24, 1971. In the statement O'Brien said: ... I served in the United States Army for almost five years. My last four years on active duty were spent as an Army Intelligence Agent, the first three in Western Germany, where I was trained as and performed the duties of an Army Intelligence Case Officer. During these three years I worked in the defensive counterespionage field and most of my work was directed against non-Americans, whose activities were thought to be inimical to the national defense interests of the United States. My last year on active duty with the United States Army was spent assigned to Region I, 113th Military Intelligence Group, in Evanston, Illinois. At Region I, I performed the duties of an Army Intelligence Case Officer. My duties at Region I were similar in nature to my duties while assigned to Western Europe, except that at Region I my activities were directed almost exclusively against United States citizens. I was honorably discharged from the United States Army on June 8, 1970, with the rank of staff Sergeant.

From June 1969 until approximately December 1969, I was assigned to the Special Operations Section of Region I. During that period, I worked primarily in undercover operations. These undercover operations included the recruitment, training and controlling of undercover agents utilized by the United States Army. On several occasions, I personally performed as an undercover agent as part of my assigned military duties. Special Operations activities at Region I consisted of the screening, investigation, recruitment, training, targeting, and controlling of individuals performing in an undercover capacity for the United States Army. Such activities were primarily directed against civilian organizations and individuals. . . .

I also assisted the CONUS/Liaison Section at Region I. The CONUS/Liaison Section compiled personalia information concerning and monitored organizations and individuals engaged in activities to oppose the United States military involvement in Vietnam and in other activities and associations thought to be inimical to the national defense interests of the United States. Individuals included within the sphere of interest of CONUS included Adlai Stevenson III, Abner Mikva, the individual plaintiffs in the trial in Chicago, and many others including, newspapermen, university professors, public officials and businessmen. At one period in late 1969, CONUS maintained dossiers concerning approximately 800 civilian organizations and individuals. These dossiers were commonly called the subversives files. The policy throughout Region I was to obtain any information available concerning organizations and individuals whose names were in a CONUS dossier....

Rep. Abner J. Mikva (D, Ill.), mentioned by O'Brien as one the persons kept under Army surveillance in the Illinois operation, appeared before the subcommittee to demand a complete Congressional ban on domestic spying by the military and "a complete purging of every command official who was responsible for establishing and operating this spy network." Mikva said he believed that much of the activity was unknown to top civilian officials in the Defense Department.

Christopher H. Pyle, a former captain of military intelligence, said a Justice Department unit had become "the government's headquarters for civil disturbance and political protest information." Pyle also claimed that some military intelligence units, particularly the 113th Military Intelligence Group at Fort Sheridan, Ill., continued to collect political information months after orders to stop the activity were issued in June 1970. He said information on individuals, forbidden under the Army directives, was being hidden in files on organizations, which were permitted in some instances.

The subcommittee also received a statement from Edward D. Sohier, who said:

In August 1970 I was separated from the Army, honorably, with the Army Commendation Medal and the rank of Specialist 5, E–5. I had spent nearly three years on active duty, 15 months of which on duty with the Counterintelligence Analysis Division (CIAD), Directorate of Counterintelligence, Office of the Assistant Chief of Staff for Intelligence (OACSI)....

My first encounter with the so-called CONUS intelligence program was in my first job at CIAD. That was assisting in the preparation of the two-volume publication, *Personalities, Organizations, and Cities of Interest,* called by CIAD, the Compendium. This book, which was to be updated five times in the period I was with CIAD, was a compilation of information on individuals and organizations in this country which were regarded as potentially involved in domestic disturbances, in particular, in connection with anti-war and civil rights activities. Included in the lists were organizations such as Women's Strike for Peace, Southern Christian Leadership Conference, National Association for the Advancement of Colored People, American Civil Liberties Union, Quaker Action Committee, National Mobilization Committee (to End the War in Vietnam), American Friends Service Committee, and many other such peace and civil rights groups, as well as more radical groups such as Students for a Democratic Society, Black Panther Party, and Weathermen. Individuals listed included the late Dr. Martin Luther King, Dr. Benjamin Spock, Dr. Ralph Abernathy, H. Rap Brown, and Eldridge Cleaver.

The Compendium was very widely distributed by OACSI. It was sent to elements of the armed forces in the continental U.S. (CONUS) and worldwide. It was sent to other branches of the government including the Justice Department (Federal Bureau of Investigation), Treasury Department (Secret Service), and State Department. It was augmented five times with changes (additions and deletions of pages of information), and, when the order was given to destroy all copies of the Compendium in the summer of 1970, a sixth change was in the works. The Compendium was classified SECRET.

CIAD also provided the armed forces and branches of the government with other publications regarding this area of interest. One was what was called an estimate, which provided an analysis of past events in the nation and an estimate of the potential for domestic disorders for the upcoming period. I believe this publication was prepared annually. Its purpose was to inform the Army commands of the potential need for Army support required to keep the order in the nation in case of disorders.

OACSI, and in particular, CIAD, was tasked with the responsibility of providing the Army with information regarding potentially disrupting situations in the United States. Since the Army has the responsibility of responding to a national call for aid in restoring order, it needs an agency to keep it informed of the potential for that call for aid, and thus, the potential for civil disturbances. In doing so OACSI kept a sharp eye and ear on potential "trouble-makers" both individuals and organizations, and their activities.

Much of the information was gathered by CIAD from the press....

The subcommittee took testimony from Laurence F. Lane, a legislative aide of

Rep. Robert N. Giaimo (D, Conn.). Lane had worked in the office of the G2 (Intelligence & Security) Section of the 5th Infantry Division at Ford Carson, Col. from December 1968 to June 1970. Lane told the subcommittee:

Part of the recent investigation by the Department of Defense centered on the use of personnel of the 5th Military Intelligence Counter-Intelligence Section to obtain raw intelligence on civilians. Guidelines reportedly were established which prevented the use of tactical units from interfering with the areas of operations of non-tactical intelligence commands. The intelligence gathering mission in Colorado by the military reportedly was the responsibility of the Denver based Region IV Headquarters of the 113th Military Intelligence Group. Field offices of the 113th M.I. were maintained in Colorado Springs and Fort Collins, besides the Denver headquarters. Whether the 5th M.I. was in violation of standing orders or whether it was not is a moot point. The Counter-intelligence Section actively engaged in off-post, civilian oriented intelligence collection. . . .

Both commanders of the 5th Infantry Division and Fort Carson under whom I served were ambitious Generals with successful military careers. A civil disturbance mission was levied on the division and these men were responsible for accomplishing that mission. Their determination to be totally prepared placed a major burden on the G2 (Intelligence and Security) Section of the General's Staff. Faced with the responsibility to keep the commander informed, the intelligence system including linkage with the national intelligence system and the gathering of local raw intelligence developed. . . .

When I joined the G2 Operations staff in mid-December, 1968, two officers and two men had just started molding the intelligence machine which we affectionately called the "monster." The month before, a Brigade of troops had been placed on full alert to cope with a demonstration of several hundred outside of the gates to the Fort. Rumors of violence magnified by the rise of student, Chicano and Black groups laid heavy demands on the G2 to provide timely intelligence to the Commanding General. Prominent in the news was the trouble at the San Francisco State College. Two questions asked were, what is happening and will Federal troops be needed? . . .

Colorado College sponsored a "Symposium on Violence." The Symposium attracted many leading spokesmen for the New Left including Mike Klonsky, National Secretary, SDS; Jon Sunstrom, spokesman for the East Side New York Service Organization; Arnold Kaufman, a founder of the teach-in movement; John Sack, an outspokesn critic of the war in Vietnam and author; Ivanhoe Donaldson, a founder of SNCC; Richard (Dick) Gregory, comedian and civil rights activist; Andrew Kopkind, staff writer for the "New Republic"; Richard Flacks, an early anti-war critic; Sidney Peck, co-chairman of the National Mobilization Committee to End the War in Vietnam; Joe Boyd, reportedly a member of the Denver Black Panther organization; and numerous other spokesmen on violence as a tactic. An elaborate intelligence operation was instituted to cover the event. Agents from the 113th MI field office in Colorado Springs and the headquarters in Denver covered the event for the purpose of feeding information to the intelligence command. The G2 at Fort Carson mobilized the few agents of the 5th Military Intelligence Detachment and of the then separate 241st Military Intelligence Detachment to monitor the activities of the Symposium in order that the Commanding General be forewarned of possible violence. Another analyst, a Harvard graduate who was a reservist called to active duty, and I, were asked to attend the symposium not as undercover agents, but as observers. Our mission was to interpret the week of lectures, panels, and performances within the perspective of national and state-wide trends.

Viewed as an intelligence operation, the symposium coverage was excellent. The information transmitted to Fort Holabird included daily summaries of activities and rumors of upcoming demonstrations. A volume of information was compiled to include agent reports, pictures and the two independent appraisals of the symposium. . . .

. . . The second G2 for whom I worked was suspicious of dissent, and mistrustful of other intelligence-gathering activities. During his term of service as G2, the counter-intelligence section grew to over thirty men. The tactical responsibilities on the on-post counter intelligence operation were minimal while the section was extremely overstrength. The answer was to use these men to monitor the activities of activists in the community. Deep concern was expressed in particular in a family extremely active in the anti-war movement in Colorado Springs. Files were maintained on the family as well as a photograph book to make sure they were easily identified. Individuals who attended SDS meetings or Radical Education Programs meeting were of great interest. The small, but vocal anti-war faction within the community was viewed as a major threat.

It was about this time, that the jurisdictional battle between the 113th M.I. and the G2, 5th M.I. broke into the open. Two agents from the 5th M.I. Counter-intelligence Section attended the State SDS Convention, Colorado State College, Greeley, Colorado, in mid-April. The 113th M.I. commander had cautioned the G2 that having personnel there would be a violation of an informal agreement between the two intelligence units. The G2 sanctioned the mission of the two agents, and upon their return a report was filed by the G2 of the intelligence command listing the source as "two reliable sources, no further identification." The squabble developed into a game similar to two kids throwing mud at each other. The passing of information through liaison all but ceased. The G2 authorized the semi-permanent off-post activities of at least two agents. Their job became one of beating the 113th M.I. to the information and the monitoring of the activities of 113th M.I. personnel.

The classic illustration of the "spy versus spy" activities occurred at a demonstration in Colorado Springs—Fort Carson area, in mid-September 1969. Rumors of a huge demonstration bringing as many as 5,000–10,000 participants spurred the fort to an unusual state of preparedness. Elaborate preparations were made to monitor events. A newly installed Citizens' Band radio setup to include mobile car units and walking units was used. The demonstration, which had nationwide billing, attracted intelligence personnel from neighboring Air Force installations, NORAD, law enforcement agencies, 113th M.I. Region IV, and even two Navy intelligence officials from somewhere on the West Coast. The preparation included a special assignment crew with the mission to monitor the activities of the other intelligence personnel and, in particular, the personnel of the 113th M.I. To make a long story short, 119 demonstrators participated in the protest. Of the 119 individuals at the B Street Gate to Fort Carson, almost one-half (53) were intelligence gathering personnel or representatives of the press. Attempts to tape the speeches of well-known activists produced 45 minutes of the best sound effects of helicopters—at least six were airborne. The commander of the 113th M.I. walked into the G2 Operations Command Post just in time to hear one of the special assignment crew caution the headquarters that he was headed that way....

The activities of the G2 Operations staff shifted with greater emphasis on civil disturbance target areas, rather than the obsession with Colorado activists. However, during the Fall, 1969, the Counter-Intelligence Section of the 5th M.I. remained interested in local, off-post issues. There was great interest in rumors that efforts were being made to establish an anti-war coffee house in Colorado Springs. Also, during the Fall, an "underground" newspaper, *aboveground*, appeared on the fort and throughout the local community. Counter-Intelligence operations were particularly interested in military personnel participating in these reportedly "anti-military" programs, but concern was also expressed about civilians involved.

It was reported that a bar which had recently come under new management was the rumored coffee house. Counter-intelligence agents were directed to check it. I was in the area that evening and stopped out of curiosity. There sat six counter-intelligence agents, the owner and myself in this dingily lighted dive making small talk but attempting not to let on that you knew who the guy next to you really was and what he was doing there. . . .

Assistant Defense Secretary Robert F. Froehlke testified March 2 on the circumstances surrounding the Army surveillance controversy and on government action to end abuses. "Prior to the summer of 1967, the involvement of the military services in collection of civil disturbance information could be characterized as minimal but increasing," he said. Following the Newark and Detroit riots of July 1967, however, there was "a turning point," Froehlke reported. He continued:

It is significant that around 1967, the character of the major disturbances underwent a change. Prior to this point in time, the civil disturbances had largely arisen in connection with racial matters, and had apparently been precipitated by a chance incident. Later, although racial incidents continued, a new potential for major civil disturbances also arose. This potential centered on planned and usually pre-announced assemblies of persons from across the nation to protest the war. Many of the potential participants in these pre-announced assemblies announced their intention to disrupt the government. It was the cumulative impact of these developments which led to the Army being tasked to plan for possible commitment of Federal troops in as many as 25 major cities concurrently.

On April 10, 1968, the National Advisory Commission on Civil Disturbances, known as the Kerner Commission, filed its report. This Commission reported that the Army Staff Task Group had conducted a study on which the Commission had relied heavily. The . . .

It is . . . significant to note that a Commission finding stated that "the absence of accurate information, both before and during disorder, has created special control problems for police."

It was against this general background, and in this period of crisis, that the involvement of the Military Services in collection and analysis of information on civilians and organizations not affiliated with the Department of Defense occurred. These so-called intelligence activities were only one facet of the overall planning and operations required from the Military Services in connection with civil disturbances.

Although all of the Military Services were subjected to requirements connected with information collection related to civil disturbances, the Department of the Army had the responsibility for the principal effort. The other military departments had a collateral role consisting primarily of responding to intelligence requirements developed by the Army planners to the extent the other Services possessed information which filled the specified need. . . .

Investigative and related counterintelligence collection activities can be divided into categories based on the nature or techniques utilized for collection of the information. Generally, these categories are: (1) liaison, (2) public media, (3) direct agent observation, and (4) covert. Liaison collection involves the obtaining of information from Federal, state and local authorities by personal contact and written inquiry. Collection by public media involves the clipping and noting of news publications, and the monitoring of commercial telecasts and radio broadcasts. Direct agent observation involves the use of personnel to personally observe activities and events and would include personal surveillance. Covert collection involves deception and the attempt to preclude awareness by those on whom information is being collected. Covert collection includes, for example, agent penetration of an organization by the use of credentials other than those identifying the agent as a military investigator.

The involvement of Army investigative and related counterintelligence organizations in the collection and utilization of information related to civil disturbances had its genesis in 1963. At that time, after several deployments of Federal troops, the Chief of Staff of the Army was designated as Executive Agent for the Joint Chiefs of Staff to command Federal troops committed to civil disturbances. Concurrent with this designation, the investigative and counterintelligence organizations of the Army, at that time organic components of the several Continental Armies, were assigned the mission of briefing the personal representative of the Army Chief of Staff on the scene. In addition, directives specified that upon the issuance of an executive order by the President committing Federal troops in connection with the civil disturbances, the investigative and related counterintelligence units in that particular Continental Army area immediately came under the operational control of the personal representative of the Chief of Staff of the Army.

From 1963 to 1965, the investigative and related counterintelligence units of the Continental Armies had the mission, in connection with civil disturbances, of being prepared to provide initial briefings to the Commander at the time of commitment of Federal troops by the President. In addition, they were to be prepared thereafter to provide the informational needs of the Task Force Commander during the period of troop commitment. In order to prepare for the requirement of an initial briefing, civil disturbance information began to be collected. The collection means which were authorized

by directives of the Continental Army Command were by liaison and reviewing the public media. Generally, direct agent observation could be resorted to in an emergency situation by authority of the Continental Army Commander. Covert collection was prohibited without the specific approval in each case of the Commander, Continental Army Command, after coordination with the Federal Bureau of Investigation as provided in the Delimitations Agreement.

On January 1, 1965, the United States Army Intelligence Command was activated. It included all Army investigative and counterintelligence units in the United States which had formerly been parceled out among the various Continental Armies. It did not, of course, include the tactical units assigned to combat operations organizations. The same policies authorizing and restricting methods of collection which previously pertained were incorporated into the directives of the Intelligence Command. The Commander of the United States Army Intelligence Command reserved to himself the authority to approve any covert collection.

As early as 1963, there are records of complaints about the failure, or inability, of the Army's investigative and counterintelligence units to provide adequate civil disturbance information prior to the commitment of Federal troops. In retrospect, it is clear that such Army units could not satisfy the requirements for civil disturbance information by authorized collection means, namely, liaison and public media review.

Early in 1965, it appears that the Army staff was tasked to provide a daily Civil Disturbance Situation Report. There is no record to indicate who imposed this requirement. However, in September 1965, the Secretary of the Army, in a memorandum to the Deputy Secretary of Defense, recommended that the daily Civil Disturbance Situation Report be discontinued. The recommendation of the Secretary of the Army was based on a similar recommendation by offices in the Army Intelligence Command. The recommendation was approved.

Nevertheless, the number and variety of requirements for specific information related to civil disturbance continued to increase through 1967. Following Detroit, direct agent observation was increasingly used to fill requirements. . . .

It is . . . evident that both civil and military authorities continued to be dissatisfied with the quality and quantity of civil disturbance information provided.

The increased concern, activity and planning led to the issuance of the comprehensive Army Civil Disturbance Plan in January 1968. On February 1, 1968, the Intelligence Annex to the Civil Disturbance Plan was issued. The Intelligence Annex contained a one page list of general essential elements of information, and there was limited tasking by specific units and types of units.

In the first six months of 1968, however, the level of riots continued high and at an even greater intensity. It was in this period that the extensive riots following the assassination of Dr. Martin Luther King occurred. Official concern grew. Law enforcement agencies, including Federal agencies, made known to the high civil authorities their lack, in quantity and quality, of the necessary resources to cope with the increasing demands for information. As a consequence, a more comprehensive and detailed intelligence document was issued on May 2, 1968. This was the Department of Army Civil Disturbance Information Collection Plan. It was classified Confidential. It was rescinded on June 9, 1970 and declassified on February 24, 1971. . . .

This Civil Disturbance Information Collection Plan provided that predisturbance information would be obtained by drawing on other Federal as well as state and local forces. These forces secure such data in the course of carrying out their primary duties and responsibilities. It further provided that United States Army Intelligence Command personnel would not be directly used to obtain civil disturbance information unless specific direction to do so had been received from Headquarters, Department of Army. Covert operations by United States Army Intelligence Command personnel were prohibited without it the prior approval and direction of the Assistant Chief of Staff of Army for Intelligence.

This collection plan contained the following preamble:

"It is recognized that Army assistance to local or state authorities in peacetime, as well as in wartime emergency, is a long standing tradition in our country. In most instances to the past, such assistance was rendered with a minimum of advance information concerning the situation. The current civil disturbance situation dictates a change in the degree to which the Army must seek advance information concerning potential and probable trouble areas and trouble makers.

"The Army is well aware that the overwhelming majority in both the anti-war and the racial movements are sincere Americans. It also realizes that in both groups there is a small but virulent number who are out to tear America apart. During demonstrations and disturbances these are the activists that control the violent action. These are people who deliberately exploit the unrest and seek to generate violence and terror for selfish purposes. If the Army must be used to quell violence it wants to restore law and order as quickly as possible and return to its normal protective role—to do this it must know in advance as much as possible about the well springs of violence and the heart and nerve causes of chaos. To

do less means the professional violence purveyors will have a better chance to achieve their end aims—law breaking, social disintegration, chaos, violence, destruction, insurrection, revolution.

"In obtaining the information called for in this plan the Army seeks only to collect that needed to exercise honest and sound judgment of the measures to be taken in suppressing rampant violence and restoring order—to assure that only the mildest effective measures are exercised—to insure that no overstepping of the degree of force or circumscription needed is applied—to conserve military resources and to avoid infringement on the responsibility and authority of civil government agencies—to insure pervasive vigilance for the fundamental rights of private citizens by the selective and enlightened use of force in restraint against those who are truly violating the rights of their fellow citizens." . . .

Despite the limitations in the Civil Disturbance Information Collection Plan on the methods of collection, it is apparent that many of the requirements which the United States Army Intelligence Command was asked to satisfy could not conceivably be collected by liaison or public media-type collection. It is highly improbable that many of the requirements listed could be obtained by other than covert collection. Indeed, many of these requirements could not be satisfied by any collection means and certainly not with the resources available. So comprehensive were the requirements levied in the Civil Disturbance Information Collection Plan that any category of information related even remotely to people or organizations active in a community in which the potential for a riot or disorder was present, would fall within their scope. Information was sought on organizations by name or by general characterization. Requirements for information were even levied which required collection on activities and potential activities of the public media, including newspapers and television and radio stations.

In summary, the Department of Army Civil Disturbance Information Collection Plan was widely distributed throughout the Federal Government, and to officials of each state government. It expressed the need and desire for every conceivable type of information related to civil disturbances and the people and organizations who were or might become involved in civil disturbances. The United States Army Intelligence Command vigorously attempted to comply with the Civil Disturbance Information Collection Plan was rescinded on June 9, 1970. . . .

Basic authority for the use of the Armed Forces in connection with civil disturbances is Article IV, Section 4 of the Constitution and Sections 331, 332 and 333 of Title 10 of the United States Code.

The civil disturbance information collection activities of the Military Services were

all integrally connected to the use or potential use of Federal troops under this authority. This information collection was obviously considered necessary and essential
to the effective use of Federal military forces
in connection with the widespread riots and
domestic disorders occurring in this period.

In none of the documents of record, however, during this period of crisis do we find
a specific legal rationale for this use of military resources to collect civil disturbance information. Indeed, it would be surprising,
had such a rationale been prepared, since the
information collection was so inseparably a
part of the total use of Federal troops. In order to carry out the President's order and
protect the persons and property in an area
of civil disturbance with the greatest effectiveness, military commanders must know
all that can be learned about that area and
its inhabitants. Such a task obviously cannot be performed between the time the President issues his order and the time the military is expected to be on the scene. Information gathering on persons or incidents which
may give rise to a civil disturbance and thus
commitment of Federal troops must necessarily be on a continuing basis. Such is required by Sections 331, 332 and 333 of Title
10 of the U.S. Code since Congress certainly
did not intend that the President utilize an
ineffective Federal Force.

It is worthy of note that none of the activities referred to above were prohibited by
Federal or state law. . . :

In December 1968, at a meeting of the
Civil Disturbance Steering Committee, the
Under Secretary of the Army expressed concern at the Army's efforts to obtain civil
disturbance information which might not
be worth the effort. He expressed a desire
that the civil disturbance information collection efforts be more sharply focused on
essential requirements and that the mission
be more precisely delineated. As a result, efforts were undertaken in the Army staff to
accomplish this objective. In early January
1969, the Army staff proposed a new mission
statement for the Army's counterintelligence
role in civil disturbances. The staff also proposed a primary mission for the civil disturbance branch of the Office of Army Assistant Chief of Staff for Intelligence. It was
to "foster Department of Justice leadership
in development of agreed roles and missions
for various Federal agencies in civil disturbance intelligence collection and production."

On February 5, 1969, the Under Secretary
of the Army wrote a memorandum to the
Vice Chief of Staff. In this memorandum, the
Under Secretary expressed concern that the
Army's intelligence activities related to civil
disturbance problems might exceed the strict
requirements. He noted that past Army intelligence activities had resulted from gaps in
the effort of civilian agencies who "have
been unable or unwilling to pursue collection efforts in a satisfactory manner." The

Under Secretary further expressed concern
that the efforts related to civil disturbances
intruded into essentially civilian areas of
concern and could result in a diffusion of
the Army's limited manpower. The Under
Secretary then expressed what he believed
to be proper concept for the role of the Army
concerning collection and utilization of information related to civil disturbances.

The Under Secretary, in this memorandum,
approved with modifications, the revised
mission which had been recommended to
him by the Director, Civil Disturbance Planning and Operations. He directed that in the
collection of civil disturbance information,
primary reliance be placed on liaison with
local, state, and Federal police and law enforcement authorities. He directed that covert
collection operations were prohibited unless
approved by the Federal Bureau of Investigation and approved in advance in each specific case by the Under Secretary of the Army.
The Under Secretary concurred in the recommendation that efforts be made to persuade
the Department of Justice to accept a larger
role in systematically reviewing the entire
civil intelligence area. He designated the
General Counsel of the Army to explore the
matter with the Department of Justice.

The Under Secretary also designated the
General Counsel of the Army to develop for
consideration of the Secretary of the Army
appropriate guidelines for future collection
activities, and directed that the Assistant
Chief of Staff for Intelligence provide information and assistance to the General
Counsel.

Following the memorandum of the Under
Secretary of the Army on February 5, 1969,
a detailed review was made on many aspects
of the civil disturbance related activities of
the U.S. Army Intelligence Command. During this period, specific requests for civil disturbance collection were forwarded from
higher authority to the Army's Assistant
Chief of Staff for Intelligence. They were
consistently returned with a recommendation that the Department of Justice be requested to fulfill the collection requirement
in accordance with the intent of the memorandum from the Under Secretary of the
Army dated February 5, 1969.

The discussions between the General
Counsel of the Army and the Department
of Justice continued during this period and
on March 18, the Department of Justice
established an Inter-Agency Committee to
coordinate and evaluate intelligence pertaining to civil disorders. . . .

On April 24, 1969, the Under Secretary of
the Army directed that distributions by the
Army of civil disturbance information be
limited to Department of Defense agencies
and to specified Federal agencies unless permission was obtained from the Under Secretary of the Army for distribution to others.
In May, 1969, the Army Assistant Chief of
Staff for Intelligence advised the U.S. Army

Intelligence Command not to initiate civil disturbance studies and collection activities unless specifically approved in advance by Headquarters, Department of the Army. On June 17, 1969, the same guidance was forwarded to the Continental Army Command and through them to all Army units based in the Continental United States.

As a result of an internal review, the civil disturbace and biographic data bank at Fort Holabird was ordered destroyed on February 19, 1970 by the Army Assistant Chief of Staff for Intelligence. Just prior to that time, the U.S. Army Intelligence Command was directed to take a number of specific actions with reference to civil disturbance information. These included the destruction of personality lists, the discontinuance of spot reports to the Department of the Army, except those which indicated situations likely to require use of Army troops, the discontinuance of the daily civil disturbance summary to the Department of the Army, and the discontinuance of input of civil disturbance information into computer programs. On 5 March 1970, the Continental Army Command was advised to destroy its computerized civil disturbance data bank and so ordered on April 1. On March 6 the Secretary of the Army in a memorandum to the Chief of Staff, established new policy on the use of data banks for civil disturbance information. This memorandum resulted in a Department of the Army letter on April 1, requiring approval at the Secretary of the Army level for use of automated data banks for civil disturbance information, and requiring destruction of any such computerized data bank operations unless they could be justified to the Secretary under the new policy. . . .

On June 9, 1970, the Department of the Army promulgated a new and comprehensive policy on the collection, reporting, processing, and storing of civil disturbance information.

The cornerstone of this new Army policy is that the Department of the Army relies on the Department of Justice at the National level for civil disturbance planning, threat, and early warning information.

This new policy prescribes that Army intelligence resources will not be used for collection of civil disturbance information until the Director for Civil Disturbance Planning and Operations has made a determination that there is a distinct threat of civil disturbance beyond the capability of local and state authorities to control. The policy further provides that even after such a determination had been made, that collection will be limited to liaison. Overt collection, other than liaison, requires approval by Headquarters, Department of the Army. Covert methods of collection continue to require concurrence of the Federal Bureau of Investigation and specific prior approval by the Under Secretary of the Army. All civil disturbance information reporting was ordered stopped and not resumed except by order from Headquarters, Department of the Army.

The policy further provides that civil disturbance plans and support material will not include listing of organizations and personalities not affiliated with the Department of Defense, with the exception of listings of local, state, and Federal officials who have duties related to the control of civil disturbances and appropriate data on vital installations and facilities. Material prohibited by this policy, then in storage, was required to be destroyed. . . .

On December 15, 1970, the Department of the Army issued a formal policy on counterintelligence activities concerning civilians not affiliated with the Department of Defense. The intent and purpose of this policy was to make applicable to all counterintelligence activities concerning civilians not affiliated with Department of Defense the type of constraints that had been imposed in the June 9 policy with respect to civil disturbance activities. . . .

DoD Directive 5200.27 was issued effective March 1, 1971.

This directive provides for the first time a Department of Defense wide policy on this subject. It establishes for the Defense Investigative Program general policy, limitations, procedures, and operational guidance pertaining to collecting, processing, storing, and disseminating information concerning persons and organizations not affiliated with the Department of Defense.

This Directive is applicable to all Department of Defense personnel, components, and organizations within the 50 States, the District of Columbia, the Commonwealth of Puerto Rico, and U.S. territories and possessions.

It prohibits collecting, reporting, processing, or storing information on individuals or organizations not affiliated with the Department of Defense except where essential to the accomplishment of the following Department of Defense missions:

1. Protection of DoD functions and property.

2. Personnel Security.

3. Operations related to civil disturbances.

With respect to the mission of protection of DoD functions and property, the Directive specifies that acquisition of information is justified by only the following types of activities:

1. Subversion of loyalty, discipline, or morale of Department of Defense military or civilian personnel by actively encouraging violation of law, disobedience of lawful order or regulation, or disruption of military activities.

2. Theft of arms, ammunition, or equipment, or destruction or sabotage of facilities, equipment, or records belonging to DoD units or installations.

3. **Acts jeopardizing the security of DoD elements or operations or compromising** classified defense information by unauthorized disclosure or by espionage.

4. Unauthorized demonstrations on active or reserve DoD installations.

5. Direct threats to DoD military or civilian personnel in connection with their official duties or to other persons who have been authorized protection by DoD resources.

6. Activities endangering facilities which have classified defense contracts or which have been officially designated as key defense facilities.

7. Crimes for which DoD has responsibility for investigating or prosecuting.

With regard to the third Department of Defense mission—operations related to civil disturbance—the Directive specifies:

"Upon specific prior authorizations of the Secretary of Defense or his designee, information may be acquired which is essential to meet operational requirements flowing from the mission assigned to the Department of Defense to assist civil authorities in dealing with civil disturbances. Such authorization will only be granted when there is a distinct threat of a civil disturbance exceeding the law enforcement capabilities of state and local authorities."

DoD Directive 5200.27 specifies a number of prohibited activities which include the following:

1. There shall be no physical or electronic surveillance of Federal, state, or local officials or of candidates for such offices.

2. There shall be no electronic surveillance of any individual or organization except as authorized by law.

3. There shall be no covert or otherwise deceptive surveillance or penetration of civilian organizations unless specifically authorized by the Secretary of Defense or his designee.

4. No DoD personnel will be assigned to attend public or private meetings, demonstrations, or other similar activities for the purpose of acquiring information the collection of which is authorized by this Directive without specific prior approval by the Secretary of Defense or his designee. An exception to this policy may be made by the local commander concerned, or higher authority, when, in his judgment, the threat is direct and immediate and time precludes obtaining prior approval. In each such case a report will be made immediately to the Secretary of Defense or his designee.

5. No computerized data banks shall be maintained relating to individuals or organizations not affiliated with the Department of Defense, unless authorized by the Secretary of Defense or his designee.

I would like to call your attention particularly to the third prohibition which I enumerated. It states that there shall be no covert or *otherwise deceptive surveillance.* As I noted earlier in my statement, there has been confusion as to the demarcation between direct agent observation and covert collection. The prohibition of "deceptive surveillance" is specifically designed to prevent the occurrence of any marginal or even slightly questionable cases. . . .

Ervin asserted Feb. 24 that "the Army was not alone in keeping tabs on civilians." He said the Navy was active in domestic surveillance as late as December 1970 and "had the Episcopal bishop of California, Bishop [C. Kilmer] Myers, under surveillance for his antiwar activities" in 1969. He said the Air Force Office of Special Investigations "has collected and does maintain information" on student and minority organizations.

Widespread political spying by Army. Sen. Sam Ervin, in a brief entered Feb. 28, 1972 in a Supreme Court case, reported that Army surveillance of domestic political activity had been more widespread than previously reported.

According to information supplied by the Army to the Senate Constitutional Rights Subcommittee from reports and intelligence data bank printouts, the Army's 1967–70 program of surveillance had extended to the political activities of a Supreme Court justice (which the New York Times identified as Thurgood Marshall), leading Democratic senators, and representatives and governors of both parties.

A spokesman for Ervin said the objects of surveillance included Sens. Edmund Muskie, George McGovern, Edward Kennedy, Harold Hughes and Fred Harris, and former Sens. Ralph Yarborough and Eugene McCarthy; also Reps. Philip M. Crane (R, Ill.) and John Rarick (D, La.), both outspoken conservatives, and former Reps. Adam Clayton Powell and Allard Lowenstein, both New York Democrats.

Governors included were Francis W. Sargent (R, Mass.) and Kenneth Curtis (D, Me.), and former Gov. Philip Hoff (D, Vt.).

In filing his brief, Ervin entered as amicus curiae the case of Arlo Tatum, head of the Central Committee for Conscientious Objectors, who had obtained an appeals court injunction against Army surveillance.

Ervin said in the brief:

Sometime in the 1960's prompted by an increase in civil violence, the United States Government, acting through the armed forces and primarily the Army, began a massive program of investigation and surveillance of the thoughts, habits, attitudes, political activities and associations of individual American citizens. This Army program took the form of the development and maintenance of investigative files in manual and computerized systems. It was an expansion of pre-existing investigative operations of the armed forces, such as personal background investigations, and was in many aspects inseparable from these other functions. The program was ostensibly developed in connection with the increased use of the Army to put down civil violence. Although there is little evidence available to support the contention, it has been explained as an effort to "predict" situations in which the use of military force would be required.

At the height of the program in the late 1960's, thousands of agents of the United States Army Intelligence Command were involved. In addition, numerous other investigative personnel and other sources of military manpower from the Continental Army Command, the Navy and the Air Force were employed. According to Army documents, the responsibility of these investigators was to gather information on persons and organizations engaged in various activities associated with racial problems, antiwar, antidraft, and other controversial public issues. Intelligence activities have been conducted in public places, on college campuses, at high schools, in churches, and at private meetings. Persons subjected to this program have ranged from leaders of active organizations, to ordinary members, the curious and the passerby. Individuals expressing support or sympathy with subjects of the surveillance have also come under investigation. Subjects have included numerous Congressmen and United States Senators and family members of a Senator, state and local officials, a member of this Court, newspaper reporters, clergymen, and thousands of other Americans. Although no total number can be estimated, it is not an exaggeration to talk in terms of hundreds of thousands of individuals, organizations, events, and dossiers.

The information gathered on these citizens has included their participation or presence at political events, their political views, their relationships with other political activities, their travel, their family associations, finances, education, and other types of personal data. Once a person becomes the subject of investigation, the data gathered about him and his activities is unlimited.[4] Information for the Army dossiers has been obtained by observation of public activities, by covert infiltration, by electronic devices, tape-recorders, cameras, and by videotape, as well as by requesting data from other governmental agencies and from private sources. The Army analyzed and attempted to categorize and label individuals according to their utterances and the way they exercised their rights of free speech, assembly, association, and petition.

The bulk of investigative activity by the Army's own personnel occurred at the field level. Agents collected information and filed "spot reports," "agent reports", and "summaries of investigation". Most of this data was forwarded up the chain of command but record copies were kept in data centers at every level of command. Manual files were maintained at every level. At least four and possibly more computer systems were employed to store, analyze, and retrieve the information collected. Many files were microfilmed and integrated with other files on persons who were suspected of violations of security and espionage laws. These were located at the headquarters of the Intelligence Command (Fort Holabird), the Continental Army (Fort Monroe), the Third Army Corps (Fort Hood), and in the Pentagon. More than one computer data bank was maintained in some of these locations.

Information gathered in this program and political analyses produced as part of it were indiscriminately shared and exchanged by the Army and were distributed to other military record systems, and to other federal, state, and local agencies maintaining investigative files. Although subsequent to the filing of this lawsuit, many of the Army computer systems and other collections of data were ordered destroyed, much of the data still exists in files maintained by the Department of the Army, the Defense Department, and the other federal, state, and local agencies to which it was regularly sent. The Department of the Army has been unwilling or unable to ensure the complete elimination of the information collected under this program from its own and other governmental records.

Examples of the type of organizations put under investigation include the following: The Southern Christian Leadership Conference, the National Association for the Advancement of Colored People, the State Rights Party, the Presbyterian Interracial Council of Chicago, the American Civil Liberties Union, Clergy and Laymen Concerned About Vietnam, the Congress of Racial Equality, the Mexican-American Youth Organization, National Organization for Women, Operation Breadbasket, United Christian Community Service, the Urban League, Young Americans for Freedom, SANE, Milwaukee United School Integration Committee, American Friends Service Committee and hundreds of others. . . .

The subcommittee Aug. 1, 1973 issued a report entitled "Military Surveillance of Civilian Politics." It said in the report:

Army surveillance of civilians engaging in

political activities in the 1960's was both massive and unrestrained. At the height of the monitoring, the Army engaged over 1,500 plainclothes agents to collect information which was placed in scores of data centers around the country. While most of the information collecting consisted of activities such as the clipping of newspaper accounts and attending public events, there were many more serious instances of surveillance in which covert means were used to observe or infiltrate groups. No individual, organization, or activity which expressed "dissident views" was immune from such surveillance and, once identified, no information was too irrelevant to place on the Army computer. Apparently, the impetus for the surveillance were the ghetto riots and mass demonstrations which marked the mid-1960's, and which had required the use of Armed Forces. The Army claims these earlier disturbances had indicated the need for more information to predict future riots and disturbances, and to deploy troops and conduct operations when called upon by the President.

The chief subjects of the surveillance were protest groups and demonstrators whose activities the Army attempted to relate to its civil disturbance mission. Little distinction was made between peaceful and non-peaceful groups. Protests and demonstrations of a peaceful, non-violent nature, which have come to be recognized as significant parts of this country's legitimate political process, were all targets for the Army's agents. More traditional forms of political activity were similarly monitored if they involved dissident groups or individuals.

The mushrooming of surveillance has been explained by the sense of panic and crisis felt throughout the government during this period of extremely vocal dissent, large demonstrations, political and campus violence, and what at the time seemed the inauguration of a period of widespread anarchy. While officials testifying before the Subcommittee suggested that these crises justified the surveillance, they failed to recognize that the rights guaranteed by the Constitution are constant and unbending to the temper of the times. . . .

The subcommittee has been unable to conclude what particular official or officials were responsible for ordering the expansion of the surveillance operation in the late 1960's. Senior officials, both civilian and military, in the Departments of Defense and Army should have been aware of these operations. Several comprehensive intelligence-gathering plans were circulated to the upper echelons of both departments. There is no satisfactory explanation why these officials should have remained unaware of the program or, if aware, why they failed in their responsibility to perceive the violations of constitutional law and traditions taking place. The failure of senior civilian officials to know of this program, or if knowing, to halt it, represents one of the most serious breakdowns of civil-

ian control of the military in recent years.

It took over two full years—from the Army's discovery of surveillance excesses late in 1968 and early in 1969 until the creation of DIRC and its inspections beginning in spring of 1971—for the civilian superiors to bring the military under control. Once set in motion, the bureaucratic inertia proved all but impossible to halt, finally requiring as it did congressional hearings, prohibitions by the Secretary of Defense and the President, law suits, reprimands of senior officers and threats of courts-martial, great public outcry, and finally unannounced inspections, before the military, if not the American people, could be assured that the surveillance had been ended.

In any case, it is now apparent that domestic surveillance was undertaken in earnest in 1967 by several Army offices and commands. There was apparently no centralized control—each appeared to proceed on its own initiatives.

Participants in the domestic intelligence collection program were the U.S. Army Intelligence Command (USAINTC) and the Continental Army Command (CONARC). The Office of the Director of Civil Disturbance Planning and Operation (DCDPO), under the Army Chief of Staff, produced intelligence analyses predicting future disturbances. A similar function was performed at Department of Army level by the Counterintelligence Analysis Branch (CIAB) which was under the supervision of the Assistant Chief of Staff for Intelligence.

USAINTC was the principal intelligence-gatherer. It was comprised of 304 stateside offices, manned by over a thousand agents. CONARC, in reality a huge "holding company" of stateside armies, had intelligence units assigned to it, and these also engaged in intelligence gathering. Both commands maintained huge data banks of information obtained from these agents, and from external sources, including the intelligence units of other branches of service and the FBI. DCDPO and CIAB also maintained computerized intelligence files. . . .

The collection plans promulgated by these commands and agencies were vague and overbroad. This lack of definition resulted in collections of irrelevant, incorrect, ambiguous, and ultimately useless information which bore no conceivable connection with the Army's civil disturbance mission.

The methods used in conducting surveillance were also objectionable. While most of the intelligence was gathered by agents at public meetings or from clipping printed publications, there is considerable evidence of the frequent use of undercover agents and other covert means to obtain information. The collection plans provided little restriction on how the intelligence was to be collected.

Army intelligence data was circulated not only to Army commands, but also to other branches of service, and to civilian agencies, in particular, the FBI.

The domestic intelligence was used by the Department of Army to prepare briefings and written analyses for use by the Pentagon. These briefings and analyses appear to be as far removed from the Army's domestic mission as the information from which they were gleaned.

Storage of domestic intelligence was not confined to the computers of USAINTC and CONARC. Substantial files were maintained in virtually every subordinate command and field office across the country.

Despite efforts by certain Department of Army officials to limit the nature and scope of surveillance, it continued largely unabated until public pressure began to build in early 1970.

In March 1970 the Secretary of the Army ordered surveillance of civilian political activity to cease, and the data banks containing the intelligence to be destroyed. An Army directive to this effect, but not without loopholes, followed in June.

The Secretary of Defense issued similar orders in December 1970 which applied to all services. A Defense Department directive appeared in March 1971 reiterating the prior orders and directives. It furthermore provided for a Defense Investigative Review Council (DIRC) to be established to monitor the intelligence activities of the services and insure compliance with the directive.

The experience from early 1970 through the period following the subcommittee's hearings in March 1971 demonstrates the difficulty that the senior civilian faced in trying to impose controls and obedience to their orders in lower echelons. Even during our hearings, a full year after the first attempts by the Secretary of the Army to control the surveillance, the subcommittee was receiving reports of efforts to frustrate higher orders. If one agrees with the Army's contention that it discovered and sought to control surveillance as early as February 1969, then the evidence of disobedience to civilian control is even more striking. In any case, it was only after the creation of the DIRC and the institution of periodic unannounced inspection tours that the Congress and the people could begin to have confidence that the surveillance was in fact being stopped.

Nonetheless, the subcommittee has only the assurance of the Army and the executive branch that the domestic intelligence files have been destroyed. No independent inspection has been permitted, nor can the subcommittee evaluate the adequacy of the assurance it has received....

There is no question that military surveillance of civilian political activity is illegal, at least in the sense that it was not authorized by law. Finding no explicit sanction in the constitutional mandate to suppress domestic violence, or in the statutes which have been promulgated under it, the sub-committee cannot imply the need for such domestic operations from the military's limited domestic mission....

... Military surveillance inhibits the exercise of constitutionally-guaranteed rights of free speech, free association, and privacy. The Constitution denies government the power to inhibit as well as prohibit the exercise of first amendment rights. The effect of Army surveillance is to cast the pall of official disapproval upon the views and activities of those whom it makes its subjects. Once so identified, these civilians and civilian organizations have more difficulty in making converts or attracting sympathizers because of an implicit fear that some type of official retribution may one day be visited upon those who have been recorded as having espoused views contrary to those of the Government. Furthermore, the outspoken citizens or organizations may themselves be reluctant to continue to express unpopular opinions in the face of official disapproval and diminishing acceptance of their positions. In short, military surveillance infringes upon first amendment rights because it increases the reluctance of citizens to voice their opinions. It is difficult to perceive a more effective method of stifling the public willingness to engage in controversial public debate than by the specter of military surveillance....

Challenge to Army surveillance dismissed. The Supreme Court ruled June 26, 1972 that the Army could not be brought into court to defend the mere existence of its surveillance of civilian political activities against charges that the surveillance discouraged freedom of speech.

The justices held 5–4 that surveillance by the Army could be challenged in court only if and when individuals could demonstrate "actual or threatened injury" by having been watched by Army agents. In other instances, the court said, control of such surveillance must be left in the hands of Congress and the executive branch.

Chief Justice Warren E. Burger wrote the majority opinion. Joining him were Justices Harry A. Blackmun, Lewis F. Powell Jr., William Rehnquist and Byron White.

Justices William J. Brennan Jr., William O. Douglas, Thurgood Marshall and Potter Stewart dissented.

Burger said that to permit such a trial of the Army for the mere existence of its surveillance apparatus would make federal courts "virtually continuing monitors of the wisdom and soundess of executive judgment."

At issue in the case was a lawsuit filed by Arlo Tatum, executive director of the Central Committee for Conscientious Objectors, and 12 other individuals and groups who said they were targets of the Army's surveillance.

The plaintiffs had sought an injunction seeking to prevent further surveillance and a court order to require the Army to destroy the dossiers compiled by its agents.

The four dissenting justices held that Tatum and the other plaintiffs had judicial precedents to take the Army to court over the surveillance issue.

Army curbs spying on civilians. Secretary of the Army Howard H. Callaway, issued an order, effective Oct. 1, 1974, that would curtail surveillance by Army intelligence of most U.S. citizens. Under the terms of the order, the Army would still be empowered to investigate U.S. civilians working for the Defense Department abroad. Surveillance of civilians not affiliated with the Defense Department would not be permitted unless there was "substantial evidence" of illegal activities that threatened Army troops, property or functions.

Callaway, in a memo to Congress made public June 13, 1975, said that a survey of Army files had found 9,200 documents on the activities of U.S. civilians. Callaway, who said the documents should have been destroyed in accordance with a 1971 Pentagon order to purge Army files on political dissidents, indicated that an action to eliminate all such documents had been recently begun but later suspended until the completion of congressional investigations of U.S. intelligence activities.

In a related development, David O. Cooke, a deputy assistant secretary of defense, told the House Government Operations Subcommittee on Government Information and Individual Rights June 8 that the Army's files on political dissenters might exist in U.S. intelligence agencies that exchanged information with the Pentagon in the late 1960s. Although the Army had destroyed its own files, Cooke said, it did not know what the CIA, the FBI and other agencies had done with the data from the Army. "I assume the files are retrievable, but not by us," Cooke said.

FBI & Other Agencies Under Attack

FBI Files Stolen

Government and private intelligence organizations were under increasing attack by Congressional and other critics by 1971. Information-gathering agencies were accused of violating constitutionally protected rights of privacy. The FBI in particular was widely criticized. Censure of the bureau frequently focused on its director, J. Edgar Hoover, who was attacked in some quarters for his power and his apparent immunity from retribution as well as for what was seen as his agency's excesses. A group that dubbed itself the Citizens Commission to Investigate the FBI burglarized the FBI's local headquarters in Media, Pa. March 8, 1971 and made off with a collection of FBI intelligence files.

Stolen FBI files disseminated. Stolen Federal Bureau of Investigation (FBI) intelligence files were received March 22 by Sen. George McGovern (D, S.D.) and Rep. Parren J. Mitchell (D, Md.). The documents, most of them relating to peace and black activist groups, were sent by the Citizens Commission to Investigate the FBI, which admitted stealing the files after breaking into the FBI office at Media, Pa. March 8.

Both McGovern and Mitchell returned the documents immediately. McGovern said he refused to be associated with "this illegal action by a private group" and said he favored Congressional investigation of the bureau. Mitchell said in a speech March 23 that burglary was a crime and should be dealt with as such. However, he added that "the investigation and surveillance of individuals, peace groups and black student groups," as indicated by the files, was also criminal.

Attorney General John N. Mitchell said March 23 that copies of the stolen records had also been distributed to the press. He urged that the information be withheld so as not to "endanger the lives or cause other serious harm to persons engaged in investigative activities on behalf of the United States." He also said disclosure of national defense information "could endanger the United States and give aid to foreign governments whose interests might be inimical to those of the United States."

The Washington Post, which received the documents March 23, published a description of the files in its March 24 editions but omitted most names and specific locations. Copies were also received by the New York Times and the Los Angeles Times.

According to a Justice Department source, the 14 documents distributed were among nearly 800 stolen. Most of them were marked "United States Government Memorandum."

One was a Nov. 4, 1970 memorandum by FBI Director J. Edgar Hoover ordering investigations of all groups "organized to project the demands of black students." The memo said, "Increased campus disorders involving black students pose a definite threat to the nation's stability and security and indicate need for increase in both the quality and quantity of intelligence information on Black Student Unions and similar groups which are targets for influence and control by violence-prone Black Panther party and other extremists."

Another document, a newsletter from the Philadelphia FBI office, encouraged agents to increase interviews with dissenters "for plenty of reasons, chief of which are it will enhance the paranoia endemic in these circles and will further serve to get the point across there is an FBI agent behind every mailbox." The document, dated Sept. 16, 1970, added, "some will be overcome by the overwhelming personalities of the contacting agent and volunteer to tell all—perhaps on a continuing basis."

One of the documents related to a philosophy professor at a Philadelphia-area college evidently suspected of harboring fugitives. The file indicated that a college switchboard operator had agreed to report on long distance calls received by the professor and that the agent had the cooperation of a campus security guard. Another reported attempts to infiltrate a 1969 war-resisters' conference at Haverford (Pa.) College and a 1970 convention of the National Association of Black Students at Wayne State University (Detroit). The documents contained a report from the Swarthmore (Pa.) police department on black militant activities at Swarthmore College.

Other groups under surveillance included the Philadelphia Black Panthers and the National Black Economic Development Conference. Muhammad Kenyatta, 27, head of the conference in Philadelphia and who was mentioned prominently in three of the documents, said March 24 he had received the documents concerning him before they were made public. Asked how he came into possession of the files, he replied, "Let it suffice to say that revolutionary information networks are growing all across America. . . . Both sides can play the 'I Spy' game," a reference to a popular TV series.

In the March 30 Harvard Crimson (Cambridge, Mass.), the first group of 14 documents were printed in their entirety "except for the removal of the names and numbers in cases which might be harmful to those who have been spied upon." The paper received copies of the memos from Resist, a draft resistance organization.

Haverford College President Dr. John R. Coleman, in a memo March 29, and Swarthmore College president Dr. Robert D. Cross, in statements March 29 and April 9, warned that it was against the policies of the colleges to supply unauthorized information about colleagues to the government. Activities at both of the Philadelphia area institutions were the subject of FBI documents stolen from the Media office. Cross announced April 9 the appointment of a committee to recommend ways to safeguard confidential information. He said some persons on the campus may have gone "beyond the limits of reasonable cooperation" with the FBI and warned that those who divulged confidential information risked dismissal.

The Washington Post and several other newspapers received 11 more of the stolen FBI documents from the Citizens Commission to Investigate the FBI April 5.

One of the documents, reported by the Post April 6, noted a "few instances where security informants in the New Left [movement] got carried away during a demonstration, assaulted police, etc." The document said agents should advise informants that "they should not become the person who carries the gun, throws the bomb, does the robbery or by some specific violative, overt act becomes a deeply involved participant."

Another document related to the sending of anonymous radical material to college educators who "have shown reluctance to take decisive action against the 'New Left.'" Another described efforts to set up a network of informers in black neighborhoods in Philadelphia by recruiting "men honorably discharged from the armed services, . . . employes and owners of businesses in ghetto areas, . . . persons who frequent ghetto areas on a regular basis such as taxi drivers, salesmen. . . . Installment collectors might also be considered [as sources] in this regard."

File on Reuss' daughter disclosed. A memorandum containing biographical information about the daughter of Rep. Henry S. Reuss (D, Wis.) was contained in a new packet of stolen Federal Bureau of Investigation (FBI) documents distributed April 10, 1971 by the Citizens Commission to Investigate the FBI.

The document on Jacqueline Reuss, 21, a senior at Swarthmore (Pa.) College, was written Nov. 19, 1970 and contained routine educational background based on information obtained from a secretary in the college registrar's office. The memo did not indicate why the information had been collected.

Reuss, a critic of the Vietnam war, said in an April 12 statement the FBI's "mission is not to compile dossiers on millions of Americans, congressmen's daughters or not, who are accused of no wrongdoing." Miss Reuss said April 10 that she thought the reason for the FBI investigation was "the typical sort of thing leftist activity."

In distributing the new packet of documents April 10, the Citizens Commission also released the text of a letter it had mailed March 30 to persons identified as informers in the stolen FBI memos. The letter stated that persons or organizations against whom they had informed would be notified, and copies of the pertinent documents were sent to the subjects of the FBI investigations April 3. The commission's letter to the informers said, "We regret that this action was necessary" but that "the struggle for freedom and justice in this society can never succeed if people continue to betray their brothers and sisters."

Later releases, received by the press April 23–27, included documents on draft resisters in the U.S. and Canada,

files on plans for a Black Panther convention and on a black student group at Pennsylvania Military College (Chester) and reports on U.S. citizens who traveled in Communist countries or had dealings with Communist visitors to the U.S.

Another document reported acquisition of biographical data on nominees to the board of Women's International League for Peace and Freedom.

A file received by the Washington Post April 27 revealed wider spying on Miss Reuss, involving contributions by the Central Intelligence Agency and the Milwaukee and Philadelphia police departments.

Stolen files analyzed. The Citizens Commission to Investigate the FBI, in a mailing received by the Washington Post May 8, 1971, sent out an analysis of the files it had stolen from the FBI. It said 40% of the documents revealed political surveillance while only 1% concerned organized crime.

Included in the packet, sent to the Washington Post and other newspapers and radical groups, were several copies of FBI documents. They brought to more than 60 the number of stolen files made public. The analysis was made of all the stolen documents.

Included in the 40% listed by the Citizens Commission as evidence of political surveillance were two documents concerning what the group defined as right-wing groups, 10 concerning immigrants and more than 200 about "left or liberal groups."

The right-wing files, both included among the documents made public that day, included one on the militant Jewish Defense League (JDL) and one on plans for a Ku Klux Klan meeting in Darby, Pa.

Besides the 40% dealing with political groups and the 1% which the commission said concerned organized crime, mostly gambling, the breakdown on the remaining documents was reported as follows: 25% involved bank robberies; 20% involved murder, rape and interstate theft; 7% on draft resistance; and 7% on military desertion or AWOL cases. The group said the analysis did not include about 30% of the documents dealing with procedural matters.

Besides the files on the JDL and the KKK, the latest release contained a document on a rally protesting chemical and biological warfare and one indicating an arrangement with the Philadelphia office of the Bell Telephone Co. whereby the company would supply the FBI with names and addresses of all its customers, including those with unlisted numbers.

(Copies of other FBI documents, received by the Washington Post May 15 from the Citizens Commission to Investigate the FBI, involved a prominent Philadelphia civil rights leader. A letter from the commission accompanying the documents said the black leader, unnamed in the report, had been an FBI agent for several years.)

Quaker group releases FBI memos. A Philadelphia project of the American Friends Service Committee released a series of additional stolen FBI documents May 17, 1971 about police community activity and riot control. The Quaker group said it had received the papers from the Citizens Commission to Investigate the FBI.

Among the memos released by the group, called National Action-Research on the Military-Industrial Complex (NARMIC), was a document praising a Rochester, N.Y. program through which Boy Scouts were recruited as 20,-000 "extra eyes and ears for the police department." The program involved distribution of cards to Boy Scouts with police, FBI and other emergency numbers and instructions to report unusual activity, criminal acts and "suspicious acts—persons loitering . . . around schools, neighborhoods and parks."

(A statement by the Boy Scouts of America, issued from its national headquarters in New Brunswick, N.J. May 18, said the Rochester program only asked the scouts to exercise the same surveillance demanded of any citizen. The statement said it was a "positive program" to reduce crime and there was no "follow-up" beyond distribution of a pamphlet prepared by the Rochester Emergency Services Committee.)

Another document distributed by NARMIC described a Pontiac, Mich. program where police worked in schools and summer programs for children to "exert a positive influence upon the individual's values and attitudes." The memo advocated "pre-prevention" of "pre-offenders."

Also included were a "police instructor's bulletin" listing four types of riot control gases available to police departments and a "riot control information bulletin" dated 1967 that said "officers in Philadelphia have orders to shoot anyone who either fires at police or throws missiles of any type." A document on the organization of police anti-sniper patrols advised the use of "former members of the military or avid hunters" and said squads should have "high-powered rifles and machine-guns" for use from helicopters.

NARMIC was consolidating several of the documents into a booklet, "Police on the Homefront." Anne H. Flitcraft, an employe of the American Friends Service Committee who was working on the booklet, said FBI agents had raided her apartment May 16, armed with a warrant, and had confiscated her notes, books and typewriter along with copies of the stolen documents.

Residents of Powelton Village, the Philadelphia community near the University of Pennsylvania where Miss Flitcraft lived, organized a "Know Your FBI Street Fair" June 5. Photographs of alleged FBI agents and copies of stolen documents were displayed to about 1,000 persons who attended the fair. Members of the community charged harassment by FBI agents in connection with the Media theft investigation. The night after the raid on Miss Flitcraft's apartment, Powelton residents set up an alarm system designed to organize legal and community support in the event of other FBI raids.

Stolen FBI papers printed. "A virtually complete collection" of 271 documents on political surveillance stolen from the FBI's Media, Pa. office in March 1971 was printed in the March

1972 issue of Win, an antiwar magazine, which had received the files from the Citizens Commission to Investigate the FBI.

The documents, some of which had been released earlier, further detailed FBI surveillance of peace, student and black groups. According to a statement by the commission included in the Win article, over 200 documents concerned "left or liberal" groups, while only two referred to "right-wing" groups, the Philadelphia branches of the Ku Klux Klan and the Jewish Defense League.

Responding to Justice Department charges that the documents previously released overemphasized the proportion of FBI activity devoted to political surveillance, the commission said that about half the substantive documents from among the 800 stolen pertained to this area, equal to the attention paid all criminal activities and military desertion together.

Other documents told of a program of regular "liaison contact" with 10 Philadelphia area hotels, 8 colleges, 15 newspapers and broadcast stations, 16 banks, and various other businesses, in order "to create goodwill and develop sources of new cases."

FBI Spying Assailed

Wiretapping of Congressmen charged. Rep. Hale Boggs (D, La.), in a speech on the floor of the House April 5, 1971, accused the FBI of tapping telephones of congressmen. The House majority leader asked that FBI Director J. Edgar Hoover be fired.

Boggs accused the bureau of adopting "the tactics of the Soviet Union and Hitler's Gestapo" and called on Attorney General John N. Mitchell to "have enough courage to demand [Hoover's] resignation." He said: "When the FBI taps the telephones of members of this body and members of the Senate, when the FBI stations agents on college campuses to infiltrate college organizations, . . . then it is time that the present director no longer be the director."

Mitchell issued a statement April 5 in which he "categorically" denied that the FBI had ever tapped a congressman's phone. He accused Boggs of "slanderous falsehoods" and said his charges "reached a new low in political dialogue. He should recant at once and apologize to a great American."

Boggs repeated his charges April 6 and said he would produce evidence "in the near future" to support the allegations. He stated "categorically" that the FBI "had me under surveillance, but he said the bureau would not comment on whether Boggs had been investigated in the past. The spokesman said, "We are not and never have been tapping senators and congressmen."

Mitchell said in an April 6 press release, "Mr. Boggs's statements . . . now confirm the plain fact that his charges . . . have no factual basis whatever." White House Press Secretary Ronald L. Ziegler said April 6, "the President, of course, does not favor the tapping of phones of members of Congress."

Senate Majority Leader Mike Mansfield (Mont.) and Minority Leader Hugh Scott (Pa.) both said April 6 they had received no complaints from their colleagues about suspected FBI phone taps. However, Sen. Joseph M. Montoya (D, N.M.) had said March 19 that several congressmen suspected they had been the subjects of Justice Department wiretaps.

Deputy Attorney General Richard G. Kleindienst said April 7 that Boggs was "either sick or not in possession of his faculties" when he made his charges on the House floor. Kleindienst said he would "welcome an investigation by the responsible members of Congress" of the allegations. "Unless that is done or Mr. Boggs retracts his statements," Kleindienst said, "you have hanging in the air the charge itself—wiretapping the telephones of members of Congress."

Rep. Bella S. Abzug (D, N.Y.) introduced a resolution April 7 calling on the House Judiciary Committee to conduct "a full and complete investigation" of the FBI, including "investigation of the ability of the director." Rep. Charles H. Wilson (D, Calif.) introduced a bill to limit the tenure of the head of the bureau to 10 years and to set a mandatory retirement age of 65. Hoover, 76, had been director of the bureau since 1924.

Rep. Wayne Hays (D, Ohio), chairman of the House Administration Committee, said April 7 he would commission a "reputable firm" to check whether House members' phones were being tapped or their offices bugged. Robert G. Dunphy, the Senate sergeant-at-arms, had said April 6 that he periodically received requests from senators to check their telephone lines. He said he might receive one or two such requests a month and said he knew of no evidence that taps had been found.

Boggs later attempted to back up his case against the FBI in an hour-long House speech April 22. He denounced the "secret police spying and prying" of the FBI and asked President Nixon to appoint an investigatory commission "to go to the core of this cancer and remove it before the poisons spread further."

Boggs said the telephone line in his private home had been tapped in 1970. He said a Chesapeake and Potomac Telephone Co. investigator had determined that his line had been tapped but that the tap had been removed. He said that later, in an official report, the telephone company stated that no taps were discovered. Boggs said he learned subsequently that the company's policy was to deny the existence of a tap if it had been placed by the FBI.

The House majority leader also suggested that an electronic surveillance device had been used at the home of Sen. Charles H. Percy (R, Ill.) and that listening devices had been placed in the offices of former Sen. Wayne Morse of Oregon and Sen. Birch Bayh (D, Ill.). However, Boggs did not directly accuse the FBI of installing the surveillance devices.

Rep. Clarence J. Hogan (R, Md.), who had formerly worked for the FBI, immediately rebutted Boggs' charges. Hogan said Boggs had offered "innuendoes" but had "failed completely" to substantiate his charges with positive proof.

Attorney General John N. Mitchell said April 23 that Boggs had failed to produce "one iota of proof of the reckless charges" made in his speech and that he was suffering from "a new type of paranoia—called Tappanoia."

Muskie charges Earth Day spying. Sen. Edmund S. Muskie (D, Me.) charged in the Senate April 14, 1971 that the FBI had spied on 40–60 Earth Day conservation rallies April 22, 1970, including the Washington gathering where he was a speaker. Muskie called the surveillance a "fishing expedition" that represented "a threat to our privacy and freedom."

In support of his charge, Muskie made public an FBI intelligence report on the Washington rally. He said he had obtained the report, which mentioned his speech, from "a third party" and that it was in no way connected with a Media, Pa. theft of FBI documents.

Muskie said he knew of at least one other senator, "and probably others," whose Earth Day speeches and actions were "subject to surveillance." He said, "If there was widespread surveillance over Earth Day last year, is there any political acitivity in the country which the FBI does not consider a legitimate subject for watching? If antipollution rallies are a subject of intelligence concern, is anything immune? Is there any citizen involved in politics who is not a potential subject for an FBI dossier?"

Presidential Press Secretary Ronald L. Ziegler said he was "exercised" over Muskie's speech as well as recent charges by Rep. Hale Boggs that the FBI had tapped the telephones of several Congress members. Ziegler said that such statements were "aimed at getting big headlines" and gave "a totally misleading impression" about Administration policy. He said the "President's attitude is that snooping or surveillance of private citizens is quite repugnant to this administration."

Muskie proposed establishment of a domestic intelligence review board to oversee the surveillance activities of the FBI and other agencies. He said the board, to be composed of members of government intelligence agencies, Congress, the judiciary and the bar, could recommend actions and legislation "required to curb the unnecessary use of surveillance in our society."

The document Muskie released was a June 10, 1970 memorandum bearing the Justice Department-FBI seal, which was evidently distributed among other government agencies. The report included a chronology of preparations for the Washington rally, a list of individuals involved and a detailed description of speeches made and songs sung at the rally. Muskie said two appendixes attached to the report—describing the Students for a Democratic Society and the Progressive Labor party—"underscores my concerns" since it could be inferred that the Earth Day activity was "somehow related" to the radical groups.

Muskie charges answered—Attorney General John N. Mitchell, in a statement released by the Justice Department April 15, said FBI agents had attended the 1970 Washington Earth Day rally, as charged by Muskie. He said they were there because of "advance information" indicating that individuals with records of violence would attend the rally.

Mitchell said, "The FBI has no interest with an Earth Day meeting as such, but it does have a most legitimate interest in the activities of persons whose known records reveal a likelihood of violence, incitement to riot or other criminal behavior." Mitchell mentioned no names, but Sen. Robert P. Griffin (R, Mich.) said April 15 that FBI agents had been at the meeting to watch "such individuals as Rennie Davis," one of the Chicago Seven defendants convicted of inciting a riot at the 1968 Democratic National Convention.

White House Press Secretary Ronald L. Ziegler called Muskie's charges "blatantly political" April 16 and accused the senator and others of trying to create "a feeling of fear and intimidation among the people." Similar charges were made April 18 by Republican National Chairman Robert Dole.

Muskie said April 16 the Administration's "reluctance to come to grips with the facts is of considerable interest." He called on Mitchell to make public all FBI reports concerning Earth Day and "Let us judge for ourselves."

Mitchell said April 23 that Muskie had deliberately "twisted the facts to make a political headline." Muskie said the next day that Mitchell "deliberately distorted my statement. I don't even know if he has read it."

Nixon backs Hoover & FBI. President Nixon said April 16, 1971 that much of the criticism of FBI Director J. Edgar Hoover was "unfair and malicious." Responding to questions from a panel of newspapermen during a Washington convention of the American Society of Newspaper Editors, Nixon said Hoover was "taking a bad rap on a lot of things, and he doesn't deserve it."

Nixon defended the FBI as the "best law enforcement agency in the world." He said he would not comment on Hoover's tenure in office since he had not discussed the matter with the FBI director, but he added, "I believe it would be most unfortunate to allow a man who has given 50 years, over 50 years, of dedicated service to this country to go out under a cloud, maligned unfairly by many critics." Nixon said he thought such criticism would cause Hoover to "dig in" rather than hasten his retirement.

The President asserted that "despite all the talk about surveillance and bugging and the rest, let me say I have been in police states, and the idea that this is a police state is just pure nonsense. And every editorial paper in the country ought to say that."

Nixon said, "I can assure you that there is no question in my mind that Mr. Hoover's statement that no telephone in the Capitol has ever been tapped by the FBI is correct." On the question of telephone taps in national security cases, Nixon said the "high, insofar as those taps are concerned," was in 1961–63 when there were between 90 and 100 taps each year. He said in his two years of office, the total number of taps had been "less than 50 a year."

Agnew also supports FBI—Vice President Spiro T. Agnew, in New Orleans April 26, denounced critics of Hoover and the FBI as political "opportunists" and said they were trying to win the favor of the radical left. Agnew devoted his half-hour speech, before the Southern Gas Association convention, to a defense of the FBI and its director.

Agnew said persons trying to drive Hoover out of office used the issue of his age—76 years—but that "a more likely explanation" of the opposition to Hoover "is the fact that he is anathema to the New Left and extremists of every stripe."

Agnew referred specifically to two Democratic Presidential aspirants, Sens. George McGovern (D, S.D.) and Edmund S. Muskie (D, Me.), and their criticism of Hoover. He said, "These opportunists are being aided and abetted by certain of their friends in the liberal news media who automatically shout 'Right on!' every time someone claims his civil liberties have been threatened, regardless of the transparency of such charges." While not mentioning him by name, Agnew also dismissed charges by Rep. Hale Boggs (D, La.), the House majority leader, that the FBI had tapped the telephones of congressmen.

Rep. Dowdy 'bugged.' Documents released by a federal judge April 16, 1971 revealed that the FBI had tape-recorded four telephone conversations between Rep. John Dowdy (D, Tex.) and an FBI informant. The documents also showed that agents had escorted the informant to Dowdy's Capitol Hill office where a conversation with the congressman was recorded by a tape machine concealed on the informant's person.

The documents, which appeared to contradict recent statements by Justice Department officials that the FBI did not use electronic surveillance on congressmen or tap their lines, were released by U.S. District Court Judge Roszel C. Thomsen in Baltimore. The FBI actions, connected with a bribe conspiracy charge against Dowdy, had been reported in the New York Times April 16. Thomsen said he had kept the papers secret at Dowdy's request but said the article in the Times "removed the principal reason for keeping them sealed."

According to the court papers, Dowdy's telephone conversations had been monitored at the informer's end of the line, and no listening device was ever placed on the congressman's telephone. FBI agents had wired the informer's telephone and equipped him with a tape recorder on his visit to Dowdy. The activity had been approved in a court warrant and had been undertaken with the knowledge of Attorney General Mitchell and FBI Director Hoover. (The Supreme Court later ruled April 5 that such surveillance, when conducted through an informer, did not need court approval.)

In an interview with a Washington Post reporter April 17, Deputy Attorney General Richard G. Kleindienst said the recording of Dowdy's conversations did not constitute "surveillance" as defined by the Justice Department. Kleindienst had been asked to explain the Dowdy incident in light of his statement April 7 that the FBI had not used "electronic surveillance or the tapping of telephones of senators and congressmen" even in criminal investigations.

Kleindienst said April 17 that "surveillance" occurred when neither party to a conversation knew that it was being recorded. He said Dowdy's conversations were recorded with the informer's permission and that this action constituted "consensual conversation" and not "surveillance."

Senate Majority Leader Mike Mansfield (D, Mont.), who had said April 15 that the recent criticism of the FBI and Hoover contained "more noise than substance," said April 17 that the Dowdy incident was "a cause for grave concern." He said the eavesdropping on Dowdy had not been a proper use of FBI powers "even though they acted under a court order."

Sen. Sam J. Ervin Jr. (D, N.C.) called the actions of the FBI in the Dowdy case "reprehensible" April 18, but he said, "I'm not sure it's illegal."

Hoover defends informers. In an annual report to Attorney General John Mitchell, FBI Director J. Edgar Hoover Oct. 26, 1971 defended the use of "confidential informants" as having led to over 14,000 arrests by the FBI and other law enforcement agencies in the year ending June 30.

The informants had not only solved and prevented crimes, he said, but helped clear innocent persons of false charges.

Conference asks probe of FBI. A two-day conference of lawyers, academics, journalists and former government aides on the FBI was held in Princeton, N.J. Oct. 29–30, 1971. It ended with a call for Congress to investigate the bureau's aims and practices.

The three co-chairmen called for a "national commission of inquiry" to probe charges made at the conference that the agency had violated civil liberties and discouraged dissent while failing to fight organized crime. The chairmen were Burke Marshall, a former assistant attorney general, and Professors Norman Dorsen of New York University and W. Duane Lockard of Princeton University, where the meeting was held under the auspices of the university's Woodrow Wilson School and the private Committee for Public Justice.

Much of the criticism centered on alleged intimidation of peaceful dissent. Yale Professor Thomas I. Emerson Oct. 29 asked that the FBI, which he said "conceives of itself as an instrument to prevent radical change," be prevented from photographing peaceful protests or gathering files on "people not charged with a crime or reasonably suspected of a violation of the law."

But Richard Wright, one of two representatives of Americans for Effective Law Enforcement at the conference, responded that "the FBI has a basic duty to make sure the radicals don't get away with intimidating the rest of us." He suggested that surveillance might be justified to prevent violence.

Newsman Victor Navasky Oct. 29 criticized FBI wiretap practices, but placed major responsibility for abuses on past presidents and attorneys general. He warned that no reform would be possible without an "external overseeing body."

Congressional funding of the FBI was criticized Oct. 29 by Walter Pincus,

former Senate Foreign Relations Committee aide. He charged that the House Appropriations Subcommittee avoided the usual line item review of budget requests in the FBI's case because some subcommittee investigators were on loan from the bureau. In 21 years, he said, Congress had always appropriated at least as much as the bureau requested.

Two former FBI agents were among its detractors Oct. 29. William Turner, who had been asked to resign in 1961, charged that the bureau had regularly put pressure on local authorities to protect agents accused of petty crimes. Robert Wall, who resigned in 1970, said individuals had been put under FBI surveillance merely for opposing the Vietnam War.

William Hundley, chief of the Justice Department organized crime division in 1958–66, charged Oct. 30 that the FBI had not been diligent in probing organized crime in order to remain on good terms with congressmen who had criminal connections. An FBI spokesman denied the charge and challenged Hundley to produce specific evidence.

The bureau was defended Oct. 30 by John Doar, former assistant attorney general in the civil rights division. Doar defended the use of informers and electronic surveillance to combat organized crime and probe violations of civil rights.

Probe of Daniel Schorr. Press Secretary Ronald Ziegler admitted Nov. 11, 1971 that the White House had ordered an FBI investigation of Columbia Broadcasting System (CBS) correspondent Daniel Schorr, but denied that the probe was related to criticism of Schorr's reporting by President Nixon and Administration aides. Ziegler and Frederic V. Malek, White House personnel aide, said Schorr had been under consideration in August for an unspecified federal job, which occasioned the investigation.

Schorr said Nov. 10 that he had never been told of any job offer, even when he questioned Malek about the probe in October.

Ziegler said the FBI investigation had

been started in accord with a "tightly administered procedure," which he said he was unable to explain, with Malek's knowledge. Malek said, however, that the investigation had been "kicked off " by an assistant without his knowledge.

Schorr had been criticized by Nixon, Ziegler and Charles W. Colson, a Presidential aide, for his coverage of the anti-ballistic missile program, federal aid to parochial schools and Nixon's new economic program.

Congressional Action; Government Policy Attacked

Ervin hearings. Sen. Sam J. Ervin Jr. Feb. 23, 1971 opened a series of hearings by his Senate Subcommittee on Constitutional Rights to determine the effect of government and private surveillance and computer data banks on individual privacy in the U.S. The subcommittee was also considering the Army's activity in gathering domestic intelligence information.

In opening the Feb. 23 session, Ervin said: "When people fear surveillance, whether it exists or not, when they grow afraid to speak their minds freely to their government or anyone else, . . . then we shall cease to be a free society." Ervin said people were concerned about information being fed into government or commercial data banks without screening or control over who would see it.

The first witness, Arthur R. Miller, University of Michigan law professor and author of "Assault on Privacy," said, "each time a citizen files a tax return, applies for life insurance or credit card, seeks government benefits, or interviews for a job, a dossier is opened under his name and an informational profile on him is sketched." He said the information gathering activities, "by and large . . . are well-intended efforts to achieve socially desirable objectives" but warned that ."it is simply unrealistic to assume that the managers or proprietors of computer systems—government or private—will take it upon themselves to protect the public against misuse." He

said that with "no effective restraints" on the data gatherers and disseminators, the nation was being led toward a "dossier dictatorship."

Rep. Edward I. Koch (D, N.Y.) urged support for a federal privacy bill he introduced Jan. 22 with the support of 20 other congressmen of both parties. The bill would require government agencies who keep records on individuals to notify the individual of the record and to inform him when information was transferred to another agency. Another bill introduced the same day by Koch would require the same procedure by the House Internal Security Committee.

John M. O'Brien, a former Army intelligence agent whose letter to Ervin prompted the hearings, told the senators Feb. 24 that despite Army denials, agents had spied on Sen. Adlai E. Stevenson III (D, Ill.) during 1969–70 when he was Illinois state treasurer. He said he had complained to superiors about the files on Stevenson and on the American Civil Liberties Union, which he said had been described in the files as a Socialist-Communist organization.

During a March 4 hearing, Ervin disclosed an Army file of cards that apparently indexed dossiers on persons or organizations under surveillance at the University of Minnesota and in the St. Paul-Minneapolis area. Included in the file were Harry Davis, the Democratic-Farmer-Labor party candidate for mayor of Minneapolis in 1970; members of the university faculty; the elected student government group; and the St. Paul Department of Human Rights, an official arm of the city government.

Dispute on privacy policy—Assistant Attorney General William Rehnquist told the Ervin subcommittee March 9 that the Nixon Administration would oppose legislation that would hamper the government's domestic intelligence gathering activity.

Rehnquist said, "Self-discipline on the part of the executive branch will provide an answer to virtually all of the legitimate complaints against excesses of information gathering." He said such activity was essential in crime control and that the Administration "will vigorously oppose any legislation which, whether by opening the door to unnecessary and unmanageable judicial supervision of such activities or otherwise, would effectively impair this extraordinarily important function of the federal government."

Sen. Birch Bayh (D, Ind.) had introduced a bill Feb. 25 that would compel government agencies to inform citizens of files kept on them and allow subjects of such files to correct information in them. Similar legislation had been introduced in the House by Rep. Edward I. Koch (D, N.Y.).

However, another Administration spokesman, Health, Education and Welfare Secretary Elliot L. Richardson, told the subcommittee March 15 that the nation "must develop the means of controlling the potential for harm inherent" in the government's computer banks of information on citizens. Richardson said if present safeguards were inadequate, "statutes designed to define and protect an individual's rights in computerized information storage and exchange can be enacted."

Explaining the apparent divergence of views between Richardson and Rehnquist, spokesmen for HEW and the Justice Department said March 15 that the two officials spoke only for their respective departments.

Ervin questioned Richardson March 15 on the increased use of Social Security numbers for identification purposes by both government and private agencies. Richardson said, "It is not illegal for a non-federal organization to use the Social Security number in its record keeping system." He said the "potential for invasion of privacy or breach of confidentiality" did not lie in the use of the number itself, "but rather in how the organization uses computerized collections of data which are indexed by the number" and "the existence of a universal identifier." (Richardson had said Feb. 7 that the government had begun to investigate the growing practice of using Social Security numbers as identification by private firms. Richardson said he was "concerned that if the Social Security numbers were used too broadly, such widespread use and dependence upon the number might lend itself to abuses of individual privacy.")

The Justice Department's position on the government's right to collect information was questioned when Rehnquist again appeared before the subcommittee March 17 along with Assistant Attorney General Robert Mardian, in charge of the Internal Security Division. Ervin told Rehnquist, "There is not a syllable in there [the Constitution] that gives the federal government the right to spy on civilians."

Mardian said "we do not have specific, published documents" to regulate surveillance activities of the Federal Bureau of Investigation. He said internal memorandums provided operating instructions to the FBI. Sen. Edward M. Kennedy (D, Mass.), who had asked Mardian about Justice Department guidelines, said, "you haven't been terribly reassuring." He added, "It appears that on behalf of the attorney general you have washed your hands of any responsibility for surveillance."

Rehnquist was also questioned March 17 by Sen. John V. Tunney (D, Calif.), who accused the Justice Department of failing to fully investigate charges that San Francisco Mayor Joseph L. Alioto made before the subcommittee March 3. Alioto had accused six federal agencies and two California police departments of supplying confidential information to writers from Look magazine in connection with a 1969 article linking Alioto to the Mafia.

Accusing the government of having "not only a big ear, but a big mouth as well," Alioto had said the information given to the writers was "characteristic of what finds its way into investigatory files." He said it was "raw, unverified, unedited, unevaluated, hearsay information."

In answer to Tunney's challenge March 17, Rehnquist said only one San Francisco FBI agent had been involved in the Alioto leakage and that agent had been disciplined and retired.

Ervin cites data-bank danger & abuse. Sen. Sam J. Ervin Jr. said May 20, 1971 that computers and data banks had been used to feed "the insatiable curiosity of government to know everything about those it governs." Ervin, whose Constitutional Rights subcommittee was investigating government information gathering, made his remarks at an Atlantic City, N.J. meeting of the American Federation of Information Processing Societies.

Ervin said, "if the attitude of the present Administration is any indication," computer technology would become increasingly central in the government's "pursuit of its current claim to an inherent power to investigate lawful activities and to label people on the basis of their thoughts." He said he had learned from Federal Communications Commission Chairman Dean Burch that the FCC checked all license applications against a computerized list of about 11,000 persons considered suspicious by such agencies as the Justice Department, the Internal Revenue Service, the Central Intelligence Agency, and the House Internal Security Committee.

Sen. Ervin had said Feb. 9 during a four-day symposium on data banks at Dickinson College (Carlisle, Pa.) that the U.S. Passport Office kept a secret computerized file of 243,135 Americans. He said the computer was programed to report to various law enforcement and intelligence agencies—without the subjects' knowledge—the passport applications of persons suspected of being "subversive" or who might fail to "reflect credit" upon the U.S. abroad.

Miss Frances Knight, Passport Office director since 1955, admitted the existence of the file Feb. 10 but claimed that "a vast majority" of the subjects were persons of "questionable citizenship." A spokesman for Ervin, however, said Feb. 10 that the State Department had reported to the senator that the largest group on the list were "known or suspected Communists or subversives."

■ Four individuals and the Socialist Workers party filed suit Feb. 24 in federal court in New York City demanding destruction of the Passport Office file. The suit denounced the file as potential "political blacklisting" and said it

threatened "freedoms of speech, association, belief and travel."

Administration policy in dispute. Attorney General John N. Mitchell, speaking at a Kentucky Bar Association meeting in Cincinnati April 23, 1971, upheld what he described as the Administration's right to use wiretaps against domestic subversives without obtaining court warrants. A federal appeals court in Cincinnati had ruled that such taps could only be installed under court order, and on April 27, the Justice Department announced it was appealing that ruling to the Supreme Court.

Rep. Emanuel Celler (D, N.Y.), chairman of the House Judiciary Committee, in an interview April 25, disputed Mitchell's claim that unwarranted wiretaps were justified "when, in his opinion, the national security is involved." Celler said, "that's a huge umbrella that can cover thousands of actions. . . . Who is to be judge of national security? . . . He is to be the judge? That's not government by law, that's government by personality."

In two rival Law Day speeches, delivered to opposing factions of the District of Columbia Bar Association and the Federal Bar Association in Washington April 27, Assistant Attorney General Robert C. Mardian defended the Administration's security policies and Sen. Harold E. Hughes (D, Iowa) sharply attacked the Administration for fostering "a private climate wherein official spying is the name of the game."

Mardian, invited as the official speaker, told about 100 lawyers and judges that the need for information made government intelligence gathering "an obligation rather than a right or privilege." He said proper information might have prevented the assassination of President Kennedy. He also suggested that miscalculations based on inadequate information might have contributed to the situation in which four Kent State University students were killed by National Guardsmen in May 1970.

Hughes' address was heard by some 300 lawyers who attended a rival Law Day meeting set up by young lawyers who objected to the invitation extended.

to Mardian, the Justice Department's chief security official. Hughes, considered an unannounced candidate for the Democratic presidential nomination, accused the Nixon Administration of creating a "trend toward repression." He cited "the relentlessly increasing emphasis on wiretapping, bugging, no-knock entry, subpoenaing of private notebooks and tapes from news reporters, increased surveillance by the government of dissident political groups and the attempts by the government to intimidate the communications media."

Ex-official urges curb on FBI powers—

William C. Sullivan, third ranking official of the FBI before his retirement in 1971, warned that the agency represented a threat to U.S. civil liberties and urged that its power and budget be reduced. He also called for a three-year moratorium on electronic surveillance by all federal agencies, during which time a study would be undertaken to assess the effect on criminal justice and internal security operations. An independent commission would determine the need for an internal security apparatus, he said. If such activity were necessary, Sullivan said, it should be conducted by an independent board chosen by Congress, not the FBI.

Sullivan, whose recommendations were in a paper presented to the annual Earl Warren Conference of the Roscoe Pound-American Trial Lawyers Association and released Nov. 24, 1974, said: "FBI headquarters was wrong in releasing to the American people propaganda that pictured us as an elite corps far superior to any other government organization. . . . The gulf between public relations and our actual performance was indeed very great."

Beginning in 1939, when the agency first took on internal security duties, Sullivan said, "To be candid, the 'right to privacy' was not at issue nor was it an impediment to solving cases. . . . The primacy of civil liberties on occasions gave way to expediency."

CIA role defended. Richard Helms, in his first public address since he became director of the Central Intelligence Agen-

cy in 1966, defended the CIA's role in a democratic society April 14, 1971. Speaking to the American Society of Newspaper Editors in Washington, Helms cited "an inherent American distaste for the peace-time gathering of intelligence" but said the "nation must to a degree take it on faith that we too are honorable men devoted to her service."

Herbert G. Klein, President Nixon's director of communications, said April 14 that Nixon had approved Helms' appearance as an opportunity to explain the role of the CIA. The agency had come under heavy attack in 1967 when it was discovered that the CIA gave financial support to the National Student Association and to various unions, foundations and publications.

Helms emphasized that the CIA had no domestic security functions. He said "we do not have any such powers and functions; we have never sought any; we do not exercise any. In short, we do not target on American citizens." He also said the agency had "no stake in policy debates." He said the "role of intelligence in policy formulation is limited to providing facts."

Helms said: "I can assure you that what I have asked you to take on faith, the elected officials of the United States government watch over extensively, intensively and continuously." He mentioned the "constant supervision and direction" of the National Security Council, the President's Foreign Intelligence Advisory Board and other agencies and Congressional committees.

Supreme Court & LBJ tapped. Justice William O. Douglas reported Oct. 15, 1973 that the Supreme Court's secret conference room had been "bugged," and he said that Lyndon Johnson complained when he was president that his phone had been tapped.

Douglas' assertion came in a dissenting opinion he wrote for a case in which the court had refused to grant bail to a defendant who claimed her phone had been improperly tapped by the government. He wrote: "I am indeed morally certain that the conference room of this court has been bugged, and President Johnson during his term in the White House asserted to me that even his phone was tapped." Douglas refused to elaborate.

Hoover barred Capitol Hill surveillance—An unnamed, former high ranking FBI official told the Washington Post Dec. 30, 1974 that the late J. Edgar Hoover had declared the grounds of the U.S. Capitol in Washington "off limits" to FBI agents. Hoover feared criticism from congressmen, who periodically accused him of tapping their telephones and compiling dossiers on their private lives, the official said. Soviet agents quickly learned of the prohibition and scheduled meetings there, the former official added.

Disclosures Continue; Executive Branch Action

Domestic CIA spying reported. The New York Times reported Dec. 21, 1974 that the Central Intelligence Agency (CIA), in violation of its 1947 Congressional charter, conducted "a massive, illegal domestic intelligence operation during the Nixon Administration against the antiwar movement and other dissident groups." (The report was written by Seymour Hersh.)

An extensive investigation, the Times said, had established that a special, top secret unit of the CIA had maintained files on 10,000 U.S. citizens. At least one antiwar congressman was among those under CIA surveillance, the Times said.

The Times also said former CIA Director James Schlesinger had found evidence of dozens of illegal domestic operations by the CIA beginning in the 1950s, including "break-ins, wiretapping and surreptitious interception of mail." These activities, which were also prohibited by the agency's charter,* the Times said, had been directed against foreign intelligence

---

*According to the 1947 law creating the CIA (Title 50, Section 403 of the United States Code), the agency "shall have no police, subpoena, law enforcement powers, or internal security functions."

operatives in the U.S. and not dissident U.S. citizens.

Richard Helms, director of the CIA during the first term of the Nixon Administration and current ambassador to Iran, issued a statement through the State Department Dec. 24 denying that "illegal domestic operations against antiwar activists or dissidents" had occurred during his stewardship of the CIA.

The newspaper quoted several unnamed sources, who insisted that the CIA had discontinued all domestic operations.

One Times source said the domestic spying had been directed during the Nixon Administration by James Angleton, chief of the CIA's counterintelligence department since 1954. Officially, Angleton's job was to insure that foreign agents did not penetrate the CIA.

Along with assembling domestic intelligence dossiers, one Times source said, Angleton's department recruited informants to infiltrate the more militant dissident groups. " 'They recruited plants, informers and doublers [double agents],' " the source said. (It was reported Dec. 24 that Angleton had resigned from his post, effective Dec. 31. He also publicly denied the Times' allegations.)

A number of former Federal Bureau of Investigation (FBI) officials, the Times said, felt that the CIA's decision to mount domestic counterintelligence operations "reflected, in part, the long-standing mistrust between the two agencies." By the late 1960s, one former FBI official said, "all but token cooperation between the two agencies on counterintelligence and counterespionage had ended." (Under U.S. law, the FBI was empowered to conduct domestic intelligence operations.)

Other unnamed Times sources noted that J. Edgar Hoover, director of the FBI, in 1970 had broken off all but formal liaison contact between the CIA and the FBI. This lack of a working relationship, another Times source said, might have provided impetus to the CIA's domestic surveillance program.

President Ford said Dec. 22 that William Colby, current director of the CIA, had assured him that "nothing comparable" to what was described in the article was happening now. Ford also said that he had told Colby "that under no circumstances would I tolerate any such activities under this administration."

Ford received a report from Colby about the Times' allegations Dec. 26. The Los Angeles Times reported Dec. 31 that Colby's report confirmed the allegations. Colby said the CIA had compiled files on at least 9,000 U.S. citizens and had engaged in other illegal clandestine activities. The article said some of the activities, "including at least three illegal entries," had been directed against CIA employes suspected of "slipping over to the other side."

The New York Times reported Dec. 29 that a former undercover CIA agent had said that much of the spying against domestic radicals had been done by the highly secret Domestic Operations Division of the agency.

During the late 1960s, the former agent told the Times, New York City became a prime target for CIA domestic spying because it was considered a "training ground" for radicals. At the height of antiwar activity at Columbia University and elsewhere, he said, more than 25 CIA operatives were assigned to the city. His own involvement, the former agent said, began with the Black Panther movement in 1967 and increased as antiwar dissent escalated in the last months of the Johnson Administration. "And then it started to snowball from there," he said.

The former agent also admitted participating in wiretaps and break-ins meant to closely monitor activities of radicals in New York City. He added that the CIA supplied him with "more than 40" psychological assessments of radical leaders during his spy career.

(The Times said it had been able to verify that its source had worked for the CIA as an undercover agent, but the newspaper said it was unable to check all of his information. A high-ranking, unidentified U.S. intelligence officer familiar with CIA operations said the former agent's description of life as a domestic spy "'seemed a little bit far out.'")

FBI's 1956–71 anti-radical activities. Attorney General William B. Saxbe and Clarence M. Kelley, who had become FBI director, Nov. 18, 1974 released some details of a Justice Department report on FBI counterintelligence operations conducted during 1956–71 under the designation COINTELPRO.

The Justice Department report revealed that COINTELPRO had been composed of seven different programs, with five directed at domestic organizations and individuals and two aimed at foreign intelligence services, foreign organizations and individuals connected with them. Among the domestic targets of COINTELPRO were two black civil rights groups not considered radical by many observers: the Southern Christian Leadership Conference (SCLC) and the Congress of Racial Equality (CORE). All the programs were abruptly terminated in mid-1971 by J. Edgar Hoover, the late FBI director.

The Justice Department committee, headed by Assistant Attorney General Henry E. Petersen, said in its draft report that some of the operations could "only be considered abhorrent in a free society." But the report added that such "improper activities were not the major purpose or indeed the major characteristic of the FBI's COINTELPRO efforts."

The first COINTELPRO operation, which was against the Communist Party U.S.A., was an outgrowth of the "Red Scare" of the mid-1950's, the report said. Begun in 1956 on Hoover's orders, COINTELPRO—Communist Party USA was the FBI's response to the then-prevailing "view in Congress and the American people" that the federal government should act against domestic subversion. Moreover, the report noted, later activities were based on the COINTELPRO—Communist Party USA model, but reflected "changing threats to the domestic order" during the 1960s.

Other COINTELPRO operations and their effective dates were: Socialist Workers Party (1961–1971), White Hate Groups (1964–1971), Black Extremists (1967–1971) and New Left (1968–1971). The other two COINTELPRO efforts were Espionage or Soviet Satellite Intelligence (1964–1971) and Special Operations (1967–1971). According to the Petersen committee, which for national security reasons declined to provide any details, the overall objectives of the latter two programs were to encourage and stimulate counterintelligence efforts against hostile foreign intelligence sources and foreign communist organizations. In all, various FBI field offices submitted 3,247 proposals for domestic counterintelligence; 2,370 were approved and implemented. More than half the proposals concerned the Communist Party USA, the report said.

The COINTELPRO activities were characterized in the report as sending anonymous or fictitious materials to groups to create internal dissension; leaking of informant-based or non-public information to friendly media sources; use of informants to disrupt a group's activities; informing employers, credit bureaus and creditors of members' activities; informing or contacting businesses and persons with whom members had economic dealings of members' activities; attempting to use religious and civil leaders and organizations in disruptive activities; and informing family or others of radical or immoral activities.

The report also singled out over 20 instances that it called "most troubling" or "egregious" examples of COINTEL-PRO actions. Among them: investigating the love life of a group leader for dissemination to the press; obtaining income tax returns of members of a group; mailing an anonymous letter to a member of a group who was a mayoralty candidate in order to create distrust toward his comrades; sending an anonymous letter, purported to be from a concerned parent, to a local school board official alerting him that candidates for the school board were members of a group; and making an anonymous phone call to a defense attorney, after a federal prosecution had resulted in a mistrial, "advising him (apparently falsely) that one of the defendants and another well known group individual were FBI informants."

According to the report, COINTEL-PRO programs were reported to at least three attorneys general, as well as key White House personnel between 1958 and 1969, although none of the activities was revealed during the period in which it was implemented. No activity involving improper conduct was so reported nor did Hoover ever allow use of the term COINTELPRO outside of the FBI, the report added.

Saxbe and Kelley said the New Left groups targeted by the FBI were Students for a Democratic Society (SDS), the Progressive Labor Party, the Weathermen and the Young Socialist Alliance. Black groups subject to FBI operations were CORE, the SCLC, the Student Nonviolent Coordinating Committee (SNCC), the Black Panther Party, the Revolutionary Action Movement and the Nation of Islam. So-called White Hate groups that were objects of FBI counterintelligence efforts were various Ku Klux Klan organizations, the Minutemen, the American Nazi Party and the National States Rights Party.

The Justice Department Dec. 6, 1973 had already made public internal FBI memos disclosing that in May 1968 Hoover had ordered a campaign to "expose, disrupt and otherwise neutralize" the New Left. He had ordered bureau offices to take advantage "of all opportunities for counter-intelligence and also inspire action in instances where circumstances may warrant." The "organizations and activists who spout revolution and unlawfully challenge society to obtain their demands must not only be contained, but must be neutralized," Hoover said.

A second memo, issued April 28, 1971, ordered that the campaign be discontinued immediately.

The memos were released after the Justice Department decided not to appeal a federal district court decision ordering that they be turned over to National Broadcasting Co. newsman Carl Stern, who had sued for their release under the Freedom of Information Act.

(The Justice Department made it known Jan. 3, 1975 that it had decided not to prosecute anybody accused in connection with COINTELPRO. It had been determined, the department said, that there was "no basis for criminal charges against any particular individual involving particular incidents.")

FBI allowed to watch Socialist parley. Supreme Court Justice Thurgood Marshall Dec. 27, 1974 refused to set aside an appellate court order allowing the FBI to send agents and informants to the convention of the Young Socialist Alliance, which opened in St. Louis Dec. 28.

The 2nd U.S. Circuit Court of Appeals Dec. 24 had reversed an injunction issued Dec. 16 by U.S. District Court Judge Thomas P. Griesa that prohibited the FBI from conducting surveillance of the Young Socialist Alliance, the youth affiliate of the Socialist Workers Party.

Griesa had acted on a complaint that FBI surveillance of the Trotskyite political group inhibited people from attending meetings and exercising their freedom of speech. Ordering the FBI to keep its informants and agents away from the convention, Griesa said, "You've been looking at this group for 35 years and you haven't produced one single solitary crime or incitement to violence in the U.S. by anyone in this organization."

The three-judge appellate court panel ruled that Griesa's injunction had been based on inadequate information and represented an "abuse of discretion." In vacating Griesa's injunction, the panel said that the FBI could watch the convention on the condition it did not transmit the names of those attending to the U.S. Civil Service Commission or other government agencies that might use the information against persons seeking employment.

Judges Henry J. Friendly, William H. Timbers and Murray Gurfein comprised the appellate panel.

IRS watched 'subversives.' The National Council of Churches and the Urban League were on the list of potentially subversive organizations the Internal Revenue Service kept under tax surveillance during 1969–73, the Tax Reform Research Group said Nov. 17, 1974. The group, a Washington affiliate of Ralph Nader's Public Citizen, obtained the list as part of IRS data released to it in a Freedom of Information Act case.

According to the data, the IRS set up a special group, eventually named the Special Services Staff (SSS), July 2, 1969, one day after a White House aide, Tom Charles Huston, informed the IRS that President Nixon wanted the agency "to move against leftist organizations." The SSS was to monitor tax records and keep watch over "ideological, militant, subversive, radical and similar type organizations," the documents revealed.

Files were collected on 2,873 organizations and 8,585 individuals before the SSS was dismantled in August 1973. A final report said 78% of these were found to have "no apparent revenue significance or potential." The other 22% of the files were said to have been preserved. No serious tax cheating was reported discovered by the operation, which produced about $100,000 in additional tax revenues.

The National Council of Churches and Urban League were on an early list of 99 targets. Others included the Unitarian Society, Americans for Democratic Action, the John Birch Society, Welfare Rights Organization, the Congress of Racial Equality and Church League of America.

IRS returns Times phone records. The Internal Revenue Service Feb. 13, 1974 returned to the Chesapeake and Potomac Telephone Co. (C&P) telephone records of the Washington bureau of the New York Times that it had secretly subpoenaed Jan. 8. Not among the returned records, however, were logs of toll calls made from the Maryland home of Washington-based Times reporter David E. Rosenbaum, whose name had appeared on the Jan. 8 IRS subpoena for the Times records. (Rosenbaum said Feb. 12 that the IRS might have been interested in the calls he made when he was investigating charges of tax evasion against a major contributor to President Nixon's 1972 campaign.)

The IRS said it had subpoenaed the records as part of an investigation into a leak of information by an IRS employe. The records were procured by an "administrative summons," a legal instrument normally reserved for tax evasion cases and one not giving notice to the person or organization under scrutiny.

(The St. Louis Post-Dispatch had said Feb. 1 that the Justice Department had issued secret subpoenas in 1971 for the telephone records of the Post-Dispatch, Knight Newspapers Inc. and Leslie H. Whitten, an associate of syndicated columnist Jack Anderson.)

AT&T promises notice of subpoenas— AT&T announced Feb. 15 that it would notify its customers when records of their long distance phone calls were subpoenaed by government investigators. The phone company also agreed to supply the records only in response to subpoenas, not simply to written requests as had been the policy in the past. However, AT&T qualified its announcement, saying subscribers would be notified in all cases except when "the agency requesting the records directs the company not to disclose, certifying that such a notification could impede its investigation and interfere with enforcement of the law."

A spokesman for the Reporters Committee for Freedom of the Press said the exception potentially nullified AT&T's entire commitment to advance notification.

New crime data control rules. The Justice Department Feb. 14, 1974 announced a new set of regulations that would limit access to criminal information compiled by the Federal Bureau of Investigation (FBI) and state and local police agencies.

The regulations, published in the Federal Register Feb. 14, were intended as an interim measure until Congress could pass legislation restricting the use of criminal records. The Justice Department had offered a bill Feb. 2, and Sen. Sam J. Ervin Jr. (D, N.C.), chairman of the Judiciary Committee's Subcommittee on Constitutional Rights and a co-sponsor of the Justice Department measure, offered his own, somewhat stricter measure.

The Justice Department regulations, which were applicable to federal law enforcement agencies as well as state or local police agencies receiving funds from the Law Enforcement Assistance Administration, were aimed at preventing government agencies and private groups

from obtaining criminal information from police data banks for other than criminal justice purposes. State and local agencies would also have to seal arrest records of individuals not found guilty or whose cases were not disposed of in five years. Sealed records would be available only to law enforcement agencies for criminal justice purposes, to persons compiling statistics or to the individuals involved.

While the regulations contained no provisions for sealing FBI records, they restricted their dissemination to federal agencies authorized by statute or executive order to receive them.

The legislation offered by the Justice Department would go further in protecting individual rights than the interim regulations of Feb. 14. Under the proposed bill, an individual could review and correct information in his record, and bring lawsuits against persons who improperly disclosed his records.

Another provision would require sealing of arrest records seven years after release in felony cases and five years in misdemeanor cases, although seals could be broken after subsequent arrests for other crimes. Another section would bar police agencies from giving incomplete records to noncriminal justice agencies, and forbid disclosure of information for purposes of employment or credit unless specifically authorized by statute or executive order.

Blacklists, Subversive Lists & Loyalty Oaths

HEW ends blacklists. Health, Education & Welfare (HEW) Secretary Robert H. Finch had announced Jan. 2, 1970 that the department had abandoned a controversial security-clearance procedure for part-time advisers that had led to the blacklisting of some prominent scientists, including Nobel Prize winner Dr. Salvador E. Luria. Finch said the action was "the first step in a long overdue updating of our appointment procedure."

In the future, Finch said, a prospective part-time consultant would be asked to submit three character references and to sign an affidavit stating that he did not advocate the violent overthrow of the government. The affidavit would be checked against Federal Bureau of Investigation files, and if a question arose, the nominee would have the right to challenge evidence against him.

Finch said department agency heads would have the sole right to appoint part-time advisers, on the basis of professional competency alone. Final approval would be up to the discretion of the HEW secretary and would no longer be with the department's Office of Internal Security. The new procedures applied only to part-time consultants.

The relaxation of the security rules was based on recommendations by H. Reed Ellis, a Harvard Law School graduate, whose study of HEW's security procedures was released along with Finch's statement. Ellis concluded that the old procedures were "supported by a logic all their own" and that "no reasonable man would design the present system as it has evolved." He contended that blacklists were officially condemned but said "the operation of the system itself encourage[d] bureaucrats in the bowels of the appointing agencies to make them up and use them anyway." Ellis continued: "The whole operation takes on a Kafkaesque aura in the public mind when Nobel laureates are excluded from the government service for whatever reason."

Ellis said the loyalty oath he recommended was "constitutionally permissible" after a Washington, D.C. U.S. District Court had ruled that the standard federal loyalty oath was invalid. (The court had ruled June 4, 1969 that the federal loyalty oath was based on an unconstitutionally vague federal statute. After federal lawyers failed to appeal the decision, the Civil Service Commission issued a directive Sept. 29 to heads of departments and independent agencies stating that the loyalty oath section of federal appointment affidavits would no longer be applicable. The directive said applicants would be permitted to "strike through" the loyalty oath. According to a New York Times Jan. 7 report, most federal government officials had overlooked the directive, and the D.C.

American Civil Liberties Union had called attention to the commission's action in connection with plans for the new HEW loyalty oath.)

Subversives list abolished. The attorney general's controversial list of subversive organizations—27 years old and not updated since 1955—was abolished by presidential order June 4, 1974. William B. Saxbe, then attorney general, said it was "now very apparent that it [the list] serves no useful purpose."

According to the Justice Department, all but about 30 of the 300 organizations still on the list had been out of existence for five years or more. A spokesman said a recent survey of government agencies had found only the Defense Department still using the list as an "investigative device in background checks."

President Nixon had attempted to have the Subversive Activities Control Board update the list in 1971, but the board was later eliminated from the budget.

File ordered destroyed—The FBI was ordered Aug. 29 to destroy its file on Lori Paton, a Chester, N.J. girl who had sought information from an allegedly subversive group as part of a high school classroom project.

U.S. District Court Judge James A. Coolahan refused, however, to grant a class action request that the FBI be generally prohibited from conducting the type of mail cover surveillance that had led to the existence of a "subversive" file on Miss Paton. Coolahan also denied her claim for $65,000 in damages.

In early 1973, Miss Paton had sent a letter to the Young Socialist Alliance, an affiliate of the Socialist Workers Party. The party was on the subversive list then maintained by the attorney general and subject to an FBI mail cover.

The FBI received Miss Paton's name from a postal inspector and began an investigation, which included a check on her family and a visit to her high school. The agent who investigated was reportedly surprised to learn the reason for her letter to the party, and recommended that "the case be closed administratively." The FBI, however, maintained a file under her name, with a notation signifying "subversive matter—Socialist Workers Party."

In his ruling, Coolahan said there was no legal justification for her file, which could become an unfair detriment in later life.

Army admits use of subversive list—The Army admitted Nov. 12 that it still used the attorney general's list of subversive organizations to discharge suspect military personnel, despite a June 4 presidential order abolishing use of the list for "any purpose." Continuing Army use of the list came to light when Steven Wattenmaker, a leader of the Young Socialist Alliance, challenged his involuntary dismissal from the Army Reserve because he belonged to an organization on the subversive list. The notice of discharge received by Wattenmaker said his retention was not in the interests of national security since he was a member of the Young Socialist Alliance, which was "controlled and dominated by the Socialist Workers Party, which has been designated as a subversive organization by the attorney general."

Bar loyalty oaths. In three 5–4 decisions Feb. 23, 1971, the Supreme Court held that a state may require applicants for licenses to practice law to take an affirmative loyalty oath. But the court banned wide-ranging questions on membership in organizations or requirements that the applicant disclose membership in alleged subversive organizations. Justice Potter Stewart cast the deciding vote in all three rulings.

The court rejected an Arizona test for bar applicants that asked a law school graduate if he had ever joined a subversive organization. The ruling reversed the Arizona Supreme Court in the case of Sara Baird of Phoenix, who had been denied a license because she refused to say whether she belonged to any organization "that advocates overthrow of the United States by force and violence."

The justices also said that Ohio illegally asked bar applicant Martin R. Stolar to list all organizations to which

he had ever belonged. Dissenters in both the Arizona and Ohio cases were Chief Justice Warren E. Burger and Justices John M. Harlan, Byron R. White and Harry A. Blackmun.

Stewart joined the dissenters in the Arizona and Ohio cases to form the majority in the third ruling, whereby the court allowed an affirmative New York State loyalty oath for prospective members of the bar. Unlike the Arizona test, New York asked bar applicants whether they belonged to a subversive group and whether they had "the specific intent to further the aims of such organization." Writing for the majority, Stewart emphasized that no known applicant had ever been denied a license to practice law in New York because of his beliefs.

Dissenting Justices Black, Douglas, Marshall and Brennan argued that the New York procedure examined too deeply an applicant's political beliefs.

Oaths for passports. The State Department confirmed Nov. 3, 1971 that Secretary of State William P. Rogers had reinstated a requirement for a loyalty oath to be taken by persons applying for a U.S. passport.

The loyalty oath swearing allegiance to the Constitution had been an optional activity for issuance of passports since 1967, but it had been challenged by the American Civil Liberties Union as a restriction of the right to freedom of belief.

U.S. District Court Judge June L. Green ruled on the challenge July 28, holding that an optional oath unfairly discriminated among U.S. citizens and requiring the State Department to decide whether to require the oath or not. Rogers' decision to require the oath was based on a provision of the U.S. Code that no passport should be issued to "any other persons than those owing allegiance, whether citizens or not, to the United States." The move to make the oath optional had been taken out of consideration of objections of a few citizens on religious, political or other grounds.

Other Developments

Court upholds Nader's right to sue GM. In another step in the three-year legal battle between consumer advocate Ralph Nader and General Motors Corp. (GM), which developed after Nader had published a book criticizing the safety and design of GM products, the New York State Court of Appeals ruled Jan. 8, 1970 that Nader had valid grounds to sue GM for invasion of privacy. Nader had accused GM of tapping his phone, harassing him with "obnoxious" phone calls and women seeking to trap him with "illicit proposals," and hiring detectives to delve into his personal life. The court's decision, written by Chief Justice Stanley H. Fuld, upheld similar rulings in the state's Supreme Court and its appellate division.

GM had contended that invasion of privacy suits applied only to commercial cases. Nader had argued that his right to sue was based on common law (rules and principles outside the purview of legislative actions). The court's majority decision said that privacy was not invaded (1) by "the mere gathering of information about a particular individual"; (2) "if the information sought is of a confidential nature and the defendant's conduct was unreasonably intrusive"; (3) "where the information sought is open to public view or has been voluntarily revealed to others." The court ruled that Nader had cause for action because GM's private detective had "engaged in unauthorized wiretapping and eavesdropping by mechanical and electronic means." The court suggested that Nader could sue GM for "defamation" and "intentional infliction of emotional distress."

The company settled Nader's suit out of court Aug. 13, 1970 for $425,000.

1972 party platforms. Both political parties made statements on the "right to privacy" in their 1972 party platforms.

The Republican statement, the shorter of the two, was:

We will continue to defend the citizen's right to privacy in our increasingly interdependent society.

We oppose computerized national data banks and all other "Big Brother" schemes which endanger individual rights.

The Democratic platform pledged to work for fulfillment of:

The rights of free speech and free political expression, of freedom from official intimidation, harassment and invasion of privacy, as guaranteed by the letter and the spirit of the Constitution.

The Democratic document also included this fuller statement:

Free Expression and Privacy. The new Democratic Administration should bring an end to the pattern of political persecution and investigation, the use of high office as a pulpit for unfair attack and intimidation and the blatant efforts to control the poor and to keep them from acquiring additional economic security or political power.

The epidemic of wiretapping and electronic surveillance engaged in by the Nixon Administration and the use of grand juries for purposes of political intimidation must be ended. The rule of law and the supremacy of the Constitution, as these concepts have traditionally been understood, must be restored.

We strongly object to secret computer data banks on individuals. Citizens should have access to their own files that are maintained by private commercial firms and the right to insert corrective material. Except in limited cases, the same should apply to government files. Collection and maintenance by federal agencies of dossiers on law-abiding citizens, because of their political views and statements, must be stopped, and files which never should have been opened should be destroyed. We firmly reject the idea of a National Computer Data Bank.

The Nixon policy of intimidation of the media and Administration efforts to use government power to block access to media by dissenters must end, if free speech is to be preserved. A Democratic Administration must be an open one, with the fullest possible disclosure of information, with an end to abuses of security classifications and executive privilege, and with regular top-level press conferences.

Bank Secrecy Act upheld. The Supreme Court April 1, 1974 upheld the 1970 Bank Secrecy Act, which gave the government broad access to bank customer records.

Justice William H. Rehnquist, writing for the 6–3 majority, conceded that the authority conferred on the Treasury Department by the act "might well surprise or even shock those who lived in an earlier era . . . ," but he added that "the latter didn't live . . . to see the heavy utilization of our domestic banking system by the minions of organized crime. . . ."

Under regulations established by the Treasury Department, banks were required to record all customer checks and microfilm those over $100, keep records of depositors' identities and all loans over $5,000 except mortgages, and report domestic deposits or withdrawals larger than $10,000 and foreign financial transactions exceeding $5,000. The regulation of foreign transactions was aimed at preventing leakage of untaxed money to secret Swiss bank accounts.

Justices William O. Douglas, William J. Brennan Jr. and Thurgood Marshall dissented. All wrote separate opinions. Calling the Treasury regulations resulting from the act "a sledgehammer approach to a problem that only a delicate scalpel can manage," Douglas warned that a government agent could invade an individual's private life merely by scrutinizing the checks he wrote. Marshall conceded that law enforcement officials would be aided by the "dragnet requirements" of the act, but added, "Those who wrote our Constitution, however, recognized more important values."

In a concurring opinion, Justice Lewis F. Powell Jr., joined by Harry A. Blackmun, cautioned that the Treasury Department's domestic reporting requirement would pose "substantial and difficult constitutional questions" if it were extended to transactions smaller than $10,-000.

Several California banks, which had challenged the act, argued that the domestic reporting requirement violated their rights against unreasonable searches and seizures—a contention rejected by the court majority, which quoted a 1950 court ruling that "neither incorporated nor unincorporated associations can plead an unqualified right to conduct their affairs in secret." The court avoided dealing with similar search and seizure claims by individual depositors, ruling they had failed to prove the reporting requirement would affect them.

IBM loses bid to avoid data disclosure— The court refused to review lower court decisions requiring the International Business Machines Corp. (IBM) to yield 700 documents to the Justice Department that the government contended were necessary to prosecute a civil antitrust suit against IBM. The court also let stand a $150,000-a-day contempt of court fine, which the court said was to be imposed, beginning immediately, until IBM surrendered the papers. (An IBM spokesman said May 13, "Since the Supreme Court has chosen not to hear our appeal, we are making the documents available to the Justice Department today.")

Houston police kept files on citizens. Fred Hofheinz, mayor of Houston, said Jan. 6, 1975 that the city's police had compiled dossiers on substantial numbers of Houston residents. Among those with police files was Rep. Barbara Jordan (D, Tex.), Hofheinz said.

Houston Police Chief Carrol M. Lynn said, "I found numerous names of persons on file who were never suspects in any case under investigation. . . ."

Hofheinz, who asked Lynn to purge the files of the dossiers, indicated that those responsible would be punished.

Watergate Revelations

Scandal Discloses Political Spying

The most serious political scandal in U.S. history began to unfold in the early hours of June 12, 1972 with the seizure of five men who had broken into the Democratic national headquarters in the Watergate building in Washington. Investigations resulting from the arrest of these five burglars led to the first resignation of an American President. The inquiries implicated top government and political leaders in misdeeds ranging from the solicitation of illegal political contributions to such invasions of privacy as electronic spying on the election campaign offices of the competing political party.

Watergate break-in crew seized. Five men were seized at gunpoint at 2 a.m. June 17, 1972 in the headquarters of the Democratic National Committee in the Watergate office-and-hotel complex in Washington. Alerted by a security guard, police apprehended five men, along with cameras and electronic surveillance equipment in their possession, after file drawers in the headquarters had been opened and ceiling panels removed near the office of Democratic National Chairman Lawrence F. O'Brien.

Those arrested and charged with second-degree burglary were: Bernard L. Barker, alias Frank Carter; James W. McCord, alias Edward Martin; Frank Angelo Fiorini, alias Edward Hamilton; Eugenio L. Martinez, alias Frank A. Sturgis, originally listed as Gene Valdes; Virgilio R. Gonzales, alias Raul Godoy. All but McCord were from Miami.

McCord, who had retired from the CIA in 1970 after 19 years with the agency, currently was employed as a security agent by both the Republican National Committee and the Committee for the Re-Election of the President.

Barker, apparently the leader of the raid, reportedly played some role for the CIA in the abortive invasion of Cuba in 1961 and had met in Miami in early June with E. Howard Hunt Jr., CIA official in charge of the invasion. Hunt recently was a consultant to Charles W. Colson, special counsel to President Nixon and other high White House officials. The White House confirmed this June 19 and said Hunt had ended his consulting work March 29.

Nixon's campaign manager, John N. Mitchell, said June 18 that none of those involved in the raid were "operating either on our behalf or with our consent."

At a news conference June 20, O'Brien called the raid a "blatant act of politi-

67

cal espionage" and said that his party was filing a $1 million civil lawsuit against the Committee to Re-Elect the President and the raiders on charges of invasion of privacy and violation of civil rights of the Democrats.

Citing the "potential involvement" of Colson, O'Brien said there was 'a developing clear line to the White House."

Mitchell responded later June 20 with a statement deploring the raid and denouncing the Democratic lawsuit as "demagoguery" by O'Brien. White House Press Secretary Ronald L. Ziegler said June 20 Colson had "assured me that he has in no way been involved in this matter."

(O'Brien, citing later evidence, said Aug. 15 that the Democrats' headquarters had been wiretapped for some time before the June 17 break-in.)

Nixon denies White House involvement. President Nixon told reporters attending an impromptu news conference in his office June 22 that "the White House has had no involvement whatever" in the Watergate raid. Such a raid, Nixon said, "has no place in our electoral process or in our governmental process."

Evidence Involves Nixon Election Group & White House

Watergate tied to Nixon committee. A report by the General Accounting Office (GAO), Congress' auditing agency, cited a connection between one of the Watergate conspirators and funds from the Finance Committee to Re-Elect the President. The GAO reported Aug. 26, 1972 that it had found "apparent and possible" violations of the Federal Election Campaign Act by the Nixon committee involving amounts of up to $350,000.

The GAO cited failure to keep adequate records concerning (a) a $25,000 contribution made to the Republicans by Minnesota businessman Dwayne O. Andreas through Kenneth H. Dahlberg,

chairman of the Minnesota re-election committee for Nixon, (b) $89,000 from four checks drawn on a Mexican bank and (c) the balance of some $350,000 in cash deposited May 25 to a media affiliate of the Nixon committee.

Funds from the Dahlberg check and the Mexican checks had turned up in possession of Bernard L. Barker.

At the time of his arrest, Barker was found to be in possession of bills traced to part of $114,000 he had withdrawn in cash from a Miami bank after having deposited the Mexican bank drafts and the Dahlberg check. Both instances apparently involved contributions from normally Democratic backers who desired anonymity. The Mexican bank checks were said to have come from GOP campaign funds collected in Texas.

The $25,000 contribution from Andreas was collected in cash near April 7. Andreas had put the cash in the custody of a third party in a Miami area hotel April 5. Dahlberg arrived April 7, when the hotel vault was closed, so he collected the money April 9 and, for security, converted it to a cashier's check to himself April 10, endorsed it and handed it to President Nixon's campaign finance chairman, Maurice Stans, April 11. Stans reportedly turned the check over without delay to Hugh W. Sloan Jr., treasurer of a separate GOP committee, the Committee to Re-elect the President (who resigned July 14). Sloan turned it over to G. Gordon Liddy, lawyer for the Finance Committee to Re-elect the President (who was later dismissed).

McGovern charges 'bugging' attempt. Sen. George S. McGovern (S.D.), the Democratic Party's Presidential candidate, during a campaign trip to New Mexico, referred Sept. 9 to an attempt by "our opponents" to bug his headquarters early May 27, an attempt that was apparently foiled when the raiders discovered McGovern workers present. McGovern commented that "it is but a single step from spying on the political opposition to suppressing that opposition and the imposing of a one-party state in which the people's precious liberties are lost."

Democrats accuse GOP of spying. The Democratic party accused Republicans Sept. 11 of conspiring "to commit political espionage" against Democrats, and the Republicans accused the Democrats Sept. 13 of using the federal courts as "an instrument for creating political headlines."

The Democrats Sept. 11 sought to amend a court action initiated against the five raiders by including as defendants Maurice H. Stans, finance chairman of the Nixon campaign, three other campaign aides and the Committee to Re-elect the President. The three other aides named were Hugh W. Sloan Jr., former treasurer of the committee, G. Gordon Liddy, former finance counsel to the committee, and E. Howard Hunt Jr., a former White House counsultant who was an intelligence agent for the committee.

The Democrats also sought to raise the amount of damages being sought from $1 million to $3.2 million.

The broadened complaint charged that Stans and Sloan had delivered $114,000 to finance an "espionage squad" and had stated that the funds were accounted for in the committee's records although the records had been destroyed. It also charged that Liddy and Hunt led an espionage squad formed to break into Democratic offices to obtain and photograph documents and install wiretaps and eavesdropping devices. The complaint also charged that Liddy and Hunt were with the raiders seized at Democratic headquarters June 17 but were warned the police were coming and withdrew.

Other Democratic charges in the new complaint were that: (a) the spy squad had broken into the Democratic National Committee offices before May 25 and stolen and photographed private documents of committee chairman Lawrence F. O'Brien; (b) O'Brien's phone was tapped from May 25 to June 17 and a listening post set up across the

street from the Watergate at a motor lodge; (c) Liddy, Hunt and James W. McCord, chief security officer of the Committee to Re-elect the President and one of those arrested at the Watergate, made periodic visits to the listening post and McCord prepared confidential memorandums of the conversations; (d) the squad tried to break into the headquarters of Sen. George McGovern to install wiretaps; (e) the break-in June 17 at Watergate was to repair existing wiretaps, establish new ones and steal and photograph documents.

■ Michael Richardson, a Miami photography processor, disclosed Aug. 31 that he had processed, the week before the Watergate raid, 35 mm pictures of Democratic party documents, many of them to or from O'Brien, for two of the men arrested at Watergate—Bernard L. Barker and Frank Sturgis.

The GOP countersuit—Clark Mac-Gregor, President Nixon's campaign director, announced Sept. 13 that the Committee to Re-elect the President had filed a countersuit that day in federal court seeking $2.5 million in damages from O'Brien. It accused O'Brien of having used the court "as a forum in which to publicize accusations against innocent persons which would be libelous if published elsewhere" and of "using his civil action to improperly conduct a private inquisition while a grand jury investigation is in progress."

Watergate burglars indicted. E. Howard Hunt Jr., the men seized in the Watergate and G. Gordon Liddy, the ex-presidential assistant and currently counsel to the Finance Committee of the Committee to Re-elect the President, were indicted by a federal grand jury Sept. 15.

According to the indictment: Liddy had been in telephone communication with Barker before the raid, and Barker with Hunt; McCord had rented a room at a motor lodge across from the Watergate from about May 5 through June 17, had bought a device to intercept wire and oral communications, had met with Liddy and Hunt May 26 and on May 27

had inspected with them the headquarters of Sen. George McGovern,
then seeking the presidential nomination;
Liddy gave McCord $1,600 in cash
June 11–15; Liddy, Hunt, McCord and
the four men from Miami, having in
their possession a device to intercept oral
communication and another to intercept
wire communication, broke into the
Democratic headquarters June 17 to
steal property, tap phones and intercept
telephone calls.

The indictment also accused Liddy,
Hunt and McCord of intercepting phone
calls from about May 25 up to or about
June 16 in the Democratic offices, primarily the telephone of Robert Spence
Oliver, executive director of the Associations of State Chairmen.

The indictment alleged burglary and
possession of eavesdropping devices,
brought under District of Columbia law,
and conspiracy and interception and
disclosure of telephone and oral communications, brought under federal law.

In announcing the indictment, Attorney General Richard G. Kleindienst said
the investigation was "one of the most
intensive, objective and thorough ... in
many years, reaching out to cities all
across the United States as well as into
foreign countries." John W. Hushen,
director of public information for the
Justice Department, said "we have
absolutely no evidence to indicate that
any others should be charged."

The seven men charged in the case
pleaded not guilty Sept. 19 and were
released on bonds ranging from $10,000
to $50,000.

McGovern commented Sept. 15 that
"the indictments do point up the seriousness in the matter and what now needs to
be pursued is how it was funded and
whether there are violations there, which
there seem to be."

In a statement Sept. 16, McGovern
accused Nixon of ordering a "whitewash," deplored the "questions left unanswered" by the grand jury and linked
the affair to "the moral standards of
this nation."

McGovern said the "unanswered
questions" in the case were: "Who

ordered this act of political espionage?
Who paid for it? Who contributed the
$114,000 that went from the Nixon cam-
paign committee to the bank account of
one of the men arrested, and that paid
off the spies for their work? Who received the memoranda of the tapped
telephone conversation?"

McGovern indicated disbelief that
the seven men indicted "dreamed up and
carried out this shabby scheme to spy on
the Democratic party all on their own,
with no authority from above."

Mitchell linked to secret GOP fund.
The Washington Post reported Sept. 29
that former Attorney General John N.
Mitchell controlled a secret Republican
fund utilized for gathering information
about the Democrats. The fund was said
to have fluctuated between $350,000 and
$700,000, and Mitchell was said to have
approved withdrawals for almost a year
before he left the Cabinet to become
President's Nixon's campaign manager.

The Post said former Commerce Secretary Maurice H. Stans later was
among four persons in addition to
Mitchell permitted to approve payments
from the secret fund.

A spokesman for the Committee to
Re-elect the President said there was
"no truth" to the charges.

The Administration Oct. 25 denied a
new report linking H. R. Haldeman,
President Nixon's White House chief of
staff, with the secret fund, which was
allegedly used in part to finance intelligence gathering and political espionage.
The report, published by the Washington
Post Oct. 25, said Haldeman was one of
five persons authorized to approve payments from the GOP fund. The other
four authorized to approve payments
were said to be Mitchell, former Commerce Secretary Maurice C. Stans, Jeb
Stuart Magruder, a former White House
assistant to Haldeman and currently
deputy director of the President's re-
election campaign, and Herbert W.
Kalmbach, the President's personal
lawyer.

The secret fund was reported to have
been used in part to pay for an under-

cover effort to discredit or hinder Democratic campaigns. Funds involved in financing the break-in at Democratic national headquarters in the Watergate building in Washington also reportedly derived from the secret fund, whose only record reportedly had been destroyed by a Nixon campaign official after the Watergate arrests. The General Accounting Office previously had reported the existence of a $350,000 fund in cash kept in a safe in Stans' office.

The Washington Post story Oct. 25 cited sources as federal investigators and accounts of sworn grand jury testimony taken in the Watergate case.

The report carried Haldeman's denial of the story as "untrue."

The story also was denied Oct. 25 by White House Press Secretary Ronald L. Ziegler and Nixon campaign director Clark MacGregor. Ziegler said Haldeman never had access to such a fund and, in fact, such a fund never existed. MacGregor said he had been assured by Haldeman that he had never had authority to disburse campaign funds for the President's re-election.

Ex-FBI agent delivered information. A former agent for the Federal Bureau of Investigation (FBI) disclosed Oct. 5 that he had delivered information obtained by espionage from the Democratic headquarters at the Watergate building in Washington to an official at the Nixon campaign office. In an interview published in the Los Angeles Times, the ex-FBI agent, Alfred C. Baldwin 3rd, said he had monitored telephone and other conversations at Watergate for three weeks while employed by the Committee to Re-elect the President, working from a room in a motor lodge across from Watergate.

Baldwin said the official to whom he delivered the information was not one of those indicted in the Watergate headquarters raid. Baldwin revealed that he, himself, was a member of the raid crew. He was not indicted after agreeing to cooperate with the Justice Department. He was a key witness for the government in the case.

The Washington Post reported Oct.

6 that Baldwin had informed the FBI that memorandums describing the intercepted Democratic conversations were sent to members of the White House staff and Nixon campaign staff.

The Post reported Oct. 10 that the Watergate raid was but part of a larger espionage and sabotage effort against the Democrats on behalf of the Nixon re-election effort. The newspaper quoted federal investigators as describing the intelligence operation by the Nixon campaign organization as "unprecedented in scope and intensity." The story reported attempts to disrupt campaigns of Democratic candidates for president.

The Post article also related an account from three attorneys that they had been offered, and rejected, proposals to work as agents provocateurs on behalf of the Nixon campaign. The Post report said the FBI had information that at least 50 undercover Nixon operatives were at work throughout the country in an attempt to disrupt and spy on Democratic campaigns.

GOP spying linked to White House. A report in the Oct. 23 issue of Time Magazine (made available Oct. 15) linked a Republican political sabotage effort against the Democrats directly to the White House. It said Los Angeles attorney Donald H. Segretti, previously identified as a recruiter for an undercover spy operation against Democratic campaigns, had been hired in September 1971 by Dwight Chapin, a deputy assistant to President Nixon, and Gordon Strachan, a White House staff assistant. Time said the information came from Justice Department files.

The report said Segretti was paid more than $35,000 for his services by Herbert Kalmbach, Nixon's personal attorney, provided by the Committee to Re-elect the President out of funds kept in the safe of Maurice Stans, chief political fundraiser for Nixon.

According to the Washington Post Oct. 15, California attorney Lawrence Young, in a sworn statement, said Segretti had told him "Dwight Chapin was a person I reported to in Washington" and he received political sabotage and spying assignments from E. Howard Hunt Jr.

The New York Times Oct. 18 linked Segretti to a number of telephone calls made in the spring to the White House and to Chapin's home and to Hunt's home and office.

The Administration Oct. 16 rebutted the charges that a political sabotage and spying effort involved high Nixon aides. White House Press Secretary Ronald L. Ziegler called the charges "hearsay, innuendo and guilt by association" and said he refused to "dignify" them by discussing them. Clark MacGregor, chairman of the Nixon re-election effort, attacked the Post for using "unsubstantiated charges" to "maliciously" link the White House to Watergate.

Neither spokesman would discuss specific items of the charges. MacGregor left the room after reading his statement, although Ziegler denied that Segretti had ever worked for the White House and MacGregor said he had not worked for either the political or financial branches of the campaign structure.

The Washington Post carried a report Dec. 8, based on an interview with a former White House personal secretary, that Hunt was one of a team of officials, known as the "plumbers," assigned by the White House to investigate leaks to the news media. A private, non-government telephone installed for use in the effort was apparently used almost exclusively for conversations between Hunt and Bernard L. Barker, another of the Watergate defendants, according to the secretary. She said the bills for the phone service were submitted for payment to an aide in the office of John Ehrlichman, President Nixon's chief domestic affairs aide.

Ziegler confirmed the "plumbers" operation Dec. 12 and said the work was supervised by Ehrlichman, but he said he did not believe Hunt had worked on the project. It "would be folly," Ziegler said, to associate use of the phone with the alleged bugging of Democratic headquarters in May and June since the spe-cial line was in use only from August 1971 to March 15, 1972.

Trials Add to Disclosures

Hunt pleads guilty. E. Howard Hunt Jr. pleaded guilty Jan. 11, 1973 to all six charges against him. He made the guilty plea on the second day of the conspiracy trial of the seven defendants indicted in connection with the June 1972 break-in and alleged bugging of Democratic party national headquarters at the Watergate complex in Washington.

Hunt had offered the preceding day to plead guilty on three charges, but Chief Judge John J. Sirica of U.S. District Court in Washington said Jan. 11 he would refuse the offer, because of "the apparent strength of the government's case" against Hunt, and because the public must be assured "not only the substance of justice but also the appearance of justice."

The six counts against Hunt were conspiracy to obtain information illegally from the Democrats, breaking into and entering the Watergate headquarters, knowingly intercepting wire communications, attempting to intercept wire communications, attempting to intercept oral communications, and an additional breaking and entering charge.

The chief prosecutor at the trial was Assistant U.S. Attorney Earl J. Silbert.

Silbert's two-hour opening statement Jan. 10 depicted the Watergate incident as part of a well-financed espionage program against the Democratic party and Democratic presidential candidates. According to Silbert, G. Gordon Liddy, one of the defendants and at that time counsel to the Committee to Re-elect the President, had been given $235,000 by other committee officials, Jeb Stuart Magruder and Herbert L. Porter, to uncover plans for demonstrations against Republicans campaigning for Nixon or against the Republican National Convention, and for other "special intelligence assignments," including a probe of certain campaign contributions made to a Democratic presidential candidate. Silbert said the committee kept few if any records on the funds, and said the prosecution could only account for $50,000.

The prosecutor charged that Liddy and Hunt were seen at the Watergate the night their co-defendants were arrested, and had demonstrated prior knowledge of the break-in attempt. One witness, Silbert said, would testify to having monitored about 200 personal and political phone calls from a tap on a telephone at the Democratic headquarters before June 17.

Defense attorneys, in opening arguments Jan. 10, stressed their contention that the defendants' had acted with "no criminal intent" or "no evil motive."

4 more plead guilty. Four more defendants in the Watergate case pleaded guilty Jan. 15 to all counts of a federal indictment charging them with conspiracy, second-degree burglary and wiretapping. The four were Bernard L. Barker, Frank A. Sturgis, Eugenio Rolando Martinez and Virgilio R. Gonzalez.

The four pleading guilty Jan. 15 all denied that pressure had been put on them by "higher-ups," as Sirica phrased it in questioning them, or money offered them to plead guilty. Gonzalez and Sturgis, in response to further questioning, indicated, as Barker previously had in interviews, that their participation in the Watergate affair was based on a belief they were furthering the cause of Cuban liberation from Communist control.

A report that "great pressure" was being exerted upon Sturgis, Gonzalez, Barker and Martinez to plead guilty was carried by the New York Times Jan. 15 in an article by Seymour M. Hersh. Another report in Time magazine Jan. 22 said the Watergate defendants had been promised a cash settlement as high as $1,000 a month if they pleaded guilty, with additional funds to come after release from prison. Hersh had reported in the Times Jan. 14, that, according "to sources close to the case," at least four of those arrested in the Watergate raid were still being paid, by unnamed sources. The Times sources also claimed that Martinez was an active employe of the Central In-

telligence Agency at the time of the raid and was dropped from the CIA payroll a day later, that high officials of the Committee to Re-elect the President had acknowledged privately that they were unable to account for $900,000 in campaign contributions, that a Nixon supporter working in Democratic headquarters had taped open doors to permit entry by those apprehended there.

■ Thomas James Gregory, a student of Brigham Young University, testified at the trial Jan. 11 he was recruited and paid by Hunt to spy on Democratic presidential candidates McGovern and Sen. Edmund S. Muskie (Me.).

Liddy, McCord convicted. G. Gordon Liddy and James W. McCord Jr. were convicted by a jury in U.S. district court in the District of Columbia Jan. 30, 1973 of attempting to spy on Democratic headquarters in the Watergate.

The jury, which deliberated less than 90 minutes, found Liddy and McCord, former officials of President Nixon's political organization, guilty of conspiracy, second-degree burglary, attempted wiretapping, attempted bugging and wiretapping. McCord was also found guilty of possessing wiretapping and bugging equipment.

Liddy's defense contended that he thought the other defendants, five of whom were arrested during the break-in, had been engaged in a legitimate intelligence operation and he, like other officials at Nixon headquarters, was "on the safe side of the line of innocence." The lawyer, Peter L. Maroulis, disclosed in summation Jan. 30 that Liddy had destroyed memoranda based on information from the wiretap at Watergate when he realized, after the arrests at Watergate, that the information could be "tainted" and cause embarrassment to the re-election committee.

McCord's defense was that he had not participated in the raid with "criminal intent" and was therefore not guilty as charged. The prosecution had charged that McCord was in the operation for financial gain and more power within the re-election committee.

A proposed defense argument that McCord had acted at Watergate out of "duress" to prevent harm to officials, including President Nixon, was disallowed Jan. 24 by Chief Judge John J. Sirica, who dismissed it as "ridiculous."

Several times during the trial Sirica had interrupted examination of witnesses by both the defense and prosecution to conduct the questioning himself. In doing so Jan. 22, he said neither side was developing "all the facts." It was under probing by Sirica that Hugh W. Sloan Jr., former treasurer of the Nixon re-election finance committee, disclosed Jan. 23 that $199,000 in campaign funds had been paid to Liddy after verification from former Attorney General John N. Mitchell, also former Nixon campaign manager, and former Commerce Secretary Maurice H. Stans, Nixon's chief fundraiser. However, Sloan said that Mitchell and Stans had verified that Jeb Magruder, a deputy campaign director, was authorized to make the payments. However, he said no one had "indicated" to him how the $199,000 was to be used.

Magruder testified Jan. 23 that about $235,000 had been budgeted by the Nixon organization for an intelligence operation, assigned to Liddy, to (1) learn plans of radical groups that might disrupt political rallies or inflict "possibly bodily harm" on presidential surrogates, and to (2) discover the intentions of demonstrators at the Republican National Convention.

One such assignment, he related, was to investigate reports that a Democratic presidential candidate known for his anti-pollution stand, presumably Sen. Edmund S. Muskie (Me.), had received money from a major polluter.

The Sloan testimony was elicited in the absence of the jury, a frequent occurrence during the trial, and Sirica called the jury back Jan. 26 to hear an edited transcript of it.

The court had been under a higher court ruling not to admit without further advice testimony concerning information discovered by wiretap if the testimony were contested. The situation existed with the key prosecution witness, Alfred C. Baldwin 3rd, who said he had been ordered by McCord to monitor wiretapped telephone conversations at Watergate. The content of his testimony became an issue, and the U.S. Court of Appeals ruled Jan. 19 he should not say what he had overheard nor name anyone outside the Watergate offices who had talked over the tapped telephone.

Baldwin testified Jan. 19 he had delivered some of the wiretapped information to Nixon's political organization but could not remember the identity of the official to whom the material had been addressed. Baldwin could not remember, again in persistent questioning on the point Jan. 22 by Sirica with the jury absent.

Congress Begins Inquiries

Senate authorizes probe. The Senate, by a 70–0 vote Feb. 7, 1973, resolved to establish a seven-member select committee—four Democrats and three Republicans—to probe all aspects of the Watergate bugging case and other reported attempts of political espionage against the Democrats in the 1972 presidential election campaign.

Sen. Sam J. Ervin Jr. (D, N.C.) was named chairman of the special panel Feb. 8. The other members were Democrats Joseph M. Montoya (N.M.), Herman E. Talmadge (Ga.) and Daniel K. Inouye (Hawaii) and Republicans Howard H. Baker (Tenn.), Edward J. Gurney (Fla.) and Lowell P. Weicker Jr. (Conn.).

A preliminary report on the same subject by a Senate panel Feb. 1 stated that the federal government had failed to conduct a substantial investigation. Sen. Edward M. Kennedy (D, Mass.), chairman of a Judiciary Committee subcommittee that had conducted the study, said his panel had found evidence that "strongly indicates that a wide range of espionage and sabotage activities did occur" during the recent campaign and "neither the federal criminal investigation nor the White House administrative inquiry included any substantial investigation of the alleged sabotage and espionage operations apart from those surrounding the Watergate episode itself."

Kennedy cited indications that "one key participant was in repeated contact with the White House, the White House convention headquarters and White House aides during relevant time periods" and that "at least part of the financing was arranged through a key Republican fund-raiser who is a close associate of President Nixon's." Although the names were omitted, the references, based on previous news reports, were taken to involve the activities of Donald H. Segretti, a lawyer from California, and Herbert W. Kalmbach, Nixon's personal lawyer and a leading GOP fund-raiser.

A New York Times report Feb. 7 by Seymour M. Hersh, based on government sources, named Gordon C. Strachan, a former staff assistant to H. R. Haldeman, Nixon's chief of staff, as the initial contact between Segretti, allegedly involved in political espionage and sabotage against Democratic presidential campaigners, and political intelligence operations led by Watergate figures G. Gordon Liddy, recently convicted, and E. Howard Hunt Jr., who pleaded guilty. Dwight C. Chapin, Nixon's appointments secretary, was reported to be another contact for Segretti. In a Hersh report Feb. 8, Chapin was said to have directed Kalmbach to pay Segretti for his activities and to have used a code name—"Chapman"—in his undercover intelligence work.

According to court depositions released Feb. 6, former Attorney General John N. Mitchell, who served as Nixon's campaign manager, received confidential information from someone traveling with Democratic candidates identified as "Chapman's friend," information Mitchell described as "pap." He said he did not know who "Chapman" was.

The sworn depositions had been taken in pretrial testimony in a civil Watergate action, depositions sealed during the criminal case and released Feb. 6 by U.S. District Court Judge Charles R. Richey.

Among other data disclosed in the depositions: the White House had been alerted within hours of the Watergate raid arrests of the possible involvement of one of its consultants, E. Howard Hunt Jr.; John D. Ehrlichman, Nixon's assistant for domestic affairs, had called Charles W. Colson, a special counsel to Nixon, to inquire about Hunt because of Hunt's possible involvement in the incident.

Ehrlichman confirmed Feb. 8 that the White House had been notified early, as a matter of routine whenever members of the White House staff were "arrested or in trouble."

Colson also said in the deposition that it was under his "initiative" that Hunt had been hired by the White House, to work on the "Pentagon papers controversy," that he had consulted with Ehrlichman about the hiring and that Hunt initially reported to Colson. Hunt was later transferred, Colson believed, to work or help the Nixon re-election committee, probably "in the area of convention security" and "the general area of security" for the campaign committee.

Gray faces Senate opposition. The White House announced Feb. 17 the nomination of L. Patrick Gray 3rd, acting director of the Federal Bureau of Investigation since May 1972, to be permanent director, but the nomination soon ran into opposition in the Senate committee holding hearings on the appointment after it was learned that the FBI had supplied the White House and the Nixon campaign committee with information gathered in its investigation of the Watergate break-in.

Gray acknowledged Feb. 28 that extensive records of the FBI probe had been made available to the White House and claimed that the late FBI director, J. Edgar Hoover, had provided other Administrations with progress reports of important investigations.

(Gray coupled the disclosure with a promise to open the FBI files on the Watergate breakin to any senator.)

Gray said he based his decision on advice from his legal staff after John W. Dean 3rd, a presidential counsel conducting a separate White House inquiry into the Watergate breakin, "asked us to give him what we had to date." The request was made in August 1972, according to Gray.

Gray said he had provided Attorney General Richard G. Kleindienst with the report and added, "I have every reason to believe that it then went to the White House."

Gray also revealed March 6 that White House special counsel Charles W. Colson had told FBI agents in August 1972 about a trip he had authorized in August 1972 for E. Howard Hunt.

The disclosure was made during the FBI's Watergate investigation, in which Colson and Hunt were implicated.

It was also revealed that Dean ordered Hunt's office safe emptied June 28, 1972, three days after he had been arrested for the Watergate breakin. The papers were not turned over to the FBI until a week after the safe had been opened.

When asked about the time lag between the two events, Gray said, "I see nothing irregular about it. The President's got a rather substantial interest as to what might be in those papers."

Gray also revealed Feb. 28 that FBI agents had questioned Donald H. Segretti in June 1972 regarding his involvement in alleged political espionage activities.

The Washington Post had reported Oct. 15, 1972 that Segretti had been shown FBI documents by White House aides to prepare him for grand jury testimony. Gray told the committee that he had checked these reports with Dean and that Dean had denied them.

Gray added March 7 that agents had questioned a former presidential assistant, Dwight Chapin, March 5 and that he also denied having given the FBI reports to Segretti.

Information supplied the committee by Gray March 7 indicated that Nixon's personal lawyer, Herbert W. Kalmbach, had paid Segretti between $30,000 and $40,-000 in GOP funds from Sept. 1, 1971 until March 15, 1972.

According to Gray, Kalmbach claimed that he was only a "disbursing agent" with no knowledge of Segretti's use of the money or how he obtained his instructions from the party.

Gray told the committee March 7 that Dean received FBI reports of interviews with Segretti as well as accounts of FBI interviews with Alfred C. Baldwin, who had admitted tapping Democratic party telephones. Dean received information on the "nature" and "substance" of Baldwin's eavesdropping, Gray said.

A 12-page summary of the FBI investigation on the Watergate affair, dated July 21, 1972, was submitted to the Senate committee March 5. The report charged that attorneys for the Committee to Re-elect the President had hampered FBI efforts to question GOP campaign officials.

Gray told the panel March 6 that an unspecified number of Nixon campaign officials had sought and obtained FBI interviews which were conducted when GOP lawyers were not present. Dean received reports of those interviews as well.

Dean, "in his official capacity as counsel to the President," demanded and was allowed to be present during the FBI's questioning of all White House personnel, despite his vociferous objections, Gray claimed. Had he objected, no White House interviews would have been permitted, Gray added.

As Gray was speaking before the Senate committee March 6, White House Press Secretary Ronald L. Ziegler told reporters that Dean sat in on the interviews of only those White House staff members who had requested his presence.

Gray testified March 1 that John Mitchell, Nixon's former campaign manager, prevented the FBI from questioning his wife on a matter related to the Watergate probe.

Gray amended those remarks March 7, saying that after the initial rebuff, Mitchell had offered to allow his wife to "come to Washington for an interview, if our agent thought it was necessary." The agent "stated that he did not," according to Gray.

The FBI was also unable to interview a top campaign official, Robert C. Mardian, about the destruction of campaign finance records, Gray had told the committee March 1. Gray said then that the FBI did not talk with presidential assistant H. R. Haldeman, whose staff members had been linked to political espionage charges.

Testimony from 'raw files' deplored—
After Gray had given the Judiciary Committee a report of the FBI interview with Nixon's attorney, Herbert W. Kalmbach, White House Press Secretary Ronald L. Ziegler March 8 expressed President Nixon's "concern" at the release of "raw, unevaluated material" from FBI files.

At his news conference, Nixon expressed his own annoyance with the procedure. He said he understood why Gray had acted as he had "because his hearing was involved" but the practice of the FBI furnishing "raw files" to full Congressional committees "must stop" with this particular instance. "Now, for the FBI," he said, "before a full committee of the Congress to furnish 'raw files' and then to have them leak out to the press, I think could do innocent people a great deal of damage."

(Gray's testimony about Kalmbach actually was not from "raw files" but contained in a written addition to previous testimony as a paraphrase of Kalmbach's accounting of the incident to the FBI. And the "leak" to the press apparently was this testimony by Gray for the committee's public record.)

Gray ordered not to discuss case—Gray informed the Senate Judiciary Committee March 20 that Attorney General Richard G. Kleindienst had ordered him to stop discussing the Watergate case at his nomination hearings.

Gray, who had previously told the committee he had supplied the White House and the Nixon re-election committee with data gathered in the FBI Watergate inquiry, confirmed to the panel March 20 that he had continued to send the FBI's Watergate reports to Presidential counsel Dean even after learning that Dean had recommended convicted Watergate defendant G. Gordon Liddy for his job with the Nixon re-election committee.

Gray testified March 21 that Dean had picked up the Watergate material from him in person and he had never notified Kleindienst or anyone else in the FBI or Justice Department of the transaction. He said he had kept no record on the contents of the data handed over but said Dean had been given "an integral part of the total Watergate file."

‣He would continue to give Dean any material he requested as long as Dean was the President's counsel, Gray said. He had not informed Kleindienst about releasing the material to Dean for the same reason. It was not necessary to inform Kleindienst, Gray said, "in view of the fact that I had a request from the counsel to the President."

Gray's new orders about testimony forbade answering questions that would reveal information from FBI files.

The Administration also superseded Gray's offer to the Judiciary Committee Feb. 28 to open the FBI's Watergate files to any senator who wished to examine them.

Gray explained March 20 that his new orders restricted Senate access to the files to the committee chairman and ranking minority member and their respective chief counsels of investigating panels.

This agreement had been worked out March 16 in a meeting of Kleindienst, Sen. Sam J. Ervin Jr. (D, N.C.) and Howard H. Baker Jr. (R, Tenn.), chairman and vice chairman, respectively, of the Senate select committee established to investigate the Watergate and related affairs.

Ervin said March 18 he agreed with President Nixon that raw FBI files made available to a Congressional committee should not be made public. Appearing that day on the CBS "Face the Nation" broadcast, Ervin disagreed with the President's position to invoke executive privilege to bar White House aides from testifying before Congress.

Gray admits Dean 'probably' lied—
Gray admitted March 22 that Dean "probably" lied to FBI agents investigating the Watergate case. But he reiterated, because "that man is counsel to the President," that he would continue to send Dean confidential FBI reports if he requested them.

This testimony was elicited under insistent questioning by Sen. Robert C. Byrd (W. Va.), Senate Democratic whip, who established a chronology concerning Dean and Watergate defendant E.

Howard Hunt Jr., who had pleaded guilty. Byrd recalled Gray's testimony that Dean's aides had searched Hunt's office June 19 and that material from the search had been turned over to Dean June 20. Then, on June 22, Byrd continued, during the FBI's interview with White House aide Charles W. Colson, which Dean attended, Dean responded to a remark by one of the agents that he did not know whether Hunt had an office at the White House and would "check it out."

In view of this, Byrd asked if Dean had "lied to the agents" and Gray replied that he "would have to conclude that judgment probably is correct."

A White House statement later March 22, calling Byrd's charge "reprehensible, unfortunate, unfair and incorrect," said "Mr. Dean flatly denies that he ever misled or . . . lied to an agent of the FBI." It said Dean recalled having been asked by the agents whether or not they could visit Hunt's office, not whether or not Hunt had an office there, and he had replied that he would check on it.

Gray's nomination withdrawn—Gray's nomination as FBI director was withdrawn by President Nixon at Gray's request April 5, 1973.

Fresh Charges Made

McCord implicates others. New allegations of prior complicity in the Watergate case by a White House aide and a former aide to the Committee to Re-elect the President were disclosed March 26, 1973.

The disclosures were reported to have been made in still-secret testimony by convicted Watergate defendant James W. McCord Jr.

The new development unfolded as Judge John J. Sirica convened the District of Columbia district court March 23 to deliver sentences on the convicted Watergate defendants.

He had a "preliminary matter" to dispose of first, Sirica said. It was a letter to him, delivered by a court probation

officer, from McCord. The letter contended that "others" had escaped capture at the Watergate raid, that "perjury occurred during the trial in matters highly material to the very structure, orientation and impact of the government's case and to the motivation and intent of the defendants," and that "political pressure to plead guilty and remain silent" had been brought on him and the others caught at the Watergate.

In the letter, McCord asked for a private meeting with Sirica to discuss these matters. "I cannot feel confident," he wrote, in talking of them in the presence of FBI agents, Justice Department attorneys or "other government representatives." He believed "that retaliatory measures will be taken against me, my family and my friends should I disclose such facts."

Provisional sentences for 5 others—Five of the other Watergate defendants were sentenced "provisionally" March 23 to maximum prison terms—35 years for E. Howard Hunt Jr. and 40 years each for Bernard L. Barker, Frank A. Sturgis, Eugenio R. Martinez and Virgilio R. Gonzalez. All had pleaded guilty.

G. Gordon Liddy, who was convicted with McCord, was sentenced to 6 years, 8 months–20 years in prison.

In announcing the provisional maximum sentences, Sirica pointedly told them: "I recommend your full cooperation" with the federal grand jury and the Senate select committee investigating the Watergate case. "You must understand that I hold out no promises or hopes of any kind," he told them, "but I do say that should you decide to speak freely I would have to weigh that factor in appraising what sentence will be finally imposed in each case."

McCord talks to Senate counsel—McCord made a second surprise move later March 23 when he appeared with a new lawyer, Bernard Fensterwald of Washington, for a secret discussion of the case with Samuel Dash, chief counsel for the Senate Select Committee, and Harold Lipset of San Francisco, a committee investigator. A second session was held

March 24. Dash said, in disclosing the meetings March 25, that McCord had given them, among other data, names of participants in the Watergate conspiracy who had escaped prosecution.

Dean and Magruder named—The names in McCord's allegations appeared first in the Los Angeles Times, which published a report March 26 that McCord had named John W. Dean 3rd and Jeb Stuart Magruder, former deputy director of Nixon's re-election committee, as two Administration officials who had prior knowledge of the Watergate spying operation. He also claimed, according to the report, that Hunt had put pressure on other defendants to plead guilty and told them they would receive "executive clemency" and money for remaining silent.

The Washington Star-News reported later March 26 that McCord, "encountered on a Washington street today," had verified as accurate published accounts of what he told Dash.

Later March 26, Magruder, currently an official with the Commerce Department, denied the charge of prior knowledge and White House Press Secretary Ronald L. Ziegler "flatly" denied "any prior knowledge on the part of Mr. Dean regarding the Watergate affair." The White House also said the President had discussed the reports of McCord's testimony with Dean that day and retained "absolute and total confidence" in his counsel.

More names—For several days after the Select Senate Committee had held a secret session with McCord March 28, it was reported widely that he had related, as uncorroborated hearsay from the Watergate co-conspirators (principally Liddy) that: former Attorney General John N. Mitchell approved the espionage activity and was "overall boss" of the group conducting it; John W. Dean 3rd, counsel to the President, attended a planning meeting with two of the men later convicted as conspirators and reported back that the operation had been approved; the President's chief of staff, H. R. Haldeman, "knew what was going on" at the Nixon re-election committee;

Charles W. Colson, former special counsel to the President, possibly received a detailed plan for the Watergate raid from E. Howard Hunt Jr., a Watergate defendant who pleaded guilty; McCord met with Mitchell "daily" to discuss family and Republican security arrangements.

All the officials linked by the allegations to Watergate had denied such involvement, and Mitchell was on record with a sworn statement that he met with McCord "once" for a briefing about security of the building and, aside from passing in hallways, it was his only contact with McCord.

McCord cites payoffs to defendants. James W. McCord was reported April 9 to have told a Watergate grand jury that payments had been paid to defendants in the criminal case for their silence and pressure applied for guilty pleas.

He was also reported to have named, on a hearsay basis, Kenneth W. Parkinson, then attorney for the Committee to Re-elect the President, as the person he believed responsible for applying the pressure and channeling the payments. The New York Times confirmed the testimony, originally leaked from "sources close to the case," in a telephone interview with McCord.

The reports noted that McCord's testimony concerning Parkinson's alleged role was based on talks with Mrs. Dorothy Hunt, who was named by McCord as the conduit for the cash payments. Mrs. Hunt was the deceased wife of another convicted Watergate defendant, E. Howard Hunt Jr.

Parkinson, currently a member of a Washington law firm, was also contacted by the Times and said the allegations against him were "absolutely false."

The amount of the cash payments was said to be $1,000 per month for each of the four defendants arrested with McCord and, the Washington Post reported April 10, $3,000 a month for McCord.

Mitchell involvement alleged—According to a Post report April 12, also confirmed by McCord, of his further testimony before the grand jury, McCord claimed that convicted co-conspirator G. Gordon Liddy had told him transcripts of wire-tapped conversations of Democratic officials had been hand-carried to former Attorney General John N. Mitchell. Liddy also told him, according to the report, that Mitchell had ordered a priority list of electronic eavesdropping operations against the Democrats—first the Watergate headquarters, then the campaign headquarters of Sen. George S. McGovern, then the Miami hotel rooms to be occupied by presidential candidates and party officials attending the national convention.

Mitchell's denial of both charges was relayed through the Committee to Re-elect the President.

McCord's lawyer, Bernard W. Fensterwald, told reporters April 9 that McCord had no first-hand knowledge that anybody "higher up" than Liddy knew of the Watergate operation.

The Washington Post reported April 19 that Jeb Stuart Magruder, Mitchell's former aide in the Nixon re-election campaign, had told federal prosecutors April 14 that he, Mitchell, Liddy and presidential counsel John W. Dean 3rd had planned and approved the Watergate wiretapping at a meeting in the attorney general's office in February 1972.

Magruder was said to have told the prosecutors that Mitchell and Dean later arranged to buy the silence of the seven convicted Watergate conspirators.

A New York Times report April 20 said Mitchell had disclosed in private conversations with friends that he had participated in three meetings on the proposed wiretapping plan—on Jan. 24 and Feb. 4, 1972 while he was attorney general and in March 1972, when he was manager of the Nixon re-election campaign. Mitchell was said to have confirmed that Liddy and Magruder had discussed spying on the Democrats at these meetings, but Mitchell reportedly said he had rejected the plans on each occasion. Dean was said to have been present at one or more of the sessions. Mitchell appeared before the Watergate grand jury April 20 and con-

firmed the substance of the report in the Times.

Mitchell told reporters later April 20 that he had "heard discussions" of plans to spy on the Democrats during the 1972 presidential campaign but he had "never approved any bugging plans during any period during the campaign."

There also were reports April 20 that Mitchell had told the grand jury he had approved payments of Nixon campaign funds to the seven Watergate defendants for their legal fees, not, as alleged by Magruder, to buy their silence.

Attorney William G. Hundley, retained by Mitchell April 19, told the New York Times April 20 that Mitchell had been prepared to testify "he had some knowledge that Republican re-election funds were being used to pay the legal fees for the defendants." Hundley quoted Mitchell as saying that such payments were normal practice in the business world.

The April 20 Times report said that Dean allegedly had supervised cash payments of more than $175,000 in GOP funds to the Watergate defendants and their lawyers. The allegation was denied later April 20 as "absolutely untrue" by Dean's lawyer, Robert C. McCandless of Washington.

White House Begins to Yield

Nixon permits his aides to testify. President Nixon announced April 17 there had been "major developments" from a "new" inquiry he had initiated into the Watergate case.

The President also announced he had agreed to permit testimony under certain conditions by his aides before a Senate investigating committee. "I believe," he said, an agreement had been reached with the committee on ground rules for the testimony which would "preserve," he said, "the separation of powers without suppressing the fact."

The President made the announcements in a brief statement he read to reporters at the White House.

In his statement, Nixon said he had begun "intensive new inquiries into this whole matter" March 21 "as a result of serious charges which came to my attention, some of which were publicly reported." He said he had met Sunday, April 15 in the Executive Office Building adjoining the White House with Attorney General Richard G. Kleindienst and Assistant Attorney General Henry Peterson "to review the facts which had come to me in my investigation and also to review the progress" of a separate investigation by the Justice Department.

"If any person," Nixon continued, "in the executive branch or in the government is indicted by the grand jury, my policy will be to immediately suspend him. If he is convicted, he will, of course, be automatically discharged."

The President asserted his view that "no individual holding, in the past or at present, a position of major importance in the Administration should be given immunity from prosecution." He would aid the judicial process "in all appropriate ways," he said, and "all government employes and especially White House staff employes are expected fully to cooperate in this matter. I condemn any attempts to cover up in this case, no matter who is involved."

The President said discussions for the ground rules on Watergate testimony by White House aides had been initiated several weeks ago between Sens. Sam J. Ervin Jr. (D, N.C.) and Howard H. Baker Jr. (R, Tenn.), chairman and vice chairman of the Senate Select Committee, and John D. Ehrlichman, the President's special assistant on domestic

affairs, and White House aide Leonard Garment. The committee's ground rules, Nixon said, "totally preserve the doctrine of separation of powers." "They provide," he said, that a witness could first appear in secret session, "if appropriate," and that executive privilege was "expressly reserved and may be asserted" during the testimony. He said White House staff members "will appear voluntarily when requested" and "will testify under oath and they will answer fully all proper questions."

Nixon specified that the arrangement applied to "this hearing only in which wrongdoing has been charged" and "would not apply to other hearings." "Each of them will be considered on its merits," he said.

After Nixon's statement, White House Press Secretary Ronald L. Ziegler said the President's previous statements denying Watergate involvement by White House staff members were now "inoperative" since they were based on "investigations prior to the developments announced today."

Ervin issues guidelines—Sen. Ervin, chairman of the Senate's Select Committee on Presidential Campaign Activities, issued the committee's guidelines on the Watergate investigation April 18, noting that the panel would be the final judge on whether a witness could refuse to answer its questions.

"The guidelines say just what was the law already in any kind of a fair investigation," he said, "that if any witness claims that he is privileged for any reason against testifying, he can raise that point. But just like in court, somebody has to rule on that point, and these guidelines expressly say that the committee's going to do the ruling. If the committee rules adversely to the witness on any question of privilege, the committee shall require the witness to testify."

The rules also expressly stated that a claim of privilege against testifying could not be claimed by or for any witness prior to appearance before the committee. The committee would not rule on such a claim "until the question by which the testimony is sought is put to the witness."

---

*President Nixon's previous statements on the Watergate case:

At a news conference Aug. 29, 1972, he disclosed that his own staff had investigated the affair and he could "categorically" state that the probe "indicates that no one in the White House staff, no one in this Administration, presently employed, was involved in this very bizarre incident."

Nixon, at a news conference March 3, 1973, reiterated that the White House investigation of Watergate indicated that no one on the White House staff at the time the investigation was conducted was involved "or had knowledge of the Watergate matter."

President Nixon, at an impromptu news conference March 15, 1973, claimed confidence in all the White House staffers who had been linked to Watergate.

As for the President's stipulation that a witness could make his first appearance before the committee in secret session "if appropriate," the rules provided the committee with the power of decision. The guideline itself stipulated that "all witnesses shall testify" under oath in open hearings."

Haldeman, Ehrlichman, Kleindienst & Dean resign. The resignations of four top Nixon Administration officials were announced April 30, 1973 as a consequence of the widening Watergate affair.

Those who resigned were H. R. Haldeman, President Nixon's chief of staff; John D. Ehrlichman, Nixon's assistant for domestic affairs; Attorney General Richard G. Kleindienst and John W. Dean 3rd, Nixon's counsel.

In their letters of resignation, Haldeman and Ehrlichman said their ability to carry out their daily duties had been undermined by the Watergate disclosures and the time required to deal with them.

Kleindienst said he had resigned because of the apparent implication in "Watergate and related cases" of persons "with whom he has had a close personal and professional association."

The President said without amplification that he had "requested and accepted" the resignation of his counsel, Dean.

Kleindienst was replaced as attorney general by Secretary of Defense Elliot L. Richardson, who was to "involve himself immediately" in the Watergate investigation and to "assume full responsibility and authority for coordinating all federal agencies in uncovering the whole truth about this matter and [to] recommend appropriate changes in the law to prevent future campaign abuses of the sort recently uncovered."

Effective immediately, Nixon's special consultant Leonard Garment was to assume Dean's White House duties until a permanent successor was named, and to "represent the White House in all matters" relating to Watergate.

The President expressed regret at

Kleindienst's resignation and "deep appreciation for his dedicated service." Nixon said he "greatly" regretted the departures of Haldeman and Ehrlichman, whom he called "two of my closest friends and most trusted assistants in the White House." He emphasized that their action should not be seen "as evidence of any wrongdoing."

Nixon takes responsibility. President Nixon, in a nationally televised broadcast April 30, accepted responsibility for the Watergate affair and told the American people that he was not personally involved in the political espionage or the attempt at coverup.

Nixon said he wanted the American people "to know beyond the shadow of a doubt" that during his term justice would be pursued "fairly, fully and impartially, no matter who is involved."

The President reiterated this determination throughout his speech. "There can be no whitewash at the White House," he said, and he would do "everything in my power" to insure that the guilty were "brought to justice" and that such abuses as occurred at Watergate were "purged from the political processes." When he had assumed control March 21 over "intensive new inquiries" into the Watergate affair, Nixon said, he was determined to "get to the bottom of the matter" and have the truth "fully brought out."

Nixon said the new probe was begun after he received new information which persuaded him "there was a real possibility" of involvement by members of his Administration and indicated "there had been an effort to conceal the facts both from the public . . . and from me."

When he first learned from news reports of the Watergate break-in June 17, 1972, Nixon said, "I was appalled at this senseless, illegal action and I was shocked to learn that employes of the re-election committee were apparently among those guilty." He said he had immediately ordered an investigation "by appropriate government authorities," and had repeatedly asked those conducting it "whether there was any reason to believe that members of my Administration were in any way involved."

"I received repeated assurances that there were not," Nixon said. Because of that and because he believed the "continuing reassurances" and had faith in the persons giving them, he had "discounted" press reports that "appeared to implicate" members of his Administration or GOP campaign officials.

The President said he had remained convinced that the denials were true until March, and "the comments I made during this period, the comments made by my press secretary in my behalf, were based on the information provided to us at the time we made those comments."

The President said those who committed criminal acts must "bear the liability and pay the penalty." "For the fact that alleged improper actions took place within the White House or within my campaign organization," he continued, "the easiest course would be for me to blame those to whom I delegated the responsibility to run the campaign. But that would be a cowardly thing to do."

"I will not place the blame on subordinates," Nixon declared, "on people whose zeal exceeded their judgment and who may have done wrong in a cause they deeply believed to be right. In any organization the man at the top must bear the responsibility. That responsibility, therefore, belongs here in this office. I accept it."

"I know," Nixon said, "that it can be very easy under the intensive pressures of a campaign for even well-intentioned people to fall into shady tactics, to rationalize this on the grounds that what is at stake is of such importance to the nation that the end justifies the means. And both of our great parties have been guilty of such tactics."

"The lesson is clear," Nixon said. "America in its political campaigns must not again fall into the trap of letting the end, however great that end is, justify the means."

He urged everyone to join in working toward "a new set of standards" to insure fair elections.

Cover-up conspiracy alleged. The New York Times May 2 reported statements from "government investigators" that they had evidence that high White House officials and the Committee to Re-elect the President to cover up the Watergate investigation.

The report, by reporter Seymour M. Hersh, said the "investigators" claimed evidence that the cover-up effort was coordinated by Haldeman, Ehrlichman and former Attorney General Mitchell, and involved White House aides Dean, Jeb Stuart Magruder and Frederick C. LaRue, former campaign assistant to Mitchell.

The grand jury's investigation of possible involvement in the cover-up was reported to be focused on four other persons—then White House aides Dwight L. Chapin, Gordon Strachan, Herbert L. Porter and attorney Kenneth W. Parkinson. Parkinson had been hired by the Nixon campaign committee after the Watergate break-in.

The conspiracy was said to have involved payments to the Watergate defendants, promises of executive clemency, public denials and overall denial by everyone a party to the operation.

Nixon re-election committee treasurer Hugh W. Sloan Jr. was identified in the report as the only key official who apparently refused to participate in the cover-up, resisted subsequent pressure to conform to the conspiracy and was frustrated in efforts to get word to the President that something was wrong.

Burglary of Office of Ellsberg's Psychiatrist

Watergate conspirators accused. Two convicted Watergate defendants were reported during the Pentagon Papers trial in Los Angeles April 27, 1973 to have burglarized the office of Pentagon Papers defendant Daniel Ellsberg's former psychiatrist.* The burglary, in Beverly Hills, Calif., took place Sept. 3–4, 1971. The disclosure was made in a Justice Department memo released by the trial judge, William M. Byrne.

An FBI interview with Presidential aide John D. Ehrlichman, made public May 1, disclosed that Ehrlichman, at President Nixon's request, had ordered a secret White House investigation of the Pentagon Papers and that this inquiry had led to the burglary.

Judge Byrne announced from the bench April 30 that he both had met with Ehrlichman and had been "introduced" to the President "for approximately one minute or less." At the meeting with Ehrlichman, Byrne was offered a new government position, which he refused to specify and which he said he had refused to discuss until the conclusion of the trial.

Byrne confirmed from the bench May 2 he had met with Ehrlichman, and he offered more details. He said two meetings had taken place April 5 and 7, one in San Clemente and the other in Santa Monica, Calif., at which the possibility of his appointment as director of the FBI had been broached.

According to an FBI summary of the Ehrlichman interview, events leading to the break-in and photocopying of files of Dr. Lewis J. Fielding, who treated Ellsberg in the late 1960s and the first half of 1970, began in 1971 after the President "had expressed interest" in the leak of classified information and had asked Ehrlichman "to make inquiries independent of concurrent FBI investigation which had been made relating to the leak of the Pentagon papers."

Ehrlichman said he had assumed this responsibility, and had asked the aid of White House assistant Egil Krogh Jr. and David Young of the National Security Council. After the decision was made to work "directly out of the White House," G. Gordon Liddy and E. Howard Hunt

Jr. were "designated to conduct this investigation," Ehrlichman said.

Ehrlichman said Hunt and Liddy determined that Ellsberg had emotional and moral problems, which through further investigation, they hoped could be used as the basis of a "psychiatric profile."

Ehrlichman told the FBI that he knew Liddy and Hunt had conducted an investigation in the Washington area and had gone to California in connection with the inquiry. However, he said, he was not told they had broken into the psychiatrist's office until after the incident had taken place.

Ehrlichman said he did "not agree with this method of investigation" and when he learned of it, he cautioned Liddy and Hunt "not to do this again."

The information made its way to Judge Byrne after federal investigators, who learned of the burglary April 15, brought the events to the attention of the President, according to the Washington Post May 3. When Nixon heard about the burglary, he "endorsed without hesitation" the decision to send to Byrne a confidential memo on the subject from Earl J. Silbert, chief Watergate prosecutor, to Assistant Attorney General Henry E. Petersen, chief of the Justice Department's criminal division, the Post said.

The prosecution May 4 gave the court a dossier on Ellsberg that Hunt had compiled. The dossier, which had been in the possession of the Justice Department for 10 months, contained a 28-page chronology of Ellsberg's life, including notations of private phone calls and visits he had made to two psychiatrists. The Justice Department had no explanation for its earlier failure to disclose the file.

Four Justice Department officials submitted affidavits May 9 to Judge Byrne in which they swore they had not become aware of the burglary of the office of Ellsberg's former psychiatrist until April 16, 1972. They were Assistant Attorney General Henry E. Petersen; Kevin T. Maroney, a deputy assistant attorney general; John L. Martin, another Justice Department lawyer; and David R. Nissen,

---

*The Pentagon Papers case involved a voluminous file of secret defense Department documents on U.S. involvement in the Vietnam War. Ellsburg admitted that he had given copies of the documents to various newspapers.

chief prosecutor in the Pentagon Papers case.

CIA involved. The CIA admitted that its former deputy director, at the request of the White House, had assisted Liddy and Hunt as they planned the burglary of the office of Ellsberg's former psychiatrist.

The CIA involvement was disclosed in testimony given by Hunt May 2 to the Washington grand jury investigating the Watergate break-in.

The New York Times reported May 7 that Gen. Robert E. Cushman Jr., present commandant of the Marine Corps and then deputy director of the CIA, gave aid to Liddy and Hunt in the form of false identification papers, disguises, a tape recorder, and a miniature camera. This aid, the Times said, came at the request of Ehrlichman.

In testimony May 9 before the Senate Appropriations subcommittee on CIA operations, CIA director James R. Schlesinger admitted the agency had been "insufficiently cautious" in providing materials for the break-in. He denied that the CIA was aware that Liddy and Hunt had decided to break into Fielding's office. Schlesinger noted that aid to Hunt and Liddy had been discontinued one week before the Los Angeles break-in occurred because Cushman was becoming "increasingly concerned" over Hunt's repeated requests for assistance. The agency chief also said that former director Richard Helms had personally ordered CIA officers to assist in the preparation of a personality profile of Ellsberg.

In his grand jury testimony May 2, Hunt told how he and Liddy had been hired by White House aides Egil Krogh Jr. and David Young to investigate leaks of the Pentagon Papers. One offshoot of this was the question of the prosecutability of Daniel Ellsberg, a topic that led to the suggestion of a "bag job" (break-in) at the office of Ellsberg's former psychiatrist.

Hunt then testified that he and Liddy flew to Los Angeles Aug. 25, 1971, where they reconnoitered the office of Dr. Fielding. One of their devices was a camera fitted into a tobacco pouch.

Hunt said the camera had been sup-

plied by a technical services representative of the CIA at a "safe house" on Massachusetts Avenue in Washington, "the same one we used when we were given disguises and other physical equipment." Hunt added that Krogh told him where to make contacts with the CIA.

After he and Liddy returned from their first trip to Washington, they submitted a report to Krogh through Young, recommending that the operation continue, Hunt stated.

At this point Hunt traveled to Miami, where he recruited three men to aid in the mission. They were Bernard L. Barker, Eugenio Rolando Martinez, both later convicted for the Watergate break-in, and Felipe de Diego, who reportedly assaulted Ellsberg on the steps of the Capitol May 2, 1972 while he spoke at a rally.

On Labor Day weekend in 1971 the five met in Los Angeles. Two of the Miami men had a cleaning woman Sept. 3 let them into the office of Fielding. Disguised as delivery men, they left a suitcase containing a camera in the office. Later that night, while Liddy remained nearby and Hunt watched Fielding at his home, either two or three of the Miami operatives broke into the office, and searched for files on Ellsberg.

Hunt said the men were unable to find any material with Ellsberg's name on it.

Hunt and Liddy then returned to Washington, where they reported their lack of results to Krogh, Hunt testified.

Hunt denied he had spoken to Ehrlichman about the burglary and that Ehrlichman told him not to do it again.

The role of the CIA in the Los Angeles burglary was further detailed in four Justice Department memos made public by Pentagon Papers trial defendants Ellsberg and Anthony J. Russo Jr. May 8.

One memo dated Dec. 4, 1972 told of secret meetings of an unnamed CIA agent, "Mr. Blank," with Hunt and Liddy, at which they were given documents and disguises, as well as the tobacco pouch camera. It also said Hunt called "Mr. Blank" Aug. 26, 1971 and asked "Mr. Blank" to meet him at Dulles Airport outside Washington at 6 a.m. the following morning because he had film that had to be developed by that afternoon.

A second undated memorandum told of a July 22, 1971 meeting between Hunt and Cushman, at which time Hunt asked for CIA aid. Cushman said he would look into the matter and get in touch with Hunt at his White House office.

Subsequently Cushman complied with Hunt's requests until the day the CIA received the film that was to be developed. On that day the "Mr. Blank" instructed CIA technical personnel not to comply with further Hunt requests because they had gone beyond the original understanding. More important, they appeared to involve the CIA in domestic clandestine operations. The unnamed agent reported his findings to Cushman, who then called the White House to inform the "appropriate individual" that there would be no more CIA aid.

The testimony given by CIA Director Schlesinger May 9 amplified these facts. He said Ehrlichman had originally requested CIA aid, and Ehrlichman was telephoned by Cushman and told there would be no more CIA aid.

Schlesinger also testified that CIA officials had given ex-Acting FBI Director L. Patrick Gray 3rd an account by letter July 5 and 7, 1972 of the CIA involvement with Hunt in the Ellsberg case, which they repeated in a July 28, 1972 meeting. Attorney General Richard Kleindienst and Assistant Attorney General Henry E. Petersen reviewed the report in October 1972, Schlesinger added. Chief Watergate prosecutor Earl Silbert was also briefed on the incident during the same period, Schlesinger said.

Krogh resigned as undersecretary of transportation May 9. Krogh had submitted an affidavit to Judge Byrne. In the affidavit, made public May 7, he had stated that "general authorization to engage in covert activity to obtain a psychological history" on Daniel Ellsberg was given by Ehrlichman.

Krogh stated that Liddy and Hunt developed the plans for acquiring information from Dr. Fielding's office. Krogh admitted he had told Hunt and Liddy to hire Cubans to accomplish the mission, and that he told Hunt and Liddy

not to be in "close proximity of Dr. Fielding's office."

In his letter of resignation to President Nixon, Krogh said the mission was "my responsibility, a step taken in excess of instructions and without the knowledge or permission of any superior." He said his actions had been dictated by the "vital national security interests of the U. S."

Cuban admits break-in. A Cuban real estate broker admitted May 10 he had participated in the 1971 burglary of the office of Daniel Ellsberg's former psychiatrist.

Felipe de Diego, after being granted immunity from prosecution by Los Angeles District Attorney Joseph Busch, said in Miami that he, Bernard L. Barker, and Eugenio R. Martinez forced open the door to the office of Dr. Lewis J. Fielding about 1 a.m. Sept. 4, 1971.

The Cuban exile said that after a short search, papers from what appeared to be a file on Ellsberg were found and photographed.

Times says Nixon tried to block data. The New York Times reported May 7 that President Nixon sought on two occasions to block release of details about the burglary of Dr. Fielding's office to Judge Byrne.

One attempt came April 16 or 17 when Nixon tried to bar release of a Justice Department memorandum revealing that the break-in had taken place, the Times said.

The second attempt reportedly came April 30, when former White House aide Egil Krogh Jr. was told by Presidential assistant John D. Ehrlichman, "the President doesn't want anymore of this to surface for national security reasons."

The White House issued the following statement May 9: "Any reference or suggestion made by anyone that the President would have proceeded in any other way than to provide information to the court is completely unfounded."

The Times cited as sources for its allegations "some of the principals, lawyers and Justice Department officials."

The sources said Earl Silbert, chief Watergate prosecutor, received a memo about the Los Angeles break-in April 16 or 17. The source of the information was said to have been former Counsel to the President John Dean 3rd, who met with federal prosecutors April 15.

A memorandum on the subject was sent from Silbert to Assistant Attorney General Henry E. Petersen, who subsequently passed it on to Nixon.

When the President "personally put the lid on it," Petersen pondered the situation for several days and finally decided "he just couldn't live with himself" if he withheld the information about Liddy-Hunt break-in, Times sources said.

Petersen then talked to Attorney General Richard Kleindienst "who—after hours of debate—agreed that the matter should be taken directly to Mr. Nixon."

Nixon agreed to forward the material after meeting with the two. Ten days after the Justice Department learned of the break-in, chief Pentagon Papers trial prosecutor David Nissen gave the memo to Byrne.

A few days after talking to Ehrlichman, Krogh reportedly had lunch with Elliot L. Richardson, whom the President had nominated to be the new attorney general. Krogh told Richardson all he knew about the Ellsberg case and about the order not to divulge any more information.

Richardson reportedly said to Krogh, "I'm not going to participate in a cover-up because it will destroy my role in the Watergate investigation. I'm not going to follow through on the President's orders. The truth has got to come out," Richardson was reported to have said.

The Times said Krogh, "apparently fortified by this meeting," decided to draft an affadavit, which he then mailed to Judge Byrne.

Krogh, who mailed the affadavit May 4, had the day before received from presidential Counsel Leonard Garment guidelines telling him not to divulge national security information.

FBI tap on Ellsberg revealed. Evidence of wiretaps on telephone calls made by Ellsberg in late 1969 or early 1970 was disclosed in a memorandum sent May 9 by Acting FBI Director William D. Ruckelshaus to Judge Byrne.

The Ruckelshaus memo said "that an FBI employe recalls that in late 1969 or early 1970 Mr. Ellsberg had been overheard talking from an electronic surveillance of Dr. Morton Halperin's residence." The memo also said a search of FBI records had failed to disclose the existence of such wiretaps. Halperin, a defense consultant and witness in the trial, headed the study group that compiled the Pentagon Papers.

Judge Byrne immediately suspended court proceedings and asked the government to produce all its logs and other records concerning the taps. He ordered both sides to prepare arguments as to why charges against Daniel Ellsberg and Anthony J. Russo Jr. should not be dismissed because of the disclosure of the wiretaps and the fact that records concerning them had disappeared.

The government contended May 10 it had "testimonial evidence" that the electronic surveillance of Halperin's home that picked up any Ellsberg conversation had been "authorized by the attorney general in accordance with national security procedures."

Taps on Times reporters disclosed
The phones of at least two reporters for the New York Times were tapped by members of the Nixon Administration in connection with the Pentagon Papers disclosure, the Washington Post reported May 3.

The Post cited one highly placed Administration source as saying the wiretapping was supervised by Watergate co-conspirators E. Howard Hunt Jr. and G. Gordon Liddy, and that former Attorney General John N. Mitchell authorized the taps.

The source said the team of wiretappers, supervised by Hunt and Liddy, operated independently of the FBI.

According to Post sources, the wiretaps followed earlier White House-ordered taps of other reporters, the purpose of which was to discover leaks of information about the strategic arms limitation talks to the news media.

The sources also said the home or office phones of at least 10 White House staffers were tapped in an effort to stem other news leaks.

"In late 1971 or early 1972, it was decided at a Nixon campaign strategy meeting that some members of the same vigilante squad responsible for the Pentagon Papers wiretapping would be used to wiretap the telephones of the Democratic presidential candidates . . . ," the Post said.

The Times reported May 11 that the Nixon Administration, concerned over the information leaks, had ordered wiretaps on the phones of reporters from three newspapers and at least one government official.

Times sources said reporters placed under surveillance were William Beecher and Hedrick Smith of the New York Times, and Henry Brandon, a Washington-based correspondent for the Sunday Times of London. Phones of unidentified reporters for the Washington Post also were tapped, the Times said.

The government official was Morton H. Halperin, a member of the National Security Council until 1971.

According to the account supplied by Times sources, former Attorney General John N. Mitchell called the late director of the FBI, J. Edgar Hoover, in the spring of 1969, requesting that the taps be placed. Hoover refused to comply without written authorization from Mitchell, who subsequently sent the late FBI chief an unspecified number of forms used to request "national security" wiretaps. (The Supreme Court had ruled in 1972 the government needed court orders before it could install wiretaps in national security cases, except where foreign connections were involved.)

In September 1971, the Justice Department retrieved the forms.

Wiretap files found—Ruckelshaus disclosed at a May 14 press conference that missing records of 17 FBI wiretaps placed on newsmen and government officials had been discovered May 11 in a safe in the outer office of former presidential adviser John Ehrlichman.

Ruckelshaus, declining to identify those

under surveillance, said he personally retrieved them May 12.

In a related development, the New York Times reported May 17 that national security adviser Henry Kissinger, acting under presidential authorization, formally submitted requests for the taps to the late FBI director, J. Edgar Hoover.

Contained in the records was information relating to the wiretap that had been placed on the home telephone of Morton H. Halperin.

Ruckelshaus said the FBI had assumed the records had been destroyed. This was based on two pieces of FBI correspondence, bearing notations in Hoover's handwriting, that indicated former Attorney General John N. Mitchell had so informed the late director. Ruckelshaus noted that Mitchell had previously denied making such a statement.

(Ehrlichman said May 14 he had the records in his safe for more than a year. He said he had "skimmed" them but was unaware they contained any material about Ellsberg. A White House spokesman said May 15 that President Nixon had not known the files were in Ehrlichman's safe.)

Ruckelshaus explained that the FBI had ascertained the records still existed in a May 10 interview in Phoenix, Ariz. with Robert C. Mardian, former assistant attorney general in charge of the now defunct Internal Security Division.

Ruckelshaus said an FBI investigation showed that after the wiretaps had been removed in 1971, the records were placed in the custody of William C. Sullivan, then assistant director of the FBI. Sullivan later contacted Mardian about the records and recommended they be transferred. According to Mardian, the recommendation had been made because Sullivan thought Hoover might use them against the attorney general or the President, Ruckelshaus said.

Sullivan confirmed the sequence of events in an interview published in the Los Angeles Times May 14. He said the records were kept in the White House because Hoover was "not of sound mind" in his later years. Sullivan gave the files to Mardian before being forced to retire Oct. 6, 1971, since he felt Hoover "could not be trusted" to keep the files confidential. However, contrary to what Ruckelshaus had said, Sullivan claimed Mitchell ordered the files given to Mardian.

Sullivan, noting that Hoover had ordered the files kept outside the regular FBI filing system, said Justice Department officials, who were aware of the files, became very upset when they learned Sullivan was leaving the FBI.

"They could no longer depend on Hoover. He had been leaking stuff all over the place. He could no longer be trusted. So I was instructed to pass the records to Mardian," Sullivan said.

Hoover, who was concerned about being fired as director, retained the records "to keep Mitchell and others in line," Sullivan continued.

"The fellow was a master blackmailer and he did it with considerable finesse despite the deterioration of his mind," Sullivan said.

Sullivan said neither Mardian nor Mitchell ever specifically told him they did not want Hoover to have the files because they could not trust Hoover. But Sullivan said he could "read between the lines."

Nixon authorized wiretaps—The White House acknowledged May 16 that President Nixon had personnaly authorized the use of 17 wiretaps against 13 members of his own Administration and four newsmen.

The New York Times reported May 17 that Henry A. Kissinger, assistant to the President for national security affairs, personally provided the FBI with the names of a number of his aides on the National Security Council (NSC), whom he wanted wiretapped. The Times cited Justice Department officials as its source.

The White House, in formally acknowledging the existence of the wire taps, said they were made in 1969 after publication in the Times May 9, 1969 of an article by William Beecher disclosing American B-52s were bombing Cambodia. (Beecher was appointed deputy assistant secretary of defense for public affairs April 20.)

Among those tapped was Helmut Sonnenfeldt, a former NSC official, who was nominated April 10 to be undersecretary of the Treasury.

Times sources revealed that Marvin Kalb, a diplomatic correspondent for the Columbia Broadcasting System (CBS), was under surveillance.

Kissinger, in an interview with the Times May 14, confirmed he had seen summaries of the wiretaps, but he said he had not asked that they be installed nor had he specifically approved them in advance. He also admitted he held one or two conversations with Hoover in 1969 in which he expressed "very great concern" that national security information be fully safeguarded.

The Washington Post reported May 18 that specific wiretaps had also been authorized by H. R. Haldeman, Nixon's former chief of staff.

Other former NSC officials whose phones were reported tapped were Anthony Lake, Daniel I. Davidson, and Winston Lord. Lord, a personal aide to Kissinger during the Paris peace talks and during his visits to Peking and Moscow, was on a one-year leave from the NSC.

Charges against Ellsberg, Russo dismissed. Government charges of espionage, theft and conspiracy against Pentagon Papers trial defendants Daniel Ellsberg and Anthony J. Russo Jr. were dismissed by presiding Judge William M. Byrne in Los Angeles May 11, 1973.

Citing government misconduct as the reason for the dismissal, Byrne said that after two weeks of extraordinary disclosures beginning April 26, the government had raised more questions than it had answers for.

Of greatest significance was not the disclosure of a wiretap on phone conversations of Ellsberg, but that the government had lost the records pertaining to the tap. "There is no way . . . [anybody] can test what effect these interceptions may have had on the government's case. . . ."

The dismissal also resulted from the

break-in at the office of Ellsberg's former psychiatrist.

Senate Inquiries

Senate hearings begin. The Senate Select Committee on Presidential Campaign Activities began hearings May 17, 1973 in Washington into the Watergate scandal and related charges of wrongdoing during the 1972 presidential campaign.

Chairman Sam J. Ervin Jr. (D, N.C.) declared in an opening statement delivered before a crowded Senate Caucus Room in the Old Senate Office Building: "A clear mandate of the unanimous Senate resolution provides for a bipartisan investigation of every phase of political espionage." He said:

"The questions that have been raised in the wake of the June 17 break-in strike at the very undergirding of our democracy. If the many allegations made to this date are true, then the burglars who broke into the headquarters of the Democratic National Committee at the Watergate were in effect breaking into the home of every citizen of the United States. And if these allegations prove to be true, what they were seeking to steal was not the jewels, money or other property of American citizens, but something much more valuable—their most precious heritage, the right to vote in a free election."

Convicted Watergate conspirator James W. McCord Jr. testified May 18 that ex-White House aide John J. Caulfield, who had served as an employe of the Nixon re-election committee, had offered him executive clemency before his trial in exchange for his silence. McCord reported the offers as coming from Caulfield in three secret rendezvous. In these sessions, the clemency offer was represented as coming from "the very highest levels of the White House." He was told President Nixon had been informed of their meeting and would be told its results.

McCord's testimony also included hearsay reports that former Attorney General John N. Mitchell and former presidential counsel John W. Dean 3rd had participated in the planning of the Watergate operation. It was McCord's personal opinion, because of the high-level participation involving the White House, that

"the President of the United States had set into motion this operation."

McCord revealed to the committee he had access in his security role for the Nixon re-election committee to confidential memorandums from the Justice Department's Internal Security Division. The data concerned activist groups suspected of planning demonstrations against the Republicans.

Caulfield, testifying May 22, corroborated much of McCord's testimony about the clemency offer, except for the remark about Nixon being told of their meeting.

Caulfield testified that the order for the offer of executive clemency came from Dean. Caulfield said he had no personal knowledge that Nixon ever approved the offer but he felt that the President "probably" knew about it and that he "was doing something for the President" when he made the offer.

Bernard L. Barker, who had pleaded guilty to the Watergate break-in, testified May 23 that his prime motive for participating was to further the cause of Cuban liberation. He said he believed that fellow conspirator E. Howard Hunt Jr. and "others in high places" in the U.S. could help his cause. According to Barker: Hunt had recruited him for the Watergate operation and Barker had responded without question. He collected his Watergate team out of friendship with Hunt for his participation in the 1961 Bay of Pigs operation. Barker had been Hunt's principal assistant in that operation.

Ten years after the Bay of Pigs, Barker testified, Hunt had recruited him for some other operations—the September 1971 break-in at the Los Angeles office of Daniel Ellsberg's psychiatrist, "infiltrating" a May 1972 Capitol demonstration where Ellsberg was expected to be a participant, and two Watergate break-ins.

In the original break-in in Los Angeles, Barker said, he was told that the operation "was a matter of national security." This sufficed for all of the operations. "At no time was I told any different from the original motivation for which I had been recruited," he declared.

Asked what national security was involved in the early operation, Barker responded, "Discovering information about a person who I had been told by Mr. Hunt was a traitor, who was passing, he or his associates, to a foreign embassy." Barker identified the embassy as that of the Soviet Union.

Barker said the documents he was seeking were not found either in the Ellsberg break-in or the first Watergate break-in May 27, 1972 prior to the intercepted one June 17, 1972.

At the Watergate, he said, the documents he was seeking—he was the document-finder, another the photographer—were those "that would prove that the Democratic party and Sen. [George] McGovern [D, S.D.] were receiving contributions nationally and national and foreign contributions from organizations that were leftist organizations and inclined to violence in the United States and also from the Castro government."

McCord had testified May 22 that G. Gordon Liddy had told him in January or February 1972 "that he was going out to Las Vegas, Nev. in connection with casing the office of Hank Greenspun," editor of the Las Vegas Sun. According to McCord:

"Liddy said that Attorney General John Mitchell had told him that Greenspun had in his possession blackmail type information involving a Democratic candidate for President, that Mitchell wanted that material, and Liddy said that this information was in some way racketeer-related, indicating that if this candidate became President, the racketeers or national crime syndicate could have a control or influence over him as President. . . .

"Subsequently in about April or May, 1971, Liddy told me that he had again been to Las Vegas for another casing of Greenspun's offices. Liddy said that there were then plans for an entry operation to get into Greenspun's safe. He went on to say that, after the entry team finished its work, they would go directly to an airport near Las Vegas where a Howard Hughes plane would be standing by to fly the team directly into a Central-American country . . .

"Around the same time Liddy made

this last statement to me about the Howard Hughes plane, Hunt told me in his office one day that he was in touch with the Howard Hughes company and that they might be needing my security services after the election.

"He said that they had quite a wide investigative and security operation and asked me for my business card and asked if I would be interested. I said I would like to know more about what was involved, gave him a card, but never heard from him again on this subject. . . ."

Burglars sought Hughes papers—Hank Greenspun said May 22 that the attempted burglary of his office during the summer of 1972 was not an attempt to obtain blackmail information about one of the Democratic contenders for the Presidency.

Instead, it was an attempt to acquire hundreds of memoranda signed by industrialist billionaire Howard Hughes, he said. Greenspun would only say of the memos that they pertained in part to problems Hughes had with the antitrust division of the Justice Department regarding his $200 million–$300 million holdings in Nevada.

Greenspun said he found it "catastrophically disturbing" that the U.S. government would be employed to "serve the private interests of Howard Hughes."

Ervin smear proposed. Former presidential chief of staff H. R. Haldeman made two attempts during March to enlist the aid of North Carolina Republicans in discrediting Sen. Sam. J. Ervin Jr., chairman of the select Senate committee investigating Watergate, the Charlotte (N.C.) Observer reported May 17, 1973.

Haldeman twice telephoned former White House aide Harry Dent asking him to approach the North Carolina GOP chairman, Frank Rouse, with a proposal "to dig up something to discredit Ervin and blast him with it," the Observer said.

Dent and Rouse discussed the matter but rejected Haldeman's proposal.

CIA involvement was sought. High Administration officials sought to involve the Central Intelligence Agency (CIA) in the Watergate affair, according to testimony presented to the Senate Armed Services Committee. The committee was inquiring into the CIA's involvement in domestic undercover work, which was barred under the 1947 National Security Act.

The hearings were closed, but Sen. Stuart Symington (D, Mo.), the committee acting chairman, said after the first session May 14, 1973 that "there were other matters besides the Ellsberg case in which the White House tried to get the CIA involved."

On the basis of testimony by Lt. Gen. Vernon A. Walters, deputy director of the CIA, Symington reported that the White House aides involved in the apparent attempt to compromise the CIA were H. R. Haldeman, John D. Ehrlichman and John W. Dean 3rd.

"Ehrlichman, and Haldeman—particularly Haldeman," Symington said, "were up to their ears in this, along with Dean, in trying to involve the CIA in this whole Watergate mess."

In releasing a summary of Walters' testimony May 15, Symington said "it is very clear to me that there was an attempt to unload major responsibility for the Watergate bugging and cover-up on the CIA." According to the summary:

■ Dean asked Walters 10 days after the Watergate break-in (in June 1972) if the CIA could provide bail or pay the salaries for the men apprehended there. Walters refused and declared he would rather resign than implicate the agency in such a scheme.

■ As recently as January or February, Dean sought to obtain CIA assistance in retrieving from the FBI "some materials" obtained from the CIA for burglarizing the office of Daniel Ellsberg's former psychiatrist.

■ Haldeman and Ehrlichman intervened in an attempt to have the CIA press the FBI to call off its probe in 1972 into Nixon campaign funds that had been routed—or "laundered" to prevent tracing—through a Mexican bank and, at one point, through several of the Watergate defendants. The CIA's approach to the FBI would be made on the ground that national security

was involved and pursuit of the probe would compromise certain CIA activities and resources in Mexico. Walters met with Acting FBI Director L. Patrick Gray 3rd several times. The first time he related to Gray that senior White House aides had told him pursuit of the FBI probe would uncover some CIA activities in Mexico. After Gray later said he would need a written statement to that effect before the FBI inquiry could be ended, Walters, apparently on word from then-CIA Director Richard M. Helms, informed Gray the CIA activity actually was not in jeopardy by the FBI probe.

Helms, currently ambassador to Iran, testified May 16 before a Senate Appropriations subcommittee, which was examining the same issue. Chairman John L. McClellan (D, Ark.) said afterward that Helms had expressed concern about the White House overtures to the CIA for domestic activity, which he considered improper, but said he had never conveyed his concern to President Nixon.

According to McClellan, Helms confirmed Walters' testimony and defended his own statements at his confirmation hearings on the ambassadorship that the CIA had never been involved in Watergate.

More testimony was released May 17, as Helms and Walters returned before the Armed Services panel. Walters said he told Gray in their meeting in early July 1972 he considered the attempts "to cover this up or to implicate the CIA or FBI would be detrimental to their integrity" and he was "quite prepared to resign on this issue."

Gray "shared my views" and "he, too, was prepared to resign on this issue," Walters said. He also recounted a conversation with Gray in a second meeting a week later: "I said that I had told Dean that the best solution would be to fire those responsible. Gray said he had made the same recommendation."

Nixon's name invoked in cover-up— Deputy CIA Director Walters was told by Haldeman that "it is the President's wish" that he ask L. Patrick Gray 3rd, then acting FBI director, to halt the FBI's investigation of the "laundering" of election campaign funds through a bank in Mexico. This disclosure was made in one of 11 memos written by Walters and given to the Senate Foreign Relations Committee. Committee member Symington made it public May 21.

One "memorandum of conversation" written by Walters related to a meeting he had with Haldeman, former presidential aide John D. Ehrlichman, and former CIA Director Richard Helms June 23, 1972, six days after the Watergate break-in. Within an hour of the meeting, an appointment for Walters with Gray had been set up.

Haldeman issued a statement May 21: "I can flatly say the President was not involved in any cover-up of anything at any time."

According to Symington, the committee had obtained two sets of documents that purported to deal with Administration plans during the summer of 1970 to commit burglary and engage in other illegal activities to gather intelligence about some U.S. citizens. Symington said the plans were never carried out.

Helms, who also appeared before the committee May 21, substantiated the Walters memoranda and added that during the June 23, 1972 meeting Haldeman had said "the opposition" was "capitalizing" on the Watergate case.

Gray says he alerted Nixon. According to sources within the Senate Watergate committee, which interrogated former Acting FBI Director Gray May 10 (the testimony was leaked May 11), Gray testified that Nixon had telephoned him about another matter July 6, 1972. Gray took the opportunity to express concern about White House interference in the Watergate probe and to caution the President that he was being "wounded" by men around him "using the FBI and CIA." According to Gray, Nixon responded that Gray should continue to press his investigation.

The July 6 date was the same day Walters visited Gray to inform him the FBI probe would not jeopardize CIA activity. In that visit, Walters identified, as he had not- in his previous talk with Gray, the White House aides who were pressing for an end to the FBI probe— Ehrlichman and Haldeman.

According to some accounts of Gray's testimony, he also reported arranging a meeting with CIA Director Helms about possible CIA complications, but received a call from Ehrlichman that firmly suggested he cancel it because of the security aspect.

Gray's reported testimony May 10 that he had also called Nixon's campaign chairman, Clark MacGregor, July 6, 1972 to express concern about the obstacles to- his probe, was confirmed May 12 by MacGregor, who said he was in California at the time, which was about 2 a.m. in Washington. He said Gray had seemed "agitated, concerned" and "wondered if I recognized how serious Watergate was." MacGregor reported being aware of the seriousness of the crimes involved in the break-in and said Gray did not bring the subject up again.

'Illegal' Government Action Against Radicals Reported

'Illegalities' began in 1969. The Washington Post reported May 17, 1973 that since 1969 the Nixon Administration had engaged in a wide pattern of illegal and quasi-legal activities against radical leaders, students, demonstrators, news reporters, Democratic candidates for president and vice president, the Congress and Nixon Administration officials suspected of leaking information to the press.

Reporters Carl Bernstein and Bob Woodward quoted "highly placed sources in the executive branch" who said that although most of the clandestine operations were political in nature, they were conducted by the Federal Bureau of Investigation (FBI), the Secret Service and special teams working for the White House and the Justice Department under the guise of "national security."

"Watergate was a natural action that came from long existing circumstances. It grew out of an atmosphere. This way of life was not new. There have been fairly broad [illegal and quasi-legal] activities from the beginning of the Administration. I didn't know where 'national security' ended and political espionage started," one source said.

The Post named former presidential chief of staff H. R. Haldeman, former Attorney General and Nixon campaign director John N. Mitchell, former domestic affairs adviser John D. Ehrlichman, former White House counsel John W. Dean 3rd and former Assistant Attorney General Robert C. Mardian as the officials who supervised covert activities.

According to the Post, seven high Administration officials cited Haldeman and former White House special counsel Charles W. Colson as the prime movers behind the espionage operations conducted during the 1972 presidential campaign.

"It was a campaign that went astray and lost its sense of fair play. Secrecy and an obsession with the covert became part of nearly every action," a highly placed former Administration official said.

Known instances of illegal and quasi-legal activities:
■ Information was gathered by the Secret Service on the private life of at least one Democratic presidential candidate. On two occasions, the Administration considered leaking some of the reports to the press. Colson admitted receiving such information about one prominent Democrat, but denied that the information originated with Secret Service agents.

(The New York Times had reported Nov. 2, 1972 that Secret Service agents were providing the White House with confidential information regarding meetings held by Sen. George McGovern [D, S.D.] and potential financial backers.)
■ The medical records of Sen. Thomas Eagleton (D, Mo.), McGovern's running mate for a brief period, were obtained by Ehrlichman several weeks before the information regarding Eagleton's treatment for nervous exhaustion was leaked to the press.

Former Attorney General Ramsey Clark said the records were in FBI files. According to Post sources, Mardian, who had left the Justice Department to become political coordinator of the Nixon campaign, gave the FBI files to the White House.

■ Paid provocateurs were used to foment violence at antiwar demonstrations during Nixon's first term of office and also during the 1972 presidential campaign.

■ Clandestine activities against persons considered opponents of the Administration were conducted by "suicide squads," which if apprehended in illegal activities would be disavowed by the FBI and the White House.

■ Paid "vigilante squads" were hired by the White House and Justice Department to conduct wiretapping and other forms of political espionage and to infiltrate radical groups for purposes of provocation.

Convicted Watergate conspirators E. Howard Hunt Jr. and G. Gordon Liddy supervised the squads, made up of former FBI and Central Intelligence Agency (CIA) operatives.

The transfer of these activities from the White House to the Committee to Reelect the President in late 1971 and early 1972 was arranged by Haldeman and Mitchell and was part of an elaborate plan to extend the "dirty tricks" operations to the 1972 campaign, the Post reported.

■ Frederic V. Malek, formerly in charge of recruiting personnel for the Nixon Administration and a deputy campaign manager, and presently deputy director of the Office of Management and Budget, established an information network in nearly 50 states to report on the McGovern campaign.

"Viola Smith" was the code-named contact at the Nixon re-election committee for the "McGovern Watch" spies. The re-election committee also provided the agents with forms marked confidential which contained space for details about staff changes, speeches and polls in the McGovern campaign. The Post based its information on a memo entitled, "Intelligence on Future Appearances of McGovern and Shriver," which Malek admitted writing although he denied its intent was espionage.

DeVan L. Shumway, Nixon re-election committee spokesman, also admitted that on orders from deputy campaign director Jeb Stuart Magruder, he had asked two reporters to provide him with McGovern's campaign schedule. (The reporters rejected the proposal.)

One Democratic presidential contender sought legal advice after determining that he and his family were under surveillance, an activity which a former Nixon campaign official acknowledged he had authorized.

Mardian supervised two spies in the McGovern campaign who reported directly to him. Other Nixon campaign aides, on loan from the Republican National Committee, regularly posed as newsmen to obtain routine data on McGovern.

■ Colson organized a group of 30 Nixon supporters to "attack" news correspondents through use of write-in, telephone and telegraph campaigns, according to Tom Girard, a former Nixon committee press aide.

Another instance of covert activity directed against newsmen was the 1971 investigation of Columbia Broadcasting System correspondent Daniel Schorr. Haldeman personally ordered the FBI probe, the Post reported.

Details of 1970 plan revealed. White House plans in 1970 to launch a massive counter-insurgency plan against the Black Panthers, Arab extremists, antiwar radicals, and Soviet espionage agents were revealed by the New York Times May 24.

Times sources said that the late J. Edgar Hoover had refused to go along with the project because President Nixon would not give him written authorization for use of FBI personnel for illegal wiretaps and illegal breaking-and-entering operations.

(The Times had reported May 21 that in 1970 the White House had established a secret Intelligence Evaluation Committee, which operated out of the Justice Department, whose purpose was to collect and evaluate information about antiwar and radical groups and then pass it on to former White House counsel John W. Dean 3rd and John J. Caulfield, then an aide to Dean.)

The plan was outlined in a secret report that was among the documents taken from the White House by Dean.

According to a Times source who worked on the report in 1970, "the facts we had available in this country then showed that we were faced with one of the most serious domestic crises that we've had. One of our greatest problems was that the informed public didn't understand it."

Another official who worked on the report told the Times the most serious issue facing the Nixon Administration in mid-1970 was the "black problem." The source said there was suspicion that the Black Panthers were being covertly financed by certain Caribbean countries and certain nations in North Africa, of which one was strongly suspected to be Algeria.

There was further fear that the "vigilante police action [killing]" against Chicago Black Panther Fred Hampton in 1969 had brought many moderate blacks over to the side of the Panthers, whom the official called "thugs and murderers."

Hoover's decision in 1966 to limit domestic intelligence operations severely hampered the FBI's ability to penetrate the Panthers and other radical groups, the source said.

A second source of concern among Administration officials was the possibility of Arab sabotage of the Middle East talks that were scheduled to be held at the United Nations in 1970.

Another project that was "wiped out" by Hoover was one involving the analysis of handwriting of immigrants to the U.S., to determine if they had attended Soviet schools and thus, were potential spies.

Ervin charges 'Gestapo mentality'—Sen. Sam J. Ervin (D, N.C.), chairman of the Senate committee investigating Watergate, said May 31 that the documents that had been held by former counsel to the President John W. Dean 3rd "would be a great shock to the American people if they were released."

Dean's papers revealed a "Gestapo mentality" in the highest levels of the Nixon Administration, Ervin said.

Ervin said, "I interpret the papers as being an effort . . . to set up an operation to spy on the American people in general or at least on those who didn't agree with the Administration."

Effort to form Miami spy ring. Ex-White House Counsel John W. Dean 3rd was said to have tried to recruit a lawyer from the Interior Department for the purpose of setting up an undercover espionage and intelligence network to infiltrate radical and antiwar groups in Miami before the national political party nominating conventions in 1972.

Kenneth C. Tapman said May 14, 1973 that in May 1972 Dean had offered him a large sum to either take part in or direct the covert operation.

Tapman had been assigned by the Interior Department in 1969 and 1970 to negotiate with antiwar groups regarding permits for demonstrations in Washington. Dean, then a Justice Department official, was charged with coordinating the government's response to the demonstrators.

Tapman said he rejected Dean's proposal.

Nixon knew of plan's illegalities. President Nixon in 1970 had approved the plan for expanded intelligence gathering operations with the knowledge that certain aspects of it were clearly illegal, the New York Times reported June 7, 1973.

According to the Times, the plan approved by Nixon involved "serious risks" to his Administration if revealed. As a result the program was approved by him through presidential Chief of Staff H. R. Haldeman after Tom Charles Huston, then a staff assistant to Nixon, told Haldeman: "We don't want the President linked to this thing with his signature on paper . . . [because] all hell would break loose if this thing leaked out."

The Times obtained three memoranda written by Huston: one dealt with recommendations to the President by the Interagency Committee on Intelligence; a second recommended means to overcome FBI Director Hoover's opposition, and the third was a presidential directive, written by Huston, to implement the plans.

The three memoranda were among documents given to Watergate Judge John J. Sirica by former White House Counsel John W. Dean 3rd.

The memo of recommendations contained among its proposals suggestions for relaxation of restrictions on the "surreptitious entry of facilities occupied by subversive elements." "This technique would be particularly helpful if used against the Weathermen and Black Panthers." "Use of this technique is clearly illegal: it amounts to burglary. It is highly risky and could result in great embarrassment if exposed."

Another committee proposal was that "present restrictions on covert [mail] coverage should be relaxed on selected targets of priority foreign intelligence and internal security interest. . . . Covert coverage is illegal and there are serious risks involved. However, the advantages to be derived from its use outweigh the risks."

"Covert coverage" involved the opening and examination of mail before delivery.

The Huston memo noted that Hoover opposed even the legal monitoring of mail, which involved recording sender and addressee without breaking any seals. Hoover's concern was said to stem from opposition by "civil liberty people."

Other recommendations by the committee as reflected in the Huston memo:

■ Permission for the National Security Agency (NSA) to monitor "the communications of U.S. citizens using international facilities. [telephone and telegraph circuits.]"

■ "Intensification of coverage of individuals and groups in the U.S. who pose a major threat to internal security." The memo said in connection with this that everyone on the committee except Hoover felt that "existing coverage is grossly inadequate."

■ An increase in the number of campus operatives to "forestall widespread" violence. Huston called campuses "the battleground of the revolutionary protest movement." The memo noted the FBI's refusal to employ campus intelligence sources younger than 21 years old for fear of risk of exposure. Committee consensus—with Hoover objecting—was that risk of exposure was minimal and that it was a price to be paid for effective campus coverage.

The second Huston memo dealt with ways to overcome Hoover's objections to the intelligence plan. He said Hoover's objections were twofold: current operations were satisfactory and "no one has any business commenting on procedures he [Hoover] has established for the collection of intelligence by the FBI." According to Huston, Hoover stood alone among committee members in his objections, which the presidential aide labeled "inconsistent and frivolous—most express concern about possible embarrassment to the intelligence community (i.e. Hoover) from public disclosure of clandestine operations."

Huston offered several suggestions to the President as means of overcoming Hoover's opposition. The President should call Hoover into his office for a "stroking session," in which the President would explain his decision to Hoover, thank him for his past cooperation, and indicate he was counting on Hoover for continuing help. Afterwards, the entire committee should be called in and an official photo, to be autographed by the President, should be taken. Later an official memorandum outlining the plan should be distributed to those involved.

Huston concluded that he was certain that Hoover would accede to Nixon's wishes, and the President should not be reluctant to override the director. "Mr. Hoover is set in his ways and can be as bull-headed as hell, but he is a loyal trooper. Twenty years ago he would never have raised the kind of objections he has here, but he's getting old and worried about his legend. . . . he'll respond to direction by the President."

On July 15, 1970 Huston sent the third memo to Hoover, Central Intelligence Agency (CIA) Director Richard Helms, Defense Intelligence Agency (DIA) Director Gen. Donald V. Bennett, and NSA Director Adm. Noel Gayler, informing them that the President had carefully studied the committee's recommendations and agreed to their full implementation.

The Times reported that when Hoover received this memo "he went through the roof." Hoover had assumed that when the President saw a number of footnotes he had attached to the original recommendations, in which he voiced his objections, the President would not approve the plan.

A Times source who participated in the report's preparation said Hoover made no principled objections to the plan; instead his opposition stemmed from the issue of "whether he was going to be able to run the FBI any way he wanted to run it."

President Nixon rescinded his approval of the plan July 28, 1970, five days after Hoover received the memo approving it.

According to the Times, Huston made one more attempt to get his plan past Hoover by composing another memorandum which he sent Aug. 5, 1970. The plan was not revived.

Break-ins against radicals reported. Newsweek magazine reported in its June 11 issue that investigators for the Senate select committee probing Watergate were looking into allegations that certain aspects of the 1970 intelligence gathering plan had been put into operation before the birth of the White House "plumbers" group in the summer of 1971.

Newsweek said illegal methods—including burglary and unauthorized wiretaps—were used to stop sensitive leaks, to monitor the domestic left, and gather information for prosecution cases against radicals. Senate investigators were told by high Administration officials that burglaries were committed in connection with the Seattle Seven, the Chicago Weathermen, the Detroit Thirteen and the Berrigan cases. Senate investigators were also reported to be studying charges that Administration operatives buglarized the offices of the Brookings Institution in Washington seeking information on Morton Halperin, a former member of the National Security Council and a friend of Pentagon Papers trial defendant Daniel Ellsberg. Time magazine June 11 said the Brookings Institution burglary was never carried out.

In a related matter, the Justice Department May 31 admitted the FBI had wiretapped the phone of a prominent radical lawyer 23 times between 1955 and 1970. The lawyer was identified as Arthur Kinoy, an associate of William Kunstler, who worked for the defense in the Chicago Seven trial.

"At the time I was handling the Chicago Seven appeals, the government was listening to my phone conversations. It was the most outrageous invasion of privacy ever admitted to," Kinoy said.

A 1969 break-in by FBI agents at the offices of the underground newspaper, the Washington Free Press, was disclosed by the New York Times June 1. Aiding the FBI were members of the Army's 116th Military Intelligence Detachment, the Times said. The raid took place just before the Nixon inauguration, when there was concern about a series of planned counter-inaugural activities. The FBI June 1 admitted entering without a search warrant, but a spokesman claimed agents had been given a key by the building landlord.

White House probed others. The New York Times reported June 6 that two previously unreported wiretaps had been authorized by former presidential Domestic Affairs Adviser John D. Ehrlichman. One was placed in 1969 against syndicated columnist Joseph Kraft and the other against an unnamed White House official.

White House investigators John J. Caulfield and Anthony T. Ulasewicz, former New York City policemen hired by Ehrlichman, besides placing the taps, were reported to have looked into the background of Rep. Mario Biaggi (D, N.Y.) for possible Mafia ties. Biaggi had criticized as "insulting to Italian-Americans" a 1969 Nixon crime message calling for an attack on organized crime.

The Times called Caulfield and Ulasewicz the precursors to the White House plumbers group.

Further Concessions by Nixon & Aides

Nixon on White House role. In a statement released May 22, 1973, President Nixon conceded the probable involvement of some of his closest aides in concealing some aspects of the Watergate affair and acknowledged that he had ordered limitations on the investigation because of national security considerations "of crucial importance" unrelated to Watergate.

He reiterated, however, his own lack of prior knowledge of the burglary and the attempted cover-up while acknowledging that aides might have "gone beyond" his directives to protect "national security operations in order to cover up any involvement they or certain others might have had in Watergate."

In a summary accompanying the statement, Nixon made the following replies to specific allegations against White House activities:

"1) I had no prior knowledge of the Watergate operation.

2) I took no part in, nor was I aware of, any subsequent efforts that may have been made to cover up Watergate.

3) At no time did I authorize any offer of executive clemency of the Watergate defendants, nor did I know of any such offer.

4) I did not know, until the time of my own investigation, of any effort to provide the Watergate defendants with funds.

5) At no time did I attempt, or did I authorize others to attempt, to implicate the CIA in the Watergate matter.

6) It was not until the time of my own investigation that I learned of the break-in at the office of [Pentagon Papers case defendant Daniel] Ellsberg's psychiatrist, and I specifically authorized the furnishing of this information to Judge [William M.] Byrne.

7) I neither authorized nor encouraged subordinates to engage in illegal or improper campaign tactics."

In his detailed statement, Nixon sought to separate secret investigations begun earlier in his term from the Watergate case. He told of a "special program of wiretaps" set up in 1969 to prevent leaks of secret information important to his foreign policy initiatives. He said there were "fewer than 20 taps" and they were ended in February 1971.

The President said that in 1970 he was concerned about increasing political disruption connected with antiwar protests and decided a better intelligence operation was needed. He appointed the late FBI Director J. Edgar Hoover as head of a committee to prepare suggestions. On June 25 1970, Nixon said, the committee recommended resumption of "certain intelligence operations that had been suspended in 1966," among them the "authorization for surreptitious entry—breaking and entering, in effect"—in specific situations related to national security.

He said Hoover opposed the plan and it was never put into effect.

Further efforts to improve intelligence operations were made in December 1970 with the formation of the Intelligence Evaluation Committee, for which he said he had authorized no illegal activity, nor did he have knowledge of any.

After the New York Times began publishing the Pentagon Papers in June 1971, Nixon said, he approved the formation of a special investigations unit in the White House to "stop security leaks." The unit, known as the "plumbers," was directed by Egil Krogh Jr. and included convicted Watergate conspirators E. Howard Hunt and G. Gordon Liddy. Nixon recalled that he had impressed upon Krogh the importance of protecting the national security and said this might explain how "highly motivated individuals could have felt justified in engaging in specific activities" he would have disapproved had he known of them.

"Consequently," Nixon said, "I must and do assume responsibility for such actions, despite the fact that I at no time approved or had knowledge of them."

Nixon said he had "wanted justice done in regard to Watergate" but he had not wanted the investigation to "impinge adversely upon the national security area." He noted that, shortly after the break-in, he was informed that the CIA might have been involved and that he instructed H. R. Haldeman and John Ehrlichman to "insure that the investigation of the break-in not expose either an unrelated covert operation of the CIA or the activities of the White House investigations unit." He said he gave similar instructions to Assistant Attorney General Henry E. Petersen April 18.

The President reiterated that in the months following the Watergate incident, he was given repeated assurances that the White House staff had been cleared of involvement. But with hindsight, Nixon conceded, it was apparent that "I should have given more heed to the warning signals I received along the way . . . and less to the reassurances." He acknowledged that "unethical, as well as illegal, activities took place in the course of that campaign."

Nixon concluded by retreating on the issue of executive privilege, saying that it would not be invoked "as to any testimony concerning possible criminal conduct or discussions of possible criminal conduct, in the matters presently under investigation, including the Watergate affair and the alleged cover-up."

At a news briefing after the release of the statement, Presidential counsel Leonard Garment, Press Secretary Ronald L. Ziegler and special counsel J. Fred Buzhardt Jr. attempted to reconcile the statement with earlier Nixon comments on the Watergate case.

Ziegler contended that the latest statement showed that Nixon had a "clearer recollection of the case," and Garment said they had been hampered earlier by "limitations on the amount of information available to the President and the staff."

Responding to a question about the President's approval of a plan which would have allowed "surreptitious entry" in certain national security cases, Garment said such activities were customary and had been "traditionally authorized by presidents in order to meet problems that go beyond the boundary of ordinary civil law."

Ziegler rejected a reporter's interpretation of the statement as an admission that Nixon had acquiesced in an alleged cover-up of Watergate to protect intelligence operations.

Both Buzhardt and Garment declined to expand on Nixon's recollection of being told that the CIA might have been involved in the Watergate break-in, despite several questions as to who had given Nixon the information.

Kissinger takes responsibility for taps. Henry A. Kissinger, President Nixon's national security adviser, May 29 conceded "his office" supplied names of some of the members of the National Security Council to the Federal Bureau of Investigation beginning in 1969 to wiretap their phones.

Kissinger, branding wiretaps as "a distasteful thing in general," defended them in safeguarding national security.

Kissinger declined to explain what he meant by "his office." "I am responsible for what happens in my office, and I won't give the names of the people who did it," Kissinger said.

He had denied authorizing any wiretaps May 14.

Nixon aides tie Mitchell to bugging. Former Attorney General John N. Mitchell personally chose three sites for electronic bugging in the 1972 presidential campaign, John D. Ehrlichman, former presidential domestic affairs adviser, said in a deposition in the $6.4 million civil suit filed by the Democratic party against the Committee to Re-elect the President.

The deposition, given in private May 22–24, was released June 5.

The information given by Ehrlichman was obtained for the most part from Jeb Stuart Magruder, Mitchell's assistant at the Nixon re-election committee, and former presidential counsel John W. Dean 3rd. As such the testimony was hearsay. Ehrlichman said the President had asked him to conduct an investigation March 30 after Dean had failed to provide a written report of his own investigation into Watergate.

In his deposition, Ehrlichman spoke of three meetings, held January–March 1972, during which proposals for an intelligence and information facility were discussed. Attending the meetings were Mitchell, Dean, Magruder, and G. Gordon Liddy, later convicted in the Watergate break-in.

Ehrlichman said Magruder told him

that at the first two meetings Liddy presented plans that were rejected as too grandiose and extreme. A third plan was finally accepted, with Mitchell giving oral approval to the bugging operation.

Ehrlichman reported Dean as saying Mitchell had approved the plans in writing "by circling or checking" three targets for bugging from a list.

The three sites were the Democratic national headquarters in the Watergate complex, the Fontainebleau Hotel in Miami Beach during the Democratic convention, and the Washington headquarters of Sen. George McGovern (D, S.D.).

Ehrlichman testified that the second Watergate break-in resulted from Liddy's initiative rather than on orders from anyone high in the Nixon re-election committee. Ehrlichman said Mitchell had been furious that a bug placed on Democratic National Chairman Lawrence F. O'Brien had failed to produce satisfactory results.

In response to Mitchell's criticism, Liddy initiated a second entry into Watergate, at which time the burglars were caught.

Ehrlichman also revealed that his former assistant, John J. Caulfield, came to him in 1971 with a proposal for a private intelligence unit to be contracted for by the Nixon re-election committee. "I gave him this prospectus back and sent him on his way," Ehrlichman testified.

Ehrlichman said Magruder had been told by former Special White House Counsel Charles W. Colson that the Nixon campaign needed information on O'Brien. Magruder said Colson had at no time mentioned illegal intelligence gathering methods.

H. R. Haldeman testified in the Democratic suit May 22–25. His testimony generally complemented Ehrlichman's deposition. But at one point there was a difference: Haldeman reported knowledge of only two meetings attended by Mitchell in which the Watergate bugging was discussed.

Haldeman revealed a March 28 meeting he held with Mitchell at the White House. Mitchell told of a conversation he had with Magruder in which Magruder related that pressure on him had been applied by Special Counsel to the President Charles W. Colson for the gathering of intelligence on the Democrats.

Colson called Magruder while Watergate conspirators G. Gordon Liddy and E. Howard Hunt Jr. sat in his office. Colson told Magruder the two had an intelligence gathering plan that merited study. (Haldeman noted Colson later said he was not aware the Liddy-Hunt plan involved anything illegal. They had come at the end of the day, at a time when Colson had felt rushed.)

In response to the pressure by Colson, Magruder launched the Liddy-Hunt plan. Mitchell told Haldeman the Watergate bugging was conducted with the full knowledge and approval of Magruder.

Haldeman also testified that:

President Nixon did not request a formal investigation of Watergate until March 22. Prior to that time Nixon addressed questions regarding Watergate to Haldeman and Ehrlichman, who in turn passed them to White House Counsel John W. Dean 3rd. Haldeman said Dean maintained until that time no White House personnel had been involved in Watergate. Dean claimed he was unable to establish the connection between Watergate and the Nixon re-election committee because of conflicting evidence and testimony. Dean was taken off the Watergate matter and Ehrlichman assigned March 30 after Dean failed to produce satisfactory explanations for Watergate, Haldeman said.

Ehrlichman tied to coast break-in. Watergate prosecutors were reported to have in their possession a memorandum addressed to John D. Ehrlichman that contained detailed plans for the break-in at the office of the former psychiatrist of Pentagon Papers trial defendant Daniel Ellsberg, the Washington Post reported June 13, 1973.

The memo sent by former White House aides David Young and Egil Krogh Jr. was dated before the burglary occurred Sept. 3-4, 1971.

Young, under a grant of immunity from prosecution, gave the document to prosecutors and agreed to testify that Ehrlichman saw the memo and approved its contents.

Ehrlichman, who had previously denied advance knowledge of the break-in, conceded to the House Armed Service Committee's Subcommittee on Intelligence Operations June 13 he had approved "some sort of proposal" involving investigation of Ellsberg. Ehrlichman admitted the proposal might have dealt with going to Los Angeles, but he "did not recollect" anything in the memo referring to an actual break-in.

Krogh, in an affidavit submitted to Pentagon Papers trial Judge William M. Byrne Jr. and made public May 7, said Ehrlichman gave "general authorization to engage in covert activity" to obtain information on Ellsberg.

According to Post sources, the Krogh affidavit was prepared from a document, whose bottom portion, describing the burglary in detail, had been clipped off. The bottom was removed at the beginning of 1973 to "sanitize" Krogh's files before Senate confirmation hearings on his nomination as undersecretary of transportation, a post he resigned May 9.

Ervin Committee Hearings

Evidence mounts. The continuing hearings of the Select Senate Committee headed by Sen. Sam J. Ervin Jr. produced additional testimony linking members of the Nixon Administration and 1972 Nixon election campaign to the various misdeeds being brought to light as a result of the Watergate scandal.

The committee heard June 5, 1973 that reports on political data gleaned from illegal wiretaps were regularly sent to former Attorney General John N. Mitchell and the White House, and that politically sensitive material in the files of the Nixon campaign committee was destroyed after the Watergate break-in.

Testimony also revealed a meeting in the White House in early February 1972 of Mitchell, then-White House counsel John W. Dean 3rd, Jeb Stuart Magruder, deputy director of the Nixon committee, and G. Gordon Liddy, a former White House and Nixon committee aide later convicted in the Watergate conspiracy. The committee was told that Magruder, who was Mitchell's assistant at the Nixon committee when Mitchell was head of the campaign, passed word to Liddy at one point, probably in March 1972, that "it was arranged."

The testimony came from Robert A. F. Reisner, who had been Magruder's administrative assistant at that time. His testimony was the first given publicly and under oath linking Mitchell to data from the illegal wiretaps at the Democratic national headquarters at the Watergate building. The wiretaps had been installed in May 1972 prior to the second break-in there June 17, 1972, when five of the conspirators were apprehended.

Reisner testified he had seen, a week or two prior to the aborted break-in, reports marked "Gemstone," the code word for material obtained from the wiretaps and other political spying activity of the committee. He said Magruder one time handed him a Gemstone document "in such a way that it was indicated to me very clearly that it was not for me to observe." He was instructed to put the document in files Magruder maintained for his daily meetings with Mitchell, Reisner said. And he testified that as each document was sent to Mitchell through him, a duplicate copy of that document was sent to the office of John D. Ehrlichman, then chief Nixon domestic adviser.

The day of the Watergate break-in, Reisner testified, Magruder, who was in California, ordered him by telephone to remove the Gemstone file, which Magruder termed "sensitive" material, from the office over that weekend. Subsequently, Reisner said, he asked Magruder what the Gemstone file was and, he said, Magruder replied, " 'I don't know what it is either. Forget about it, though. It's gone.' "

Much or all of the "sensitive" material in the files was destroyed after the break-in, Reisner testified. Magruder ordered him to go through the files "and centralize sensitive materials," he said, and "some of those were subsequently destroyed."

Ervin questioned him about what was actually "centralized." Reisner said: "Virtually everything. Well, I think Mr. Magruder's secretary and I looked through his own files. I think other people on the committee did similar things and virtually anything that concerned the opposition, contenders, that sort of thing, that would have been awkward or politically damaging to—well, no, even broader than that. Anything that would have concerned the opposition."

This apparently would have included material marked "Sedan Chair 2," which Reisner identified as that dealing with information from the Democratic presidential campaign of Sen. Hubert H. Humphrey. The information was bought by the committee, Reisner said, at the rate of $1,000 a month, he believed, probably from a "disgruntled" Humphrey worker.

Liddy's secretary testifies—Liddy's secretary at the time of the Watergate break-in, Sally J. Harmony, testified June 5 that she had typed memos for Gemstone. She said that on several occasions she transcribed directly from logs of conversations delivered to her directly from the secret listening post by James W. McCord Jr., another convicted conspirator.

She recalled little of substance for the committee. She did recall seeing some photographs of documents with Democratic National Chairman Lawrence F. O'Brien's name on them.

"Was there anything unusual about the photograph that you can remember?" she was asked.

"Yes, sir. They were being held by fingers."

"Fingers?"

"Yes, sir. I guess at this point they would have been fingers of rubber gloves."

She also recalled making a fake entry pass to the headquarters of Democratic presidential contender George McGovern and shredding her shorthand notebooks, at Liddy's request, after the break-in.

Watergate payments—Hugh W. Sloan Jr., former treasurer of the Committee to Re-elect the President (Nixon), testified June 6 that a persistent effort was made by top Nixon campaign officials to pressure him to cover up the large amount of cash payments made to the Watergate conspirators. He testified that he was put off when he attempted to warn high campaign and White House officials that something was seriously amiss at the GOP committee or possibly in the entire campaign. He also testified that John Mitchell was making decisions about campaign spending while he was attorney general months before he left to head the Nixon campaign on March 1, 1972.

Sloan's special problem at the Nixon committee involved G. Gordon Liddy, later convicted in the Watergate case. He said he gave Liddy $199,000 in cash in the spring of 1972. Liddy presented him with a budget of $250,000, Sloan said, with an initial request for $83,000 in cash. He checked the request with Nixon campaign finance chairman Maurice Stans, Sloan said, who told him, "I do not want to know and you do not want to know" what the money was for.

After the Watergate break-in, Sloan testified: About June 21 or 22, 1972, he spoke with Magruder about the funds Magruder had authorized for Liddy. "He indicated to me that we are going to have to [disclose to investigators] or suggested to me a figure of what I had given to Mr. Liddy in the range of, somewhere, $75,000 to $80,000." Sloan said he "did not know the precise amount of money that I had given to Mr. Liddy at that point. However, I did know that the sum was considerably larger than that because Mr. Magruder himself had authorized a payment for $83,000 in one single installment.

"I must have indicated to him, well, that just is not the right figure, I did not have the right figure, but that is too low. He indicated to me at that time that I said to him, he must have been insistent because I remember making to him on that occasion a statement I have no intention of perjuring myself."

Committee counsel Samuel Dash asked Sloan: "What did he say to you when you said that?"

Sloan responded: "He said you may have to."

Later that day, Sloan was approached by Frederick C. LaRue, a Mitchell campaign aide conducting an investigation of the Watergate matter for Mitchell. During their talk, Sloan was informed two FBI agents were waiting to talk to him. LaRue said he should see Mitchell first, and Sloan went, hoping to get some "guidance."

"I essentially asked for guidance, at which point he [Mitchell] told me, 'when the going gets tough the tough get going.' "

Sloan did not consider that "any particular helpful guidance at that point," but he saw the FBI agents, who asked him only about Alfred C. Baldwin 3rd, who had monitored the wiretaps at the Democratic headquarters, about whom Sloan knew nothing.

LaRue came to see him about the interview, and, "At that point he indicated to me that, and I do not have the precise words, the sense of the meaning as it came across to me, there was very brief reference something to the effect that the Liddy money is the problem, it is very politically sensitive, we can just not come out with a high figure, we are going to have to come out with a different figure. And I said, as I recall, I said, if there is a problem I cannot see that it makes any difference whether it is $200 or $200,000, at which point he dropped the conversation."

That night, Sloan attended a party along with several White House aides and arranged with them to meet the next day with Nixon's appointments aide Dwight C. Chapin and Ehrlichman.

With Chapin, Sloan said, "I believe probably the tone of the conversation was that there is a tremendous problem there, something has to be done.... He suggested that the important thing is that the President be protected.

"In the Ehrlichman meeting, . . . I believe I expressed my concern, my personal concern with regard to the money. I believe he interpreted my being there as personal fear and he indicated to me that I had a special relationship with the White House, if I needed help getting a lawyer, he would be glad to do that, but 'do not tell me any details; I do not want to know. My position would have to be until after the election that I would have to take executive privilege.' "

The committee also heard testimony, first from Sloan and then first-hand from his attorney, James T. Treese, that White House counsel Dean had called him in October 1972 and urged Sloan to take the Fifth Amendment during his scheduled appearance at the Florida trial of Watergate conspirator Bernard Barker, who was accused of falsely notarizing a Nixon campaign check. Treese, who took the call, reported it this way: Dean said Sloan "could be a real hero around here if he took the Fifth. And I said, 'John, relax . . . Hugh Sloan is not going to take the Fifth Amendment.' "

Porter admits perjury—Herbert L. Porter, former scheduling director of the Nixon campaign committee, testified June 7 that he had committed perjury when he testified in 1972 before the Watergate grand jury and at the Watergate trial in January on the funds paid Liddy. Porter admitted that he lied under oath about Watergate out of "a deep sense of loyalty" to President Nixon and because of "the fear of group pressure that would ensue from not being a team player."

Porter said "at no time did I ever have any intention of covering up a criminal act. At no time did I knowingly engage in any cover-up of the Watergate burglary." He said he had "no prior knowledge" of the break-in, "and up to this very moment I have no knowledge of the involvement of others."

He told the committee this story:

On June 28 or 29, 1972, he met with Magruder, who told him "that he had just come from a meeting with Mr. Mitchell, Mr. LaRue, himself, and a fourth party whose name I cannot remember, where my name had been brought up as someone who could be—what was the term he used—counted on in a pinch or a team player or words to that effect.

". . . He said it was apparent . . . that Mr. Liddy and others had on their own illegally participated in the break-in of the Watergate . . . , and Mr. Magruder swore to me that neither he nor anybody higher than Mr. Liddy in the campaign organization or at the White House had any involvement whatsoever in Watergate, at the Watergate break-in, and reinforced that by saying, 'Doesn't that sound like something stupid that Gordon would do?' And you have to know Mr. Liddy. I agreed with that.

"He said, 'I want to assure you now that no one did.' He said, however, he said, 'There is a problem with some of the money.' He said, 'Now, Gordon was authorized money for some dirty tricks, nothing illegal,' he said, but nonetheless, 'things that could be very embarrassing to the President of the United States and to Mr. Mitchell and Mr. Haldeman and others. Now, your name was brought up as someone who we can count on to help in this situation.' And I asked what is it you are asking me to do, and he said, 'Would you corroborate a story that the money was authorized for something a little bit more legitimate-sounding than dirty tricks. Even though the dirty tricks were legal, it still would be very embarrassing.'

". . . You were in charge of the surrogate campaign, you were very concerned about radical elements disrupting rallies and so forth, and I said yes, and he said suppose that we had authorized Liddy, instead of the dirty tricks, we had authorized him to infiltrate some of these radical groups?

"He said, how could such a program have cost a hundred thousand? And I thought very quickly of a conversation I had with a young man in California in December, as a matter of fact, and I said, Jeb, that is very easy. You could get 10 college-age students or 24- or 25-year-old students, people, over a period of 10 months. Mr. Magruder had prefaced his remark by saying from December on. And I said, you can pay them $1,000 a month, which they would take their expenses out of that, and I said that is $100,-000. I said that is not very much for a $45 million campaign. And he said, now that is right.

"He said, would you be willing, if I made that statement to the FBI, would you be willing to corroborate that when I came to you in December and asked you how much it would cost, and that is what you said? That was the net effect, the net of his question. I thought for a moment and I said, yes, I probably would do that. I don't remember saying yes, but I am sure I gave Mr. Magruder the impression I would probably do that and that was the end of the conversation."

Q. Later, did you tell the FBI what Mr. Magruder asked you to tell them?

A. **Yes, sir, I did.**

Q. What did you tell the federal grand jury?

A. **The same thing.**

Q. Were you a witness at the trial of the seven defendants who were indicted in the Watergate case?

A. **Yes, sir.**

Q. And did you give the same account?

A. **Yes sir, I did.**

On April 11, Porter continued, Magruder advised him to contact a lawyer and tell the federal prosecutor "what you know." In a chance encounter three days later, Porter said, Magruder told him, "He had just come from a meeting at the White House and that it is all over, he said, and I said, what do you mean, it is all over? He said, it is all over, the President has directed everybody to tell the truth. Those were his exact words. He said I had a meeting with Mr. Ehrlichman and I told him the whole story and, boy, was he really shocked, words to that effect."

Magruder told him then that Mitchell "was going to deny complicity until the end," Porter said.

Magruder admits perjury, links Mitchell to Watergate planning—Jeb Stuart Magruder, deputy director of the Committee for the Re-election of the President during the 1972 campaign, testified June 14 on the "true" story of the planning of the Watergate break-in and of the subsequent coverup. He admitted that he had given a "false story" to the Watergate grand jury and had testified falsely at the trial.

In an opening statement, Magruder said, "Unfortunately, we made some mistakes in the campaign which have led to a major national concern. For those errors in judgment that I made I take full responsibility.... These mistakes were made by only a few participants in the campaign. Thousands of persons assisted in the campaign to re-elect the President and they did nothing illegal or unethical. As far as I know at no point during this entire period from the time of planning of the Watergate to the time of trying to keep it from the public view did the President have any knowledge of our errors in this matter. He had confidence in his aides and I must confess that some of us failed him."

Then, under questioning by the committee's chief counsel and staff director Samuel Dash, Magruder told this story:

On Jan. 27, 1971, there was a meeting in Attorney General John N. Mitchell's office at the Justice Department attended by Mitchell, Presidential counsel John W. Dean 3rd, Magruder and G. Gordon Liddy. Using large charts on an easel, Liddy presented an espionage plan he budgeted at $1 million. The proposed projects included wiretapping, electronic surveillance and photography. One proposal was to abduct radical leaders and detain them in Mexico to prevent them from disrupting the Republican National Convention.

Another project "would have used women as agents to work with members of the Democratic National Committee at their convention and here in Washington and, hopefully, through their efforts, they would obtain information from them." The project included rental of a yacht at Miami, "set up for sound and photographs," for "call girls" to "work with" prominent Democrats.

The reaction to the plan, Magruder continued, was that "all three of us were appalled" because of "the scope and size of the project." Mitchell indicated "that this was not an acceptable project" and that Liddy should "go back to the drawing board and come up with a more realistic plan."

Magruder made a telephoned report on the meeting to Gordon Strachan, then assistant to Nixon chief of staff H. R. Haldeman. "Everything that I did at the committee," Magruder told the committee, "everything that we did was staffed to Mr. Strachan so that he could alert other officials at the White House as to our activities."

A second meeting on the Liddy plan was held Feb. 4, 1972 at the Justice Department with the same participants. The topic was "the potential target" of the Democratic National Committee headquarters and "the possibility of using electronic surveillance" at the Democratic convention headquarters and at the presidential contender's headquarters. Either Mitchell or Dean also brought up the point that information relating to Sen. Edmund S. Muskie (Me.), then a Democratic presidential aspirant, possibly could be obtained in a newspaper office in Las Vegas and Liddy "was asked to review the situation in Las Vegas to see if there would be potential for any entry."

Magruder said the information sought at the convention site concerned a plan for a business exposition to be staged, with a kickback of some or all of the fee to the Democrats (a plan never executed).

In general, he said, information also was being sought to offset the effectiveness of then Democratic National Chairman Lawrence F. O'Brien. O'Brien, he said, had "been a very effective spokesman against our position on the ITT case and I think there was a general concern that if he was allowed to continue as Democratic national chairman, because he was certainly their most professional political operator, that he could be very difficult in the coming campaign. So we had hoped that information might discredit him."

The reaction to this Liddy plan, which had been scaled down to a $500,000 cost, was "that it would not be approved at that time but we would take it up later."

Again, Magruder made a telephone report on the meeting to Strachan.

Another development at this time was word to Magruder from the White House to get the Liddy plan approved. According to Magruder, Charles Colson, then a counsel to the President, "called me one evening and asked me in a sense would we get off the stick and get the budget approved for Mr. Liddy's plans, that we needed information, particularly on Mr. O'Brien. He did not mention, I want to make clear, anything relating to wiretapping or espionage at that time."

Magruder was also pressed on the matter by Colson assistant, Richard Howard.

"But, I would like to make it clear," Magruder stressed, "there was a general, I think, atmosphere in the White House and the committee of the need to gather

information. This was not necessarily information that would be gathered illegally."

A third and final meeting on the Liddy plan was held on or about March 30, 1972. It was at Key Biscayne, where Mitchell was on vacation. The participants were Mitchell, Magruder, Liddy and Frederick C. LaRue, former White House aide and chief deputy to Mitchell at the campaign committee. This plan, scaled down to a $250,000 cost, involved entry into the Democratic National Committee headquarters (in the Watergate building in Washington) and possible later entry into the Democratic presidential contenders' headquarters and the Democratic convention headquarters. The plan included electronic surveillance and photography of documents.

"No one was particularly overwhelmed with the project," Magruder said. "But I think we felt that the information could be useful and Mr. Mitchell agreed to approve the project and I then notified the parties of Mr. Mitchell's approval."

Magruder recalled being questioned by Hugh W. Sloan Jr., treasurer of the campaign committee's finance arm, about the initial large sum of money requested by Liddy, $83,000, for the operation.

"I indicated that Mr. Liddy did have that approval. Mr. Sloan evidently then went to Mr. Stans. Mr. Stans went to Mr. Mitchell. Mr. Mitchell came back to me and said why did Gordon need this much money and I explained to him this was in effect front end money that he needed for the equipment, and the early costs of getting his kind of an operation together. Mr. Mitchell understood, evidently told Mr. Stans it had been approved and the approval was complete."

The first break-in at the Watergate occurred May 27, 1972. Liddy indicated to Magruder afterward "he had made a successful entry and had placed wiretapping equipment in the Democratic National Committee." About a week and a half later, Magruder received "the first reports" from the bugging in the form of recapitulated telephone conversations and pictures of documents. He "brought the materials into Mr. Mitchell," who "reviewed the documents" and "indicated that there was really no substance" to them.

Liddy was called in and "Mitchell indicated his dissatisfaction with the results of his work." Magruder said Mitchell "did not ask for anything more." Liddy indicated "there was a problem with one wiretap" (the one on O'Brien's phone was not working) and "he would correct these matters and hopefully get the information that was requested."

Magruder called Strachan, who came to his office "and look[ed] over the documents and indicate[d] to me the lack of substance to the documents."

The morning after the June 17, 1972 break-in, which the police intercepted, Liddy phoned Magruder, the latter testified. Magruder, in California, talked to LaRue, who contacted Mitchell. Mitchell then ordered Robert C. Mardian to ask Liddy to find out from Attorney General Richard G. Kleindienst whether "there was any possibility" that James W. McCord Jr., a campaign committee employe who was one of those arrested, "could be released from jail."

Magruder also called Strachan and told him of the problem. He also received a call from Haldeman, who "asked me what had happened" and, after being told, "indicated that I should get back to Washington immediately" to take care of the problem.

Back in Washington, Magruder met June 19 with Mitchell, LaRue, Mardian and Dean. "One solution was recommended in which I was to, of course, destroy the Gemstone [Liddy plan] file." "As I recall," Magruder said, "we all indicated that we should remove any documents that could be damaging, whether they related at all to the Watergate or not."

Magruder stressed that no one asked him to participate in the cover-up. "I personally felt that it was important to be sure that this story did not come out in its true form at that time, as I think did the other participants. So I want to make it clear that no one coerced me to do anything. I volunteered to work on the cover-up story."

There were a "series of meetings," mainly held in Mitchell's office, attended by Mitchell, LaRue, Mardian, Dean and Magruder. At one point, "there was some discussion about me and I volunteered at one point that maybe I was the guy who ought to take the heat, because it was going to get to me, and we knew that. And I think it was, there were some takers on that, but basically, the decision was that because I was in a position where they knew that I had no authority to either authorize funds or make policy in that committee, that if it got to me, it would go higher, whereas Mr. Liddy, because of his past background, it was felt that would be believable that Mr. Liddy was truly the one who did originate it."

Magruder told of a meeting with Haldeman in January before the Nixon inauguration. "... I went to Mr. Haldeman, and I said I just want you to know that this whole Watergate situation and the other activities was a concerted effort by a number of people, and so I went through a literally monologue on what had occurred. That was my first discussion with Mr. Haldeman where I laid out the true facts."

He and Mitchell met with Haldeman in late March, Magruder said, and were urged to meet with Dean to agree on a story. The three met but could not agree. "The election was now over and the reason for the cover-up [Nixon's reelection] was no longer valid," Magruder said. Then Dean was indicating "some reluctance" to abide by the story Magruder had told the grand jury, and Magruder felt "the story would not hold up" under further investigation by the Senate committee as well as the grand jury, which was reviving its probe.

So he told the "true" story to the federal prosecutors April 12.

Magruder also spoke of the atmosphere in the Nixon White House in response to queries from Sen. Howard H. Baker Jr. (R, Tenn.), who was curious about the "reluctant decision" described by Magruder on the final Watergate plan.

"I still can't quite come to grips with why you all had an expressed reservation about this and you still went ahead with it," Baker told him. Magruder then discussed the work at the White House.

There, he "was mainly engaged in the

activities trying to generate some support for the President," he said. "During that time, we had worked primarily relating to the war situation and worked with antiwar groups.... We were directly employed with trying to succeed with the President's policies." At the same time, he "saw people I was very close to breaking the law [in antiwar protests] without any regard for any other person's pattern of behavior or belief.

"So consequently, when these subjects [Liddy plans] came up although I was aware they were illegal we had become somewhat inured to using some activities that would help us in accomplishing what we thought was a cause, a legitimate cause ... That is basically, I think, the reason why that decision was made, because of that atmosphere that had occurred and to all of us who had worked in the White House, there was that feeling of resentment and of frustration at being unable to deal with issues on a legal basis."

Magruder told Baker, "I do not think there was ever any discussion that there would not be a cover-up." The planning for it, he said, began the day they "realized there was a break-in." Magruder said he felt that if the story had "gotten out that people like Mr. Mitchell and others had been involved," that Nixon's re-election "would be probably negated." "I think it was felt," he continued, "that if it ever reached Mr. Mitchell before the election, the President would lose the election."

Press & Other Reports

Colson reiterates Nixon's innocence. Charles W. Colson, former special counsel to the President, told the New New York Times June 9, 1973 that he would stake his life on President Nixon's disclaimer of any knowledge of a Watergate cover-up.

Colson, who resigned his White House position in March, said he had warned the President Feb. 14 he must force former Attorney General John N. Mitchell to admit the role he played in planning the Watergate wiretaps.

Colson said that as late as March 21 the President did not believe Mitchell or any of his senior aides were guilty nor would he consent to making a scapegoat of Mitchell, an innocent man.

Colson said he told federal prosecutors that in early February he informed Chief of Staff H. R. Haldeman of his concern over possible perjury and obstruction of justice in the first Watergate trial in January. Payments by Nixon associates to the Watergate defendants could be construed as criminal "hush money." Haldeman's response, Colson said, was that he knew about the money and he was not concerned.

Colson said the main reason he had withheld his story from reporters was fear that Haldeman and former Nixon Domestic Affairs Adviser John D. Ehrlichman would frame him.

Colson claimed he first expressed his suspicions of Mitchell's involvement to the President shortly after his inauguration in January. The President told him "Get me evidence and I'll act on it," Colson said.

Colson said the President was neither a harsh nor persistent questioner of his own staff members after they fell under suspicion with regard to Watergate. The President was a reluctant investigator and waited for outside events to force him to act, Colson said. "The Nixon style is sort of third person," Colson said with reference to events immediately following Watergate. "The President would ask about the Watergate, something like, 'Now why in the hell would somebody do that?' It would be sort of a rhetorical question giving you an opportunity to say, 'Well, Mr. President, I blew it.' But when you said, 'I have no idea, Mr. President; it seems to me, too, the stupidest thing I've ever heard,' that was taken as an answer," Colson said.

Colson recollected that the President's first reaction to the Watergate burglary was denunciation of the entire management of the Committee to Re-elect the President, which Mitchell had been directing since March 1, 1972.

Hunt blackmail reported. Convicted Watergate conspirator E. Howard Hunt Jr. "effectively blackmailed" the White

House with threats he would expose involvement of high Nixon Administration officials in secret illegal activities unless he received large sums of money and a guarantee of executive clemency, the Washington Post reported June 15.

According to Post sources, Hunt received, along with promises of clemency, amounts totaling more than $200,000. In late March, Hunt allegedly asked for an additional $130,000, which was never paid.

Reportedly, acquiescence by key White House officials was in part the result of fears that Hunt would reveal the Administration's secret plans against radicals, political opponents, and the press.

Post sources said Hunt's demands clearly established a case of obstruction of justice against White House officials. "Hunt was being paid to keep quiet. It demolishes the argument that the money was just for lawyers' fees and care for the families of the defendants," Post sources were quoted as saying.

Hunt allegedly relayed his first demand to the White House only a few days after the Watergate break-in by warning, "The writer has a manuscript or play to sell," government investigators told the Post. Hunt was the prolific author of more than 40 novels.

In the beginning, payments were made to Hunt by Nixon campaign aide Frederick C. LaRue, who delivered the cash to either Hunt directly or Hunt's attorney William O. Bittman. Bittman, sources said, admitted receiving three or four sealed envelopes, which he passed to Hunt, but Bittman denied knowledge of their contents.

By the fall of 1972 Hunt was reported to have become dissatisfied with his channels to the White House and fearful about promises of clemency, facts he had relayed to the White House in a three-page memo. Hunt reportedly upped his demands for money and for better White House channels. "It kicked up a crisis at the White House," a Post source said.

Hunt sent at least five messages to the White House, the last on March 16, one week before he was given a provisional prison sentence of 35 years and after his wife Dorothy had been killed in a plane crash. Hunt, worried that no one would

take care of his children, made a final demand for $130,000—$70,000 for personal expenses and $60,000 for legal fees, Post sources said.

White House Counsel John W. Dean 3rd, recipient of the demand, "hit the ceiling" and refused to accede to Hunt's demands, the Post reported. By then the cover-up was falling apart, one Post source said.

Haldeman ordered files destroyed. H. R. Haldeman, President Nixon's former chief of staff, ordered aide Gordon C. Strachan to destroy documents that showed he knew of "actual data" obtained from the wiretap of the Democratic National Committee headquarters in the Watergate complex.

The information was contained in a report submitted to the Senate committee investigating Watergate by member Sen. Lowell P. Weicker (R, Conn.) after he interviewed former White House Counsel John W. Dean 3rd May 3, the New York Times reported June 10.

According to the report, about June 18, 1972, "Strachan told Dean that he had been ordered by Haldeman to destroy documents which indicated that Haldeman had awareness of actual data received from the wiretap at the Democratic National Committee."

Dean told Weicker that Strachan admitted to him he had destroyed the documents in his office June 17 or 18, 1972.

Ellsberg wiretap revealed. The Washington Post reported June 14 that the White House in 1971 received information from wiretaps—previously undisclosed—on Pentagon Papers defendant Daniel Ellsberg and New York Times reporters Neil Sheehan and Tad Szulc.

According to Post sources, the wiretap information was received in the White House as early as May 1971—one month before the Pentagon Papers were published in the New York Times and one month before the White House "plumbers group" was set up on orders from President Nixon.

The Federal Bureau of Investigation

said it had no record of any such electronic surveillance.

The tap on Ellsberg continued for at least four months. The surveillance of the other two was irregular and lasted over several months, the Post said.

Sheehan prepared the Pentagon Papers for publication by the Times.

Dean's testimony leaked. Former Presidential counsel John W. Dean 3rd met June 16, 1973 with the Select Senate Committee's staff members and lawyers in a preparatory session for his public testimony. The panel's chief counsel, Samuel Dash, and its Republican counsel, Fred D. Thompson, prepared separate summaries of Dean's testimony at the session and these summaries were distributed to the seven senators on the committee. Leaked accounts of Dean's testimony began appearing in the press soon afterwards and continued through the following week at a time when public hearings for Dean had been cancelled because of a visit by Soviet Communist Party leader Leonid I. Brezhnev to the U.S.

By midweek, excerpts from a summary prepared by the committee staff were being published. Also being published at the same time were excerpts from a White House account of conversations between President Nixon and Dean that had been sent to the committee. The New York Times published both sets of excerpts June 21.

Dean's story—The Times reported June 17, from various sources, one of them "a Dean associate," that Dean had informed government investigators about being told by White House aide Egil Krogh Jr. in early January that the orders for the burglary of files belonging to Pentagon Papers defendant Daniel Ellsberg's former psychiatrist came "from the oval office" (President Nixon's office). The account pictured Dean as having become convinced of Nixon's knowledge of the Watergate cover-up and feeling that his frequent meetings with Nixon early in 1973, when the President was concerned over executive privilege and national security, were related to the cover-up. The account said Dean attempted to tell Nixon on at least two occasions in mid-

March about the scope of the scandal and, after arranging for his own personal defense and setting up a meeting with federal prosecutors, told the President the whole account of Watergate.

In the news accounts based on leaks after Dean's session with the Senate panel, Dean reportedly told the investigators:

■ Nixon asked him to keep a list of newsmen who were giving the President "trouble" during the 1972 election campaign.

■ Nixon asked Dean to see that Internal Revenue Service tax audits "be turned off on friends" of the President.

■ Dean promised to provide the committee with documents showing that he and top Nixon aides H. R. Haldeman and John D. Ehrlichman began immediately after the Watergate break-in to devise a cover-up story.

The summary of Dean's testimony before the Senate panel revealed further allegations by Dean. Among them:

■ In September 1972 Nixon directed that an effort be made to muffle a Watergate investigation by a House committee.

■ Nixon "had been bugged" in the 1968 campaign, Nixon once told Dean on the word of the late FBI director J. Edgar Hoover, and Nixon believed the information could be used to the Administration's advantage at some future time.

■ There was an attempt to persuade former Attorney General John N. Mitchell to "take the heat" off other officials by assuming the blame for the Watergate break-in.

■ Ehrlichman had instructed Dean to throw wiretapping equipment "in [the] river" after it had been found in the White House safe of one of the Watergate conspirators, E. Howard Hunt Jr.

■ Mitchell at first ignored a request to obtain money for the Watergate defendants, but Hunt sent word, through Dean to Ehrlichman and Mitchell, he wanted $72,000 for living expenses and $50,000 for lawyers' fees or, as the summary phrased it, "Hunt would have things to say about the seamy things Hunt did for Ehrlichman while Hunt was at the White House." On March 21 or 22, the account continued, "Ehrlichman asked Mitchell if Hunt's problem had been taken care of and Mitchell said 'Yes.'" The next sentence in the summary was: "Hunt's asking for money came to the attention of the President."

Dean then was said to have discussed the question of executive clemency for the defendants with Nixon in the spring.

■ Intelligence data on Democrats was coming into the White House in early 1970 and reports by a private intelligence gathering unit in the White House were sent to Nixon through Haldeman and Ehrlichman.

White House summary—The White House summary of Nixon's discussions with Dean portrayed Dean as deflecting persistent questioning by Nixon about White House involvement in the Watergate burglary and cover-up until March 21. The two met almost daily during the first three weeks of March, according to the account, with Dean insisting there was no White House involvement.

The report said on March 13 Dean told Nixon that Haldeman aide Gordon C. Strachan "could be involved" and on March 21 Dean "gave the President his theory of what happened"—revealing "that [Jeb Stuart] Magruder probably knew, that Mitchell possibly knew, that Strachan probably knew, that Haldeman had possibly seen the fruits of the wiretaps through Strachan, that Ehrlichman was vulnerable because of his approval of [Herbert W.] Kalmbach's fund-raising efforts." Kalmbach was Nixon's personal attorney and reportedly was called upon to raise contributions for a fund to pay the Watergate defendants.

According to the summary, Nixon was told March 21 that Hunt "was trying to blackmail Ehrlichman about Hunt's prior plumber [plugging news 'leaks' such as Pentagon Papers' publication] activities unless he was paid what ultimately might amount to $1 million, ..."

The summary said Nixon sent Dean to Camp David March 23 and later that day called him "to check on his progress," presumably concerning a written report on Watergate; on March 30, when it became obvious Dean "would write no report," Nixon ordered Ehrlichman to investigate; Ehrlichman reported April 14 "possible Mitchell, Magruder and Dean involvement"; Nixon called Attorney General Richard G. Kleindienst, "who followed up"; Nixon called almost everyone on April 15 and "told Dean he must go before the grand jury without immunity"; the next day Nixon "asks Dean to resign. Had two drafts prepared for Dean's signature. Dean demanded Haldeman and Ehrlichman resign also"; the federal prosecutor asked a delay on Dean's firing until he could be put before the grand jury; Nixon was told April 27 there was no use trying to get Dean before the jury since he was demanding immunity; on April 30 Nixon announced "Haldeman's and Ehrlichman's resignations and Dean's firing."

Watergate Ramifications

Dean Implicates Nixon & White House Staff

Dean's testimony. Former presidential counsel John W. Dean 3rd testified for five consecutive days before the Senate Watergate committee June 25–29, 1973.

Dean's reading of a statement—245 triple spaced legal-size pages—occupied the full June 25 session and lasted more than six hours. In addition, Dean submitted 47 documents to the committee to accompany his statement.

Dean admitted to the committee his own involvement in the effort to cover up the Watergate conspiracy and related how that effort spread among the White House staff, the Committee to Re-elect the President, the Justice Department and President Nixon.

While Dean's account was the first before the committee to directly accuse Nixon of involvement in the Watergate cover-up, Dean asserted that Nixon did not "realize or appreciate at any time the implications of his involvement." Dean said, however, that Nixon had permitted the cover-up to continue even after Dean had told him about some of the cover-up plans. Dean added that Nixon had discussed with him the possibility of executive clemency for some of the Watergate conspirators and "hush money" payments to maintain the cover-up.

Dean's statement detailed the "excessive concern" in the White House for data on antiwar activists and other political opponents of the Administration. Dean suggested that this concern, along with the "do-it-yourself White House staff, regardless of the law," created the climate for the Watergate affair.

Dean described his superiors in the White House—former presidential aides H. R. Haldeman and John D. Ehrlichman—as the principals in the efforts to conceal the ramifications of the Watergate break-in. But he also implicated, among others, former Attorney General John N. Mitchell, former special counsel to the President Charles W. Colson, U.S. District Court Judge Charles R. Richey, Assistant Attorney General Henry E. Petersen, former Acting FBI Director L. Patrick Gray 3rd, White House Press Secretary Ronald L. Ziegler, presidential aide Richard Moore and former presidential aides Frederick C. LaRue and Gordon C. Strachan.

In summary, his statement said:

"The Watergate matter was an inevitable outgrowth of a climate of excessive concern over the political impact of demonstrators, excessive concern over leaks, an insatiable appetite for

113

political intelligence, all coupled with a do-it-yourself White House staff, regardless of the law. However, the fact that many of the elements of this climate culminated with the creation of a covert intelligence operation as part of the President's re-election committee was not by conscious design, rather an accident of fate."

"The White House was continually seeking intelligence information about demonstration leaders and their supporters that would either discredit them personally or indicate that the demonstration was in fact sponsored by some foreign enemy. There were also White House requests for information regarding ties between major political figures [specifically members of the U.S. Senate] who opposed the President's war policies and the demonstration leaders."

There was a lack of information showing such ties between the demonstrators and either foreign governments or major political figures, and this "was often reported to a disbelieving and complaining White House staff that felt the entire system for gathering such intelligence was worthless."

Soon after joining the White House staff in July of 1970, Dean learned about "the project to restructure the government's intelligence gathering capacities vis-a-vis demonstrators and domestic radicals." He was "told of the presidentially-approved plan that called for bugging, burglarizing, mail covers and the like." White House Chief of Staff H. R. Haldeman instructed him "to see what I could do to get the plan implemented."

Dean considered the plan "totally uncalled for and unjustified." He talked about it with Attorney General John N. Mitchell, who opposed it.

In early March, "as a part of the planned counteroffensive for dealing with the Senate Watergate investigation," Nixon "wanted to show that his opponents had employed demonstrators against him during his re-election campaign." But, he said, "We never found a scintilla of viable evidence indicating that these demonstrators were part of a master plan; nor that they were funded by the Democratic political funds; nor that they had any direct connection with the McGovern campaign. This was explained to Mr. Haldeman, but the President believed that the opposite was, in fact, true."

There was also considerable concern at the White House about news leaks. This concern "took a quantum jump" when the Pentagon Papers were published in June 1971.

Another concern at the White House was obtaining "politically embarrassing" information on leading Democrats.

In the spring of 1971, Haldeman discussed with Dean "what my office should do" during the coming campaign year. "He told me that we should take maximum advantage of the President's incumbency and the focus of everyone in the White House should be on the re-election of the President."

Part of Dean's task, in addition to "keeping the White House in compliance with the election laws," was "improving our intelligence regarding demonstrators," he said.

This brought him in touch with G. Gordon Liddy, who was being considered for a post as general counsel for the Nixon campaign committee. Dean interviewed Liddy and told him one of his responsibilities "would be keeping abreast of the potential demonstrations that might affect the campaign."

The next time Dean met Liddy was at a meeting Jan. 27, 1972 in Mitchell's office, with Magruder also there, when Liddy presented a "mind-boggling" plan for "mugging squads, kidnapping teams, prostitutes to compromise the opposition and electronic surveillance."

Liddy explained: The mugging squad could "rough up demonstrators that were causing problems. The kidnapping teams could remove demonstration leaders and take them below the Mexican border. The prostitutes could be used at the Democratic convention to get information as well as compromise the person involved."

Mitchell told Liddy the plan "was not quite what he had in mind and the cost was out of the question." He suggested that Liddy "go back and revise" it, "keeping in mind that he was not interested in the demonstration problem."

At a second meeting of the same four men Feb. 4, 1972, Dean ended the meeting by interjecting that such discussions could not be held in the attorney general's office. He said he did not know "to this day who kept pushing for these plans." He told Liddy he "would never again discuss this matter with him" and "if any such plan were approved," he "did not want to know."

Dean then informed Haldeman of "what had been presented by Liddy" and "that I felt it was incredible, unnecessary and unwise. I told him that no one at the White House should have anything to do with this. . . . Haldeman agreed and told me I should have no further dealings on the matter."

Dean returned from a Far East trip June 18, 1972 when he was told of the Watergate break-in. Liddy June 19 told him that "Magruder had pushed him into doing it." That afternoon, Ehrlichman instructed Dean "to call Liddy to have him tell Hunt to get out of the country." He did this without thinking, then "realized that no one in the White House should give such an instruction." He checked with special presidential counsel Charles W. Colson and Ehrlichman, who agreed. Liddy was recalled but said he had already passed the message.

Also on June 19, Gordon Strachan told Dean he had been instructed by his superior, Haldeman, to go through the files and "remove and destroy damaging materials." Strachan said the "material included such matters as memoranda from the re-election committee, documents relating to wiretap information from the D.N.C., [Democratic National Committee], notes of meetings with Haldeman, and a document which reflected that Haldeman had instructed Magruder to transfer his intelligence gathering from Senator Muskie to Senator McGovern."

On June 20, 1972, Dean investigated the contents of Hunt's safe, including a briefcase with electronic equipment.

"Among the papers were numerous memoranda to Chuck Colson regarding Hunt's assessment of the plumbers unit, a number of materials relating to Mr. Daniel Ellsberg, a bogus cable, that is other cables spliced together into one cable, regarding the involvement of persons in the Kennedy Administration in the fall of the Diem regime in Vietnam, a memorandum regarding some discussion about the bogus cable with Colson and [writer] William Lambert, some materials relating to an investigation Hunt had conducted for Colson at Chappaquiddick, some materials relating to the Pentagon papers."

Ehrlichman told Dean "to shred the documents and . . . toss the briefcase into the river."

Then acting FBI director L. Patrick Gray told Dean on or about June 21, 1972 that the FBI had checked banking transactions of one of those arrested at the Watergate and had traced checks for $114,000 to a Mexico bank. "The fact that the FBI was investigating these matters was of utmost concern to Mr. [Maurice] Stans when he learned of it."

Mitchell, Ehrlichman and Haldeman thought Dean "should see the FBI reports," and in early July 1972 Dean broached the matter with Gray. Gray wanted assurance that the information would be reported to the President.

Dean assured him, "Even though I was not directly reporting to the President at that time, I was aware of the fact that Ehrlichman or Haldeman had daily discussions with the President, and I felt certain, because Haldeman often made notes, about the information I was bringing to their attention, that this information was being given to the President."

A summary report of the investigation to that stage was sent to Dean sometime after July 21, 1972. Former Assistant Attorney General Robert C. Mardian, who served as a top Nixon campaign official, "clearly thought that Gray was being too vigorous" and he "demanded that I tell Gray to slow down, but I never did so."

Several days later, Mardian proposed "that the CIA could take care of this entire matter if they wished." "Mitchell suggested I explore with Ehrlichman and Haldeman having the White House contact the CIA for assistance. Ehrlichman thought it was a good idea. He told me to call General [Vernon A.] Walters because he was a good friend of the White House and the White House had put him in the [CIA] deputy director position so they could have some influence over the agency."

"When Gen. Walters came to my office I asked him if there was any possible way the CIA could be of assistance in providing support for the individuals involved. Gen. Walters told me that while it could, of course, be done, he told me that he knew the director's feelings about such a matter and the director would only do it on a direct order from the President. He then went on to say that to do anything to compound the situation would be most unwise and that to involve the CIA would only compound the problem because it would require that the President become directly involved. When I reported this to Ehrlichman, he very cynically said that Gen. Walters seems to have forgotten how he got where he is today."

There was a discussion in Mitchell's office June 28, 1972 "of the need for support money in exchange for the silence for the men in jail." But only $70,000 or $80,000 was on hand and "more would be needed." Mitchell asked Dean to get approval from Haldeman and Ehrlichman for Herbert Kalmbach to raise the necessary money. This was done. Mitchell told Dean that the White House, in particular Ehrlichman, should be "anxious to accommodate the needs of these men. He was referring to activities that they had conducted in the past that related to the White House, such as the Ellsberg break-in."

On the day the Watergate indictments were handed down, Sept. 15, 1972, Dean went to Nixon's office, where "the President told me that Bob [Haldeman] had kept him posted on my handling of the Watergate case, told me I had done a good job and he appreciated how difficult a task it had been and the President was pleased that the case had stopped with Liddy."

Dean also recalled "the President telling me to keep a good list of the press

people giving us trouble, because we will make life difficult for them after the election."

"The conversation then turned to the use of the Internal Revenue Service to attack our enemies." Dean said not much use had been made because the White House "didn't have the clout," the IRS was "a rather Democratically oriented bureaucracy and it would be very dangerous to try any such activities. The President seeemed somewhat annoyed and said that the Democratic Administrations had used this tool well and after the election we would get people in these agencies who would be responsive to the White House requirements."

In about late November 1972, after the election was over, Mitchell called and said part of a $350,000 White House fund under Haldeman's aegis would have to be used "to take care of the demands that were being made by Hunt and the others [defendants] for money." Neither Dean nor Haldeman liked the idea of using White House money for that purpose, but no other answer was found and, under the assurance the amount would be returned, some funds were turned over to the campaign committee. Dean thought the amount was "either $40,000 or $70,000."

But the demands "reached the crescendo point once again" shortly before the trial, Mitchell made another request for funds and "Haldeman said send the entire damn bundle to them but make sure that we get a receipt for $350,000."

An attorney for the campaign committee, Paul L. O'Brien, informed Dean "that Hunt was quite upset and wished to plead guilty but before he did so he wanted some assurances from the White House that he would receive executive clemency."

Colson met with Ehrlichman in Dean's presence. He said "he felt it was imperative that Hunt be given some assurances of executive clemency ... Ehrlichman said that he would have to speak with the President. Ehrlichman told Colson that he should not talk with the President about this. On Jan. 4th, I learned from Ehrlichman that he had given Colson an affirmative regarding clemency for Hunt."

Colson later told Dean he thought the matter so important he had discussed it with Nixon himself.

Dean said the President raised the subject with him on two occasions—March 13 and April 15.

At a Feb. 27 meeting, "the President directed that I report directly to him regarding all Watergate matters. He told me that this matter was taking too much time from Haldeman's and Ehrlichman's normal duties, and he also told me that they were principals in the matter, and I, therefore, could be more objective than they."

At a March 1 meeting, Nixon told Dean that "there should be no problem with the fact that I had received the FBI reports [on its Watergate probe]. He said that I was conducting an investigation for him and that it would be perfectly proper for the counsel to the President to have looked at these reports. I did not tell the President that I had not conducted an investigation for him because I assumed he was well aware of this fact and that the so-called Dean investigation was a public relations matter, and that frequently the President made reference in press conferences to things that never had, in fact occurred. I was also aware that often in answering Watergate questions that he had made reference to my report and I did not feel that I could tell the President that he could not use my name."

When Dean and Nixon met March 13, Dean told Nixon about the money demands by the defendants and, after Haldeman came in, that there was no money to pay the demands. Nixon asked Dean "how much it would cost. I told him that I could only make an estimate that it might be as high as a million dollars or more. He told me that that was no problem."

"He then asked me who was demanding this money and I told him it was principally coming from Hunt through his attorney. The President then referred to the fact that Hunt had been promised executive clemency. He said that he had discussed this matter with Ehrlichman and ... expressed some annoyance at the

fact that Colson had also discussed this matter with him."

In reply to a question, Dean told Nixon the payment money "was laundered so it could not be traced" and the deliveries were secret.

Dean told the President March 15 that he had received a new demand for support money from Hunt, through O'Brien, "that he wanted $72,000 for living expenses and $50,000 for attorney's fees and if he did not receive it that week, he would reconsider his options and have a lot to say about the seamy things he had done for Ehrlichman while at the White House." Dean felt he "had about reached the end of the line and was now in a position to deal with the President to end the cover-up."

Dean met with Nixon March 21 and warned him that "a cancer ... on the Presidency" was "growing more deadly every day" and must be "removed" or "the President himself would be killed by it."

Dean said he told the President that he had been told Mitchell had received wiretap information; Haldeman had received such information through Strachan; Kalmbach had been used to raise funds to pay the defendants for their silence on orders from Ehrlichman, Haldeman and Mitchell; Dean had relayed the orders and assisted Magruder in preparing his false story for the grand jury; cash at the White House had been used to pay the defendants; more funds would be required for the cover-up to continue; and Dean "didn't know how to deal" with the blackmail problem.

Dean concluded "by saying that it was going to take continued perjury and continued support of these individuals to perpetuate the cover-up and that I did not believe it was possible to continue it; rather I thought it was time for surgery on the cancer itself and that all those involved must stand up and account for themselves and that the President himself get out in front of this matter. I told the President that I did not believe that all of the seven defendants would maintain their silence forever. In fact, I thought that one or more would very likely break rank.

"After I finished, I realized that I had not really made the President understand because after he asked a few questions, he suggested that it would be an excellent idea if I gave some sort of briefing to the Cabinet and that he was very impressed with my knowledge of the circumstances but he did not seem particularly concerned with their implications."

Dean, Haldeman and Ehrlichman met with Nixon again later March 21, and it then became "quite clear that the cover-up as far as the White House was going to continue."

"I for the first time said in front of the President that I thought that Haldeman, Ehrlichman and Dean were all indictable for obstruction of justice and that was the reason I disagreed with all that was being discussed at that point in time."

Dean told Ehrlichman aide Egil Krogh Jr. March 28 or March 29 that it was very likely the Ervin committee "could stumble into the Ellsberg burglary" because documents at the Justice Department contained pictures left in a camera of Liddy standing in front of the break-in site. He said Ehrlichman wanted him to retrieve the documents and return them to the Central Intelligence Agency (CIA) "where they might be withheld" from Congressional committees probing the CIA but the CIA was "unwilling."

Krogh made a statement that startled Dean into asking him to repeat it. Dean had asked Krogh "if he had received his authorization to proceed with the burglary from Ehrlichman. Krogh responded that no, he did not believe that Ehrlichman had been aware of the incident until shortly after it had occurred: Rather, he had received his orders right out of the 'Oval Office'."

Dean's attorneys informed the prosecutors April 2 that "I was willing to come forward with everything I knew about the case." Dean felt he should tell Haldeman he was going to meet the prosecutors. Haldeman told him he should not.

Dean said he told Mitchell April 9 if he were called he would testify honestly. Mitchell understood "and did not suggest that I do otherwise." But he told Dean he should avoid testifying if at all possible be-cause his testimony "would be very harmful to the President."

Haldeman and Ehrlichman at that time still "talked about pinning the entire matter on Mitchell."

Dean had a meeting with Nixon April 15. As the meeting progressed, Dean realized Nixon was asking him "a number of leading questions, which made me think that the conversation was being taped and that a record was being made to protect himself."

Nixon recalled a previous discussion in which he said there was no problem raising a million dollars to keep the defendants silent. "He said that he had of course, only been joking when he made that comment." Dean became more convinced "that the President was seeking to elicit testimony from me and put his perspective on the record and get me to agree to it."

Nixon had Dean come to his office April 16 and asked him to sign a letter of resignation or an alternative letter of indefinite leave of absence, which had been prepared. Nixon said "he would not do anything with them at this time but thought it would be good if he had them." Dean read the letters, then "looked the President squarely in the eyes and told him that I could not sign the letters. He was annoyed with me, and somewhat at a loss for words. . . . I told him that the letters that he had asked me to sign were virtual confessions of anything regarding the Watergate. I also asked him if Ehrlichman and Haldeman had signed letters of resignations. I recall that he was somewhat surprised at my asking this and he said no they had not but they had given him a verbal assurance to the same effect. I then told him that he had my verbal assurance to the same effect. . . ."

"On April 30th, while out of the city, I had a call from my secretary in which she informed me that . . . my resignation had been requested and accepted and that Haldeman and Ehrlichman were also re-signing."

Dean cross-examined — Committee members and counsel began to cross-examine Dean June 26. Dean then disputed the President's public statements on Watergate as "broad," misleading, unfounded or simply untruthful.

He said an "enemies list" of persons considered unfriendly to the Nixon Administration was maintained and kept updated. And he told of incidents of harassment against some individuals considered unfriendly, incidents utilizing federal services such as the Internal Revenue Service, the Secret Service and the FBI.

The committee's Democratic chief counsel Samuel Dash opened the cross-examination.

Is it not true, Dash asked, that you played a role in the cover-up activities? "That is correct," Dean said. Was it on his own initiative or under orders from someone? "I inherited a situation," Dean said. "The cover-up was in operation when I returned to my office" two days after the Watergate break-in "and it just became the instant way of life at that point in time."

He was "a conveyor of messages" between the White House and the Mitchell committee, Dean testified, and his reporting relationship was directly to Haldeman and to Ehrlichman.

When Nixon complimented him on Sept. 15, 1972 about the good job he had done, did he have any doubt what the President was talking about? "No, I did not," Dean replied. Whatever doubts he may have had prior to Sept. 15, 1972 about the President's involvement in the cover-up, did he have any doubts about this after Sept. 15? "No, I did not."

Dean was confronted June 27-28 with a White House response to his charges in the form of a memorandum and questions submitted to the committee by special presidential counsel J. Fred Buzhardt Jr. The memo, read by Sen. Daniel K. Inouye (D, Hawaii), portrayed Dean as the "mastermind" of the cover-up and Mitchell as his "patron." Buzhardt's charges failed to shake Dean's insistence that he fell into an existing cover-up situation as a conduit between Haldeman and Ehrlichman and the campaign committee.

In a statement released June 28, Buzhardt insisted that the memo "does not represent a White House position" and

had not been reviewed by the President. Its sole purpose, the statement said, was "to facilitate the examination" of Dean by the committee.

The White House statement charged:

It is a matter of record that John Dean knew of and participated in the planning that went into the break-in at Watergate, though the extent of his knowledge of that specific operation or of his approval of the plan ultimately adopted have not yet been established. There is no reason to doubt, however, that John Dean was the principal actor in the Watergate cover-up, and that while other motivations may have played a part, he had a great interest in covering up for himself, pre-June 17th.

. . . It must have been clear to Dean as a lawyer when he heard on June 17 of Watergate that he was in personal difficulty. The Watergate affair was so clearly the outgrowth of the discussion and plans he had been in on that he might well be regarded as a conspirator with regard to them. He must immediately have realized that his patron, Mitchell, would also be involved.

Dean and Mitchell were Magruder's principal contacts on the cover-up. Dean was not merely one of the architects of the cover-up plan. He was also its most active participant. Magruder correctly concluded that Dean 'was involved in all aspects of this cover-up,' and this is from the Magruder testimony.

Dean was perfectly situated to mastermind and to carry out a cover-up since, as counsel to the President and the man in charge for the White House, he had full access to what was happening in the investigation. He sat in on FBI interviews with White House witnesses and received investigative reports.

Dean's activity in the cover-up also made him, perhaps unwittingly, the principal author of the political and constitutional crisis that Watergate now epitomizes. It would have been embarrassing for the President if the true facts had become known shortly after June 17th, but it is the kind of embarrassment that an immensely popular president could easily have weathered. The political problem has been magnified one thousand-fold because the truth is coming to light so belatedly, because of insinuations that the White House was a party to the cover-up, and above all, because the White House was led to say things about Watergate that have since been found untrue. These added consequences were John Dean's doing.

Dean responded to the White House statement frequently, often basing his defense on previously stated testimony that his role within the Administration during the period preceding and following the Watergate break-in was an exponent of reason and caution. While continuing to admit his active role as a participant in the cover-up, Dean repeated his assertions that he served principally as a point of contact for top level White House personnel and re-election committee officials with lesser Nixon aides who actually carried out the cover-up.

He emphasized the essentially mundane

and passive nature of his role in the Watergate affair by telling the committee that, "based on what I know, and knowing the position I held in the White House staff, there is no way conceivable that I could have done and conceived and implemented the plan that they are trying to suggest I did."

'*Political enemies*'—Among documents Dean submitted in evidence June 27 were lists "several inches thick" of Nixon's "political enemies."

The "Opponents List and Political Enemies Project" turned over to the Senate committee, Dean said, was compiled beginning in 1971 by various Administration officials and was frequently updated.

In one of the documents, written by Dean Aug. 16, 1971, intended to accompany the undated master list of opponents, Dean suggested ways in which "we can use the available federal machinery to screw our political enemies." Methods proposed included Administration manipulation of "grant availability, federal contracts, litigation, prosecution, etc."

Dean testified that the memo was sent to Haldeman and Ehrlichman.

Although Dean later recommended that the Administration utilize Internal Revenue Service (IRS) audits to harass political enemies, other documents which were provided to the committee showed that the White House had been unable to win IRS cooperation. An undated memo, submitted by Dean, identified "the problem: Lack of guts and effort. The Republican appointees appear afraid and unwilling to do anything with the IRS that would be politically helpful. For example: We have been unable to crack down on the multitude of tax exempt foundations that feed left-wing political causes. We have been unable to obtain information in the possession of IRS regarding our political enemies. We have been unable to stimulate audits of persons who would be audited. Walters [IRS Commissioner Johnnie M.] should be told that discreet political action and investigations are a firm requirement and responsibility on his part." [See below]

In the August 1971 memo, Dean wrote:

"I feel it is important that we keep our targets limited for several reasons: (1) A low visibility of the project is imperative; (2) It will be easier to accomplish something real if we don't overexpand our efforts; and (3) We can learn more about how to operate such an activity if we start small and build."

The master list of political enemies was prepared by the office of then White House counsel Charles W. Colson, Dean said. A condensed list of 20 prime political enemies slated for reprisals was also produced by Colson's office, according to Dean. Others named by Dean who had direct input in the lists were former White House aide Lyn Nofziger and Haldeman aide Gordon Strachan.

The larger list, divided in categories, included 10 Democratic senators, all 12 black House members, more than 50 newspaper and television reporters, prominent businessmen and labor leaders, and entertainers. Another list included large and small contributors to Sen. Edmund S. Muskie's (D, Me) presidential campaign.

The revelation about an "enemies list" was elicited by Sen. Lowell Weicker (R, Conn.), who questioned Dean primarily about the Administration's establishment of a domestic interagency intelligence operation and the sources of White House intelligence.

During the course of it, Dean said there was "a continual request" in the White House "for information regarding demonstrations and particularly information that would embarrass individuals in connection with their relationship with demonstrators or demonstration leaders." There was an effort, he said, to obtain "politically embarrassing information on individuals who were thought to be the enemies of the White House. There was also maintained what was called an 'enemies list,' which was rather extensive and continually being updated." Weicker asked about these documents, and Dean said he would supply them.

Dean told Weicker of involvement in such activities of several federal agencies. Haldeman once requested, he related, an FBI investigation of CBS newsman Daniel

Schorr. The investigation "proceeded," but, "to the dismay of the White House," it was "sort of a full field wide open investigation and this became very apparent. So this put the White House in a rather scrambling position to explain what had happened. The long and short of the explanation was that Mr. Schorr was being considered for a post and that this was a part of a preliminary investigation."

Another incident involved the Secret Service. An official from there once supplied him with a "small intelligence printout" alleging that Democratic presidential contender George McGovern would attend a fund-raising affair in Philadelphia with some involvement of "either Communist money or former Communist supporters." Dean passed the item to Charles W. Colson, then White House special counsel, who told him later he had arranged to have it published.

Political pressure on IRS confirmed. Former Internal Revenue Service (IRS) Commissioner Randolph W. Thrower revealed a 1970 Administration plan to launch an IRS investigation of radical organizations and individuals in a Washington Post report June 27. Thrower resigned his post in January 1971 after he had successfully resisted White House pressure on him to hire John J. Caulfield, implicated in the Watergate cover-up, and G. Gordon Liddy, convicted Watergate conspirator, to direct the investigations.

Also in December 1970, Thrower said, the White House pressured him to make the bureau's enforcement division "a personal police force" reporting directly to him as part of a crackdown on "subversive organizations allegedly engaged in acts of terrorism." Although he resisted this suggestion, Thrower admitted acquiescing in a White House plan to set up an IRS unit, the Special Service Group, to conduct tax audits on radical groups and individuals. Thrower insisted that both right and left wing extremist groups were investigated.

As other witnesses before the Watergate hearings had testified, Thrower said political conditions in the country, as perceived by the Nixon Administration, justified these special measures.

"You've got to go back to the atmosphere that existed at that time in early 1970. There was great concern in the country about the use of explosives and firearms by subversive groups. [The Special Service Group] was set up partly in response to the wave of subversive bombings that was just reaching its peak then," Thrower declared.

One of the memos submitted June 27 to the Senate Watergate hearings by former White House counsel Dean revealed Administration displeasure with Thrower's efforts to balk the politicization of the IRS. The memo, written by Dean based on "material provided to me by Caulfield," outlined a plan to make "the IRS politically responsive to the White House." Although the memo was written after Thrower had left the IRS, Dean termed Thrower "a total captive of the Democratic assistant commissioners. In the end, he was actively fighting both Treasury and the White House," according to the memo.

"In brief, the lack of key Republican bureaucrats at high levels precludes the initiation of policies which would be proper and politically advantageous. Practically every effort to proceed in sensitive areas is met with resistance, delay and the threat of derogatory exposure," Dean wrote.

A Thrower report, dated Sept. 19, 1970, submitted to the Watergate hearings by Dean, to Tom Charles Huston, a member of the Special Service Group, made the disclosure that data on 1,025 organizations and 4,300 individuals had been completed. "Enforcement action" on 26 groups and 43 persons had resulted, Thrower said.

Dean also revealed that a politically motivated IRS audit of the tax returns of Robert Greene, a Newsday reporter, was requested by Caulfield. Greene had headed a team of reporters investigating President Nixon's friend, Charles G. Rebozo.

2nd 'enemies' list revealed. The Joint Committee on Internal Revenue Taxation said in a report Dec. 20, 1973 that the White House gave the Internal Revenue Service (IRS) in September 1972 a list of 575 persons "to see what type of information could be developed concerning the people on the list." The report was based on testimony from Johnnie Walters, then IRS commissioner, who said he received the list from former White House counsel John W. Dean 3rd as an intermediary for former Nixon aide John D. Ehrlichman.

Walters told the panel he apprised Treasury Secretary George P. Shultz of the matter and was directed to "do nothing" about it. The panel's own investigation concluded that there was "no evidence" that the IRS had acted on the matter and that, in fact, there was evidence some persons on the list should have received closer scrutiny by the IRS.

The list, composed primarily of contributors to Sen. George McGovern's Democratic presidential campaign and of McGovern staffers, was separate from the first White House "enemies" list previously disclosed by Dean to the Senate Watergate committee.

Parallel Developments

Hunt probed Sen. Kennedy. Convicted Watergate conspirator E. Howard Hunt Jr. said June 28, 1973 that he had used equipment supplied to him by the Central Intelligence Agency (CIA) in 1971 to interview an individual he thought might have politically useful information concerning Sen. Edward M. Kennedy (D, Mass.).

Hunt, testifying before the House Armed Services Committee's Subcommittee on Intelligence Operations, said he had informed Charles W. Colson, then an aide to President Nixon, of his need for CIA equipment, and that Colson said he would arrange for it.

Colson, appearing before the committee June 29, denied knowing that Hunt was using CIA material in the Kennedy probe. However, Colson acknowledged contacting presidential domestic affairs adviser John D. Ehrlichman about getting CIA assistance for Hunt. Colson said Ehrlichman later told him, he [Ehrlichman] had contacted the CIA on Hunt's behalf. (Ehrlichman May 30 denied calling the CIA to ask for aid for Hunt.)

Hunt told the House panel, which was investigating the role of the CIA in Watergate affair, that he interviewed Clifton DeMotte in August 1971 to determine if he had any scandalous material relating to Kennedy. DeMotte, a General Services Administration employe in Rhode Island, was the public relations director of the Yachtsman Motor Inn in Hyannisport, Mass. in 1960, when John F. Kennedy used the hotel as his headquarters during the 1960 presidential campaign. Hunt indicated DeMotte hadn't said "anything worthwhile." The Washington Post had reported in February that DeMotte had rejected a request from Hunt that he "do work on Chappaquiddick."

In his interview with DeMotte, Hunt used false identification papers in the name of Edward Warren, as well as a wig, a device to alter his voice and a tape recorder. These devices were supplied by the CIA. Hunt emphasized to the subcommittee that the Kennedy probe prompted his request for the CIA-furnished disguise.

In his testimony, Colson said he had sought CIA help for Hunt after being told by Hunt that he wanted to interview former agency operative Lt. Col. Lucien E. Conien about Pentagon Papers defendant Daniel Ellsberg.

The former special counsel to the President further denied he had ordered Hunt to break into the Milwaukee apartment of Arthur H. Bremer after Bremer shot Alabama Gov. George C. Wallace in May 1972 during a Wallace presidential campaign rally. Colson said President Nixon had immediately ordered the Federal Bureau of Investigation to secure Bremer's apartment, thus eliminating any need for action by Hunt.

More White House probes. Senior White House aides ordered 16 private investigations into the private lives of such individuals as House Speaker Carl Albert (D, Okla.), former Rep. Richard H. Poff (R, Va.), the Smothers brothers comedy team and the producers of the movie

Millhouse, the Washington Post reported Aug. 1.

Among the schemes was one involving the use of a New York City apartment to seduce and subsequently blackmail female friends of Mary Jo Kopechne, who drowned in July 1969 in an accident involving Sen. Edward M. Kennedy (D, Mass.), the Post reported. The apartment was rented in 1971 by Anthony T. Ulasewicz, a secret investigator for the White House. Ulasewicz allegedly hoped to extort from the women details about the party that occurred just before the accident.

Attorney William O. Bittman said July 31 that his client, Watergate conspirator E. Howard Hunt Jr., informed government attorneys in private about what he had been told of the plan, the Post reported. Ulasewicz denied the allegations.

According to the Post, Ulasewicz investigated Albert in 1972 following rumors that Albert had been drunk at the time of an automobile accident in Washington, the Post reported.

Ulasewicz looked into the background of Poff when he was being considered for an appointment to the Supreme Court in 1971, Post sources said.

Tom and Dick Smothers were investigated after their network television program was dropped because of disputes with the network in 1969.

The probe of the producers of Millhouse, an anti-Nixon film, was ordered by White House Chief of Staff H. R. Haldeman, the Post said.

Colson sought IRS aid. Charles W. Colson, then President Nixon's special counsel, directed other White House aides to ask the Internal Revenue Service (IRS) for the names of contributors to the National Council of Senior Citizens, a Washington lobbying group which Colson described as an "outfit giving us trouble," according to a court document filed Aug. 2.

According to Roy Kinsey, a former aide to White House Counsel John W. Dean 3rd, Colson also ordered inquiries into the possibility of withdrawing tax exempt status from two other organizations regarded by the Nixon Administration as "political enemies"—Common Cause and Vietnam Veterans Against the War.

Kinsey's statements were contained in a deposition in connection with a lawsuit brought by the Center for Corporate Responsibility. The center claimed that it had been the target of political reprisals by the IRS, which had denied it tax exempt status.

Colson's instructions to Dean were passed to him, Kinsey said. His contact at the IRS on "sensitive" matters was Roger V. Barth, deputy chief counsel, according to Kinsey.

He was unable to obtain information on the senior citizens group, Kinsey reported. He did not reveal what action was taken against the Vietnam veterans but he said the Common Cause issue was not pursued because the group had obtained only a limited tax exempt status.

IRS to disband activists study unit—The IRS announced Aug. 9 that it was dismantling a special division that had studied liberal and radical organizations for possible violations of tax laws. The group was created in August 1969 as a result of Senate investigations of extremist groups, according to Donald C. Alexander, IRS commissioner.

Testimony before the Senate Watergate committee had linked the IRS unit to planned White House reprisals against political enemies.

Alexander said that since 1972 the IRS unit had been limited to investigations of "tax rebels," which he defined as those "tax-resistance organizations and those individuals who publicly advocate noncompliance with the tax laws."

Rogers scores taps on aides. Secretary of State William P. Rogers was reported to have repudiated the White House-approved wiretapping of three top foreign service officers during a 1969–71 program acknowledged by the Administration as authorized to find and plug security leaks. Acting State Department spokesman Paul J. Hare said Aug. 24 that Rogers had told him he was never informed by the White House about the wiretaps and he "would not have approved them."

Rogers' position was made known in

reference to a New York Times report that three top foreign service officers had been among 13 government officials whose telephones were tapped on the President's authority during the 1969–71 program.

The officers were identified as William H. Sullivan, formerly department liaison to the Paris Vietnam peace talks and currently ambassador to the Philippines; Richard F. Pedersen, formerly the department's counselor and currently ambassador to Hungary; and Richard L. Sneider, formerly on the National Security Council staff and currently deputy assistant secretary of state for East Asian affairs.

Kissinger & wiretaps. Henry A. Kissinger's nomination to succeed Rogers as secretary of state was confirmed by 78–7 Senate vote Sept. 21 after Senate Foreign Relations Committee hearings in which Kissinger's role in the wiretapping of government officials and newsmen* had been a major issue.

Kissinger Sept. 7 had defended the taps as needed to stop leaks to the press. He said he had consented to the practice in 1969 on the advice of then Attorney General John N. Mitchell and the late director of the Federal Bureau of Investigation (FBI), J. Edgar Hoover. He disclaimed deep involvement in the operation and said his office's involvement ended by the summer of 1970. Kissinger urged the committee to deal directly with Attorney General Elliot L. Richardson in further pursuit of the matter. In response to a question, he said "there were cases in which the sources of some leaks were discovered and corrective action taken."

---

*Disclosure of the identities of the 13 government officials and four newsmen subjected to the wiretapping was completed Aug. 31 when the New York Times identified three more officials on the list. They were James W. McLane, then on the White House Domestic Council staff, currently deputy director of the Cost of Living Council; John P. Sears, then deputy White House counsel and a former law partner of President Nixon; and Lt. Gen. Robert E. Pursley, then a colonel and military aide to the defense secretary, currently commander of American forces in Japan. Among those identified previously were Richard Moose, then on the National Security Council, currently a consultant to the Senate Foreign Relations Committee; and William Safire, then a presidential speechwriter, currently a columnist for the New York Times.

Wiretapping report requested—The panel had requested from the Justice Department the FBI report on the wiretap operation. Committee access to the report became a central factor. Committee member Clifford P. Case (R, N.J.) told Kissinger it was "very clear that the committee will not be in the position to act on the nomination until that report has been received." Committee Chairman J. W. Fulbright (D, Ark.) agreed with Case.

Richardson met in closed session with the committee Sept. 10 and provided a memorandum on Kissinger's role in the wiretapping. The panel released the memo, which was based on FBI records. The memo said Kissinger's role "included expressing concern over leaks of sensitive material and when this concern was coupled with that of the President and transmitted to the director of the FBI it led to efforts to stem the leaks, which efforts included some wiretaps of government employes and newsmen." The memo continued, "His role further involved the supplying to the FBI of names of individuals in the government who had access to sensitive information and occasional review of information generated by the program to determine its usefulness."

The committee voted later Sept. 10 14–0 to authorize two of its members, Case and Sen. John J. Sparkman (D, Ala.), to meet with Richardson "to obtain information on Dr. Kissinger's role respecting his initiative, or concurrence in wiretap surveillance."

At the committee's public session later Sept. 10, Kissinger was asked by Sen. Edmund S. Muskie (D, Me.) whether he would continue to approve wiretapping as secretary of state.

"The issue of wiretapping raises the balance between human liberty and the requirements of national security," Kissinger replied, "and I would say that the weight should be on the side of human liberty and that if human liberty is infringed, the demonstration of national security must be overwhelming and that would be my general attitude."

Richardson complied with the committee's action and made the FBI report available to Case and Sparkman Sept. 11. Later, the two senators met with Kissinger and Richardson to discuss it. Sparkman told newsmen there was no data in the report to jeopardize Kissinger's confirmation. Case said the committee's access to the report seemed to remove a major threat to the confirmation.

In a letter requested by Fulbright on the current policy on wiretapping, Richardson said Sept. 12 that wiretaps without court warrant would be used only "in a limited number of cautiously and meticulously reviewed instances" that involved "a genuine national security interest." He listed three criteria to be applied to determine such instances, that the surveillance would be ordered only if it met one of these conditions: "1. To protect the nation against actual or potential attack or other hostile acts of a foreign power; 2. To obtain foreign intelligence information deemed essential to the security of the United States; or 3. To protect national security information against foreign intelligence activities."

Halperin affidavit on wiretap. Morton H. Halperin, a former National Security Council (NSC) official, asserted in a sworn statement released Nov. 27, 1973 that three days after NSC member Henry A. Kissinger had orally agreed to limit Halperin's access to sensitive national security data, Halperin's telephone was tapped as part of a White House effort to stop leaks of such information.

The statement was part of an affidavit given by Halperin in connection with his civil suit against Kissinger and others, whom he held responsible for illegal wiretaps that were placed on him for 21 months beginning in May 1969.

According to his affidavit, Halperin made an arrangement with Kissinger May 9, 1969 that Halperin would continue to advise the NSC, although he would no longer have access to sensitive data. Kissinger had told Halperin that Administration officials suspected Halperin, a Democrat, of leaking information regarding the secret bombing of Cambodia, Halperin testified.

In a brief filed in the suit Sept. 30, the

Justice Department had acknowledged that the tap continued on Halperin nine months after he had ceased to have any connection with the NSC. In April 1970, Halperin became an unsalaried foreign policy adviser to then presidential aspirant Sen. Edmund S. Muskie (D, Me.).

In its brief, the Justice Department admitted that former Attorney General John N. Mitchell failed to renew the authorization for the tap on Halperin every 90 days, although Justice Department rules required it.

In a related development, the New York Times, citing authoritative sources, reported Oct. 15 that a second former NSC official, Anthony Lake, was the object of an Administration wiretap until February, 1971—two months after Lake also became a foreign policy adviser to the Muskie campaign.

Secret Service agent passed data. The Secret Service Aug. 16 announced the resignation of one of its agents, James C. Bolton Jr., who had divulged confidential information about the Presidential campaign of Sen. George McGovern (D, S.D.) that eventually found its way to the White House.

While at a family dinner, Bolton allegedly told his father of a McGovern meeting with a subversive—a later memo showed no such meeting had occurred. Bolton Sr., an assistant to Rep. Glenn R. Davis (R, Wis.), passed the item to the White House.

Bolton Sr. denied he had given any other information to the White House, but a White House memo obtained by the Washington Post said Bolton Jr. had "promised to keep his dad informed" on the McGovern campaign.

The Secret Service said it had determined the incident was an "isolated" one occurring through a family relationship.

McGovern camp spy unmasked. A freelance journalist admitted Aug. 18 she was paid $1,000 a week, plus expenses, by former White House aide Murray M. Chotiner to travel with and spy on the Presidential campaign of Sen. George

McGovern from Labor Day to election day, 1972.

Lucianne C. Goldberg, who said she took the assignment only after Chotiner agreed to let her write a book on her experiences, indicated that she transmitted her intelligence to Washington by telephone under the codename "Chapman's Friend."

Denying that he had asked Goldberg to dig up "dirt" on the McGovern campaign, Chotiner conceded Aug. 20 that he paid her from his own funds and then was reimbursed by the Committee to Re-elect the President.

Freidin preceded Goldberg—Chotiner confirmed Aug. 28 that he had hired journalist Seymour K. Freidin, also at $1,-000 a week, to supply intelligence on Democratic candidates to the Nixon campaign.

Freidin preceded Goldberg as an intelligence source. Freidin quit his job with the Republicans in September 1972 to take a position as chief of the London bureau for the Hearst newspaper group.

Freidin denied he had spied on the Democrats and said he took the job to write a book about his experiences.

Chotiner commented on the use of Goldberg and Freidin: "We didn't get anything we couldn't have gotten in the public press. . . . I guess it was worth the $1,000 just to know the stuff the newspapers were reporting was quite accurate."

Nixon's brother wiretapped. On direct orders from President Nixon, the Secret Service wiretapped the telephone of F. Donald Nixon, the President's brother, the Washington Post reported Sept, 6, 1973.

According to what the Post called "four highly reliable sources," the President feared that Donald Nixon's financial activities could result in embarrassment to the Administration.

One Post source indicated that the President was concerned in part over his brother's "involvement with the financial empire of billionaire Howard Hughes."

A White House spokesman said Sept. 7, "If there was any monitoring of the President's immediate family by the Secret Service, it would have been related to the protective function of the Secret Service."

Mitchell & Others Testify, White House Tapes Revealed

Mitchell feared exposure of 'horror stories.' After a holiday recess, the hearings of the Senate committee investigating Watergate and other campaign irregularities resumed July 10, 1973 with the appearance of former Attorney General John N. Mitchell.

In three days of testimony, Mitchell maintained that Nixon had not been involved in the Watergate break-in scheme or the subsequent cover-up. Mitchell said July 10 that he had withheld information from Nixon to prevent damage to the re-election campaign and the presidency.

He said he was concerned not so much about Nixon's ability to withstand exposure of the Watergate case as the fact that an inquiry might lead to the exposure of other "White House horror stories," such as the break-in at the office of Daniel Ellsberg's psychiatrist, the proposed fire-bombing of the Brookings Institution and the falsification of cables relating to the 1963 death of South Vietnamese President Ngo Dinh Diem.

Mitchell sought, however, to blunt earlier charges of his own involvement in the Watergate affair. He said July 10 that he "had to violently disagree" with the testimony of former campaign aide Jeb Stuart Magruder that Mitchell approved the break-in plan and gave instructions to destroy related documents.

Mitchell also disputed the testimony of former presidential counsel John W. Dean 3rd concerning discussions of payments to the Watergate defendants.

At the July 11 session, Mitchell conceded that he had failed in his obligations to Nixon by not informing him of the ramifications of the Watergate affair, but he also implicated former presidential advisers John D. Ehrlichman and H.R. Haldeman in participating in a "design not to have the stories come out." Mitchell insisted that Nixon had not asked him for a complete account of Watergate.

Sens. Daniel K. Inouye (D, Hawaii) and Howard H. Baker Jr. (R, Tenn.) sought to attack Mitchell's credibility before the committee, pressing him on how far he might go to shield Nixon. Mitchell maintained that he had never needed to fabricate stories about Watergate; he simply withheld information.

Under intense questioning July 12 by the committee's chief counsel, Samuel Dash, Mitchell conceded that some of his testimony during the hearings differed from earlier statements. Mitchell attributed this to memory lapses and the fact that he was not "volunteering" information to earlier Watergate investigators—including the FBI—in the months following the break-in.

Mitchell had told Dash July 10 that he was aware of the 1970 White House plan for a secret intelligence operation, some of it illegal. He had "joined" then FBI Director J. Edgar Hoover in "opposing its implementation," Mitchell said. He had talked to President Nixon and his aide H. R. Haldeman about it, and the plan was reconsidered and dropped. He did not recall receiving any formal notice of its demise; Mitchell said he was 'just told verbally that it was nil." He said he opposed the plan because it dealt with surreptitious entry, mail covers and the like.

Liddy's plans—Mitchell July 10 described the plan presented in his office Jan. 27, 1972 by G. Gordon Liddy, later convicted as a Watergate conspirator, as "a complete horror story that involved a mish-mash of code names and lines of authority, electronic surveillance, the ability to intercept aircraft communications, the call girl bit and all the rest of it." It was "just beyond the pale." His reaction: "I told him to go burn the charts and that this was not what we were interested in. What we were interested in was a matter of information gathering and protection against the demonstrators."

Mitchell contended there were "faulty recollections" about the discussion during the second meeting Feb. 4, 1972 on the Liddy operation. "I violently disagree with Mr. [Jeb Stuart] Magruder's testimony to

the point that the Democratic National Committee was discussed as a target for electronic surveillance for the reasons that he gave, number one with respect to the Democratic kickback story. . . . These targets were not discussed." To the best of Mitchell's recollection, no targets were discussed.

What about previous testimony before the committee that Mitchell himself had volunteered a target, a Las Vegas newspaper office? To the best of his recollection, Mitchell said, "there was no such discussion."

What was the reaction to this plan? "Dean, just like myself, was again aghast" and "was quite strong to the point that these things could not be discussed in the attorney general's office. I have a clear recollection of that and that was one of the bases upon which the meeting was broken up." Mitchell's observation at the meeting was "that this was not going to be accepted. It was entirely out of the concept of what we needed."

Unaware of bugging—Mitchell said he was unaware at the time of the early break-in at the Democratic offices at Watergate in May 1972. He said he did not know of the "Gemstone" file of wiretap information generated from it "until a great deal later," "much after" June 17, 1972, the second break-in date.

Dash asked whether Mitchell recalled Magruder's testimony that he had shown these documents to Mitchell.

A. I recall it very vividly because it happens to be a palpable, damnable lie.

Among other things, he had a White House appointment at the time period he was said to have been shown the files. And he never saw or talked to Liddy from Feb. 4, 1972 until June 15, 1972 so he could not have berated Liddy about the inadequate results of the first break-in, as Magruder also testified.

Mitchell said the June 15 meeting with Liddy involved a letter being sent to a newspaper about campaign financing charges.

Mitchell related "there was considerable concern" about the June 17 break-in when he learned about it while he was in California. The name of James L.

McCord Jr., the campaign committee security aide, "had surfaced" and "obviously, there was an involvement" in the campaign committee.

When Mitchell talked with Nixon June 20, 1972, shortly after the break-in, "I apologized to him for not knowing what the hell had happened and I should have kept a stronger hand on what the people in the committee were doing."

Mitchell on 'horror stories'—After the break-in, Mitchell testified, Liddy was debriefed and Mitchell learned for the first time of what he repeatedly referred afterwards to as "the White House horrors"— the surveillance of McGovern headquarters, the "plumbers" group and Liddy's extensive activity while at the White House in connection with "the Ellsberg matter . . . and a few of the other little gems."

Other items cited by Mitchell as "horror stories" were a false cable purporting to link President Kennedy to the death of South Vietnamese President Ngo Dinh Diem, the proposal to firebomb the Brookings Institution and what he termed other "extracurricular" eavesdropping.

There was a Watergate discussion at his Washington apartment June 19, 1972, but he was unaware at that time of the Gemstone file and nobody at the meeting "knew of the wiretapping aspects" or had any connection with that. He did not recall any discussion at that time of destruction of documents, either.

Did he become aware during that June and July of Magruder's involvement in the break-in? He was aware that Magruder had provided the money, and the focus seemed to be at that time on how much money had been given Liddy.

Mitchell said Magruder was shifting his story and, facing grand jury testimony, was asked to put his statement in writing. "It got to the point where I had a very, very strong suspicion as to what the involvement was," Mitchell said, but he did not know at the time Magruder's story was not a true one. He learned later, "sometime" before Magruder went to the grand jury.

Prior to Magruder's third appearance before the grand jury, Magruder, Dean and Mitchell met, not primarily to discuss the question of how to handle Magruder's testimony, but to discuss "what the recollection was" of the planning meeting and "what could be said about it to limit the impact."

Q. And you were aware, then, in December that he would testify not completely, if not falsely, concerning the meetings on Jan. 27 and Feb. 4?

A. Well, that is generally correct. As I say again, this is something that Dean and I were listening to, as to his story as to how he was going to present it.

Q. Well, wasn't it the result of your effort or program to keep the lid on? You were interested in the grand jury not getting the full story. Isn't that true?

A. Maybe we can get the record straight so you won't have to ask me after each of these questions: Yes, we wanted to keep the lid on. We were not volunteering anything.

Mitchell said he became aware "in the fall sometime" that payments were being made to the defendants. He also learned of the involvement in the payoffs of Nixon's personal lawyer, Herbert W. Kalmbach, and Mitchell's aide Frederick C. LaRue.

Dash explored Mitchell's opinion about Nixon's awareness of the Watergate events and aftermath.

Did he believe the President was aware of the events prior to or after the break-in, the actual bugging or the cover-up?

A. I am not aware of it and I have every reason to believe, because of my discussions and encounters with him up through the 22nd of March, I have very strong opinions that he was not.

Asked to explain, Mitchell said of Nixon, "I think I know the individual, I know his reactions to things, and I have a very strong feeling that during the period of time in which I was in association with him . . . that I just do not believe that he had that information or had that knowledge; otherwise, I think the type of conversations we had would have brought it out."

Had he told Nixon what he discovered from Liddy's debriefing? "No, sir. I did not." Why not?

A. Because I did not believe that it was appropriate for him to have that type of

knowledge, because I knew the actions that he would take and it would be most detrimental to his political campaign.

Q. Could it have been actually helpful or healthy, do you think?

A. That was not my opinion at the particular time. He was not involved; it wasn't a question of deceiving the public as far as Richard Nixon was concerned, and it was the other people that were involved in connection with these activities, both in the White House horrors and the Watergate.

Money for the defendants—Mitchell told the committee that sometime in the fall of 1972 one of the Watergate defendants, E. Howard Hunt Jr., called White House aide Charles W. Colson to demand money. Mitchell heard in March about oral communications from Hunt or his attorney "relating to requests for legal fees and so forth, which were communicated to the White House." Mitchell said his informant was probably LaRue, who told him "in this context: I have got this request, I have talked to John Dean over at the White House, they are not in the money business any more, what would you do if you were in my shoes and knowing that he had made prior payments? I said, if I were you, I would continue and I would make the payment."

Eventually, the source of the funds being paid to the defendants ran out, and Mitchell suggested seeing if the $350,000 fund "sitting" in the White House since April "was available for the purpose."

On the subject of executive clemency, Mitchell thought the only conversations he had on that had to do with Colson and Hunt, that in early 1973 Hunt approached Colson about it and Colson's word "was the only word" Hunt would take on the clemency, "whatever that meant."

Mitchell had "never promised" executive clemency to anybody. "Obviously, there is no basis upon which I could." When Magruder came to see him in March, he told him "I thought he was a very outstanding young man and I liked and I worked with him and to the extent that I could help him in any conceivable way, I would be delighted to do so."

"And this was exactly the same conversation that we had the next day down

at Haldeman's office," Mitchell added. Haldeman made no promises to Magruder "other than the fact to help him as a friend."

Moore disputes Dean's testimony. Richard A. Moore, a special counsel to the President, followed former Attorney General John N. Mitchell to the Senate committee's witness table July 12.

Called at the request of Leonard Garment, counsel to the President, Moore read a 20-page statement centering on his "deep conviction that the critical facts about Watergate did not reach the President" until White House counsel John W. Dean 3rd supplied them March 21.

According to Moore, Dean had met with Haldeman, Ehrlichman and Moore Feb. 11 and said "he had been told by the lawyers [for the Watergate defendants] that they may be needing some more money and did we have any ideas?" When Mitchell's name was mentioned, Moore, a former aide to Mitchell, was asked to enlist his help. Moore said that Mitchell turned him down Feb. 15; "I believe he said something like, 'Tell them to get lost.' "

Moore said, "Mr. Dean has testified we left the meeting together and that . . . he cautioned me against conveying this fund-raising request when I saw Mr. Mitchell. I have absolutely no recollection of any such conversation and I am convinced it never took place."

A series of meetings, attended only by Nixon, Dean and Moore, were held March 15, 19 and 20 to discuss executive privilege, Moore said. Another meeting had occurred March 14, with presidential press secretary Ronald L. Ziegler present. "At no time during this meeting [March 14] or during succeeding meetings . . . did anyone say anything in my presence which related to or suggested the existence of any cover-up or any knowledge of involvement by anyone in the White House, then or now, in the Watergate affair," Moore stated.

In the interval between the March 19–20 meetings, Moore said Dean told him that convicted Watergate conspirator E.

Howard Hunt Jr. was threatening to "say things that would be very serious for the White House" if he were not given a large sum of money. Moore said this was blackmail and he urged Dean to have nothing to do with it.

Moore related that Dean had told him earlier of being present at the two meetings in which Watergate conspirator G. Gordon Liddy had presented intelligence plans that were rejected.

"This," Moore said, "brings me to the afternoon of March 20, when Mr. Dean and I met with the President in the Oval Office. . . . As I sat through the meeting . . . . I came to the conclusion in my own mind that the President could not be aware of the things that Dean was worried about or had been hinting at to me, let alone [Watergate defendant] Howard Hunt's blackmail demand. Indeed, as the President talked about getting the whole story out— as he had done repeatedly in the recent meetings—it seemed crystal clear to me that he knew of nothing that was inconsistent with the previously stated conclusion that the White House was uninvolved in the Watergate affair, before or after the event.

"As we closed the door of the Oval Office and turned into the hall, I decided to raise the issue directly with Mr. Dean. I said that I had the feeling that the President had no knowledge of the things that were worrying Dean. I asked Dean whether he had ever told the President about them. Dean replied that he had not, and I asked whether anyone else had. Dean said he didn't think so."

That evening Moore received a call from Dean, who said he had arranged a private meeting the next day with the President. Meeting Moore after seeing the President, Dean said he had told Nixon "everything." "I asked if the President had been surprised and he said yes," Moore testified.

White House taping system revealed. The existence of a recording system installed to secretly tape President Nixon's White House conversations was revealed July 16 at the continued Watergate hearings of the Select Senate Committee. The commit-

tee then received a letter in which J. Fred Buzhardt Jr., special counsel to President Nixon, wrote to confirm that "the President's meetings and conversations in the White House" had been recorded. Buzhardt asserted that "this system, which is still in use, is similar to that employed by the last Administration and which had been discontinued from 1969 until the spring of 1971."

Joseph A. Califano Jr., one of the late Lyndon B. Johnson's top advisers, called the Buzhardt statement "an outrageous smear" and asserted there "was absolutely no secret wiring in the place" during the Johnson Administration. Califano said there had been open recordings of some cabinet meetings. He also noted that Johnson had occasionally told his secretary to make notes of telephone conversations while listening on an extension.

A Secret Service spokesman acknowledged July 16 that the agency had installed Nixon's recording system but said the agency had never done similar work for any other administration.

The Associated Press reported July 18, however, that the Nixon Administration had obtained affidavits from two former Johnson aides alleging the installation of manually-operated, hidden recording devices in several of Johnson's offices.

The director of the John F. Kennedy Library in Waltham, Mass. said July 17 that the library had 193 dictaphone belts and tapes of telephone conversations and meetings involving Kennedy. Dan H. Fenn Jr., the library director, said a "cursory check" showed the tapes dealt with "highly sensitive foreign policy and national defense matters." Fenn did not say whether the tapes had been made secretly.

The General Services Administration, which operated the Dwight D. Eisenhower Library in Abilene, Kan., said July 17 that there were stenographic transcriptions of presidential conversations in the library. On some transcriptions, the agency said, it was clear all parties knew the conversation was being recorded; on others it was not.

The existence of the Nixon White House's

recording system was revealed at the committee's televised hearings by Alexander P. Butterfield, a former presidential aide then serving as administrator of the Federal Aviation Administration. Butterfield said that the system automatically recorded the President's meetings and telephone conversations in his offices in the White House and the adjacent Executive Office Building for "historical purposes." He said that the President's conversations with dismissed White House counsel John W. Dean 3rd and other persons involved in the Watergate case would have been recorded by the system routinely.

According to committee sources July 16, staff members uncovered the story of the secret recordings almost by accident July 13 while privately questioning Butterfield. Donald G. Sanders, the assistant minority counsel, said that Butterfield was asked, "out of the blue," about Dean's testimony June 25 that he suspected Nixon was recording one of their meetings. Butterfield then described the recording system, which he and Secret Service agents had maintained. He was summoned to testify July 16 on three hours' notice and appeared without benefit of counsel.

Butterfield's testimony made it clear that the President's conversations with key figures in the Watergate affair, including the meetings described by John Dean in his appearance before the committee, would have been routinely recorded by the system.

Butterfield, who had served as a deputy assistant to the President from the beginning of Nixon's first term until March 14, said that the secret recording system had been installed to make tapes for "historical purposes" and had been in operation since the summer of 1970. Butterfield said that the system's existence was known only to himself, his immediate superior, H. R. Haldeman, Lawrence M. Higby of Haldeman's staff, the President and the Secret Service, which maintained the system. (After being informed that presidential counsel J. Fred Buzhardt Jr. had confirmed to the committee the system's existence since spring 1971, Butterfield said he accepted that date.)

Butterfield described the operation of a White House network of "presidential locator boxes," which, in following Nixon's movements, "triggered" recording devices in the Oval Office in the White House and in Nixon's office in the Executive Office Building (EOB). The recorders in these offices were automatically activated by the sound of a voice when the locators indicated that the President was in the room. A manually-operated recorder was concealed in the White House Cabinet room.

There also were tape devices on four of Nixon's telephones: in the two offices, the Lincoln Room of the White House and in Nixon's private quarters at Camp David, Md.

Butterfield was questioned by minority counsel Fred D. Thompson:

Q. So far as the Oval Office and the EOB Office is concerned, would it be your testimony that the device would pick up any and all conversations no matter where the conversations took place in the room and no matter how soft the conversations might have been?

A. Yes, sir.

The tapes were stored and periodically checked by the Secret Service, Butterfield said. He was responsible for seeing that the system remained in working order.

"Were any of these tapes ever transcribed as far as you know?"

A. To my recollection, no.

Q. To your knowledge, did the President ever ask while he was in the Oval Office to have the system not operate, the locator light not show in that office so as to trigger the device?

A. No sir. As matter of fact, the President seemed to be totally, really oblivious, or certainly uninhibited by this fact. . . .

Q. And so that if either Mr. Dean, Mr. Haldeman, Mr. Ehrlichman, or Mr. Colson had particular meetings in the Oval Office with the President on any particular dates that have been testified before this committee, there would be a tape recording with the President of that full conversation, would there not?

A. Yes sir.

Responding to questions by Sen. Herman E. Talmadge (D, Ga.), Butterfield said none of Nixon's visitors were informed that their conversations were being taped. Nor were there audible signals to indicate telephone taping.

Kalmbach on use of funds. Herbert W. Kalmbach, Nixon's former personal attorney and political fund raiser, testified before the committee July 16–17. Kalmbach detailed how he had raised and channeled $220,000 to the original seven defendants in the Watergate break-in. He said he had been acting on orders from John Dean and John D. Ehrlichman, then a top Nixon adviser. But Kalmbach insisted he had thought the funds were "humanitarian" and only for the defendants' legal fees and family support.

Kalmbach testified that Ehrlichman had stressed the payoffs must be kept secret to prevent "misinterpretation" of White House motives in paying the Watergate defendants.

In his statement, Kalmbach denied having any prior knowledge of the Watergate break-in or of participating in a conspiracy to cover-up the burglary or other acts of campaign sabotage.

Throughout the day's questioning, Kalmbach maintained that by collecting payoff money for the Watergate defendants, he was discharging a "moral obligation" to raise funds for their legal defense and family support. "The fact that I had been directed to undertake these actions by the Number 2 and Number 3 men on the White House staff [Ehrlichman and Dean] made it absolutely incomprehensible to me that my actions in this regard could have been regarded in any way as improper or unethical," he said.

He described the transfer of $350,000 in cash from the finance committee to the White House in the "last week of March or very early in April." The request was made by Haldeman's aide Lawrence Higby.

Kalmbach testified that on June 28, 1972 Dean made an urgent request for a meeting in Washington to discuss raising $50,000–$100,000 "for the legal defense of these [Watergate] defendants and for the support of their families." Kalmbach said he and Dean met June 29, 1972 in Lafayette Park, across from the White House. According to Kalmbach, he urged Dean to establish a public committee for the purpose of raising the funds.

Dean rejected the idea, Kalmbach said, because a "public committee might be misinterpreted." According to Dean, the project required "absolute secrecy" in order not to jeopardize Nixon's re-election chances. Anthony T. Ulasewicz, identified in previous testimony as the White House contact with convicted Watergate conspirator James W. McCord Jr., should distribute the money Kalmbach collected, Dean told him.

Kalmbach testified that his meetings and conversations with Ulasewicz were secretive, utilizing codewords and clandestine meetings in hotel rooms and cars to exchange money. According to Kalmbach, Mrs. E. Howard Hunt Jr., wife of one of the convicted Watergate conspirators, received the money from Ulasewicz. A total of $220,000 was collected for payoff purposes.

Kalmbach said his doubts about the project prompted him to request a meeting with Ehrlichman. Kalmbach recalled the meeting July 26, 1972 in Ehrlichman's office:

"I said, John, I want you to tell me, and you know, I can remember it very vividly because I looked at him, and I said, John, I am looking right into your eyes. I said, I know that my family and my reputation mean everything to me, and it is just absolutely necessary, John, that you tell me, first, that John Dean has the authority to direct me in this assignment, that it is a proper assignment and that I am to go forward on it.

"He said, Herb, John Dean does have the authority. It is proper, and you are to go forward.

"Now, he said, in commenting on the secrecy, . . . this . . . could get into the press and be misinterpreted. And then I remember he used the figure of speech, he said, they would have our heads in their laps, which again would indicate to me that it would jeopardize the campaign."

In mid-August 1972, Kalmbach was asked to collect more money for the Watergate defendants but he refused to comply with the request because "this whole degree of concern had come back to me to the level that I knew that I did not want to participate any longer in this assignment." The fund raising request was repeated at a meeting Jan. 19, 1973 in Mitchell's Washington office, with Mitchell, Dean and LaRue present. Kalmbach said he again rejected the bid.

Kalmbach conceded in his testimony July 17 that he now realized his fund raising efforts for Watergate defendants represented an "improper, illegal act."

In retrospect, Kalmbach told the committee, he felt "used" by Nixon's chief aides: Haldeman, Ehrlichman, Mitchell and Dean. "It is just as if I have been kicked in the stomach," he said.

Kalmbach's role as paymaster for the cover-up attempt was examined in detail. Senators Montoya and Weicker appeared incredulous that Kalmbach would risk his legal career to act as an accomplice in silencing the Watergate defendants.

Kalmbach cited his "implicit trust" in Dean and Ehrlichman as justification for his actions. "It is incomprehensible to me, and was at that time, I just didn't think about it that these men would ask me to do an illegal act," he said.

Sen. Talmadge tried to establish that Kalmbach undertook the assignment because "the President himself might have approved it," but Kalmbach rejected that explanation.

Despite his belief that Dean "was standing, really standing in the shoes of the President" when discussing Nixon's legal affairs with Kalmbach and his law partner, Kalmbach refused to concede that Dean issued the cover-up orders with similar presidential authority.

What was there about the "nature of the White House or the presidency or the aura that surrounds it" that would cause Kalmbach to have such enormous faith and trust in the propriety of the cover-up requests, Sen. Baker inquired.

Kalmbach replied, "It was a composite of all those factors"—reverence for the institution of the presidency, personal friendship for Nixon and long acquaintanceship with Dean. It never occurred to him to talk to Nixon about his doubts, Kalmbach testified, because he knew that

Ehrlichman, and Dean "had the absolute trust" of Nixon.

Kalmbach testified about the transcript of a recorded phone conversation between Ehrlichman and Kalmbach, taped by Ehrlichman without Kalmbach's knowledge on April 19—one day before Kalmbach's scheduled appearance before the federal grand jury investigating the Watergate scandal.

Kalmbach characterized the taping by Ehrlichman as "self-serving," adding again he felt that "it was just as if I had been kicked in the stomach."

According to the transcript, Ehrlichman told Kalmbach that Dean, who was "cooperating with the U.S. attorney in the hopes of getting immunity," was "throwing off on Bob [Haldeman] and me [Ehrlichman] heavily."

Sen. Ervin advanced the proposition, and Kalmbach agreed, that Ehrlichman's taping of this "conversation represented an effort on his part to advance the theory that John Dean should be made a scapegoat and sent out into some wilderness, legal wilderness, bearing the full responsibility for any impropriety or unethical aspects of the disuse of the money."

(On April 19 Dean had told reporters that he was not going to be made the "scapegoat" for the Watergate cover-up.)

In the transcript, Kalmbach said he had phoned Ehrlichman to express concern "that there is a massive campaign underway to indict all the lawyers . . . and I was a little shocked and I guess what I need to get from you, John, is assurance that this is not true."

Ehrlichman told him, "I would never knowingly have put you in any kind of spot." Ehrlichman said he knew of no attempt to "target" Kalmbach, but added that through Dean, the prosecutors were "trying to get at me."

During the conversation, Ehrlichman appeared to be laying the groundwork for a cover story that would protect himself, and secondarily, Kalmbach. Dean was "taking the position [with federal investigators] that he was a mere agent," Ehrlichman said. He told Kalmbach that "as far as propriety [of the coverup project] is concerned, I think we both were relying entirely on Dean."

Ehrlichman warned Kalmbach, according to the transcript, "They'll ask you to whom you've spoken about your testimony and I would appreciate it if you would say you've talked to me in California because at that time I was investigating this thing for the President."

Kalmbach agreed with Ervin that the inference in this request was that Kalmbach not reveal to the prosecutors anything about the phone conversation.

Ulasewicz tells of payoffs. Anthony T. Ulasewicz July 18 offered testimony complementing that of Herbert Kalmbach. Ulasewicz described how he clandestinely disbursed $219,000—sometimes unsuccessfully—to Watergate conspirator G. Gordon Liddy; Dorothy Hunt, the late wife of conspirator E. Howard Hunt Jr.; Hunt himself; lawyers for the conspirators; and Frederick C. LaRue, former campaign strategist for Nixon.

Under examination by the committee's assistant majority counsel, Terry Lenzner, Ulasewicz related the details of a June 30, 1972 meeting he had with Kalmbach in a Washington hotel room. Ulasewicz, assured by Kalmbach on the question of legality, agreed to provide funds to the lawyers of the Watergate defendants and "payment to assist their families during some troublesome period." Kalmbach insisted on confidentiality, ordering Ulasewicz to use pay phones for communication and the name Novak as an alias, or Rivers if the need arose.

His first contact, M. Douglas Caddy, the original attorney for the five men caught in the Watergate, failed to keep an afternoon rendezvous in a Washington restaurant. A call by Caddy to the waiting Ulasewicz revealed that the lawyer preferred a meeting at his law office; Ulasewicz, instructed not to negotiate, demurred and said he would call back. A call to Kalmbach resulted in instructions to drop the "Caddy business."

Ulasewicz next called Paul L. O'Brien, attorney for the Committee to Re-elect the President. O'Brien, too, "showed no interest in any script, players or any type of message I would give," Ulasewicz said.

Ulasewicz finally met success when William O. Bittman, attorney for Hunt, agreed to accept an advance legal fee of $25,000.

Another recipient of funds from Ulasewicz was Dorothy Hunt, killed in a plane crash Dec. 8, 1972. On three separate occasions—the last Sept. 19, 1972—Mrs. Hunt picked up a locker key taped to the underside of a phone in Washington's National Airport, allowing her to collect a total of $136,500; in a like manner her husband accepted another $18,000.

Ulasewicz testified that Mrs. Hunt was his main contact to channel funds to the Watergate defendants. He said that each time he talked to her, she increased her demands. In the end, Ulasewicz calculated she wanted $450,000.

In a series of phone conversations in July, 1972, Mrs. Hunt suggested $3,000 per month per person for the main Watergate defendants—her husband, Liddy, and James W. McCord Jr. Moreover, she requested the payments in multiple amounts so as to avoid monthly meetings. She asked a total of $23,000 for conspirator Bernard L. Barker, as well as smaller sums for the other three Watergate defendants: Eugenio R. Martinez $2,000, Frank A. Sturgis $4,000 and Virgilio R. Gonzalez $2,000. For attorneys' fees, Mrs. Hunt requested $105,000, including $25,000 for Bittman.

Ulasewicz testified that he made two other payments. In July 1972 he left $8,000 in a National Airport locker for Liddy. Two months later he gave LaRue an envelope containing $29,900.

Ulasewicz said Mrs. Hunt's demands caused him concern over the role he was playing and eventually led to his resignation. He said he had told Kalmbach, at a California meeting in August 1972, that "something here is not kosher" and then informed Kalmbach of his plans to quit.

LaRue testifies. Frederick LaRue testified July 18. While much of his testimony concerned payments he made as part of the Watergate cover-up, LaRue also offered a third version of the March 30, 1972 meeting at which former Attorney General John Mitchell was alleged to have approved a $250,000 intelligence plan against the Democrats.

According to LaRue, Mitchell neither approved the bugging plan, as former deputy campaign director Jeb Stuart Magruder had testified June 14, nor flatly rejected the project, as Mitchell himself had claimed. LaRue recalled that Mitchell said of the plan, "Well, this is not something that will have to be decided at this meeting."

The bulk of LaRue's testimony, which extended to July 19, related to $230,000 he had distributed after Ulasewicz quit. LaRue indicated that he had funnelled $210,000 to William O. Bittman, attorney for E. Howard Hunt Jr. LaRue testified he used the code name "Baker" to contact Bittman and then dispatched messengers to the lawyer's home or office with bundles of bills totaling $25,000 in Sept. 1972, $50,000 in Dec. 1972, $60,000 in Jan., and $75,000 in March.

LaRue said he also sent $20,000 to Peter Maroulis, Liddy's attorney.

LaRue said he had obtained the funds from a secret $350,000 kitty of surplus 1968 campaign funds kept in the White House.

LaRue further testified that before he made the final payment of $75,000 to Bittman, he became concerned over his own criminal liability. He said he had voiced his apprehension to Mitchell and asked if he should make the payment. Informed by LaRue the money was for legal fees, Mitchell counseled him to make the payment, LaRue said.

LaRue further testified that Mitchell advised Magruder to burn documents relating to the Watergate bugging scheme.

Mardian denies any role in cover-up. Robert C. Mardian, a former assistant attorney general and official of the Committee to Re-Elect the President, testified July 19. Mardian disputed earlier witnesses, denying he played an illegal role in trying to conceal the events surrounding the Watergate case.

In his opening statement, Mardian said that immediately after the Watergate burglars' arrests June 17, 1972, in the Democratic National Committee's head-

quarters, he was relieved of his political duties at the re-election committee and was named the committee's attorney on matters related to the Watergate case. He cited this role at several points as his justification—under the canon of attorney-client confidentiality—for not revealing the information he gained as the scandal unfolded.

Questioned by James Hamilton, an assistant committee counsel, Mardian related how, after the arrests, he was asked by Jeb Stuart Magruder, then the re-election committee's deputy director, to help with the "slight problem" of the arrested burglars.

Hamilton asked if Magruder had described events leading to the break-in:

Q. Did Mr. Magruder inform you who had approved the budget for dirty tricks . . . ?

A. Yes.

Q. Whom did he say?

A. He told me that the budget had been approved by Mitchell.

Q. Did Mr. Mitchell later that afternoon confirm that he had approved such a budget?

A. I would like to put it this way: It is my best recollection that I think the subject was discussed and he didn't deny it. And again, it may have come up when Mr. Mitchell wasn't in the room. I want to be fair on that point.

Hamilton pressed Mardian on the meetings held in the few days after the break-in. Mardian replied, describing a June 21, 1972 interview of conspirator G. Gordon Liddy at LaRue's apartment.

Liddy, who had been portrayed to Mardian as "some kind of nut," entered the apartment, turned on a radio and asked LaRue and Mardian to sit beside it—so that "this conversation can't be recorded," as Mardian quoted Liddy. Liddy then told of the break-in and assured LaRue and Mardian there was no need to worry because the job had been done by "real pros" who would divulge nothing. Mardian said he told Liddy "his best bet was to give himself up," but Liddy rejected the suggestion.

According to Mardian, Liddy told the details of his involvement in other operations by the White House "plumbers" unit—the burglary of the office of Daniel Ellsberg's psychiatrist and the removal of Dita Beard, a lobbyist for International Telephone & Telegraph Corp., to a Denver hospital to keep her away from Congressional investigators.

Mardian said he asked Liddy on whose authority he carried out the burglary of Ellsberg's psychiatrist, and, Mardian said, ". . . I don't know that he used the name of the President, but the words he did use were clearly meant to imply that he was acting on the express authority of the President of the United States, with the assistance of the Central Intelligence Agency."

Mardian testified that former presidential counsel John Dean had been "dead wrong" in telling the Ervin committee that Mardian had access to confidential FBI files on the Watergate investigation and had tried to involve the CIA in the cover-up.

Mardian also denied participating in discussions of Magruder's plans to maintain the cover-up by giving perjured testimony to the Watergate grand jury.

Under questioning by Sen. Lowell P. Weicker Jr., Mardian testified July 20 that in 1971 Nixon had personally asked him to transfer from FBI files to John D. Ehrlichman the logs of wiretaps authorized by the White House on National Security Council employes and newsmen.

The logs, found May 11 in a safe in Ehrlichman's office, included one of Ellsberg's conversations. A White House spokesman had said May 15 that Nixon had not known the logs were in Ehrlichman's safe.

Mardian acknowledged that while he was director of the Justice Department's Internal Security Division (from November 1970 to May 1972) there was an "extreme concern" in the Administration over news leaks, but he said his division "never ordered a single wiretap." Mardian rejected Weicker's suggestion that the division had been used "to stifle political dissent."

On another matter, Mardian denied the testimony of convicted Watergate conspirator James W. McCord Jr. that Mardian had furnished McCord with

confidential Justice Department files suggesting that information on anti-Republican activist groups might be found in the Democratic Party's Watergate headquarters.

Strachan says Haldeman knew of spy plan. Gordon C. Strachan, 29, an aide to White House chief of staff H. R. Haldeman, testified under a grant of immunity from the committee July 20. In his opening statement, Strachan declared that much of the information he would disclose "is politically embarassing to me and the Administration," adding that he was told little about the Watergate break-in by the people "at the White House . . . who have confessed to criminal wrongdoing."

Strachan, who served as liaison between the White House and the Committee to Re-elect the President, said he had told Haldeman two months before the Watergate break-in about a "sophisticated political intelligence gathering system" set up by the re-election committee. Strachan said he had destroyed documents that might link the burglars to the White House. Strachan also said he was the courier who transmitted $350,000 in White House "polling" funds to others who used the money to pay off the Watergate defendants.

Strachan testified that neither Haldeman nor John Dean had informed him of "the series of meetings with Mr. Mitchell, Dean, Liddy and Magruder" in which the Watergate operation was discussed. Strachan said that after the March 30, 1972 meeting at Key Biscayne, Magruder had called him and reported on "about 30 major campaign decisions" that included "a sophisticated political intelligence gathering system [that] has been approved with a budget of 300 [$300,000]." Strachan said that soon after the conversation, he wrote a "political matters" memo for Haldeman that included the matter along with a sample of a political intelligence report, entitled "Sedan Chair II," dealing with the Pennsylvania campaign organization of Sen. Hubert Humphrey (D, Minn.).

Strachan described a meeting with Haldeman on June 19 or 20, two or three days after the break-in, during which he showed Haldeman the political matters memo. Strachan said that "after speaking to [Haldeman], I destroyed that memo and Sedan Chair II, as well as several other documents I have told this committee and prosecutors about. I also told Mr. Dean that I had destroyed [the memo] . . . and three confidential source memos which I said could possibly have been wiretap reports."

Strachan's statement placed major responsibility for the Watergate operation on Jeb Magruder. Strachan disputed Magruder's testimony that Strachan had been informed of the three meetings in early 1972 at which the intelligence schemes were discussed. Strachan also said that John Dean, and not he, had been responsible for keeping Haldeman informed of political intelligence matters.

Strachan rejected Magruder's testimony that he "automatically sent all memos, including Watergate documents, to Strachan." In his testimony, Strachan told the committee that, although Magruder was supposed to report to Haldeman through him, he "frequently tried to avoid the reporting system" by giving a "full report" directly to Haldeman or to his aide, Lawrence M. Higby.

Describing his role in turning over $350,-000 in White House funds to Fred LaRue after the election, money subsequently paid to the Watergate defendants, Strachan said that he "was not told by anyone, nor did I know what use was being made of this money." He said that he "became more than a little suspicious" when he delivered about $10,000 to LaRue who "donned a pair of gloves" before touching the money, "and then said, 'I never saw you'."

Strachan said in his testimony of July 23 that Haldeman had told him three days after the Watergate break-in to "make sure our files are clean."

In response to a question by majority counsel Samuel Dash, Strachan said "I believe I was following his orders" in destroying the papers. Strachan testified that he had no doubt that the papers showed Haldeman had knowledge of the intelligence plan. Among the papers

shredded were the memo Strachan had sent to Haldeman describing the Liddy plan and its budget and a "talking paper" Haldeman had used in an April 1972 meeting with John Mitchell that mentioned the plan.

Strachan said he believed Haldeman was aware of Liddy's intelligence activities before the break-in because Haldeman had told him in April 1972 "to contact Mr. Liddy and tell him to transfer whatever capability he had from Muskie to McGovern with particular interest in discovering what the connection between McGovern and Sen. [Edward] Kennedy was." Strachan told the committee that Haldeman had held a series of meetings with John Mitchell in 1971-72 to discuss intelligence gathering. He testified that Haldeman had proposed putting a "24-hour tail" on Sen. Kennedy because he was "particularly interested in the area of political intelligence and information" on the Senator.

In response to interrogation, Strachan said that Magruder did not report to him about the Feb. 4 meeting, as he had testified. Strachan denied that Magruder had showed him the Gemstone papers—transcripts of the wiretap at the Democratic National Committee headquarters. Strachan also testified that Magruder had unsuccessfully attempted to persuade him to commit perjury before the Watergate grand jury.

Ehrlichman & Haldeman Defend Themselves & Nixon

Ehrlichman defends actions. One of the two men closest to President Nixon, John D. Ehrlichman, until April 30 Nixon's assistant for domestic affairs, appeared before the Select Senate Committee July 24, 1973.

In testimony that was described as confident and aggressive and at times quarrelsome, Ehrlichman defended every aspect of his and the President's actions before, during and after the Watergate break-in and wiretapping. Declaring that his testimony would "refute every charge of illegal conduct on my part, he singled out former White House counsel John Dean as the principal source of information implicating him and the President in the case and he rejected it as false.

He challenged Dean's contention that the Watergate issue was a major preoccupation of the Nixon Administration during the three months following the June 17 break-in. Under questioning, Ehrlichman explained his role in the Labor Day 1971 burglary of the office of Daniel Ellsberg's psychiatrist and in the events surrounding it. Despite the committee's disbelief, Ehrlichman insisted that the President had statutory authority to order the break-in in the name of national security.

Ehrlichman's 30-page opening statement began with a rejection of charges by Dean that the White House was neurotic in its fear of demonstrators. He said that events of 1969–70—described as bombings of public buildings, radicals' harassment of political candidates, violent street demonstrations that endangered life and property—had to be taken as "more than a garden variety exercise of the 1st Amendment." The President felt that these events affected his ability to conduct foreign policy and he gave them "balanced attention along with other events and factors."

Ehrlichman was forceful in his denial that Watergate was the main interest of the White House in the period June 17–Sept. 15, 1972. "I do not suggest that we were all just too busy to have noticed. We did notice and we kept informed through John Dean and other sources on the assumption that he was giving us complete and accurate information," he stated. "A chain of delegation" of authority was "only as strong as its weakest link," Ehrlichman added with reference to Dean.

Countering Dean's statement that the White House was engaged by the events of the campaign, Ehrlichman said, "in 1972 with the foreign situation as it was, the President decided quite early that he simply could not and would not involve himself in the day-to-day details of the presidential primaries, the convention and the campaign. He made a very deliberate

effort to detach himself from the day-to-day strategic and tactical problems."

"In 1972, the President had to delegate most of his political role and it went to people not otherwise burdened with governmental duties. As a result, I personally saw very little of the campaign activity during the spring and early summer of 1972."

Ehrlichman rejected Dean's contention that he and Haldeman blocked access to the President. Dean, like others, had only to submit a memorandum to get the President's attention, Ehrlichman testified.

Ehrlichman admitted discussing the Watergate affair with Dean, but he said this was only to keep posted on campaign issues. He said he devoted only half of 1% of his time to the campaign and Watergate.

Ehrlichman's interrogation began with questioning by Samuel Dash on the 1971 break-in at the office of Ellsberg's psychiatrist.

After being assured by Ehrlichman that he played no role in the stillborn 1970 interagency intelligence plan, Dash asked if he had been requested to develop a White House capability for intelligence gathering. Ehrlichman responded that Egil Krogh Jr., a White House aide, had been ordered to form a special unit, and he was designated as the person Krogh should see in connection with the unit.

Q. So there came a time when you were administering an investigative unit?

A. Yes. In a literal sense, that is true.

Ehrlichman recalled how the special unit became operational in 1971. A copy of the Pentagon Papers had been turned over to the Soviet Embassy in Washington. According to then-Assistant Attorney General Mardian's report to the President, the theft was the work of a conspiracy, some of whose members had ties to domestic Communist activities.

Soon afterward, Krogh came to him, Ehrlichman said, with the complaint that the FBI was not pressing its investigation into the matter. Ehrlichman said a call to Attorney General Mitchell revealed that FBI Director J. Edgar Hoover was blocking the investigation because of friendship with Ellsberg's father-in-law, Louis Marx.*

"So it was this set of facts, and the real strong feeling of the President that there was a legitimate and vital national security aspect to this, that it was decided, first on Mr. Krogh's recommendation, with my concurrence, that the two men in this special unit who had had considerable investigative experience, be assigned to follow up on the then leads." (The two men were E. Howard Hunt Jr. and G. Gordon Liddy; the special unit was the group later known as the White House "plumbers.")

Ehrlichman said the break-in at the psychiatrist's office "was totally unanticipated. Unauthorized by me."

Dash then read part of an August 11, 1971 memorandum from Krogh and David R. Young Jr., his associate in the unit, to Ehrlichman which referred to a planned meeting with a CIA psychiatrist who was doing a personality profile of Ellsberg: "In this connection," the memo said, "we would recommend that a covert operation be undertaken to examine all the medical files still held by Ellsberg's psychoanalyst covering the two year period in which he was undergoing analysis." At the bottom, Dash pointed out, was Ehrlichman's approval and a short note in his handwriting, "If done under your assurance that it is not traceable."

Under probing by Dash, Ehrlichman argued that "covert" as used in the memo meant a "covered operation" in which the investigators were not to identify themselves as being from the White House. Ehrlichman denied he had agreed to a break-in and added "there are a lot of perfectly legal ways that medical information is leaked."

Noting the trip made to Los Angeles by Liddy and Hunt to study the feasibility of a covert operation to obtain Ellsberg's

*Ellsberg July 25 denied that Marx had been a friend of Hoover's. He said that Marx, a wealthy industrialist, had been interviewed by the FBI in 1971. This assertion was also in conflict with Ehrlichman's testimony. W. Mark Felt, former associate director of the FBI, said July 27 that the bureau's investigation of Ellsberg in 1971 was "extensive and exhaustive." At no time, Felt said, did the White House tell the FBI it was dissatisfied with the probe.

medical records, Dash then asked Ehrlichman:

Q. Well, those who read it [the memo] undertook to also interpret what you thought you were approving. Did Mr. Young and Mr. Krogh call you while you were in Cape Cod after Mr. Hunt and Mr. Liddy came back, and tell you that they had established that it was feasible that they could get access and that you said, "Okay, go ahead and let them do it. . . ."

A. I don't recall any business calls while I was up there at all.

Q. Would you be surprised if I told you that Mr. Young would so testify?

A. Yes, I would.

Dash asked Ehrlichman if it would have been embarrassing if it had been revealed that the same two men who were connected to the Watergate break-in had been linked to the Los Angeles burglary. Ehrlichman's response was that Liddy and Hunt would never have revealed the Ellsberg burglary.

Ehrlichman strongly disagreed with John Mitchell's view, as cited by Dash, that revelation to the President of the Ellsberg break-in and other "White House horrors"—Mitchell's epithet for Liddy's activities—would have forced Nixon to pursue publicly the matters and that this might have cost him the presidency in 1972. Ehrlichman replied, with reference to the Ellsberg break-in, that the President had been protected by the fact that it involved national security.

". . . At that time, I considered the special unit's activities to be well within the President's inherent constitutional powers, and this particular episode, the break-in in California, likewise to have been within the President's inherent constitutional powers as spelled out in 18 U.S. Code 2511. . . .

"I think if it is clearly understood that the President has the constitutional power to prevent the betrayal of national security secrets, as I understood he does, and that is well understood by the American people, and an episode like that is seen in that context, there shouldn't be any problem. . . .

"In point of fact, on the first occasion when I did discuss this with the President, which was in March of this year, he expressed essentially the view that I have just stated, that this was an important, a vital national security inquiry, and that he considered it to be well within the constitutional, both obligation and function of the presidency."

Sen. Ervin asked whether the Committee to Re-elect the President were such an "eleemosynary institution" that it would give the Watergate defendants $450,000 simply because it felt sorry for them. When Ehrlichman pointed out that black militant Angela Davis and Pentagon Paper trial defendant Ellsberg had had defense funds, Ervin responded that these were public funds, publicly subscribed.

Ervin asked Ehrlichman if the contributors to radical defense funds believed in the causes involved. A "yes" from Ehrlichman brought from Ervin, "Well, certainly, the Committee to Re-elect the President and the White House aides like yourself did not believe in the cause of burglars and wiretappers, did you?" Ehrlichman said no, adding he hadn't "contributed a nickel."

Referring to Ehrlichman's claim that U.S. Code Section 2511 Title 18 was legal justification for the break-in at Ellsberg's psychiatrist's office, Ervin said the statute provided the President with the power to do anything necessary to protect the country against potential attacks or hostile acts of a hostile power, but he denied it sanctioned the break-in. Ervin said he failed to see how Ellsberg's psychiatrist was a threat to the U.S. He asserted that the CIA "had no business" doing a profile on Ellsberg because it was prohibited from engaging in domestic intelligence.

Ehrlichman: I think that basically you have to take this in context. We had here an unknown quantity in terms of a conspiracy. We had an overt act in the turning over of these secret documents to the Russian embassy, and moreover we have a technique here in the development of a psychiatric profile which apparently, in the opinion of the experts, is so valuable that the CIA maintains an entire psychiatric section for that purpose.

Now, putting those all together, I submit that certainly there is in 2511

ample constitutional recognition of the President's inherent constitutional powers to form a foundation for what I said to this committee.

Ervin: Well, Mr. Ehrlichman, the Constitution specifies the President's powers to me in the 4th Amendment. It says: "The right of the people to be secure in their persons, houses, papers, and effects, against unreasonable searches and seizures, shall not be violated, and no warrant shall issue, but upon probable abuse, supported by oath or affirmation, and particularly describing the place to be searched and the person or things to be seized."

Nowhere in this does it say the President has the right to suspend the 4th Amendment.

Ehrlichman: No, I think the Supreme Court has said the search or seizure or whatever it is has to be reasonable and they have said that a national security undertaking can be reasonable and can very nicely comply with the 4th Amendment.

But, Mr. Chairman, the Congress in 1968 has said this: Nothing contained in this chapter or in Section 605 of the Communications Act and so forth, "shall limit the constitutional power of the President to take such measures as he deems necessary to protect the nation against," and then it goes on, "to protect national security information against foreign intelligence activities."

Now, that is precisely what the President was undertaking. . . .

Ervin: Yes, I have studied that statute. I have committed that statute. And there is not a syllable in there that says the President can suspend the 4th Amendment or authorize burglary. It has no reference to burglary. It has reference only or interception and disclosure of—interception of wire or oral communications.

Under questioning by minority counsel Fred Thompson, Ehrlichman partially contradicted testimony given by Herbert W. Kalmbach. Ehrlichman denied he had told Kalmbach July 26, 1972 that payments to the Watergate defendants were legal and proper.

Ehrlichman reiterated his denial that

he had sought CIA aid for E. Howard Hunt Jr. He denied any part in asking the CIA to formulate an excuse to block FBI investigation of financial links between the Watergate conspirators and the Committee to Re-elect the President.

Asked later about his having taped his July 26 conversation with Kalmbach, Ehrlichman replied that this was no different than having his secretary listen in on another line and take it down in shorthand.

Ervin & Wilson debate extent of surveillance powers—Before resuming the questioning of Ehrlichman July 25, Sen. Ervin and the witness's attorney, John J. Wilson, engaged in a colloquy about the President's power to authorize illegal acts, among them burglary, in the name of national security.

Wilson cited a 1972 ruling in which the Supreme Court unanimously held that the government could not conduct electronic surveillance of domestic radicals without first obtaining a court order. He acknowledged that under this ruling, limits had been set regarding domestic surveillance, but he argued that the court had purposely not ruled on government surveillance powers with respect to foreign subversion.

Wilson quoted Justice Lewis F. Powell's opinion: ". . . this case involves only the domestic aspects of national security. We have not addressed and express no opinion as to the issues which may be involved with respect to the activities of foreign powers or their agents."

Moreover, Wilson pointed out, Powell argued that the Constitution (Article 2, Section 4) gave the President a source of power in his oath of office. We note "that the President . . . has the fundamental duty under Article 2 Section 1 of the Constitution 'to preserve, protect and defend the Constitution of the United States.' Implicit in that duty is the power to protect our government against those who would subvert or overthrow it by unlawful means," Powell wrote.

Wilson further contended that Section 2511 Title 18 U.S. Code indicated that there existed "a reservoir of power . . . for the purpose of permitting the Presi-

dent . . . to protect the nation against foreign intelligence and for the purpose of obtaining foreign intelligence." He added that Ervin had issued no dissent when the Judiciary Committee had reported 2511.

Ervin said he recalled the paragraph and he added: "they put that in there because there was a controversy between some members of the committee having an opinion that the President almost has powers that would make an Eastern potentate turn green with envy."

Ervin did not question the interpretation of the Supreme Court ruling; he told Wilson he differed on the facts. Ervin said he failed to see how the psychiatric records of Daniel Ellsberg were related to foreign subversion.

Ervin cited the 1952 Supreme Court decision that voided President Truman's seizure of the steel industry, a case in which Wilson had successfully represented the industry.

"Now, I think your steel case, which I think is one of the remarkable cases, they held in that case, and I am sure largely on the basis of a very persuasive argument that you made, that the President, even though the U.S. was engaged in war in Korea and needed steel in order that the men fighting that war might have weapons and munitions, and even though industrial disputes were about to close down the source of that steel, namely, the steel plants, they held that the President of the U.S. did not have any inherent power under the Constitution to seize steel mills for the purpose of securing a flow of munitions and weapons to American soldiers locked in battle with a foreign force.

"If the President does not have any inherent power under the Constitution to seize steel mills in order that he might carry on a war and furnish the weapons and munitions that will enable the soldiers to fight and prevent the destruction of themselves at the hands of the enemy, I think that is authority that he has no inherent power to steal a document from a psychiatrist's office in time of peace."

Wilson replied that the case did not apply to the burglary of the psychiatrist's office. Regardless, Wilson said, the decision was superseded by 2511.

Wilson concluded by reading what the Judiciary Committee had said on national security:

"It is obvious that whatever means are necessary should and must be taken to protect the national security interest. Wiretapping and electronic surveillance techniques are proper means for the acquisition of counter-intelligence against the hostile action of foreign powers. Nothing in the proposed legislation seeks to disturb the power of the President to act in this area. Limitations that may be deemed proper in the field of domestic affairs of a nation become artificial when international relations and internal security are at stake."

The interrogation of Ehrlichman resumed with Sen. Herman Talmadge (D, Ga.) asking the witness at what point he thought there were limits on the President's power. When Ehrlichman said he did not know, Talmadge asked,

"Do you remember when we were in law school we studied a famous principle of law that came from England and also is well known in this country, that no matter how humble a man's cottage is that even the King of England cannot enter without his consent?"

Ehrlichman replied, "I am afraid that has been considerably eroded over the years, has it not?"

Asked by Talmadge if the President could authorize a murder, Ehrlichman replied that he did not know.

Talmadge elicited from Ehrlichman that the President had not "in express terms" authorized the break-in at Ellsberg's psychiatrist's office. The President had told Egil Krogh, at the time he chartered the special unit, that he wanted Krogh to take whatever steps were necessary to perform his assignment, Ehrlichman testified.

Ehrlichman asserted that the break-in had occurred more than 60 days after the Pentagon Papers had been published in the press because FBI Director Hoover had declined to fully cooperate in the investigation of Ellsberg. Ehrlichman added that the White House feared the documents acquired by the Soviets were not the same as those printed by the newspapers.

Ehrlichman denies clemency offer—Sen. Edward J. Gurney (R, Fla.) turned the questioning to the allegation that the Watergate defendants had been offered executive clemency to secure their silence about others connected with the case. Gurney asked: had Ehrlichman, as John Dean testified, told Charles Colson Jan. 3 that he had checked with the President and he could assure attorney William O. Bittman that his client, E. Howard Hunt Jr., would receive clemency?

Ehrlichman denied the allegation. He said he had been told by the President in July 1972 that it was a closed subject "and we must never get near it, and that it would be the surest way of having the actions of these [Watergate] burglars imputed to the President." All Colson told Bittman, Ehrlichman claimed, was that he had not forgotten his [Colson's] friendship with Hunt. Ehrlichman said he felt Dean had concocted this story as a cover for his own offer of executive clemency to Watergate burglar James W. McCord Jr.

Under further questioning by Gurney, Ehrlichman challenged Dean's testimony that Ehrlichman ordered him to throw into the Potomac River politically sensitive documents found in Hunt's White House safe. Ehrlichman noted that he had helped arrange the opening of Hunt's safe in the presence of witnesses and it "would have been folly for me at some time later . . . to suggest that the briefcase be thrown into the flood tide of the Potomac." Ehrlichman said that if he wished, the documents could easily have been put in a burn bag, sealed, and thrown in the White House furnace.

Ehrlichman similarly took issue with a statement made by former Acting FBI Director L. Patrick Gray 3rd. Gray had told government investigators that at a June 28, 1972 meeting with Ehrlichman and Dean, Ehrlichman had told him the Hunt documents should "never see the light of day." Consequently he burned them, Gray said.

Ehrlichman contended that before the meeting Dean had suggested splitting the Hunt documents into two parcels: one for the FBI's Washington field office, the other, containing politically sensitive papers, for Gray. (Ehrlichman and Dean feared news leaks from the FBI field office.) At the June 28, 1972 meeting, Dean handed Gray the parcel, and Ehrlichman warned it was to be kept secret, Ehrlichman testified.

Not only had he not ordered Gray to destroy the documents, Ehrlichman testified, but he was "nonplussed" when informed of their destruction.

In a phone conversation April 15, Gray told Ehrlichman of his intention to deny that Dean had given him the documents, Ehrlichman claimed. Ehrlichman said he called Gray back to make clear that if asked he would have no choice but to say that he had been present when Dean gave Gray the documents.

Sen. Daniel Inouye's (D, Hawaii) interrogation dealt mainly with the propriety of the offer of appointment as FBI director made by Ehrlichman April 5 to the judge presiding at Ellsberg's trial, William M. Byrne Jr. Ehrlichman told Inouye that he had been quite willing to delay their discussion, but Byrne had failed to see why the Ellsberg case was an obstacle to it. Ehrlichman said he met Byrne twice and nothing improper was said. The second meeting had come at the request of Byrne, Ehrlichman said. Ehrlichman denied the offer was an effort to compromise Byrne. It was an effort to find the best man for the FBI job, he argued.[*]

Why had Ehrlichman not told Byrne of the burglary of Ellsberg's psychiatrist's office? Inouye asked. Ehrlichman replied: he was enjoined from doing so for reasons of national security, and it was properly the province of the attorney general.

Ehrlichman said that contrary to John Mitchell's testimony, he had briefed the

former attorney general in 1971 on the activities of the plumbers.

Dispute about Hoover—Sen. Weicker July 25 expressed doubt about Ehrlichman's contention that J. Edgar Hoover's refusal of cooperation with the White House in the Ellsberg matter was the primary reason for creation of the plumbers unit. Weicker read into the record a letter written by Hoover to Krogh Aug. 3, 1971. The letter told of the FBI's efforts to gather information relating to the Pentagon Papers and its readiness to pursue the inquiry.

Ehrlichman responded that the letter was a "bureaucratic device" to give the appearance of action on the part of the FBI.

Weicker asked Ehrlichman July 26 whether he was aware of the fact that the FBI had interviewed Louis Marx in June 1971. Ehrlichman replied, 'no,' and requested a copy of the FBI report on the interview. However, the committee was unable to produce the data because Attorneys General Richard Kleindienst and Elliot Richardson had restricted its access to raw FBI files.

Ehrlichman maintained that the intervention of the plumbers in the Ellsberg matter was justified because the FBI investigation was marked by "lassitude," a fact borne out, he said, by the Bureau's waiting 60–90 days to designate the case "class A" priority.

Weicker, in doubt about the motive for the plumber's investigation of Ellsberg, read into the record part of an Aug. 26, 1971 memo from Krogh to Ehrlichman: "It is important to point out that with the recent article on Ellsberg's lawyer, [Leonard B.] Boudin, we have already started on a negative press image for Ellsberg. If the present Hunt/Liddy project number 1 is successful, it will be absolutely essential to have an over-all game plan developed for its use in conjunction with the congressional investigation. In this connection, I believe that the point of [White House aide Patrick J.] Buchanan's memorandum on attacking Ellsberg through the press should be borne in mind; namely, that the situation being attacked is too big to be undermined by planted leaks among the friendly press."

---

[*]Judge Byrne July 26 gave his own version of the two meetings he had held with Ehrlichman about a White House offer to name him as FBI director. Byrne told newsmen that he had had no foreknowledge of the offer. He only knew the meeting did not concern the Pentagon Papers trial itself. Byrne said he had informed Ehrlichman April 5 that he "could not consider such a proposal but would reflect upon the matter." The second meeting occurred, he said, because he felt he owed a representative of the President the courtesy of a face to face meeting, although his answer would be "no."

Ehrlichman denied there was any intent to "persecute" Ellsberg. Rather, the White House wanted to air the matter once the facts were known and hoped a Congressional committee would call witnesses and expose how such "treachery" could happen in the government, he said.

Ehrlichman testified July 26 that the plumbers had undertaken in 1971 a mission so important to the nation's security that it justified Nixon's efforts to kept the plumbers' existence secret. He said he was under White House orders not to disclose the mission, but added he would be willing to discuss the matter privately with the committee if he received White House approval. The committee would have to pledge absolute secrecy, Ehrlichman said.

Sen. Ervin assailed Ehrlichman for statements he felt denigrated J. Edgar Hoover. Ervin asserted that at the time Tom Charles Huston was promoting his partially illegal 1970 interagency intelligence plan, Hoover was encouraging Ervin in his fight against government incursions on civil liberties. Ervin read a letter from the FBI director in 1970 that praised Ervin as "one of the guardians of our liberties and promoters of our freedom. All Americans owe you [Ervin] a debt of gratitude."

Ehrlichman reiterated he had been ordered by the President, through Haldeman, to seek assurances from the CIA that an FBI investigation of Nixon campaign funds found in the possession of the Watergate burglars would not impinge on CIA operations in Mexico. Ehrlichman insisted Nixon had given Acting FBI Director Gray authority to determine the scope of the Bureau's investigation.

Ervin expressed skepticism that the President had in the summer of 1972 sought a vigorous inquiry into the Watergate scandal. Ehrlichman replied that Dean and Kleindienst told the President that the "most vigorous" FBI investigation since the assassination of John F. Kennedy had shown that the break-in had been perpetrated only by the seven men already implicated.

In later questioning by Sen. Gurney, Ehrlichman stated he had felt in August 1972 that the President could "take the shock" of the disclosure that campaign officials had been involved in the bugging.

However, his proposal to "lay out the whole story" was rejected at a meeting that month, attended by John Mitchell, Charles Colson, then-campaign director Clark MacGregor, and former White House official Bryce N. Harlow. Thus, on the basis of information given him, Nixon made his Aug. 29, 1972 statement that no one at the White House was involved in Watergate, Ehrlichman stated.

Under questioning by Sen. Joseph M. Montoya (D, N.M.), Ehrlichman denied that 915 White House requests for tax checks by the Internal Revenue System in 1972 had been for any other purpose than to insure that potential appointees did not have income tax problems.

Conflicting testimony—Ehrlichman testified July 27 that Nixon had not received a thorough report on Watergate until April 14.

Ehrlichman's sworn testimony was at variance with the official White House account and with testimony of ousted White House counsel John W. Dean 3rd. Those versions indicated that Dean March 21 gave the President "his theory of what happened" in the Watergate affair. White House special counsel Richard A. Moore had corroborated the White House and Dean in this respect July 12.

Ehrlichman's testimony also conflicted with Dean concerning a Feb. 27 meeting Dean had with the President, in which Nixon ordered Dean to assume full responsibility for matters relating to Watergate.

According to Ehrlichman, who was being interrogated by Sen. Gurney, the President at the Feb. 27 meeting told him and Haldeman that they were to divorce themselves from Watergate. Nixon, Ehrlichman testified, wanted them to "press on" entirely different projects. In their stead Nixon ordered Dean to concentrate on executive privilege, the Senate Watergate committee, the Watergate grand jury and collateral questions.

Asked by Gurney why Nixon Feb. 27 had referred to him and Haldeman as "principals" in the Watergate matter, Ehrlichman replied that Nixon meant principals in question of the availability of presidential assistants to testify before

Congress. Nixon feared that if Haldeman and Ehrlichman appeared before Congressional panels, his foreign affairs adviser Henry A. Kissinger would be next. The net result would be a breakdown in the White House staff system, since everyone, such as Cabinet secretaries, would be testifying each day and unable to find time for work, Ehrlichman said.

Asserting that nothing important transpired in the ensuing three weeks, Ehrlichman then gave his own story of the events of March 21. Ehrlichman denied that Dean that afternoon reported to him or Haldeman what he had revealed in his morning meeting with Nixon. Ehrlichman's version held that Dean in the afternoon had focused on the "question of testimonial availability of White House staff people."

According to Ehrlichman, Dean advanced a theory that the President should obtain from the attorney general blanket immunity for the entire White House staff, thus allowing the staff to testify freely. Dean explained that immunity was the kind of "lubricant" needed to clear the air, Ehrlichman said.

Ehrlichman said he told Dean he was wrong on two counts: wrongdoers ought to be subject to penalties and the move "would just be terribly misunderstood by the American people."

At the request of the President, another meeting was called for the next day, with former Attorney General John N. Mitchell also in attendance. Mitchell was invited because his views on executive privilege were at considerable variance with the White House staff, Ehrlichman said.

Like the previous one, Ehrlichman said, this meeting centered on executive privilege. It ended when the President told Dean to go to Camp David, Md. to formulate a complete statement on the matter.

Under further questioning by Gurney, Ehrlichman said he was brought into the Watergate matter by the President March 30, when Nixon concluded that Dean was so heavily involved that he could no longer have anything to do with it.

In an April 5 interview with Paul O'Brien, an attorney for the Committee to Re-elect the President, Ehrlichman said he first learned of Watergate conspirator G. Gordon Liddy's plans against the Democrats. Among the information Ehrlichman claimed to have gleaned in the O'Brien interview:

■ Deputy Nixon campaign director Jeb Stuart Magruder named Mitchell as the person who approved plans to bug the Democratic National Committee headquarters.

■ Watergate conspirator E. Howard Hunt Jr. supervised undercover agents planted in the headquarters of Democratic Presidential contenders.

■ A Magruder statement to O'Brien that "the President wants this project [the bugging] to go on" was based on a statement White House aide Gordon C. Strachan allegedly made to Haldeman, his superior.

■ The President's former personal lawyer Herbert W. Kalmbach arranged a $70,000 blackmail payment to Hunt through Hunt's attorney, William O. Bittman.

When he had finished his own investigation, Ehrlichman said, he brought what he had learned to the President April 14–15. The President immediately instructed him to contact the attorney general, which Ehrlichman said he did.

In other testimony, Ehrlichman alluded to an April 8 meeting he and Haldeman had with Dean. While Dean said neither was indictable, each would have an awkward time explaining his connection with money that ended in the hands of the Watergate defendants, Ehrlichman testified.

Ehrlichman also suggested that the Watergate cover-up was intended to mask the role played by Mitchell in the intelligence plan that culminated in the Watergate burglary. He said Haldeman had asked if it were possible "we are taking all this anguish just to protect John Mitchell?" Ehrlichman denied that he and Haldeman tried to set up Mitchell to take the blame for Watergate.

Use of 'political dirt'—Ehrlichman and Sen. Weicker debated the White House's use of Anthony T. Ulasewicz to dig up "political dirt" on opponents.

Ehrlichman: "I think that each candidate who contests the candidacy of an incumbent has the obligation to come forward and contest the fitness of that incumbent for office both in terms of his voting record and in terms of his probity, and in terms of his morals, if you please, and any other facts that is important or germane to the voters of his district or state or the country, for that matter. I think a candidate for office assumes that burden of proof. He assumes the burden of proof of showing the unfitness of the incumbent and I don't think in our political system that is limited to his voting record or his absenteeism. If it were, we would countenance the perpetuation of scoundrels in office who were thieves or who were fraudulent or who were profligate or who were otherwise unfit for office, so I think it's perfectly competent for a challenger to meet head-on the issue of the fitness of an incumbent."

Weicker; "Do you mean to tell me and this committee that you consider private investigators going into sexual habits, drinking habits, domestic problems and personal social activities as a proper subject for investigation during the course of a political campaign?"

Ehrlichman: "Senator, I know of my own knowledge of incumbents in office who are not discharging their obligation to their constituents because of their drinking habits, and it distresses me very much, and there is a kind of an unwritten law in the media that it is not discussed, and so the constituents at home have no way of knowing that you can go over here in the gallery and watch a member totter onto the floor in a condition which, of at least partial inebriation, which would preclude him from making any sort of a sober judgment on the issues that confront this country."

Ehrlichman testified July 30 that in the period September 1972 to the end of March 1973, Nixon asked one or another of his aides eight times to prepare a definitive statement on Watergate, but none was ever written. Ehrlichman said he was not asked to prepare a statement.

Asked why he had not told Nixon about the burglary of Daniel Ellsberg's psychiatrist's office, Ehrlichman replied, "There was nothing the President could do about

it. I just made the judgment it would unnecessarily tax his attention."

Haldeman presents defense. H(arry) R(obbins) Haldeman, the other of the two men closest to President Nixon and until April 30 the President's chief of staff, testified before the Select Senate Committee beginning July 30, 1973.

He read an opening statement containing a vigorous defense of the President and a general denial of their guilt in the Watergate affair. In addition to the declaration of innocence, his statement contained a startling admission that on two occasions and at Nixon's request, Haldeman had listened to tapes of two controversial meetings between the President and John Dean. (Haldeman had been present during all of one meeting and part of another. Dean had based his testimony that the President was involved in the Watergate cover-up on recollections of those meetings held Sept. 15, 1972 and March 21, 1973.)

A refutation of Dean's charges was at the heart of Haldeman's defense. He denied that he or the President had "knowledge of or involvement in" either the Watergate break-in or the subsequent cover-up.

He declared they were unaware of the cover-up attempt until March 1973, when the President "intensified his personal investigation into the facts of the Watergate."

Haldeman said:

The question is asked: "How could the President not have known?" Very easily. Reverse the question. How could the President have known?

Only if he were directly involved himself or if he were told by someone who was either directly involved or had knowledge. The fact is that the President was not directly involved himself and he was not told by anyone until March, when he intensified his own investigation. Even then, he was given conflicting and unverified reports that made it impossible to determine the precise truth regarding Watergate or the cover-up and, at the outset at least, he was relying primarily on one man, John Dean, who has admitted that he was a major participant in the illegal and improper cover-up, a fact unknown to the President until March 1973.

"There is absolutely no question in my mind," Haldeman said, "that John Dean was in fact conducting an investigation for the White House regarding the Watergate as it might involve the White House."

Dean "apparently did not keep us [Ehrlichman and Haldeman] fully posted and it now appears he did not keep us accurately posted," Haldeman declared. "As it now appears, we were badly misled by one or more of the principals and even more so by our own man [Dean], for reasons which are still not completely clear."

Haldeman's version of the post-break-in events closely resembled Ehrlichman's. Both insisted that they and the President had been too busy with other matters to investigate the Watergate affair.

"The view of all three of us through the whole period was that the truth must be told, and quickly; although we did not know what the truth was. Every time we pushed for action in this direction we were told by Dean that it could not be done," he testified.

Haldeman denied he had ordered Dean "to cover up anything," although he admitted it was "obvious that some people at the [re-election] committee were involved."

He admitted there had been a White House effort during the 1972 election year "to contain the Watergate case in several perfectly legal and proper aspects."

One effort was made "to avoid the Watergate investigation possibly going beyond the facts of the Watergate affair itself and into national security activities totally unrelated to Watergate." Haldeman cited discussions with Central Intelligence Agency officials June 23, 1972 as part of this effort to limit the Watergate probe.

We discussed the White House concern regarding possible disclosure of non-Watergate-related covert CIA operations or other nonrelated national security activities that had been undertaken previously by some of the Watergate participants, and we requested Deputy Director [Vernon A.] Walters to meet with Director Gray of the FBI to express these concerns and to coordinate with the FBI so that the FBI's area of investigation of the Watergate participants not be expanded into unrelated matters which could lead to disclosures of earlier national security or CIA activities.

Other steps were taken to "reduce adverse political and publicity fallout" arising from the many lawsuits and investigations related to the actual Watergate break-in. There was a third concern about "distortion or fabrication of facts in the heat of a political campaign that would unjustly condemn the innocent or prevent discovery of the guilty."

Haldeman insisted that underlying this "containment effort" and "counterattack" strategy was a "concurrent effort" to obtain facts about the Watergate and make that information public.

Payoff money—Haldeman testified he did not recall authorizing Dean to have Herbert Kalmbach raise money for the Watergate defendants. (Like Kalmbach and Ehrlichman, Haldeman insisted that the money was intended for the defendants' legal fees and family support.) All his information about the fund came from Dean and John Mitchell, according to Haldeman.

Haldeman echoed a theme familiar in past Senate testimony about the payoff money: "The rest of us relied on Dean and all thought that what was being done was legal and proper." They remained convinced of that, Haldeman said, until March 1973 when Dean said the payoff money could prove to be a "political embarrassment."

Denial re cover-up—Haldeman said Dean had not advised Nixon of a Watergate cover-up during their Sept. 15, 1972 meeting. He "totally disagreed" with Dean's conclusion that the President was aware of any cover-up.

According to Haldeman's statement:

Turning to the Sept. 15 [1972] meeting, I was in meetings with the President all afternoon on Sept. 15, 1972. At the end of the afternoon, the President had John Dean come in. This was the day that the indictments had been brought down in the Watergate case, and the President knew John Dean had been concentrating for a three-month period on the investigation for the White House. . . .

There was no mood of exuberance or excitement on the President's part at the time the indictments were brought down. . . . [I]t was good news as far as the White House and the Administration were concerned that when the indictments were brought down, after a thorough investigation, it had been established there was not any involvement by anyone in the White House. This confirmed what Mr. Dean had been telling us, and we had been reporting to the President over the period of the past three months.

As was the case with all meetings in the Oval Office when the President was there, this meeting with Mr. Dean was recorded. At the President's request, I recently reviewed the recording of that meeting (at which I was present throughout) in order to report on its contents to the President. . . .

The President did not open the meeting of Sept. 15th with the statement that "Bob has kept me posted on your handling of the Watergate" or anything even remotely resembling that. He said, "Hi, this is quite a day, you've got Watergate on the way" or something to that effect. Dean responded that it had been quite a three months and then reported to the President on how the press was handling the indictments and, apparently, a Clark MacGregor press conference.

The discussion then covered the matter of the new bug that had recently been discovered in the Democratic National Committee and the question of whether it had been planted by the D.N.C. [Democratic National Committee] and the matter of Mr. Nixon's campaign being bugged in 1968 and some discussion of whether to try to get out evidence of that. . . .

Dean indicated that the indictments meant the end of the investigation by the grand jury and now there would be the GAO audit and some Congressional inquiries, such as the Patman [Banking and Currency] committee. But he assured the President that nothing would come out to surprise us. In other words, there was apparently no information that would be harmful that had not been uncovered already.

The President did at that point commend Dean for his handling of the whole Watergate matter, which was a perfectly natural thing for him to do. Dean reported that he was keeping a close eye on possible campaign law violations by the opposition; said there were some problems of bitterness at the re-election committee between the finance committee and the political group; and said he was trying to keep notes on people who were emerging out of all this that were clearly not our friends.

There was, as Mr. Dean has indicated, quite a lengthy discussion of the Patman hearings and the various factors involved in that. There was some discussion of the reluctance of the IRS to follow up on complaints of possible violations against people who were supporting our opponents because there are so many Democrats in the IRS bureaucracy that they won't take any action. . . .

Dean's investigation—Dean and Nixon held numerous meetings between Feb. 27 and March 21 that were "primarily concerned with executive privilege," according to Haldeman, but Nixon was also "intensifying pressure on Dean to find out a way to get the full story out."

"Dean at this time point was clearly in charge of any matters relating to the Watergate. He was meeting frequently with the President and he still indicated that he was positive there was no White House involvement," Haldeman said.

Haldeman said Dean's "erroneous conclusions" about the President's involvement in a cover-up attempt were based partially on a confusion of dates. Several events which Dean testified took place on March 13 actually occured on March 21, according to Haldeman.

Haldeman's version of the March 21 meeting depicted a President thwarted in efforts to obtain information from Dean about the Watergate but continuing to press for the facts. His addendum stated:

I was present for the final 40 minutes of the President's meeting with John Dean on the morning of March 21. While I was not present for the first hour of the meeting, I did listen to the tape of the entire meeting. Following is the substance of that meeting to the best of my recollection.

Dean reported some facts regarding the planning and the break-in of the DNC and said again there were no White House personnel involved. He felt Magruder was fully aware of the operation, but he was not sure about Mitchell. He said that Liddy had given him a full rundown right after Watergate and that no one in the White House was involved. He said that his only concerns regarding the White House were in relation to the Colson phone call to Magruder which might indicate White House pressure and the possibility that Haldeman got some of the fruits of the bugging via Strachan since he had been told the fruits had been supplied to Strachan.

He outlined his role in the January planning meetings and recounted a report he said he made to me regarding the second of those meetings.

Regarding the post-June 17th situation, he indicated concern about two problems, money and clemency. He said that Colson had said something to Hunt about clemency. He did not report any other offers of clemency although he felt the defendants expected it. The President confirmed that he could not offer clemency and Dean agreed.

Regarding money, Dean said he and Haldeman were involved. There was a bad appearance which could be developed into a circumstantial chain of evidence regarding obstruction of justice. He said that Kalmbach had raised money for the defendants; that Haldeman had okayed the return of the $350,000 to the committee, and that Dean had handled the dealings between the parties in doing this. He said that the money was for lawyers' fees.

He also reported on a current Hunt blackmail threat. He said Hunt was demanding $120,000 or else he would tell about the seamy things he had done for Ehrlichman. The President pursued this in considerable detail, obviously trying to smoke out what was really going on. . . .

He asked how much money would be involved over the years and Dean said probably a million dollars—but the problem is that it is hard to raise. The President said there is no problem in raising a million dollars, we can do that, but it would be wrong.

Dean also mentioned his concern about other activities getting out, such as the Ellsberg break-in, something regarding Brookings [Institution], the other Hunt activities for Colson on Chappaquiddick, the Segretti matter, use of Kalmbach funds, etc.

When I entered the meeting, there was another discussion regarding the Hunt threat and the President again explored in considerable depth the various options and tried to draw Dean out on his recommendation.

The meeting then turned to the question of how to deal with the situation and the President mentioned Ehrlichman's recommendation that everybody should go to the grand jury. The President told Dean to explore all of this with Haldeman, Ehrlichman and Mitchell.

There was no discussion while I was in the room, nor do I recall any discussion on the tape on the question of clemency in the context of the President saying that he had discussed this with Ehrlichman and with Colson. The only mention of clemency was Dean's report that Colson discussed clemency with Hunt and the President's statement that he could not offer clemency and Dean's agreement—plus a comment that Dean thought the others expected it.

Dean mentioned several times during this meeting his awareness that he was telling the President things the President had known nothing about.

I have to surmise that there is a genuine confusion in Mr. Dean's mind as to what happened on March 13th vs. what happened on March 21, because some of what he describes in quite vivid detail as happening on March 13 did, in fact, happen on March 21. The point about my laughing at his being more knowledgeable next time, and the question that he says he raised on March 13 regarding the million dollars are so accurately described, up to a point, as to what really happened on March 21 that I believe he is confused between the two dates.

Mr. Dean's recollection that the President had told him on March 13 that Ehrlichman had discussed an offer of clemency to Hunt with him and he had also discussed Hunt's clemency with Colson is at total variance with everything that I have ever heard from the President, Ehrlichman or Colson. I don't recall such a discussion in either the March 13 or the March 21 meeting.

Now, to the question of impression. Mr. Dean drew the erroneous conclusion that the President was fully knowledgeable of a cover-up at the time of the March 13 meeting in the sense (1) of being aware that money had been paid for silence and that (2) the money demands could reach a million dollars and that the President said that was no problem. He drew his conclusion from a hypothetical discussion of questions since the President told me later that he had no intention to do anything whatever about money and had no knowledge of the so-called cover-up. . . .

Leaks & funds—Haldeman July 30 told of the White House's efforts to deal with national security leaks. In mid-1971, he said, Nixon dubbed him "lord high executioner" directing a program to uncover leaks throughout the government and to report them to the department head involved.

Haldeman also testified that although he had authorized the transfer of $350,000 in cash from the White House to the re-election committee, his subsequent involvement in the money matter "was entirely through John Dean."

Haldeman said he had "no recollection" of seeing Gemstone material or other intelligence reports related to the Watergate break-in and had "no recollection" of ordering Gordon Strachan to destroy intelligence files.

Haldeman told the committee July 31 that he had had no knowledge of the specifics of the 1970 interagency intelligence gathering plan drawn up by Tom Charles Huston, despite the fact that Huston reported to Haldeman and Haldeman had conveyed Nixon's approval of the plan to Huston.

Haldeman contended he was unaware that the plan included illegal activities, or that Federal Bureau of Investigation (FBI) Director J. Edgar Hoover and Attorney General John N. Mitchell opposed the plan. He said he was unsure whether he had read the plan's recommendations for expanded domestic intelligence operations—recommendations he had presented to the President.

Haldeman testified he did not know the identities of those who had transmitted secret cash to Gov. George C. Wallace's opponent in a 1970 gubernatorial race.

Regarding the $350,000 cash fund held in the White House at his request and transferred to the re-election committee with his approval, Haldeman admitted that the cash had never been used by his office for "polling purposes" as previously described. The eventual use of the money, identified in earlier testimony as payoff money for the Watergate defendants, remained unknown to him, Haldeman insisted.

Haldeman claimed that his authority over budget matters involving the re-election committee was very general, but he admitted authorizing an allocation of $90,000 for "black" campaign projects conducted by White House counsel Charles Colson's office. When asked what "black" projects referred to, Haldeman said he was "not sure."

■ Haldeman admitted requesting a "background report" on Columbia Broadcasting System correspondent Daniel Schorr. "I don't know why, but the check was made," Haldeman said. Contrary to previous White House statements, Haldeman said, Schorr was not being considered for an Administration appointment. He also revealed that similar checks had been made on Frank Sinatra, Helen Hayes and others.

■ Haldeman testified that the political enemies list represented "an exclusion list" to White House social functions. "They did not have a right to be extended the courtesy of the President's hospitality in order to express their opposition," Haldeman said.

■ Haldeman could "not recall" authorizing 24-hour surveillance of Sen. Kennedy, a charge made in earlier Senate testimony. He also professed ignorance about reports Aug. 1 that other White House projects were planned to obtain information about the Chappaquiddick incident.

■ Haldeman conceded "it was quite possible" that tax audits had been made of Administration foes, but he could not recall whether efforts had been made to quash tax audits of Administration friends.

Further Senate Hearings

Helms & Cushman testify. The Senate committee took testimony from ex-CIA Director Richard Helms Aug. 2, 1973 in an effort to shed light on the role of the CIA in the Watergate break-in. The question that most concerned the committee was: had the White House attempted to use the CIA to block an FBI probe of the Mexican aspects of the Watergate burglary?

Testimony by Helms and the two succeeding witnesses—former Deputy CIA Director Robert E. Cushman and current Deputy CIA Director Vernon A. Walters—had previously been given privately before other Congressional committees investigating the CIA.

Ehrlichman and Haldeman had contended previously, when they had testified before the Watergate committee, that the White House had wanted the FBI to limit its investigation of the use of a Mexico City bank to "launder" money used by the Watergate burglars. Both had maintained they were fearful that the FBI might impinge on CIA operations in Mexico, a point that was confirmed, they said, in a June 23, 1972 meeting when Helms was

unable to assure them that this would not happen.

Helms gave the committee his version of the June 23 meeting, attended by Helms, his deputy Walters, Haldeman and Ehrlichman.

According to Helms, Haldeman, after making an "incoherent reference to an investigation in Mexico, or an FBI investigation running into the Bay of Pigs," turned to Walters and asked him to talk to Acting FBI Director L. Patrick Gray 3rd and indicate that the FBI probe might run into CIA operations in Mexico. Haldeman wanted the FBI to taper off its Mexican investigation.

Helms said Haldeman's references to Mexico were unclear but he acceded because the President often possessed information no one else had.

After the meeting, Helms said he advised Walters not to follow Haldeman's order but to confine himself to reminding Gray of a long-standing agreement between the FBI and the CIA that if either agency ran into operations of the other it would notify that agency immediately.

Helms said he learned later that funds used by the Watergate burglars had been channeled through a Mexico City bank.

Helms admitted that Watergate burglar Eugenio Martinez had been on a $100 a month retainer from the CIA. The CIA severed its ties with Martinez immediately after the break-in, Helms said.

This admission, plus the fact that at least four other Watergate conspirators had CIA ties, prompted Sen. Howard H. Baker (R, Tenn.) and Minority Counsel Fred D. Thompson to suggest that this information alone was sufficient to cause the White House to show concern about CIA involvement in Watergate.

Helms testified about meetings that Walters held June 26–28, 1972 with White House counsel John W. Dean 3rd. Helms said Dean put out "feelers" in the hope that he could get the CIA to offer support for the Watergate burglars. Helms stated that he told Walters, "to be absolutely certain that he permitted nothing to happen using the agency's name, facilities or anything else in connection with this business."

Cushman, current Marine Corps commandant and the next witness Aug. 2, had given Hunt technical assistance that was utilized in the 1971 burglary of Ellsberg's psychiatrist's office.

The committee's attention focused on whether Ehrlichman had asked Cushman to assist Hunt. In testimony before the Watergate committee and other Congressional panels, Ehrlichman consistently maintained that he could not recollect calling Cushman in July 1971 on the matter. The issue had been clouded when Cushman had first asserted that Ehrlichman had asked for assistance. Cushman then had said he could not remember who had asked for aid for Hunt. Cushman May 31 recanted and announced that after an intensive search, CIA documents had been found establishing that Ehrlichman had made the call to request CIA aid. Official minutes of a July 8, 1971 CIA staff meeting confirmed that Ehrlichman had made a request for CIA assistance the day before.

Cushman also produced for the Senate committee the transcript of the conversation he had with Hunt in his CIA office July 22, 1971. The conversation, tape recorded by Cushman, confirmed that Ehrlichman had made the call to Cushman.

Throughout their testimony, Cushman and Helms insisted they had not known that Hunt intended to use the CIA equipment to burglarize Ellsberg's psychiatrist's office. Both witnesses contended they had not learned of the break-in until it was made public during the Ellsberg trial April 27.

Gray's story. Before the committee recessed for the weekend Aug. 3, ex-Acting FBI Director Gray read an opening statement. The statement was in two sections: the first dealt with CIA involvement in aspects of the Watergate burglary, the second with Gray's handling of E. Howard Hunt's White House files, which he later destroyed.

Gray told the committee of a meeting with White House counsel John Dean June 22, 1972. Dean told him that he [Dean] was to be the liaison between the White House and the FBI in the Watergate matter and, as the President's counsel, he would sit in on FBI interviews of White House staff members. During the meeting, Gray said, he indicated to Dean that the FBI had evidence linking the Watergate burglars to the Committee to Re-elect the President.

In a second meeting that day, Gray said he discussed with Dean some of the bureau's early theories about Watergate, one of which was that the burglary might somehow have been part of a CIA operation.

During the meeting, Gray said he probably informed Dean of a conversation he had with Helms, also that day, in which Helms had stated that the CIA was not involved in Watergate. When Dean raised the possibility that the FBI would uncover a CIA operation in Mexico if it pushed its investigation, Gray said he responded "that the FBI was going to pursue all leads aggressively unless we were told by the CIA that there was a CIA interest or involvement."

Gray next spoke of a meeting he had with Deputy CIA Director Walters June 23, 1972, in which Walters "informed me that we were likely to uncover some CIA assets or resources if we continued our investigation into the Mexican money chain." Gray's statement conflicted with Walters' testimony about the meeting. Gray insisted that Walters did not say that he had just come from the White House. Gray contended, "I understood him to be stating a CIA position, not a White House message." Walters had asserted in his testimony that he had told Gray he was on a White House-ordered mission.

After his meeting with Walters, Gray received a call from Dean who asked the FBI to hold up its investigation of Manuel Ogarrio, who was a go-between in the Mexican money transactions. Four days later Dean called to ask the FBI not to interview Kenneth Dahlberg, another middle man in the Mexican money chain, because of alleged CIA interest in him. A call to Helms the next day revealed that the CIA had no interest in Ogarrio, Gray said.

Gray also testified about another meeting with Walters July 6, 1972, in which Walters delivered a letter to him saying that the CIA had no interest in either Dahlberg or Ogarrio.

During the meeting, Gray said, he and Walters concluded that the President should be informed of efforts to confuse the FBI investigation into the Mexican aspects of Watergate.

Later in the day, Gray said, he received a phone call from Nixon, who congratulated him on the way FBI agents had handled an attempted airplane hijacking.

Gray thanked Nixon and said:

Mr. President, there is something I want to speak to you about. Dick Walters and I feel that people on your staff are trying to mortally wound you by using the CIA and FBI and by confusing the question of CIA interest in, or not in, people the FBI wishes to interview. I have just talked to [campaign director] Clark MacGregor and asked him to speak to you about this.

There was a slight pause and the President said, "Pat, you just continue to conduct your aggressive and thorough investigation."

Following this conversation I experienced no further concerns of this kind. I believed that if there was anything to the concerns I expressed to the President or to Mr. MacGregor that I would hear further in the matter. I did not. Frankly, I came to the conclusion that Gen. Walters and I had been alarmists, a belief I held for many months. . . .

At a White House meeting with Ehrlichman and Dean June 28, 1972, Gray testified, Dean gave him two folders, which Dean said contained papers of a sensitive political nature that Hunt had been working on. Dean warned that the papers had national security implications and, while not related to Watergate, could not be allowed to confuse the Watergate issue, Gray said.

I asked whether these files should become a part of our FBI Watergate file. Mr. Dean said these should not become a part of our FBI Watergate file but that he wanted to be able to say if called upon later, that he had turned all of Howard Hunt's files over to the FBI.

I distinctly recall Mr. Dean saying that these files were "political dynamite," and clearly should not see the light of day.

It is true that neither Mr. Ehrlichman nor Mr. Dean expressly instructed me to destroy the files. But there was, and is, no doubt in my mind that destruction was intended. Neither Mr. Dean nor Mr. Ehrlichman said or implied that I was being given the documents personally merely to safeguard against leaks . . . The clear implication of the substance and tone of their remarks was that these two files were to be destroyed and I interpreted this to be an order from the counsel to the President of the United States issued in the presence of one of the two top assistants to the President of the United States.

Gray testified that he held the files until shortly after Christmas 1972, when he burned them at his home in Connecticut with trash that had been accumulated during the holiday. Before destroying the files, Gray opened one which contained what appeared to him to be a top-secret State Department cable.

Kleindienst & Petersen testify. Ex-Attorney General Richard G. Kleindienst appeared before the committee Aug. 7. He testified that while he ordered a thorough investigation of Watergate immediately on learning of the break-in June 17, 1972, he did not have "credible evidence" implicating high Administration officials until April 15, 1973.

Early in the morning of April 15, he heard Watergate prosecutors Seymour Glanzer, Donald Campbell, and Earl J. Silbert summarize in detail testimony they had taken from John Dean and Jeb Stuart Magruder. Among those implicated in the cover-up were two of Kleindienst's closest friends, former Attorney General John Mitchell and Robert C. Mardian, an official of the Committee to Re-elect the President.

Hours later, Kleindienst said, he and Henry Petersen met with Nixon and laid before him what they had learned from the Watergate prosecutors. Kleindienst said Nixon was "dumbfounded" at the news. In the discussion that followed, Kleindienst agreed that he must remove himself from the Watergate investigation because of his links to those who were implicated.

Kleindienst recounted for the Senate committee that on the morning of June 17, 1972—three hours after Kleindienst had learned of the Watergate break-in—he was visited at the Burning Tree golf club outside Washington by Watergate conspirator G. Gordon Liddy and Powell Moore, a campaign aide to John Mitchell. Kleindienst said Liddy had come at the suggestion of Mitchell to talk about those arrested in the break-in. Kleindienst said he responded by immediately calling Henry E. Petersen, assistant attorney general in charge of the Justice Department's Criminal Division. While Liddy and Moore listened, Kleindienst instructed Petersen not to treat the Watergate defendants any differently from anyone else.

Kleindienst told of a call he received from John Ehrlichman Aug. 8 or 9, 1972. Ehrlichman was agitated because Petersen had refused to follow his instructions, which were not to "harass" Maurice Stans, chairman of the Finance Committee to Re-elect the President. Kleindienst said he told Ehrlichman he was lucky that Petersen was someone who "does not blow off the handle." Kleindienst said he told Ehrlichman that Petersen could resign, call a press conference, repeat what Ehrlichman had said, and Ehrlichman would then be open to a charge of obstruction of justice. Kleindienst took responsibility for letting Stans give grand jury testimony in private, thus allowing him to avoid the newsmen at the federal courthouse.

Ehrlichman still was not placated, Kleindienst stated, and backed down only after Kleindienst himself threatened to resign if Ehrlichman did not stop interfering, Kleindienst testified.

The last witness before the committee recessed Aug. 7 was Petersen.

Petersen took credit for informing the President April 18 that the Watergate prosecution team had learned of the 1971 burglary of Daniel Ellsberg's psychiatrist's office. "The President said when I told him, 'I know about that. This is a national security matter. You stay out of that. Your mandate is to investigate Watergate.' Now he didn't say he knew about the burglary. He said he knew about it—about the [prosecutor's] report. I think that is a vital distinction to be made."

Petersen said he was dissatisfied with Nixon's instructions and conveyed his feelings to Kleindienst April 25. Kleindienst, Petersen said, agreed that the judge in the Pentagon Papers trial, William M. Byrne Jr., should be told. Prepared to resign, Petersen said, if Nixon did not agree with their suggested course of action, the two men met with Nixon. However, the President endorsed "without hesitation" their intention to pass information about the burglary to Byrne.

Petersen was asked by Sen. Gurney if at any time he had suspected there was a cover-up of Watergate taking place. Petersen responded that he had a "visceral re-action. The word I used to the prosecutors and Kleindienst, nobody acts innocent. You couldn't translate that. There was an overriding concern. There were no records. Things were destroyed. They didn't act like innocent people. Innocent people come in and say, 'Fine, what do you want to know?' It was not like that, it was a visceral reaction. Yes, that is the reason we were so insistent to get this thing, get them tied down to sentence and immunize them [the seven original Watergate defendants]."

Petersen's testimony—like that of Gray and Kleindienst—conflicted with part of Nixon's April 30 statement on Watergate. Petersen denied that the President directed him March 21 or any time before April 15 "to get all the facts" about Watergate.

Petersen, who accompanied Kleindienst April 15 to tell Nixon what the Watergate prosecutors had learned from Dean and Magruder, told the Senate panel that he advised the President to dismiss Haldeman and Ehrlichman.

Q. Now, did you make any recommendation with regard to Mr. Dean?

A. Yes, I did. The President said, "You know, Haldeman and Ehrlichman deny this and I have to go to find this out. Dean in effect has admitted it. Should I request his resignation?" And I said, "My goodness, no. Now, here is the first man who has come in to cooperate with us and certainly we don't want to give the impression that he is being subjected to reprisal because of his cooperation. So please don't ask for his resignation at this point."

Later that month, Petersen said he informed Nixon that the prosecutor's negotiations with Dean had reached an impasse and Dean should not be retained on the White House staff.

Nixon had another conversation with Petersen about Dean April 18. Dean had told Nixon that he had been given immunity from prosecution; Petersen said he told the President no such offer had been made. The President then responded that he had Dean's statement on tape. Petersen testified that he declined Nixon's offer to listen to the tape.

Petersen added at another point that no one in Washington had been more surprised than he when Dean implicated himself in the Watergate cover-up.

Guilty Pleas

LaRue pleads guilty to cover-up attempt. Frederick C. LaRue, former campaign strategist for President Nixon, pleaded guilty June 27, 1973 to one count of conspiracy to obstruct justice in the Watergate affair.

LaRue, a wealthy Mississippian who worked closely with Nixon's campaign director, former Attorney General John N. Mitchell, admitted taking part in a scheme to destroy incriminating documents and misleading both the Federal Bureau of Investigation (FBI) and the Watergate grand jury in 1972 with false testimony. He also acknowledged funneling more than $300,000 to the seven men arrested in the Watergate break-in, in an effort to buy their silence.

In entering his plea, LaRue admitted the following "overt acts of conspiracy":

At a meeting June 19, two days after the Watergate burglary, LaRue met with "others unnamed" and they agreed to destroy "certain incriminating records" relating to the break-in. James F. Neal of the special prosecutor's office identified these as wiretapping logs and summary sheets.

On July 19, he delivered "a sum of money" to Herbert M. Kalmbach at the Old Executive Office Building. Kalmbach was then President Nixon's personal lawyer and one of his chief fund-raisers.

LaRue delivered another unspecified sum of money to Kalmbach July 26.

Prior to Aug. 16, 1972, he met with "others unnamed" at the re-election headquarters, "where Jeb S. Magruder's false, misleading and deceptive statement, previously made to the Federal Bureau of Investigation, was further discussed."

On Aug. 16, Magruder falsely testified, as planned, before the grand jury investigating the case.

On Sept. 19, 1972, LaRue received $20,000 in cash.

On Dec. 1, he received $280,000, again in currency.

Magruder enters guilty plea. Jeb Stuart Magruder, former deputy director of the Committee to Re-elect the President, pleaded guilty in Washington Aug. 16 to a one-count indictment charging him with plotting the electronic bugging of the Democratic national headquarters at the Watergate and with the subsequent cover-up of the crime.

Magruder pleaded guilty to the following charges: plotting the Watergate break-in; obstructing a Department of Justice investigation into Watergate; perjuring himself and suborning the perjury of other unnamed co-conspirators; conspiring to misrepresent the Central Intelligence Agency as having an interest in limiting the investigation; giving false testimony to the Federal Bureau of Investigation; and secretly raising funds to buy the silence of the original Watergate conspirators.

Magruder was given a 10-month-to-four-year jail sentence May 21, 1974.

Dean's plea bargain. John W. Dean 3rd, former counsel to the President, pleaded guilty Oct. 19 to a single count of conspiring to cover up the truth about the Watergate break-in.

The plea was part of a bargain Dean made with Watergate prosecutor Archibald Cox: Dean agreed to be a witness for the prosecution in return for Cox's promise not to bring other charges against him.

Dean entered his plea before U.S. District Court Judge John J. Sirica, who delayed sentencing until after Dean had kept his part of the bargain.

In pleading guilty, Dean admitted the following: asking Watergate conspirator G. Gordon Liddy to tell fellow conspirator E. Howard Hunt Jr. to leave the U.S.; asking Deputy Central Intelligence Agency (CIA) Director Vernon Walters if the CIA would use covert funds to pay the salaries and bail of the men arrested in the Watergate break-in; asking the President's former private attorney, Herbert W. Kalmbach, to raise money to pay the Watergate defendants; suborning perjured testimony by former deputy Nixon re-election campaign director Jeb Stuart Magruder; asking former Treasury Department official John J. Caulfield to offer executive clemency to Watergate burglar James W. McCord Jr.; and asking former Acting Director of the Federal Bureau of Investigation L. Patrick Gray 3rd for reports of information acquired in the investigation of the Watergate break-in.

Krogh pleads guilty in Ellsberg break-in. Egil Krogh Jr., former head of the special White House investigations unit dubbed "the plumbers," pleaded guilty Nov. 30 to a civil rights charge stemming from the Labor Day 1971 break-in at the Los Angeles office of the psychiatrist who had treated Pentagon Papers defendant Daniel Ellsberg

Krogh's plea covered seven overt acts that constituted a conspiracy to violate the rights of Dr. Lewis J. Fielding.

In return for Krogh's guilty plea, the special U.S. prosecutor's office agreed to dismiss charges of making false declarations in connection with the break-in. Krogh told U.S. District Court Judge Gerhard Gesell he would cooperate with the special Watergate prosecutors after he had been sentenced.

Prior to entering his plea before Gesell, Krogh read a short statement, which said in part, "I now feel that the sincerity of my motivation cannot justify what was done, and I cannot in conscience assert national security as a defense. . . . I simply feel that what was done in the Ellsberg operation was in violation of what I perceive to be a fundamental idea in this country—the paramount importance of the rights of the individual. I don't want to be associated with that violation any longer by attempting to defend it."

Although there had been widespread speculation that Krogh would implicate President Nixon in illegal activities by the plumbers, Krogh said in a statement released after the sentencing that he had "received no specific instruction or authority whatsoever regarding the break-in from the President, directly or indirectly."

In his statement, Krogh detailed how his role had begun on July 15 or 16, 1971, when John D. Ehrlichman, then Nixon's domestic affairs adviser, told him he was to "perform an urgent assignment in response to the unauthorized disclosure of the Pentagon Papers." The "entire resources of the executive branch" were to be used to determine responsibility for the leaks, and to assess Ellsberg's motives and "his potential for further disclosures." Krogh added that Ehrlichman later told him the unit's activities "were to be impressed with the highest

classification and kept secret even within the White House staff."

The plumbers' mandate was expanded, Krogh continued, after his July 24, 1971 meeting with Nixon and Ehrlichman. The meeting followed the leak of the U.S. "fallback position" at the Strategic Arms Limitation Talks (SALT). Nixon called the leak "intolerable," Krogh said, and directed the "extensive" use of polygraph tests, emphasizing that "protection of national security information must outweigh any individual reluctance to be polygraphed."

The unit's work on the SALT leak, the Ellsberg case and "some other unauthorized disclosures" was completely "fired up and overshadowed" by the "intensity of the national security concern expressed by the President."

It was in this context, Krogh said, that the "Fielding incident" took place. Krogh suggested that this "deep concern" explained why John W. Dean 3rd, Nixon's former counsel, had testified that Krogh had described the authority for the Fielding burglary as coming directly from "the oval office."

Krogh said he had "just listened" to the tape of the July 24, 1971 meeting, and "Ellsberg's name did not appear to be mentioned." (The tape had been voluntarily turned over to the special prosecutor.)

That meeting, Krogh said, was the "only direct contact I had with the President on the work of the unit." As for the instructions to gather data on Ellsberg, they must have been "relayed to me by Ehrlichman."

Krogh contended that, "to [his] knowledge, the break-in netted nothing." He concluded that a mistake had been made and recommended to Ehrlichman that "no further actions of that sort be undertaken." Ehrlichman agreed "and stated that he considered the operation to have been in excess of his authorization."

Krogh related that his activity in the unit then diminished, ending "for all intents and purposes" in November 1971. He was called back briefly the following month in connection with the "India-Pakistan conflict leak," and was asked to authorize a wiretap concerning a "highly sensitive aspect of that leak." Krogh said he refused and was "removed from the unit the same day." He had since learned that the tap was carried out—along with another in the same investigation—after his removal. Krogh contended that these were the only wiretaps by the unit "of which I am aware."

Krogh said that during 1971 the goals of the Ellsberg investigation—including the "potential use of the information in discrediting Dr. Ellsberg as an antiwar spokesman"—seemed "dictated by the national security interest as I then understood it." This "strained interpretation" of security needs had led to his false statements in a sworn deposition about the travels to California by the burglary team.

Since then, Krogh continued, he had become convinced that the entire operation was a mistake, a crime and—especially the intention to discredit Ellsberg—a "repulsive and inconceivable national security goal." But in the atmosphere of 1971 it seemed "presumptuous if not unpatriotic" to question those purposes. "Freedom of the President to pursue his planned goals," Krogh said, "was the ultimate national security objective."

Gesell Jan. 24, 1974 sentenced Krogh to a prison term of two to six years but suspended all but six months of the term.

Nixon Urges End of 'Obsession'

Again accepts full responsibility. President Nixon told the nation in a nationally televised speech Aug. 15, 1973 to give up its "backward-looking obsession" with Watergate, turn the case over to the courts and start attending to "matters of far greater importance."

The speech, and an accompanying written statement, comprised the President's fifth major statement on the Watergate scandal.

In his speech, the President said it was clear that the Senate Watergate hearings and some of the commentary on them were directed toward implicating him personally in the illegalities that occurred. He accepted full responsibility for the abuses that occurred during his Administration and his re-election campaign and asserted

it was his duty to defend the office of the presidency against false charges.

He declined to offer a point-by-point rebuttal of charges in the case and restated his previous denials of complicity.

Nixon explained his actions after the Watergate break-in. His explanation was largely a restatement of his previous assertion that he had pressed repeatedly for information and was repeatedly misled until mid-April of 1973.

At this point, he said, it was clear that the situation was "far more serious" than he had believed and that the investigation should be given to the Criminal Division of the Justice Department. At that time, Nixon said, he turned over all the information he had to that department with the instruction it should "pursue the matter thoroughly," and he ordered all members of his Administration "to testify fully before the grand jury."

"Far from trying to hide the facts," the President emphasized, "my effort throughout has been to discover the facts—and to lay those facts before the appropriate law-enforcement authorities so that justice could be done and the guilty dealt with."

Nixon dealt at length with his refusal to turn over to the special prosecutor or the Senate committee his recordings of conversations he held in his office or on his telephone. There was "a much more important principle" involved in this, he said, "than what the tapes might prove about Watergate." That principle was the confidentiality of presidential discussions. He related this confidentiality to that required in conversations between members of Congress and their aides, judges and their law clerks, a lawyer and a client or a priest and a penitent.

It was "even more important that the confidentiality of conversations between a President and his advisers be protected," he said. It was "absolutely essential to the conduct of the presidency, in this and in all future Administrations."

If he released the tapes, Nixon said, the confidentiality of the presidency "would always be suspect from now on."

He said he would continue to "oppose efforts which would set a precedent that would cripple all future Presidents by inhibiting conversations between them and those they look to for advice."

Turning to "the basic issues" raised by Watergate, Nixon said he recognized "that merely answering the charges that have been made against the President is not enough. The word 'Watergate' has come to represent a much broader set of concerns."

"To most of us," he said, Watergate had come to mean "a whole series of acts that either represent or appear to represent an abuse of trust. It has come to stand for excessive partisanship, for 'enemy lists,' for efforts to use the great institutions of government for partisan political purposes." For many Americans, he continued, the term also had come to include a number of national security matters.

"No political campaign ever justifies obstructing justice, or harassing individuals, or compromising those great agencies of government that should and must be above politics," he said. "To the extent that these things were done in the 1972 campaign, they were serious abuses. And I deplore them...."

Nixon rejected "the cynical view that politics is inevitably or even usually a dirty business" and pledged "that I will do all that I can to insure that one of the results of Watergate is a new level of political decency and integrity in America."

Nixon linked the Watergate abuses to an attitude arising during the 1960s "as individuals and groups increasingly asserted the right to take the law into their own hands, insisting that their purposes represented a higher morality." He said their attitude "was praised in the press and even from some of our pulpits as evidence of a new idealism. Those of us who insisted on the old restraints, who warned of the overriding importance of operating within the law and by the rules, were accused of being reactionaries."

This new attitude, he said, "brought a rising spiral of violence and fear, of riots and arson and bombings," all in the name of peace and justice. Political discussion turned into "savage debate," he said. "Free speech was brutally suppressed, as hecklers shouted down or even physically assaulted those with whom they disagreed."

"The notion that the end justifies the means proved contagious," the President said, and it was not surprising that some persons adopted the same morality in 1972.

But, he said, "those acts cannot be defended. Those who were guilty of abuses must be punished."

The "extremes of violence and discord in the 1960s," he said, "contributed to the extremes of Watergate" and "both are wrong. Both should be condemned...."

Speaking of the Senate hearings, Nixon said "we have reached a point at which a continued, backward-looking obsession with Watergate is causing this nation to neglect matters of far greater importance."

"We must not stay so mired in Watergate," he said, that the nation failed to respond to its national and world challenges. "We cannot let an obsession with the past destroy our hopes for the future."

Nixon's written statement—The President's written statement, released just prior to his speech Aug. 15, covered much the same ground as the speech and contained sections of identical text.

The statement asserted it would be "neither fair nor appropriate" for the President" to assess the evidence or comment on specific witnesses or their credibility" since this was the function of the committee and the courts. It was not his intention to attempt "comprehensive and detailed response" to "the questions and contentions raised" during the hearings nor "attempt a definitive account of all that took place." He did not believe he "could enter upon an endless course of explaining and rebutting a complex of point-by-point claims and charges arising out of that conflicting testimony which may engage committees and courts for months or years to come, and still be able to carry out my duties as President."

The statement again repeated Nixon's denials of complicity in the break-in or cover-up, his assertions that he ordered vigorous pursuit of the federal investigation of the break-in and his repeated demands for reports on Watergate developments.

When the indictments were returned against only the seven original defendants, he stated, it seemed to confirm the reports he was getting that no one then employed at the White House was involved. "It was in that context," Nixon stated, that he met with his counsel John W. Dean 3rd Sept. 15, 1972, and Dean gave him "no reason at that meeting to believe any others were involved."

"Not only was I unaware of any cover-up," Nixon continued, "but at that time, and until March 21, I was unaware that there was anything to cover up."

Nixon cited the March 21 date on which he said he learned for the first time that the planning for the break-in "went beyond" those who had been tried and "that at least one, and possibly more, persons at the re-election committee were involved." He also learned that funds had been raised for payment to the defendants, but "not that it had been paid to procure silence," only that it was for lawyers' fees and family support. He learned "that a member of my staff had talked to one of the defendants about clemency, but not that offers of clemency had been made." And he learned that one of the defendants (E. Howard Hunt Jr.) was trying "to blackmail the White House by demanding payment of $125,000 as the price of not talking about other activities, unrelated to Watergate, in which he had engaged."

The allegations were "troubling," Nixon stated, they gave "a new dimension" to the Watergate matter. They also reinforced his determination, he stated, to have the full facts made available to the grand jury or the Senate committee and to have any illegalities "dealt with appropriately according to the law." If there was White House involvement, or involvement by high campaign committee personnel, he said, "I wanted the White House to take the lead in making that known."

This was the time Nixon began new inquiries into the case, the statement asserted. By April 15, based on reports from his aide John D. Ehrlichman and from then-Attorney General Richard G. Kleindienst and Watergate prosecutor Henry Petersen, and based on "independent inquiries" of his own, Nixon said, he realized he "would not be able personally to find out all of the facts and make them public" and he decided "that the matter was best handled by the Justice Department and the grand jury."

In his statement, Nixon corrected an inaccurate date in his May 22 Watergate statement that it was not until the time of his own investigation, March 21, that he learned of the break-in at the office of Daniel Ellsberg's psychiatrist. He had since determined that he first learned of that break-in March 17, he stated.

Acting on Kleindienst's advice at a meeting April 25, Nixon said, he authorized reporting the break-in to the Ellsberg case judge, "despite the fact that since no evidence had been obtained [in the break-in], the law did not clearly require it."

Concerning the special investigations unit in the White House, Nixon stated many of its activities should not be disclosed because that "would unquestionably damage the national security." He added that the Senate Watergate committee had learned of some of these matters and to date "wisely declined to make them public." At no time had he authorized "the use of illegal means by the special investigations unit," Nixon stated.

Press conference. Nixon answered a number of questions about Watergate during a news conference at his home in San Clemente, Calif. Aug. 22.

He was asked about his March 21, 1972 meeting with John W. Dean 3rd on the subject of raising funds for the Watergate defendants. He replied:

Basically, what Mr. Dean was concerned about on March 21 was not so much the raising of money for the defendants but the raising of money for the defendants for the purpose of keeping them still. In other words so-called hush money.

The one would be legal, in other words raising the defense funds for any group, any individual, as you know is perfectly legal and is done all the time. But you raise funds for the purpose of keeping an individual from talking, that's obstruction of justice.

Mr. Dean said also, on March 21, that there was an attempt to, as he put it, to blackmail the White House, to blackmail the White House by one of the defendants; incidentally, that defendant has denied it .

but at least this is what Mr. Dean had claimed and that unless certain amounts of money were paid, I think it was $120,000 for attorneys' fees and other support, that this particular defendant would make a statement, not with regard to Watergate but with regard to some national security matters in which Mr. Ehrlichman had particular responsibility.

My reaction very briefly was this: I said as you look at this, I said isn't it quite obvious, first, that if it is going to have any chance to succeed, that these individuals aren't going to sit there in jail for four years, they're going to have clemency. Isn't that correct?

He said yes.

I said we can't given clemency.

He agreed.

Then I went to another point. The second point is that isn't it also quite obvious, as far as this is concerned, that while we could raise the money, and he indicated in answer to my question that it would probably take a million dollars over four years to take care of this defendant and others on this kind of a basis, the problem was, how do you get the money to them? And also, how do you get around the problem of clemency because they're not going to stay in jail simply because their families are being taken care of.

And so that was why I concluded, as Mr. Haldeman recalls, perhaps, and did testify very effectively, when I said John, it's wrong, it won't work, we can't give clemency, and we've got to get this story out. . . .

Nixon's Watergate informants—Nixon was asked who had been his principal informants on the case after he had ordered Watergate investigations in June of 1972 and March 21, 1973.

In June I of course talked to Mr. MacGregor first of all who was the new chairman of the committee. He told me that he would conduct a thorough investigation as far as his entire committee staff was concerned. Apparently that investigation was very effective except for Mr. [Jeb Stuart] Magruder who stayed on, but Mr. MacGregor does not have to assume responsibility for that, . . . he believed Mr. Magruder, and many others had believed him, too. He proved, however, to be wrong.

In the White House, the investigation's responsibility were given to Mr. Ehrlichman at the highest level and, in turn, he delegated them to Mr. Dean, something of which I was aware of and of which I approved. Mr. Dean, as White House counsel, therefore sat in on the F.B.I. interrogations of the members of the White House staff because what I wanted to know was whether any member of the White House staff was in any way involved. If he was involved, he would be fired.

And when we met on Sept. 15 and again throughout our discussions in the month of March, Mr. Dean insisted there was not—and I use his words—a scintilla of evidence indicating that anyone on the White House staff was involved in the planning of the Watergate break-in.

Now in terms of after March 21st, Mr. Dean first was given the responsibility to write his own report but I did not rest it there—I also had a contact made with the Attorney General himself, and Attorney General Kleindienst told him—this was on the 27th of March—to report to me directly anything that he found in this particular area, and I gave the responsi-

bility for Mr. Ehrlichman on the 29th of March to continue the investigation that Mr. Dean was unable to conclude, having spent a week at Camp David and unable to finish the report.

I met at great length with Mr. Ehrlichman, Mr. Haldeman, Mr. Dean, Mr. Mitchell on the 22d. I discussed the whole matter with them. I kept pressing for the view that I had had throughout, that we must get this story out, get the truth out, whatever and whoever it's going to hurt, and it was there that Mr. Mitchell suggested that all the individuals involved in the White House appear in an executive session before the Ervin committee.

We never got that far. But at least that was, that's an indiction of the extent of my own investigation.

Approach to Ellsberg judge—Nixon was questioned about his and Ehrlichman's contacts with U.S. District Judge W. Matthew Byrne Jr. while he was presiding at the Pentagon papers trial of Dr. Daniel Ellsberg. "Could you give us some reason why the American people shouldn't believe that that was at least a subtle attempt to bribe the judge in that case and it gave at least the appearance of a lack of moral leadership?" he was asked.

Nixon said he met Byrne "for perhaps one minute outside my door here in full view of the whole White House staff and everybody who wanted to see. I asked him how he liked his job. We did not discuss the case."

The meetings occurred because the attorney general had recommended Byrne as "the best man" to succeed Gray as FBI director.

"Under those circumstances," Ehrlichman called Byrne. "He said under no circumstances will we talk to you, he, Ehrlichman will talk to you, unless if he felt that it would in any way compromise his handling of the Ellsberg case. Judge Byrne made the decision that he would talk to Mr. Ehrlichman. . . . The case was not discussed at all. Only the question of whether or not at the conclusion of this case Mr. Byrne would like to be considered as director of the FBI.

"I understand, incidentally, that he told Mr. Ehrlichman that he would be interested."

In response to questioning about the break-in at the offices of Ellsberg's former psychiatrist, Nixon said he considered the break-in "illegal, unauthorized as far as I was concerned, and completely deplorable." But he said since it "was a dry hole" and no evidence had been developed from it, "there was no requirement" that the break-in be reported to the grand jury examining the Ellsberg case.

Later, he recalled, Attorney General Kleindienst recommended "that we bend over backwards" and report the break-in to the court. Nixon said when the recommendation was made "I directed that it be done instantly."

Views on impeachment, wiretaps—The President was asked whether his authorization of a 1970 intelligence plan permitting illegal acts was a violation of his oath to execute the law. He was asked,

If you were serving in Congress, would you not be considering impeachment proceedings and discussing impeachment possibility against an elected public official who had violated his oath of office?

He replied:

I would if I had violated the oath of office. I would also, however, refer you to the recent decision of the Supreme Court or at least an opinion that even last year which indicates inherent power in the Presidency to protect the national security in cases like this. I should also point to you that in the three Kennedy years and the three Johnson years through 1966 when burglarizing of this type did take place, when it was authorized, on a very large scale there was no talk of impeachment and it was quite well known.

I should also like to point out that when you ladies and gentlemen indicate your great interest in wiretaps and I understand that the height of the wiretaps was when Robert Kennedy was Attorney General in 1963. I don't criticize him, however. He had over 250 in 1963 and of course the average in the Eisenhower Administration and the Nixon Administration is about 110.

The President later commented that in 1961–63 "there were wiretaps on news organizations, on news people, on civil rights leaders and on other people."

FBI burglaries called 'a fact.' A White House spokesman declined to elaborate Aug. 23 on President Nixon's assertion that "burglarizing" authorized by the two previous Administrations had been practiced on "a very large scale" and was "quite well known." Deputy White House Press Secretary Gerald L. Warren told newsmen who questioned the assertion that "the President said it because it was a fact."

Two former attorneys general said Aug. 23 they were unaware of any such practice during their government service. Nicholas deB. Katzenbach, who suc-

ceeded the late Robert F. Kennedy as attorney general in 1964, denied knowledge of such "official" burglaries. His successor, Ramsey Clark, in the post until 1969, said he "never heard of it" and "never authorized any burglaries." Clark said he had been approached by late FBI Director J. Edgar Hoover with a request to authorize the burglary of a foreign mission in New York City. He believed it was a "North African country," but had rejected it as "unthinkable" for an attorney general to authorize such activity.

There were reports that the FBI had engaged in burglarizing over a 30-year period ending in 1966, that the practice generally was targeted against foreign embassies and missions in the U.S. to discover cryptographic, or code, materials or against organized crime figures, that the practice was a well-kept secret within the FBI and that approval of the practice came from no higher authority than Hoover. He ordered the practice ended in 1966 because of the risk to his agency's reputation from such an activity, which benefitted another agency, the National Security Agency, it was reported.

Nixon's news conference statements about wiretaps also were at variance with statistics released in June by Senate Republican Leader Hugh Scott (Pa.). Nixon said "the height of the wiretaps was when Robert Kennedy was attorney general in 1963" and that the average annual number of taps in his and Eisenhower's Administration had been "about 110." According to the June data, the largest number of wiretaps, 519, were in place between 1945 and 1954, and the average for each of the Eisenhower years of 1953–1960 was about 200.

George Christian, a former press secretary to President Johnson, Aug. 23 disputed another Nixon news conference statement that he found a "rather complex situation set up" in the White House when he took office, designed to record conversations in the President's office, the Cabinet room and at Camp David, a presidential retreat.

Christian said "what recording equipment there was at the White House was taken out before Mr. Nixon took office" and he "never heard of any" such equipment at Camp David.

Senate Hearings Resume

Hunt testifies. The Senate Watergate committee resumed its televised hearings Sept. 24, 1973 with convicted Watergate conspirator E. Howard Hunt Jr. in the witness chair.

Hunt, testifying under a grant of immunity from prosecution, gave his first public testimony on the case, although he had been questioned under oath by various judicial and Congressional panels behind closed doors on more than 25 occasions.

The witness testified about both his activity in the Watergate break-in and, before that, as a member of the White House "plumbers" group. The latter activity, which he described as "seamy activities for the White House," included the break-in at the office of a psychiatrist who had treated Pentagon Papers defendant Daniel Ellsberg.

Hunt also related his personal plight in the aftermath of Watergate, that he had been physically attacked and robbed and had suffered a stroke in his six months in jail, that he was "isolated from my four motherless children," that he had an enormous financial burden" from legal fees and that he was "crushed by the failure of my government to protect me and my family, as in the past it has always done for its clandestine agents." Hunt had been a CIA agent for 21 years before his retirement in 1970.

Hunt, visibly embittered by his Watergate involvement, pleaded abandonment by the Administration, whose high officials had encouraged his participation in Watergate for legitimate national security reasons. Hunt denied seeking executive clemency or influencing other defendants to plead guilty and said the large payments he had received after his arrest were not for his silence, but for his career of service.

When he became involved in the Watergate break-in, Hunt told the committee, "I considered my participation as a duty to my country." After a career as a spy,

"following orders without question," he said, he had never thought to question the propriety or legality of the Watergate break-in. He regretted lacking "the wisdom to withdraw," he said, but "at the same time I cannot escape feeling that the country I have served for my entire life and which directed me to carry out the Watergate entry is punishing me for the very thing it trained and directed me to do."

He frequently cited his working relationship with Charles W. Colson, then a special counsel to the President.

Hunt said he had been offered his White House job as a consultant by Colson and had worked under Colson's direction. His original work involved probing the origins of the Vietnam war and leaks of classified information, specifically the Pentagon papers. He began collecting derogatory information about Ellsberg, Hunt said, and assumed it was to be made available by Colson to selected members of the media.

The committee put in the record a July 28, 1971 memorandum from Hunt to Colson suggesting a plan to destroy Ellsberg's public image and credibility. One suggestion was, "Obtain Ellsberg's files from his psychiatric analyst." The committee also produced an Aug. 27, 1971 memo from then-Presidential adviser John Ehrlichman to Colson saying, "On the assumption that the proposed undertaking by Hunt and [G. Gordon] Liddy would be carried out, and would be successful, I would appreciate receiving from you by next Wednesday a game plan as to how and when you believe the materials should be used." Hunt told the committee the reference in the memo was to "covert entry" of the psychiatrist's office.

Hunt also said the break-in, over the Labor Day weekend in 1971, had produced no files and when he tried to inform Colson about the incident Colson told him " 'I don't want to hear anything about it.' "

Hunt also acknowledged attempts to obtain derogatory information on Sen. Edward M. Kennedy (D, Mass.) and Sen. Edmund S. Muskie (D, Me.). The move against Kennedy, in which he employed a disguise and false credentials supplied by the CIA in making a contact in Hyannis

Port, Mass., was unsuccessful. The attempt against Muskie, involving a burglary of a newspaper office in Las Vegas, was aborted.

Hunt said he believed the Watergate break-ins May 27 and June 17, 1972 were "unwise" but "lawful" and undertaken to obtain information to back up a reported contribution of campaign funds to the Democratic party from the Cuban government.

He had advised Colson beforehand, Hunt said, that he was working with Liddy on an extensive political intelligence plan for the Nixon re-election committee. Colson's reaction was that he "indicated that he was aware of the overall intelligence plan."

Hunt disclosed to the committee that he had proposed to "junk" the June 17 Watergate break-in after discovering the tape put on the door locks had been removed, but Liddy and another convicted conspirator, James W. McCord Jr., overruled him.

After the burglars were caught that night, Hunt, who was not apprehended, said he went to the White House and deposited in his safe some of McCord's electronic equipment and removed $10,-000 of "contingency" funds that were used for bail bonds for those arrested.

The committee documented two subsequent contacts between Hunt and Colson. The first was an Aug. 9, 1972 letter from Hunt to Colson expressing regret at "your being dragged into the case through association with me, superficial and occasional though the association was."

The second was a Nov. 24, 1972 telephone conversation, taped by Colson, in which Colson repeatedly advised Hunt not to give him details of his involvement in Watergate, that his value to him would be tainted unless he remained "as unknowing as I am."

The thrust of Hunt's conversation was for financial assistance for the Watergate defendants. "We're protecting the guys who are really responsible," Hunt told Colson, "but now that's that—and of course that's a continuing requirement, but at the same time, this is a two-way street and as I said before, we think that

now is the time when a move should be made and surely the cheapest commodity available is money."

"I'm reading you," Colson assured him. "You don't need to be more specific."

Hunt admitted receiving funds for his legal fees and family assistance after his indictment and conviction but denied he made threats in order to get the money. William O. Bittman, who withdrew as his attorney in August, received $156,000 in legal fees. The payments were clandestine, Hunt said.

When the anonymous packets of money stopped coming, Hunt said, he called Colson about it but eventually went to the Nixon re-election committee to see Paul O'Brien. He told O'Brien he would like his family to have the equivalent of two years' subsistence before he was jailed. And he told him of his "other activities, which I believe I described as 'seamy activities,' for the White House." Hunt denied that this was a threat to extract the funds in return for his silence about the "seamy activities." Rather, he said, he was citing his long and loyal service as grounds for receiving the subsistence.

O'Brien advised him, he said, to contact Colson, who by now had left the White House to practice law. Hunt tried but was rebuffed. He did see Colson's law partner, David Shapiro, who approached him "rather aggressively," Hunt said, "and subjected me to a lengthy monologue which I considered to be highly self-serving."

After these events, Hunt related, he received a final payment of cash on March 20 or 21, totaling $75,000, but he said he put it in a safe deposit box and eventually paid Bittman $80,000 collected from his late wife's insurance.

Hunt testified Sept. 25 that he had never been offered and had not sought executive clemency.

The committee further explored Hunt's effort to obtain psychiatric data on Ellsberg. In this and other areas, Hunt's testimony seemed to parallel in substance the more than 40 spy novels he had written during his career. He proposed that the Watergate break-in had been subverted by a "double agent." He identified the "Fat Jack" intermediary of another "double agent" deal against Sen. Muskie's campaign, and told of an assignment to assess admitted GOP saboteur Donald H. Segretti. He identified some of the material taken from his White House safe after the unsuccessful burglary at Watergate as notebooks that would have uncovered the whole "Gemstone" operation.

Hunt then described "Fat Jack" as a contact in 1972 who provided material obtained from a penetration of Muskie campaign headquarters. "Fat Jack" was in charge of an agent planted in the opposition camp. With the help of a photograph submitted by Weicker, "Fat Jack" was identified as John R. Buckley, who retired June 30 as chief of the inspection division of the Office of Economic Opportunity.

'Fat Jack's' spy role. John R. Buckley, 53, known to his campaign contacts as "Fat Jack," admitted to the comittee Oct. 9 that he had spied on Sen. Muskie while he (Buckley) was a federal employe.

Buckley related that he was paid $1,000 a month from late 1971 until sometime in April 1972 for inside information on the Muskie campaign. He had planted a messenger in Muskie headquarters, Buckley explained, who called him at the OEO whenever he obtained Muskie documents. Buckley would leave his office at lunch time, he said, pick up the documents and photograph the ones he wanted in an office he rented for that purpose.

In turn, Buckley continued, he would deliver the copied documents, during lunch hour on street corners near the White House, to Nixon campaign officials. He identified the latter as Kenneth S. Reitz, who had first given him the assignment, and later E. Howard Hunt Jr.

Buckley considered his activity "a normal transaction for an election year." "My theory is," he told the committee, "that a candidate has a right and it is proper for him to gather intelligence on the opposition, and I expect it is done in most, if not all, campaigns." Sen. Herman

E. Talmadge (D, Ga.) asked him if he did not think "taking someone else's personal documents and photographing them and delivering them elsewhere" was theft. "No, sir, I do not," Buckley responded. Sen. Daniel K. Inouye (D, Hawaii) asked him if his activity had been "absolutely proper as far as you are concerned?" "As far as I am concerned, it was," Buckley said.

"I think political espionage goes on all the time," Buckley replied to a question whether this was "an acceptable practice." "It has gone on for many, many years. I do not feel that I invented it."

McMinoway spied on Democrats. Michael W. McMinoway testified Oct. 10 that he had infiltrated three different Democratic campaigns for the Nixon re-election committee. He said he had been hired by the Nixon re-election committee at $1,500 a month to infiltrate Democratic campaigns. His contact was a man identifying himself as Jason Rainier, later identified as Roger Stone, a Nixon re-election committee employe. He was paid a total of about $6,000 for his work, he said, which he carried out from February–July 1972.

During this period, when he made daily reports to Stone, he enlisted as a Muskie campaign worker in Wisconsin, as a campaign worker for Sen. Hubert H. Humphrey (D, Minn.) in Pennsylvania and California and as a McGovern worker at the Democratic National Convention in Miami Beach. Part of his job was to collect scheduling data of the Democratic candidates and send it to a post office box in Washington. The information was circulated eventually, under the code name Sedan Chair II, within the re-election committee and the White House.

In addition to such espionage, McMinoway testified that he occasionally did minor sabotage, such as scrambling card files and dismissing volunteers who were actually needed.

McMinoway, a Louisville, Ky. resident, said he was recalled to Washington after the Watergate break-in, given assurance by Stone that his activity was not illegal and assigned one last task to infiltrate the McGovern camp at Miami Beach. He was appointed a security man for McGovern's hotel suite, he testified, and even gained entry one night to watch the convention proceedings on television with McGovern.

Watergate End Approaches

Nixon Forms Privacy Committee, Privacy & Watergate Discussed

Faced with accusations that his Administration had been guilty of serious invasions of privacy in the Watergate affair and in other "Watergate-type" activities, President Nixon announced in early 1974—the year in which the Watergate scandal forced him out of office—that he was taking action to safeguard privacy rights.

Defense of privacy. Nixon, in his State-of-the-Union message Jan. 30, promised to take steps to protect the right of privacy. He said:

One measure of a truly free society is the vigor with which it protects the liberties of its individual citizens.

As technology has advanced in America, it has increasingly encroached on one of those liberties what I term the right of personal privacy. Modern information systems, data banks, credit records, mailing list abuses, electronic snooping, the collection of personal data for one purpose that may be used for another—all these have left millions of Americans deeply concerned by the privacy they cherish.

And the time has come, therefore, for a major initiative to define the nature and extent of the basic rights of privacy and to erect new safeguards to insure that those rights are respected.

I shall launch such an effort this year at the highest levels of the Administration, and I look forward again to working with this Congress and establishing a new set of standards that respect the legitimate needs of society but that also recognize personal privacy as a cardinal principle of American liberty.

Privacy panel announced. President Nixon announced in a radio address Feb. 23 that he was creating a "top-priority" Cabinet-level committee to recommend measures to protect individual privacy against computerized data banks and other developments of "advanced technology" used by both government and private institutions.

Calling the right to privacy "the most basic of all individual rights," Nixon said "a system that fails to respect its citizens' right to privacy, fails to respect the citizens themselves." With the names of "more than 150 million Americans" in "computer banks scattered across the country," Nixon said, there was always the possibility that a citizen's rights could be "seriously damaged . . . sometimes beyond the point of repair. Careers have been ruined, marriages have been wrecked, reputations built up over a lifetime have been destroyed by the misuse or abuse of data technology in both private and public hands."

Nixon said "well-intentioned" government bureaucracies "seem to thrive" on collecting information," which "is now stored in over 7,000 government computers." The same process had been at work in the private sector, placing "vast quantities of personal information in the hands of bankers, employers, charitable organizations and credit agencies."

Nixon said the problems had grown despite a number of steps "in the right direction," including the Fair Credit Reporting Act of 1970. To meet the added "challenge of these dimensions," Nixon said he was creating the "blue-ribbon" Domestic Council Committee on the Right of Privacy, to be chaired by Vice President Gerald R. Ford and composed of six Cabinet members and four other Administration officials. Nixon directed the panel "within four months to begin providing a series of direct, enforceable measures . . . all of which we can immediately begin to put into effect."

Nixon did not refer directly to wiretapping or other forms of electronic surveillance in his speech, but a "fact sheet" issued by the White House said the President had asked the new committee "to defer recommendations" on wiretapping pending receipt of a report by the Congressionally-created National Commission for Review of Federal and State Wiretapping Laws.

The review commission was to have been composed of seven members appointed by the White House and four each by the two houses of Congress. According to the fact sheet, the commission's status was still uncertain; the Senate and White House had named their 11 prospective members, but the House—whose previous appointments had lapsed—had not named new ones.

(The President was asked by a reporter at his news conference Feb. 25 to explain, in the light of the address on privacy, the issuance in 1973 of an executive order allowing the Agriculture Department to examine farmers' individual income tax returns and a subsequent Justice Department advisory opinion calling the order a model for all government departments. Nixon replied that while he "did not raise this question specifically," he wanted "that question along with others considered" by the new White House committee, "because in the full area of privacy it isn't just a question of those who run credit bureaus and banks and others with their huge computers, but the federal government itself . . . can very much impinge on the privacy of individuals." A department official said March 6 that

while the executive order was still in effect, the plan to use tax returns as a source of mailing lists for statistical surveys was currently "inoperative.")

Hart scores 'political spying'—The Democrats' "equal time" reply to Nixon's address was delivered March 2 by Sen. Philip A. Hart (Mich.), who called on the President to "immediately" ban any wiretapping or electronic surveillance not authorized by court order and to "state without equivocation that the label of 'national security' will not be used again to hide or excuse illegal acts." Instead of "the naming of a new committee," Hart said, Nixon should have ordered "everyone in his Administration to refrain from political spying of any kind."

"Perhaps understandably in the light of Watergate," Hart said, "the President chose to paint the primary threat as one of technology. We have learned to our regret that, with or without sophisticated technology, unprincipled men can find ways to invade our privacy."

Hart noted that in addition to the acts of the Watergate burglars and the White House "plumbers" unit, the government had used Army personnel "to spy on peaceful political meetings" and had used the confidential files of the Internal Revenue Service "to harass persons on a White House enemies list."

Hart charged the Administration with a long record of opposing or failing to support legislation to prevent invasions of privacy, including bills prohibiting government employes from being asked about religious beliefs, politics and social activities, and prohibiting military spying on civilians.

Presidential power assailed. A panel of experts in public administration reported to the Senate Watergate Committee March 20 that many of the abuses associated with the Watergate scandals could be traced to a "centralization of power in the presidency," under which "the prevailing view is that the whole government should be run from the White House."

The report, by a 12-member panel from

the National Academy of Public Administration, had been commissioned by the Senate committee in preparation for the final report on its investigations.

While noting that many of the problems in the federal government had begun in earlier administrations, the report stated that Watergate was an "aberration" and culmination of "converging trends" which had seriously damaged the image of the public service.

Much of the report dealt with the White House staff system under which presidential assistants had become "assistant presidents," interposed—possibly illegally—between the President and departmental and agency heads. The panel concluded that the apparent policy of the Nixon Administration was that agency officials "must obey orders from the White House staff even in those areas where statutory powers" were vested in the agency official. Suggestions from presidential assistants were "to be construed as orders coming directly from the oval office."

The report criticized the "increasing and disturbing" politization of the White House staff and the civil service, and a tendency to appoint "political executives" to administer "duly legislated programs," sometimes with a "clear mandate from above in the hierarchy to 'gut' these programs."

A public manifestation of these trends, the report said, came in the hearings before the Senate committee, during which "almost none" of the top witnesses "mentioned any special considerations of public service for the public interest apart from the President's interest."

The report said the Nixon Administration had shown a tendency to run the government "like a corporation" with power concentrated at the top and exercised by White House staff members and "loyal followers" in executive agencies.

The report said the "most alarming" of the Watergate disclosures had been the misuse of law enforcement and intelligence agencies against supposed "enemies" and the increasingly "partisan climate" in the Justice Department. The panel urged that Congress give "special attention and oversight" to the Federal Bureau of Investigation, the Central Intelligence Agency and the Internal Revenue Service. The panel also urged Congress to prohibit the White House from conducting "intelligence activities."

The Justice Department should be "divorced from politics," the report said, and the attorney general "should be precluded from advising the President in the latter's political or personal capacity."

To deal with investigation of wrongdoing, the report suggested a permanent office of special prosecutor, established by statute and subject to Senate confirmation for a term of at least six years.

Nixon Aides Indicted

Grand juries in Washington March 1 and 7, 1974 indicted seven former key figures in the White House and President Nixon's re-election campaign. It was revealed later that the Watergate grand jury had also named Nixon as an unindicted co-conspirator.

Cover-up charges detailed. The historic indictment of seven former White House and campaign aides on charges of covering up the Watergate scandal was returned March 1 in a 15-minute session in the courtroom of Chief U.S. District Court Judge John J. Sirica.

The grand jury (the first of three dealing with the Watergate case) also delivered a sealed "report and recommendation" reportedly dealing with President Nixon's relation to the cover-up.

(The White House acknowledged June 6 that Nixon had been named in the indictment as an unindicted co-conspirator. Nixon's special counsel James D. St. Clair quoted Nixon as asserting that "They just don't have the evidence, and they are wrong.")

The defendants and the charges against them:

John D. Ehrlichman, Nixon's former

domestic affairs adviser: one count each of conspiracy, obstruction of justice and making false statements to the Federal Bureau of Investigation (FBI), and two counts of false declarations before a grand jury or court.

H. R. Haldeman, former White House chief of staff: one count each of conspiracy and obstruction of justice and three counts of perjury (before the Senate Watergate Committee).

John N. Mitchell, former attorney general and director of Nixon's 1968 and 1972 campaigns: one count each of conspiracy, obstruction of justice, perjury, and false statements to the FBI, and two counts of false declarations to a grand jury or court.

Charles W. Colson, former presidential counsel: one count each of conspiracy and obstruction of justice.

Gordon C. Strachan, Haldeman's former assistant: one count each of conspiracy, obstruction of justice and false declarations.

Robert C. Mardian, former assistant attorney general and a 1972 Nixon campaign aide: one count of conspiracy.

Kenneth W. Parkinson, attorney for the Committee to Re-elect the President: one count each of conspiracy and obstruction of justice.

All seven pleaded not guilty March 9.

The charges: *conspiracy*—The overall conspiracy charge involving all seven defendants detailed the complex scenario in which the defendants—with other persons "known and unknown"—arranged "hush money" payoffs for those first charged in the Watergate burglary and wiretapping, offered executive clemency, destroyed documents and lied to various investigative bodies—all of which formed the basis for the other charges in the indictment.

A central figure in the grand jury's narrative was former presidential counsel John W. Dean 3rd, who had already pleaded guilty to one count of conspiracy and was cooperating with the prosecution.

According to the 45 "overt acts" of conspiracy cited by the grand jury, the cover-up began within hours after the break-in at Democratic Party headquarters June 17, 1972: Mitchell told Mardian to try to arrange for the intercession of Richard G. Kleindienst, then attorney general, in getting the arrested burglars out of jail.

Over the next few days, Strachan destroyed documents on Haldeman's orders, and Mitchell suggested to Jeb Stuart Magruder, deputy campaign director for the re-election committee, that other documents in Magruder's files be destroyed. Concern over G. Gordon Liddy and E. Howard Hunt Jr., the still-unarrested burglary conspirators, led Ehrlichman to direct Dean to tell them they "should leave the United States," and to tell Dean to "take possession" of · the contents of Hunt's safe.

Liddy and Hunt did not leave, and after Liddy reminded Mardian and campaign aide Frederick C. LaRue of certain financial "commitments" to those involved in the break-in, the sequence of fund-raising and clandestine payoffs began.

On June 26 and June 28, 1972, Ehrlichman approved two suggestions relating to possible sources of funds. Dean's first approach was to the Central Intelligence Agency (CIA) for "covert funds to pay for bail and salaries." Having apparently failed, Dean went to Herbert W. Kalmbach, Nixon's personal attorney. The first payoff was delivered July 7— $25,000 in cash to William O. Bittman, Hunt's attorney.

A key "overt act" of obstruction occurred in mid-July: Mitchell, in the presence of Parkinson, told Dean to obtain FBI reports on its Watergate investigation; Mardian, meeting with Dean, examined the reports July 21.

Meanwhile, according to the indictment, the payoffs continued as demands escalated. By Oct. 13, 1972, an additional $182,500 had been delivered, mostly by Anthony T. Ulasewicz, a former New York City policeman who dealt with Kalmbach and Parkinson under "code names."

Hunt was apparently not satisfied: in a telephone conversation with Colson in mid-November 1972, Hunt pressed the need for additional payments. Colson taped the conversation, and—through Dean—the demands were relayed to Haldeman, Ehrlichman and Mitchell. In early December 1972 and early January 1973 Haldeman gave Dean his approval for the use of a $350,000 cash fund then under Haldeman's control; shortly afterwards, Strachan delivered approximately $300,000 to LaRue.

As the trial of the break-in defendants approached in early January 1973, discussions among the cover-up conspirators began to focus on the possibility of executive clemency. One such meeting of Ehrlichman, Colson and Dean centered on "assurances" for Hunt, and during the same period Mitchell instructed Dean to relay a promise of clemency to James W. McCord Jr.

Perjury: Haldeman, Dean and Nixon meeting—The key perjury charge against Haldeman concerned his testimony before the Senate Watergate Committee about the March 21, 1973 meeting with Dean and President Nixon.

The first hour of the meeting had involved only Nixon and Dean; Haldeman was present for the following 40 minutes, he told the Senate panel, but had listened to a tape of the entire session.

Giving the "best of [his] recollection" of the meeting, Haldeman said Nixon, questioning Dean on Hunt's $120,000 "blackmail threat" over the "seamy things" Hunt had done for Ehrlichman, was trying to "smoke out what was really going on" and had "led Dean on." Dean said a million dollars might be needed over the years, "but the problem is that it is hard to raise." According to Haldeman, Nixon had said, "There is no problem" in raising the money, "but it would be wrong." Haldeman told the panel the tape of the meeting confirmed his recollection.

The grand jury charged that Haldeman's statements about Nixon's "it would be wrong," as Haldeman "then and there well knew, were false."

Nixon had backed up Haldeman's testimony as "accurate" in an Aug. 22, 1973 news conference.

Perjury: Haldeman and Mitchell; money and documents—Haldeman's Senate com-

mittee testimony on the $350,000 cash fund under his control, which according to the grand jury was used for "hush money" payments to the break-in defendants, resulted in a second perjury charge. Haldeman had said he was unaware of their use for "blackmail" until told by Dean in March 1973. This, the indictment charged, was false.

(Gordon Strachan's testimony before the grand jury on the handling of the money was the basis of the false declarations charge against him.)

Haldeman's third perjury count went back to the March 21, 1973 White House meeting, which—according to Dean's testimony before the Senate Committee—had included Dean's report on the preparation of a false story on the planning of the break-in to be used by Magruder. Haldeman later told the panel, "I don't believe there was any reference to Magruder committing perjury." This statement was false, the indictment charged.

Mitchell was charged with perjury in connection with his Watergate committee testimony on the so-called "Gemstone" file of wiretap information from Democratic Party headquarters. Asked about a meeting in his apartment June 19, 1972, Mitchell said he had not heard of the Gemstone file as of that date, nor to the "best of [his] recollection" had there been any destruction of documents. The statements were false, the grand jury charged.

False statements to probers—The indictment charged that Mitchell on two occasions testified falsely before the grand jury. On the first, Mitchell said he knew of no illegal, clandestine plans against the Democrats, "because, if there had been, I would have shut it off as being entirely nonproductive at that particular time of the campaign." Mitchell testified later that he could not recall being told by LaRue or Mardian that Liddy had confessed to a role in the break-in.

Ehrlichman was also charged with two counts of lying to the grand jury. According to the first charge, Ehrlichman testified falsely when he said he could not recall discussing Liddy's role in the break-in with Dean; nor could he recall when he first learned that Liddy was implicated. The grand jury also charged that Ehrlichman lied in testifying that he could not recall discussing with Kalmbach the purpose of Kalmbach's fund-raising or telling Kalmbach that the fund-raising should be kept secret.

Both Mitchell and Ehrlichman were accused of falsely telling the FBI that their knowledge of the break-in was limited to newspaper accounts. Mitchell's statement came less than three weeks after the break-in, but Ehrlichman was charged with saying as late as July 21, 1973 "that he had neither received nor was he in possession of any information relative to the break-in . . . other than what he had read in the way of newspaper accounts. . . ."

Ellsberg burglary indictment. A second Watergate grand jury March 7, 1974 indicted six men in connection with the September 1971 burglary of the office of Dr. Lewis J. Fielding, the Los Angeles psychiatrist who had treated Pentagon Papers defendant Daniel Ellsberg. The burglary had been carried out under the aegis of the special White House investigative unit known as the "plumbers."

The charge was conspiring to violate Fielding's civil rights by acting together to "oppress, threaten and intimidate" Fielding by entering his office "without legal process, probable cause, search warrant or other lawful authority" and by concealing "the involvement of officials and employes of the United States Government."

Those charged with conspiracy were:
John D. Ehrlichman.
Charles W. Colson.
G. Gordon Liddy, Bernard L. Barker and Eugenio R. Martinez, all of whom had been convicted in the Watergate break-in.
Felipe DeDiego, who had previously been named as an unindicted co-conspirator in a California state case relating to the Fielding burglary. (The charge against DeDiego was dismissed May 21 because he had been given im-

munity by the state prosecutors in return for his testimony.)

The indictment named as unindicted co-conspirators E. Howard Hunt Jr., Egil Krogh Jr. and David R. Young Jr.

Ehrlichman was also charged with three counts of false declarations to the grand jury and one count of lying to the Federal Bureau of Investigation (FBI).

The conspiracy—In a list of 19 "overt acts," the indictment related that the conspiracy began July 27, 1971 with a memorandum from Krogh and Young [the co-directors of the "plumbers"] to Ehrlichman dealing with a request for a psychiatric study of Ellsberg. Ehrlichman was told three days later that the request had been directed to the Central Intelligence Agency.

In the interim, Hunt sent Colson a memo entitled "Neutralization of Ellsberg" containing a proposal to "obtain Ellsberg's files" from the psychiatrist's office. Krogh and Young later informed Colson they would "look into" Hunt's suggestions.

Ehrlichman approved a "covert operation" Aug. 11, provided he was given the "assurance it is not traceable." By Aug. 30, Krogh and Young were able to give Ehrlichman the assurance he required.

Meanwhile, Colson, Young and Krogh began discussing raising covert funds to pay the actual burglars. Young and Colson also concentrated on how to get "the information out" on Ellsberg. Ehrlichman instructed Colson to prepare a "game plan" on possible use of the materials taken from Fielding's office under what Ehrlichman still called Hunt's "proposed" plan.

The money problem was solved around the first of September: Colson arranged to obtain $5,000 in cash, which was repaid by a transfer from the Trust for Agricultural Political Education (a dairy industry group). Krogh delivered the money to Liddy Sept. 1, and Liddy and Hunt went to Los Angeles to meet with Barker, DeDiego and Martinez. The latter three broke into Fielding's office Sept. 3.

The final act of conspiracy cited by the grand jury came March 27, 1973, when Ehrlichman "caused the removal of certain memoranda" on the burglary "from files maintained at the White House in which such memoranda would be kept in the ordinary course of business."

Ehrlichman's false statements—The one count charging Ehrlichman with lying to the FBI involved the agency's probe into whether the Fielding burglary might taint the prosecution of Ellsberg. Ehrlichman told the FBI May 1, 1973 that he had not seen material on the White House investigation of the Pentagon Papers affair in more than a year.

Ehrlichman appeared before a grand jury May 14, 1973 and maintained repeatedly that he knew of the burglary and the instructions to prepare a psychological profile of Ellsberg only "after the fact."

Nixon an unindicted 'co-conspirator.' The White House admitted June 6 that the Watergate grand jury had voted in February to name President Nixon as an unindicted co-conspirator with his former aides, who were indicted for the cover-up of the Watergate break-in.

The grand jury's vote, reported to be unanimous, had been kept secret under an order by U.S. District Court Judge John J. Sirica. But after a report of the jury's action appeared in the June 6 editions of the Los Angeles Times, special presidential counsel James D. St. Clair said he had been informed of the vote three or four weeks earlier by special Watergate prosecutor Leon Jaworski.

St. Clair related that when he had told Nixon, the President responded: " 'They just don't have the evidence and they are wrong.' "

According to news reports, the grand jury had at first been inclined to indict Nixon, but had been dissuaded by Jaworski's contention that such action could not be taken against a President in office.

Colson plea in Ellsberg case. Charles W. Colson, former special counsel to President Nixon, pleaded guilty in Washington federal court June 3, 1974 to a charge that he "unlawfully ... did ... endeavor to influence, obstruct and impede" the trial of Pentagon Papers defendant Daniel Ellsberg. In return for the plea, the Watergate special prosecutor's office agreed to drop all other charges pending against Colson.

As part of his understanding with the prosecutor's office, Colson consented to give it sworn testimony and provide relevant documents in his possession, and in other Watergate-related cases, which observers took to mean the impeachment inquiry against the President.

Colson pleaded guilty to a one-count criminal information accusing him of "devising and implementing a scheme to defame and destroy the public image and credibility of Daniel Ellsberg and those engaged in the legal defense of Daniel Ellsberg, with the intent to influence, obstruct and impede the conduct and outcome" of the 1973 Ellsberg trial.

Colson was sentenced to one to three years in prison by Judge Gerhard A. Gesell June 3 and fined $5,000.

Before Gesell passed sentence, Colson read to the court a statement reiterating his innocence of the offenses for which he had been indicted but accepting responsibility for the charge for which he was about to be sentenced. "As to the specific offense charged, the President on numerous occasions urged me to disseminate damaging information about Daniel Ellsberg ... I endeavored to do so—and willingly. I don't mean to shift my responsibility to the President. I believed what I was doing was right."

Committee Gets Transcripts of President's Tapes

The charges that President Nixon was implicated in Watergate provoked a chorous of demands for his impeachment, and the House Judiciary Committee started an impeachment inquiry in November 1973. For its inquiry, the committee voted April 11, 1974 to subpoena all tape recordings and other materials related to 42 Presidential conversations considered relevant to the investigation. Nixon, who had consistently resisted Congressional demands that he or his aides testify or provide evidence about confidential Executive Branch discussions, said, under growing pressure, that he would provide transcripts of some of the tapes subpoenaed.

President releases transcripts. Nixon, in a television address April 29, 1974, said he would turn over to the House Judiciary Committee the next day, and also make public, 1,200 pages of edited transcripts of his conversations with key aides concerning Watergate. Asserting he had "nothing to hide," Nixon said the transcripts included "all the relevant portions of all of the subpoenaed conversations that were recorded and related to Watergate or the cover-up. The transcripts also covered other conversations, he said, which were not subpoenaed by the committee "but which have a significant bearing on the question of Presidential action with regard to Watergate."

The President cited the "wrenching ordeal" for the nation of an impeachment proceeding and "the impact of such an ordeal" throughout the world. Therefore, he was making the transcripts public and would also make public transcripts of all the parts of the tapes already turned over to the special prosecutor and the committee that related to his actions or knowledge of Watergate.

During the past year, Nixon said, "the wildest accusations have been given banner headlines and ready credence as well," leaving "a vague, general impression of massive wrongdoing, implicating everybody, gaining credibility by its endless repetition."

"The basic question at issue today," he continued, "is whether the President personally acted improperly in the Watergate matter. Month after month of rumor, insinuation and charges by just one Watergate witness, John Dean [former counsel to the President], suggested that the President did act improperly. This

sparked the demand for an impeachment inquiry."

Returning to the principle of confidentiality, he believed a reading of the raw transcripts made it "more readily apparent why that principle is essential and must be maintained in the future." "The same kind of uninhibited discussion," he said, the "same brutal candor is necessary in discussing how to bring warring factions to the peace table or how to move necessary legislation through the Congress."

The transcripts, Nixon said, would demonstrate his concern during the period covered. "The first and obvious one," he said, "was to find out just exactly what had happened and who was involved." He also was concerned, he said, for the people involved and, "quite frankly," about the political implications.

"I wanted to do what was right," he stressed. "But I wanted to do it in a way that would cause the least unnecessary damage in a highly charged political atmosphere to the Administration."

His other concerns were not to prejudice the rights of potential defendants and "to sort out a complex tangle" not only of facts but also of legal and moral responsibility. "I wanted, above all, to be fair," Nixon said.

Nixon specifically cited several conversations with Dean. The transcripts "show clearly," he said, that, contrary to Dean's charge he was fully aware of the cover-up in September 1972, "I first learned of it" from Dean on March 21, 1973 some six months later. He learned in that conversation, Nixon said, that Watergate defendant Howard Hunt was "threatening blackmail" unless $120,000 was extended to legal fees and family support, and that the blackmail involved exposure not on Watergate but on "extremely sensitive, highly secret national security matters [such as, presumably the Ellsberg case break-in]."

Later, Nixon said, he learned "how much there was that he [Dean] did not tell me then; for example, that he himself had authorized promises of clemency, that he had personally handled money for the

Watergate defendants, and that he had suborned perjury of a witness."

In his March 21 talk, he said, he kept returning to the blackmail threat, "which to me was not a Watergate problem but one which I regarded, rightly or wrongly, as a potential national security problem of very serious proportions."

"The money could be raised," he continued. "But money demands would lead inescapably to clemency demands, and clemency could not be granted, I said, and I quote directly from the tape—It is wrong, that's for sure."

Nixon also quoted from the transcripts that "in the end we are going to be bled to death" and "it is all going to come out anyway and then you get the worst of both worlds" and in effect it would "look like a cover-up. So that we cannot do."

Recognizing that the tape could be interpreted differently by different people, Nixon said in the end it showed his decision to convene a new grand jury "and to send everyone before" it with instructions to testify.

Nixon tracked his subsequent actions— assigning Dean to write a report and, when it was not forthcoming, giving the task to his aide John D. Ehrlichman; having another aide H. R. Haldeman pursue other independent lines of inquiry; having Ehrlichman inform the attorney general of his findings, and agreeing to have Assistant Attorney General Henry Petersen put in charge of the investigation and his follow-up and cooperation with Petersen.

"I made clear there was to be no cover-up," Nixon stressed. He quoted his own remarks against extending clemency and for doing "the right thing," his advice "to prick the boil and take the heat" and for Dean to "tell the truth. That is the thing I have told everybody around here."

In essence, the transcripts would show, Nixon said, "that what I have stated from the beginning to be the truth has been the truth, that I personally had no knowledge of the break-in before it occurred, that I had no knowledge of the cover-up" until March 21, 1973, that he never offered clemency and that, after March 21, "my actions were directed toward finding the facts and seeing that justice was done."

Never before in the history of the presidency, Nixon said, "have records that are so private been made so public. In giving you these records—blemishes and all—I am placing my trust in the basic fairness of the American people."

11 conversations missing—The transcripts, which were released April 30, did not cover 11 of the 42 conversations subpoenaed by the committee. Four of them, according to White House counsel J. Fred Buzhardt, were not recorded because the machine ran out of tape; five were on phones not connected to a recorder, and tapes of two were not found.

The transcripts themselves were found to be liberally sprinkled with deletions marked "unintelligible," "expletive deleted" or "inaudible." Many passages actually were unintelligible because of the markings. One entire comment attributed to Nixon, whose conversation was dotted with "expletives," was: "P. [expletive removed]! [unintelligible]"

A brief attached as an introduction to the volume of transcripts said the expletives had been removed, except where necessary to maintain relevancy, in the interest of good taste. Other deletions, allowable on the relevancy test, it said, were made to eliminate characterization of third persons and material not relating to the President's conduct.

Brief asserts innocence. A White House legal brief accompanying the transcripts April 30 asserted President Nixon's innocence in the Watergate matter. Released several hours before the transcripts, it maintained that "the raw material of these recorded confidential conversations establishes that the President had no prior knowledge of the break-in and that he had no knowledge of any cover-up to March 21, 1973."

Written by Nixon's special counsel James D. St. Clair, the brief said: "In all of the thousands of words spoken, even though they are unclear and ambiguous, not once does it appear that the President of the United States was engaged in a criminal plot to obstruct justice."

The brief, as the President did in his

speech, attacked in particular John Dean's credibility. It indicated Dean had repeatedly perjured himself in sworn testimony and accused him of trying to blackmail the President in an effort to gain immunity from prosecution.

It said Assistant Attorney General Henry E. Petersen had reported to Nixon on April 27, 1973 that Dean's lawyer was threatening to "bring the President in—not in this case [the cover-up] but in other things" if Dean did not get immunity. Nixon's reply, according to the brief, was: "All right. We have the immunity problem resolved. Do it [grant immunity] to Dean if you need to, but I am telling you—there ain't going to be any blackmail." (Dean was not extended full immunity. He pleaded guilty to one count of conspiracy to obstruct justice and was awaiting sentencing. Dean's attorney, Robert C. McCandless, denied ever making such a threat April 30.)

As another contradiction, the brief cited Dean's testimony that Nixon had never asked him to write a report on his Watergate investigation, that it was not until he went to Camp David that he received a call from a Nixon aide asking for the report. According to the March 22, 1973 transcript, Nixon told Dean "I want a written report."

Transcript excerpts. According to the transcripts provided by the White House, President Nixon (designated P.) and John Dean (designated D.) said during a discussion Feb. 28, 1973:

. . . P. [expletive deleted] Of course, I am not dumb and I will never forget when I heard about this [adjective deleted] forced entry and bugging. I thought, what in the hell is this? What is the matter with these people? Are they crazy? I thought they were nuts! A prank! But it wasn't! It wasn't very funny. I think that our Democratic friends know that, too. They know what the hell it was. They don't think we'd be involved in such.
D. I think they do too.
P. Maybe they don't. They don't think I would be involved in such stuff. They think I have people capable of it. And they are correct, in that Colson would do anything. Well, O.K.—Have a little fun. And now I will not talk to you again until you have something to report to me. D. Alright, sir.
P. But I think it is very important that you have these talks with our good friend Kleindienst. D. That will be done.
P. Tell him we have to get these things worked out.

We have to work together on this thing. I would build him up. He is the man who can make the difference. Also point out to him what we have. [Expletive deleted] Colson's got [characterization deleted], but I really, really—this stuff here—let's forget this. But let's remember this was not done by the White House. This was done by the Committee to Re-Elect, and Mitchell was the chairman, correct? D. That's correct!
P. And Kleindienst owes Mitchell everything. Mitchell wanted him for Attorney General. Wanted him for Deputy, and here he is. Now, [expletive deleted]. Baker's got to realize this, and that if he allows this thing to get out of hand he is going to potentially ruin John Mitchell. He won't. Mitchell won't allow himself to be ruined. He will put on his big stone face. But I hope he does and he will. There is no question what they are after. What the committee is after is somebody at the White House. They would like to get Haldeman or Colson, Ehrlichman.

Excerpts from a March 13, 1973 conversation on the Ervin committee hearings:
D. They would be quick [inaudible] They would want to find out who knew— P. Is there a higher up? D. Is there a higher up? P. Let's face it, I think they are really after Haldeman. D. Haldeman and Mitchell.
P. Colson is not big enough name for them. He really isn't. He is, you know, he is on the government side, but Colson's name doesn't bother them so much. They are after Haldeman and after Mitchell. Don't you think so.?
D. Sure. They are going to take a look and try to drag them, but they're going to be able to drag them into the election—
P. In any event, Haldeman's problem is Chapin isn't it? D. Bob's problem is circumstantial. P. Why is that? Let's look at the circumstantial. I don't know, Bob didn't know any of those people like the Hunts and all that bunch. Colson did, but Bob didn't. OK? D. That's right.
P. Now where the hell, or how much Chapin knew I will be [expletive deleted] if I know. D. Chapin didn't know anything about the Watergate.
P. Don't you think so? D. Absolutely not. P. Strachan? D. Yes. P. He knew? D. Yes. P. About the Watergate? D. Yes.
P. Well, then, he probably told Bob. He may not have. D. He was judicious in what he relayed, but Strachan is as tough as nails. He can go in and stonewall, and say, "I don't know anything about what you are talking about." He has already done it twice you know, in interviews.
P. I guess he should, shouldn't he? I suppose we can't call that justice, can we? D. Well, it is personal loyalty to him. He doesn't want it any other way. He didn't have to be told. He didn't have to be asked. It just is something that he found was the way he wanted to handle the situation.
P. But he knew? He knew about Watergate? Strachan did? D. Yes.
D. Yes. P. I will be damned! Well that is the problem in Bob's case. Not Chapin then, but Strachan. Strachan worked for him, didn't he? D. Yes. They would have one hell of a time proving that Strachan had knowledge of it, though. P. Who knew better? Magruder? D. Magruder and Liddy. P. Oh, I see. The other weak link for Bob is Magruder. He hired him et cetera. D. That applies to Mitchell, too.

P. Mitchell—Magruder. Where do you see Colson coming into it? Do you think he knew quite a bit and yet, he could know quite a great deal about a lot of other things and not know a lot about this. I don't know. D. Well, I have never—P. He sure as hell knows Hunt—that we know—was very close to him. D. Chuck has told me that he had no knowledge, specific knowledge, of the Watergate before it occurred. There have been tidbits that I have raised with Chuck, I have not played any games with him. I said, "Chuck, I have indications—"

P. What indications? The lawyer has to know everything. D. That's right. I said, "Chuck, people have said that you were involved in this, involved in that, involved in all of this." He said, "That is not true, etc." I think that Chuck had knowledge that something was going on over there, but he didn't have any knowledge of the details of the specifics of the whole thing.

P. There must have been an indication of the fact that we had poor pickings. Because naturally anybody, either Chuck or Bob, were always reporting to me about what was going on. If they ever got any information they would certainly have told me that we got some information, but they never had a thing to report. What was the matter? Did they never get anything out of the damn thing?

D. I don't think they ever got anything, sir. P. A dry hole? D. That's right. P. (Expletive deleted) D. Well, they were just really getting started.

Nixon and Dean March 17, 1973 discussed the burglary of the office of Daniel Ellsberg's former psychiatrist:

D. The other potential problem is Ehrlichman's and this is—P. In connection with Hunt? D. In connection with Hunt and Liddy both. P. They worked for him? D. They—these fellows had to be some idiots as we've learned after the fact. They went out and went into Dr. Ellsberg's doctor's office and they had, they were geared up with all this CIA equipment—cameras and the like. Well they turned the stuff back in to the CIA some point in time and left film in the camera. CIA has not put this together, and they don't know what it all means right now. But it wouldn't take a very sharp investigator very long because you've got pictures in the CIA files that they had to turn over to (unintelligible).

P. What in the world—what in the name of God was Ehrlichman having something (unintelligible) in the Ellsberg (unintelligible)? D. They were trying to—this was a part of an operation that—in connection with the Pentagon papers. They were—the whole thing—they wanted to get Ellsberg's psychiatric records for some reason. I don't know. P. This is the first I ever heard of this. I, I (unintelligible) care about Ellsberg was not our problem. D. That's right. P. (Expletive deleted) D. Well, anyway (unintelligible), it was under an Ehrlichman structure, maybe John didn't ever know. I've never asked him if he knew. I didn't

During a conversation March 21, 1973, Dean told Nixon that Watergate had begun as an innocent request by the White House for campaign intelligence against the Democrats. However, Liddy became involved and the final result was the bugging of the Democratic National Committee at its Watergate headquarters. When the burglars were arrested, they demanded money to see them through the November elections, as well as attorney's fees.

Nixon discussed the situation March 27, 1973 with Haldeman, Ehrlichman and Press Secretary Ron Ziegler.

One possibility, the subject of this and later conversations, was that Mitchell might be persuaded to take the blame for the entire Watergate affair and—as a high-level figure—take the pressure off the White House.

Part of the reasoning behind the concern, according to Haldeman, was the displeasure voiced by campaign officials Paul O'Brien and Kenneth W. Parkinson with seeing "all the people getting whacked around in order to keep the thing from focusing on John Mitchell when inevitably it is going to end up doing that anyway...."

P. They aren't involved in the damn thing are they? O'Brien and Parkinson? H. Yes. P. They ran this all from the beginning? H. Oh, no. P. Well, that is what I thought. H. But they are involved in the post-discovery, post-June 17th.

Ehrlichman reported to Nixon and Haldeman April 14, 1973 on a meeting he had just held with Mitchell. He had told Mitchell the President did not feel that Mitchell's only option was to agree to a guilty plea with the U.S. Attorney's office.

E. And he [Mitchell] said, well, he appreciated that, but he had not been taking the position he had for the reason that he thought he was necessarily helping or hurting the Presidency, but he said, "You know, these characters pulled this thing off without my knowledge." He said, "I never saw Liddy for months at a time." And he said, "I didn't know what they were up to and nobody was more surprised than I was. ... I didn't press him on it and I tried to play him with kid gloves. I never asked him to tell me anything. He just told me all this stuff. He says that actually Magruder is going to have a problem with all of this because Dean talked Magruder into saying the wrong things to the grand jury, and so Magruder's got a problem....

E. Well it goes on like that. His characterization of all this is that he was a very busy man, that he wasn't keeping track of what was going on at the committee—that this was engendered as a result of Hunt and Liddy coming to Colson's office and getting Colson to make a phone call to Magruder and that he, Mitchell, was just not aware that all that happened until Van Shumway brought Liddy into Mitchell's office sometime in June and that's the first he had knowledge of it....

E. Well, I said I understand that one version of the

fact is that Magruder brought you a memo with a number of targets on it, and that you checked off the targets that you wanted. And he said, "Why nothing could be further from the truth than that."

Ehrlichman met with Nixon and Haldeman after having conferred with Jeb Stuart Magruder. Magruder had just met with the U.S. Attorney General to discuss his involvement in Watergate.

The bugging of the Watergate headquarters of the Democratic National Committee, Magruder related to Ehrlichman, came after Mitchell had "chewed" out Liddy for his failure to obtain useful political intelligence against the Democrats. Moreover, the bugging operation was part of an overall plan that had been approved by Mitchell with reluctance, Magruder said:

E. In the conversation, Mitchell orally approved it. Now it involved other things besides tapes, and he was not specific. He said, "In all honesty this was a kind of a non-decision. Nobody felt comfortable in this thing but we were sort of bull-dozed into it." was the way he put it. Ah—P. By Colson? E. That's the inference. . . .

E. The one copy [of Liddy's intelligence report] that Magruder had had pictures of the kinds of papers that you'd find around with campaign headquarters. He sent a synopsis of the pictures to Mitchell. He thought it was so bad he picked up the phone and called Liddy and chewed him out. . . . Liddy was badly embarrassed by the chewing out he got. He met in a meeting with him, and said to John Mitchell, "Mr. Mitchell I'll take care of it." That was all that was said. So the next break-in was entirely on Liddy's own notion. Magruder says neither Mitchell nor Magruder knew that another break-in was contemplated. . . .

E. Dean devised a cover story, in concert with these other people, and enlisted Bart Porter who went to the Grand Jury and perjured himself in concert with the cover story. Dean prepared Magruder and others for the testimony at the Grand Jury, cross-examining and getting them ready.

P. Let me ask you, John, about Colson. Everything that has been said, despite the fact of how accurate—it would be consistent with Colson's not knowing the Watergate defendants? E. Magruder doesn't lay a glove on him.

Committee begins hearings. The House Judiciary Committee May 9, 1973 began its hearings on whether to recommend the impeachment of President Nixon.

The committee's leaders pledged in an 18-minute public ceremony to conduct a fair and nonpartisan inquiry.

Committee Chairman Peter W. Rodino Jr. (D, N.J.) opened the hearings by stressing "the importance of our undertaking and the wisdom, decency and principle we must bring to it. We understand our high constitutional responsibility. We will faithfully live up to it."

Rodino declared the committee would "thoroughly" examine six areas of inquiry, beginning with "the question of presidential responsibility for the Watergate break-in and its investigation by law enforcement agencies."

Committee issues Watergate evidence. The House Judiciary Committee released July 11, 1974 an eight-volume, 4,133-page record of the evidence assembled by its staff dealing with the Watergate break-in and its aftermath. Seven volumes consisted of the material presented by the staff to the committee members in closed sessions in May and June. The eighth volume was President Nixon's rebuttal presented to the committee by his lawyer, James St. Clair.

The staff material consisted of statements of information and supporting material; there was no attempt to present findings.

The St. Clair material—242 pages—did contain conclusions and was much narrower in scope than the staff record. It focused primarily on the controversial payment of $75,000 to Watergate conspirator E. Howard Hunt Jr. St. Clair restated the President's position that he first learned of the Watergate cover-up on March 21, 1973, then launched an inquiry and took action to bring the facts to the proper authorities. "The President had no knowledge of an attempt by the White House to cover up involvement in the Watergate affair," it declared.

The bulk of the evidence released was already on the public record, but there were some new disclosures. Among them, contained in secret grand jury testimony released as supportive material, was Hunt's admission that his demand for the money was accompanied by a threat. He was asked, according to the evidence released by the committee, if there was "any other interpretation other than the clear meaning of the words that you would review your options for alternatives other than that you would tell about these so-called seamy things unless they met your demands?" Hunt's reply was "No" and he also explained to the grand jury what the "seamy things" were—the burglary of the office of Daniel Ellsberg's psychiatrist, the forging of State Department cables and the political dirty tricks of Donald Segretti.

Also among the material released was grand jury testimony by former Nixon aide John D. Ehrlichman that when he learned of Hunt's demand, from then Nixon counsel John W. Dean 3rd, "I said it looked to me like blackmail."

Nixon Implicated, Ehrlichman Convicted in Ellsberg Case

John D. Ehrlichman was convicted in July 1974 of conspiracy in the burglary of the office of Daniel Ellsberg's former psychiatrist. He was found guilty after proceedings during which President Nixon was accused of complicity in the case.

Nixon took part in pre-break-in meeting. Former Presidential counsel Charles W. Colson said April 29 that President Nixon in a June 1971 meeting told him and H. R. Haldeman, then White House chief of staff, that leaks of classified information had to be stopped, "whatever has to be done . . . whatever the cost."

Colson, under indictment in connection with the break-in at the office of Dr. Lewis J. Fielding, who had treated Daniel Ellsberg, made this claim in a pre-trial affidavit submitted to U.S. District Court Judge Gerhard A. Gesell. Filed in support of a defense move to use national security as a defense against conspiracy charges, the statement was the most detailed account of President Nixon's anger over leaks of classified information to be made public.

Besides citing concern by the President and his national security adviser Henry Kissinger over the leaks, Colson asked the court for access to many classified government documents to prepare his case. These included federal investigatory reports "concerning the suspicion that

Dr. Ellsberg was acting on behalf of some foreign government in releasing classified information."

In his account of the June 1971 White House meeting, Colson said Nixon in effect said to him and Haldeman: "I don't give a damn how it is done, do whatever has to be done to stop these leaks and prevent further unauthorized disclosures; I don't want to be told why it can't be done. This government cannot survive, it cannot function if anyone can run out and leak whatever documents he wants to . . . I want to know who is behind this and I want the most complete investigation that can be conducted. The President went on: I want to know how and why the 'counter-government' is at work. If we do not stop them, if we do not find out who is involved and why, we will endanger everything that this government is trying to do in the most sensitive foreign policy and national security areas. I don't want excuses, I want results. I want it done, whatever the cost."

At another point, Colson said "Kissinger was even more alarmed over the leaks than the President. He believed that the leaks must be stopped at all costs, that Ellsberg must be stopped from making further disclosures of classified information. . . ." Colson stated that he had the "clear impression" that Kissinger, like the President, feared that Ellsberg's activities would "undermine the most critical and sensitive foreign policy negotiations."

Colson's affidavit also mentioned an April 1973 conversation with White House domestic affairs adviser John D. Ehrlichman, who told him that the President had informed Assistant Attorney General Henry E. Petersen that he [Nixon] had approved the "Ellsberg operation" after consultation with Federal Bureau of Investigation Director J. Edgar Hoover. The affidavit did not explain what was meant by the "Ellsberg operation."

Ehrlichman says Nixon approved break-in. Ehrlichman, Nixon's former domestic affairs adviser, said in an affidavit submitted April 30 that Nixon had twice "indicated his after-the-fact approval" of the break-in at Fielding's office.

Denying any advance knowledge of the break-in, which was perpetrated by the special White House investigations unit called "the plumbers," Ehrlichman said the President discussed the burglary twice when he had been present. The first discussion occurred during an April 18, 1973 phone conversation between Nixon and Petersen, in which the President said to Petersen in substance: "You and your department stay out of that. This is strictly a national security matter. I know you have to enforce the laws, but, as President, I have to protect the national security and that comes first. As President I am instructing you to take no action whatsoever on that matter." After hanging up, Ehrlichman said, the President said the conversation had dealt with the Fielding burglary. The President "said in substance that the break-in was in furtherance of national security and fully justified by the circumstances."

The second conversation related in the Ehrlichman affidavit took place in early May 1973 in the White House Oval Office, where the President told Ehrlichman in effect: "While I did not know of the break-in attempt in advance, I surely recognize the valid national security reasons why it was done."

At another point in his affidavit, Ehrlichman said Henry A. Kissinger, then the President's national security adviser, had been present at the 1971 meeting at the Presidential retreat in San Clemente, Calif., during which Nixon had named Kissinger's aide David R. Young Jr. a co-director of the "plumbers" unit. Kissinger had testified at Senate hearings on his appointment as secretary of state that he "did not know of the existence of the plumbers group."

Colson pleads guilty. Colson pleaded guilty June 3 to the single charge that he had tried "to influence, obstruct and impede" Ellsberg's trial in the Pentagon Papers case. In return for the plea, the Watergate special prosecutor's office agreed to drop all other charges pending against Colson.

As part of his understanding with the prosecutor's office, Colson consented to give it sworn testimony and provide relevant documents in his possession.

In a statement issued after his plea had been entered, Colson maintained that he had been innocent of charges contained in the two indictments previously returned against him—the Watergate cover-up and the Ellsberg break-in.

Colson was sentenced to one to three years in prison and fined $5,000 by U.S. Judge Gerhard A. Gesell June 21.

Ehrlichman & trio convicted. Ehrlichman was found guilty by a federal jury in Washington July 12 of conspiring to violate Dr. Fielding's civil rights. Three co-defendants—G. Gordon Liddy, Bernard L. Barker and Eugenio Martinez—were convicted of the same charge. Ehrlichman was also found guilty of three of four counts of making false statements.

Instructing the jury on the conspiracy charge, Judge Gesell said that it need not find Ehrlichman had known in advance of plans for a "covert entry" into Fielding's office files to obtain Ellsberg's psychiatric records. Moreover, Gesell told the jurors, an illegal search need not entail "physical break-in," which only tended to emphasize "lack of permission." The law had been broken if the government attempted to acquire private information without a search warrant, he said. "When a government agency invades an area in which there is a legitimate expectation of privacy to look through such papers without permission, that is a search," the judge stated.

Gesell's instructions struck at the heart of Ehrlichman's defense that he had not authorized an illegal break-in but merely a legal "covert operation."

In his other instructions, Gesell said, "An individual cannot escape criminal liability simply because he sincerely but incorrectly believes that his acts are justified in the name of patriotism, of national security or the need to create an unfavorable press image or that his superiors had the authority to suspend without a warrant the protections of the Fourth Amendment." (The 4th Amendment guaranteed against unreasonable searches.)

Ehrlichman was acquitted on a charge of false testimony to a grand jury May 14, 1973. At that time, Ehrlichman stated that he did not know who, other than Egil Krogh Jr., co-director of the White House "plumbers" unit, had files on the unit's investigation of Ellsberg. However, the jury concluded that Ehrlichman had twice made false statements to the grand jury when he said he had not been aware before the break-in of the plan to obtain Ellsberg's psychiatric files. In addition, the jury convicted Ehrlichman of the charge of falsely stating to the Federal Bureau of Investigation May 1, 1973 that he had not seen any material relating to the White House investigation of the Pentagon Papers affair for more than a year.

Ehrlichman was sentenced by Gesell July 21 to prison terms of 20 months to five years. The defendant received the same sentence for each of two other perjury charges on which he was convicted. The sentences, a minimum of 20 months, were to run concurrently.

Ehrlichman had been found guilty of lying to the FBI, but Gesell dismissed this charge July 22 as too vague.

Co-defendant G. Gordon Liddy received a sentence of one to three years in prison, to be served concurrently with his present sentence of six years, eight months to 20 years.

The two other defendants convicted of conspiracy, Bernard L. Barker and Eugenio Martinez, were placed on probation for three years by Gesell. Gesell said they had been "duped" by high government officials and had been punished enough.

Testifying in his own defense July 8, Ehrlichman had denied authorizing or seeing plans for the break-in.

Associate special Watergate prosecutor William Merrill then directed a series of questions at Ehrlichman designed to show that the defendant had known about the plan for a psychological profile of Ellsberg and that Ehrlichman, in authorizing a "covert operation" to examine Fielding's files on Ellsberg, had been aware he was authorizing an unlawful entry into Fielding's office.

Much of what Merrill asked Ehrlichman centered on an Aug. 11, 1971 memorandum, on which Ehrlichman initialed his approval of a "covert operation" as long as it was "not traceable" to the White House. Asked by Merrill what he considered a "covert operation" to be, Ehrlichman responded that it was "a private investigation, where the people don't identify themselves as from the FBI—a conventional investigation like the FBI would conduct."

Questioned about the methods that would be used to obtain the information, Ehrlichman responded that it "didn't enter my thought processes." Ehrlichman said he thought perhaps the files could be examined "by request" or "by a third party."

Under other questioning by Merrill and Judge Gesell, Ehrlichman said he had sought assurances that the operation would not be traceable to the White House because he feared it would become a "cause celebre in the press," as well as have a "big brother is watching appearance."

Nixon & Kissinger testify—The trial was highlighted July 10 by the reading to the jury of sworn testimony provided by President Nixon. The President had given written replies to six questions submitted by the defense. Prior to the reading of Nixon's testimony, Secretary of State Henry A. Kissinger had appeared as a defense witness.

The six questions and Nixon's replies were:

Q. What duties and responsibilities, if any, did you authorize the special investigations unit located in Room 16 of the Executive Office Building to perform?

A. I authorized the special investigations unit to prevent and halt leaks of vital security information and to prepare an accurate history of certain critical national security matters which occurred under prior Administrations.

Q. What instructions, if any, did you personally give John D. Ehrlichman concerning his role in the activities of the unit? (If so, please give details, including where and when such instructions were given.)

A. I instructed John D. Ehrlichman to exercise general supervisory control over the special investigations unit.

Q. Did you ever instruct John D. Ehrlichman not to discuss the activities of the unit with either (A) the FBI [Federal Bureau of Investigation] and-or (B) members of the White House staff not directly involved in the work of the unit? Please detail each such instruction and indicate the date on which it was given, the reasons for giving it and the period during which it remained in effect.

(Nixon gave a single reply to the third and fourth questions.)

Q. Did you ever instruct John D. Ehrlichman not to discuss the activities of the unit at any time after Sept. 3, 1971, as they related to Dr. Fielding's files with either (A) the FBI and-or (B) members of the White House staff not directly involved in the work of the unit? Please detail each such instruction and indicate the date on which it was given, the reasons for giving it and the period during which it remained in effect.

A. I do not have a precise recollection of instructions given to Mr. Ehrlichman with respect to any specific agencies. In substance, however, I do recall repeatedly emphasizing to Mr. Ehrlichman that this was a highly classified matter which could be discussed with others only on an absolutely "need to know" basis. I conveyed these instructions because I believed that the unit could not function effectively if its existence or the nature and details of its work were compromised by disclosure. These instructions were given at various times after the special investigations unit was formed, which was shortly after June 13, 1971. [the date of newspaper publication of the Pentagon papers]

Q. On what date were you first informed of the Fielding break-in?

A. March 17, 1973.

Q. Did you ever authorize anyone on the White House staff to search the files of Dr. Fielding for information about Dr. Ellsberg, without a warrant or the permission of Dr. Fielding, or hire others to do so? (If yes, please give details and state whether or not you authorized the CIA to cooperate with the unit by assisting it in any way in any such search of Dr. Fielding's files for information concerning Dr. Ellsberg.)

A. No.

In his brief testimony, Kissinger denied having authorized David R. Young Jr., co-director of the White House "plumbers," to ask the CIA for a psychological profile of Ellsberg. Kissinger was asked, "Did you have any knowledge whether there was a plan to obtain psychological information regarding Daniel Ellsberg or his psychological files from his psychiatrist?" Again Kissinger said, "I had no such knowledge."

Kissinger & Wiretaps

Resignation threat over charges. Secretary of State Henry Kissinger threatened June 11, 1974 to resign unless charges that he had participated in "illegal or shady" wiretapping activity were cleared up. The secretary made the remark during an emotional news conference in Salzburg, Austria, during a stopover with President Nixon preparatory to a Mideast tour.

Appearing to be hurt and angry, Kissinger, in a shaking voice, complained of "innuendoes" and said he did not believe it was possible to conduct the foreign policy of the nation "under these circumstances when the character and credibility of the secretary of state is at issue." "And if it is not cleared up, I will resign," he declared.

Kissinger's surprise threat to quit his post was prompted by reports from unidentified Congressional sources that Kissinger had a more extensive role in federal wiretapping efforts than he had led senators to believe at his confirmation hearing in 1973.

The reports suggested: he had initiated the wiretapping—which was undertaken by the government against 13 federal officials and four newsmen from 1969–71; he had prior knowledge of formation of the White House investigation unit known as the "plumbers" in 1971; the order to end the "national security" wiretaps came from his office; and then-National Security Council (NSC) aide Alexander M. Haig Jr., presumably acting for Kissinger, vetoed at least two, and possibly three, FBI proposals in mid-1969 to terminate one tap, at the home of Morton H. Halperin, because it was unproductive.

Before leaving with the presidential party for the Mideast, Kissinger had appeared before the Senate Foreign Relations Committee June 7 to defend his credibility on the issue. According to unpublished White House transcripts, circulating to members of the House Judiciary Committee, President Nixon had remarked on Feb. 28, 1973 in a White House talk that Kissinger had asked that the 1969 taps be instituted. Sen. Edmund S. Muskie (D, Me.) asked Kissinger at the hearing June 7 if he originated the recommendation for the wiretapping program. "I did not," Kissinger replied. He said he "had the impression" that the President's comments were "based on a misapprehension."

Kissinger said his role "was in supplying names as part of a program instituted by the President, the attorney general and the director of the Federal Bureau of

Investigation (FBI) to protect the national security."

The day before, during a news conference at which he expected to deal primarily with his Mideast diplomacy, Kissinger's role in the wiretapping was again raised. One question was whether he had retained counsel "in preparation for a defense against a possible perjury indictment." Kissinger, stung, retorted he did not conduct his office as a conspiracy.

After Kissinger's Salzburg news conference, Senate Democratic Leader Mike Mansfield (Mont.) disclosed that he had met Kissinger June 8 and "he was in some distress" because of the wiretapping thing "hanging over him." Kissinger had indicated, Mansfield said, "he might have to consider resigning." Mansfield added: "I told him not to even think of it."

At Salzburg, Kissinger reaffirmed his testimony before the Senate that he only provided names of individuals with access to sensitive information in the wiretapping effort from 1969 to 1971. He denied instigating the wiretapping or having prior knowledge of creation of the "plumbers."

"I find wiretapping distasteful," Kissinger said. "I find leaks distasteful, and therefore a choice had to be made. So, in retrospect, this seems to me what my role has been." Because of his concern about "egregious violations" of national security items, or leaks of classified material, he said, he had spoken to the President in 1969 and Nixon had ordered, on the advice of John N. Mitchell, then attorney general, and FBI Director J. Edgar Hoover, "the institution of a system of national security wiretaps." Kissinger said his office supplied the names of persons with access to the security data.

"The fact of the matter is that the wiretaps in question were legal," Kissinger declared. "They followed established procedures."

Kissinger said he had sent a letter to the Senate Foreign Relations Committee requesting a new review of the wiretapping charges. He read parts of the letter: "The innuendoes which now imply that new evidence contradicting my testimony has come to light are without foundation." "All the available evidence is to the best of my knowledge contained in the public and closed hearings which preceded my confirmation."

52 senators express support—A resolution backing Kissinger was introduced in the Senate late June 12 with early sponsorship of 39 Republicans and Democrats. By June 13, 52 senators had signed the resolution, including Majority Leader Mansfield and Minority Leader Hugh Scott (R, Pa.). The resolution, submitted by Sen. James B. Allen (D, Ala.), said the Senate "holds in high regard Dr. Kissinger and regards him as an outstanding member of this Administration, as a patriotic American in whom it has complete confidence, and whose integrity and veracity are above reproach."

Charges accompanied leaked papers—Sen. Barry M. Goldwater (R, Ariz.) accused the Washington Post June 12 of committing an "act of treason" when it published secret FBI documents in which it was indicated that Kissinger had initiated some of the wiretaps in question. "It's very obvious to me that any information that the government has can be obtained by the Washington Post or any other newspaper that wants to pay the price," he said. "This is plain, outright treason, and I won't stand for it."

Benjamin C. Bradlee, executive editor of the Post, in a statement later June 12, said: "That's really an outrageous charge. We neither stole the documents nor bought them." "We have a right to look at any information given to us by responsible government officials, whether it's a senator or a president or a bureaucrat," he said. "And we have a responsibility to print all information that is relevant and newsworthy."

Reports on the FBI documents had been published June 12 by the Post, the New York Times and the Boston Globe.

According to one document, entitled "Sensitive Coverage Placed at Request of White House" and dated May 12, 1973, specific requests for the wiretaps had come from either Kissinger, then national security adviser, or his aide, Gen.

Alexander M. Haig Jr., currently White House chief of staff. The document was addressed to Leonard M. Walters, then assistant director of the FBI, now retired.

The narrative at the beginning of the document read: "The original requests were from either Dr. Henry Kissinger or General Alexander Haig (then Colonel Haig) for wiretap coverage on knowledgeable NSC personnel and certain newsmen who had particular news interest in the SALT talks. The specific requests for this coverage were made to either former Director J. Edgar Hoover or former Assistant to the Director William C. Sullivan (and on one occasion by General Haig to SA Robert Haynes, FBI, White House liaison). Written authorization from the Attorney General of the United States was secured on each wiretap."

Another document, dated May 13, 1973, said "it appears that the project of placing electronic surveillance at the request of the White House had its beginning in a telephone call to Mr. J. Edgar Hoover on May 9, 1969, from Dr. Henry A. Kissinger."

Kissinger was said in the documents to have received 37 FBI summaries of the wiretapped information and to have received the summaries as late as Dec. 28, 1970. An FBI document dated May 31, 1973 was reported to have contained Kissinger's assertion that "what he was learning as a result of the [wiretap] coverage was extremely helpful to him while at the same time very disturbing." The document also said a preliminary estimate of the wiretap operation was that there had been no evidence of federal illegality gleaned from the wiretaps nor any instance that data had been leaked to unauthorized persons.

Ex-NSC aide files new wiretap suit— William Anthony K. Lake, a former staff member of the National Security Council (NSC), filed suit against Kissinger and Nixon June 12, charging that wiretaps were unconstitutionally placed on his home telephone. Lake, who served on Kissinger's NSC staff from June 1969 to June 1970, argued that the wiretap violated his civil liberties, since it was not based on evidence that he had disclosed or was likely to disclose classified information.

Lake's suit, which named other Nixon Administration officials as well as the Chesapeake & Potomac Telephone Co. as defendants, contended that the tap had been placed after he had left the NSC. The tap was ordered, Lake asserted, because he was believed to oppose some Administration policies.

A second wiretap suit by former NSC staff member Richard M. Moose, a Kissinger aide from January to September 1969, was withdrawn June 12, only hours after it had been filed. Moose's attorney, Nathan Levin, said the action came at the request of Chairman J. William Fulbright (D, Ark.) of the Senate Foreign Relations Committee, who thought it wrong for Moose, a consultant to the committee, to get himself involved in such litigation, since the committee had agreed to review Kissinger's role in initiating the wiretaps.

Ruckelshaus backs Kissinger— William D. Ruckelshaus, former acting FBI director, supported Kissinger June 16 in his account of his wiretap role in 1969–71.

Ruckelshaus, who had investigated the wiretapping and reported on it in 1973, said Kissinger's role was "pretty much as he's described it." Appearing on the CBS "Face the Nation" program, Ruckelshaus suggested an explanation for one of the questions involved: whether Kissinger did or did not initiate the wiretaps. "In the sense that he supplied the names, he initiated it," he said. "But his definition of initiation is that it wasn't his idea to tap; he simply complained about the leaks." Ruckelshaus said "in the process of supplying those names it may well have been described in FBI memoranda that this was a request coming from the National Security Council or Mr. Kissinger."

Ruckelshaus agreed there were "some questions" about one aspect of the wiretapping effort, that some persons with "only a peripheral, if any, relationship to national security" were among those tapped.

Senate panel clears Kissinger. The

Senate Foreign Relations Committee Aug. 6 reaffirmed its support for Kissinger after investigating his role in the wiretaps in question.

In a report unanimously approved, the committee concluded that there were "no contradictions" between Kissinger's testimony at his confirmation hearings in 1973 "and the totality of the new information available." In reaffirming its 1973 finding that Kissinger's role in the wiretapping did not constitute grounds to bar confirmation, the panel stated "if the committee knew then what it knows now it would have nonetheless reported the nomination favorably to the Senate."

The report noted that there were some "unexplained contradictions" between testimony of individuals and documents in the case, but it said the committee "did establish to its satisfaction" that Kissinger's role "was essentially as he described it in testimony last year."

The report cited a letter from President Nixon of July 12 asserting his full responsibility for the wiretap program.

In its closed hearings, the committee took testimony from Attorney General William B. Saxbe July 10, FBI Director Clarence M. Kelley July 15, Kissinger July 23 and Nixon chief of staff Alexander M. Haig Jr. July 30.

Ervin Committee Reports

Findings on Watergate published. In its last official action, the Senate Select Committee on Presidential Campaign Activities, known as "the Watergate Committee" or "the Ervin Committee," released a final report July 13, 1974 on its investigation of the Watergate and other scandals related to the 1972 presidential campaign.

The committee, whose televised hearings in 1973 had focused public attention on the scandals, said in an introduction to the 2,250-page report that its investigation had not been conducted, nor its report prepared, "to determine the legal guilt or innocence of any person or whether the President should be impeached."

The panel said, however, that "to be true to its mandate from the Senate and its constitutional responsibilities," it "must present its view of the facts" of the Watergate affair and related matters in addition to recommending remedial legislation to "safeguard the electoral process."

Announcing the report's release at a news conference in the committee's hearing room July 12, Chairman Sam J. Ervin Jr. (D, N.C.) contended that the report was not weaker because it did not make specific accusations. Ervin said, "There are two ways to indicate a horse. One is to draw a picture that is a great likeness. And the other is to draw a picture that is a great likeness and write under it, 'This is a horse.' We just drew the picture."

The report said the picture presented by its compilation of evidence demonstrated that "campaign practices must be effectively supervised and enforcement of the criminal laws vigorously pursued against all offenders—even those of high estate—if our free institutions are to survive."

Sen. Ervin appended to the report a "statement of individual views" studded with historical references and verbal equivalents of the arched eyebrows that had marked his appearance during the televised hearings. Ervin condemned the "illegal and unethical activities" by campaign officials and White House aides, which he said corrupted both the electoral process and the workings of government.

Answering his own question, "Why was Watergate?" Ervin said presidential aides' "lust for political power blinded them to ethical considerations and legal requirements.... They had forgotten, if they ever knew, that the Constitution is designed to be a law for rulers and people alike at all times and under all circumstances; and that no doctrine involving more pernicious consequences to the commonwealth has ever been invented by the wit of man than the notion that any of its provisions can be suspended by the President for any reason whatsoever."

Political intelligence and cover-up. The Senate Watergate Committee's report declared that the June 17, 1972 Watergate break-in had to be viewed in the context of earlier political intelligence plans and operations: a 1970 domestic spy plan proposed by presidential aide Tom Charles Huston but reportedly discarded, the White House "plumbers" unit and "Project Sandwedge," which was rejected by Presidential adviser John D. Ehrlichman. According to the report, the latter plan, for a political "detective agency," was presented to then-Attorney General John N. Mitchell in 1971, with the proposal that it operate directly under the Committee to Re-elect the President, (CRP), but Mitchell rejected it.

Intelligence plans were resurrected after the hiring of G. Gordon Liddy as counsel to CRP. The report described the series of meetings on the question involving Mitchell, Liddy, campaign aide Jeb Stuart Magruder and presidential counsel John W. Dean 3rd. Various plans, including the Watergate operation, were discussed, rejected, changed and ultimately approved.

The report noted that one meeting (Jan. 27, 1972) at which Liddy's plans were rejected as too expensive took place in Mitchell's office while he was still attorney general. Despite the rejection of the proposal, Liddy retained his position as CRP counsel and "continued to have the responsibility of developing an intelligence-gathering plan."

Although a plan was eventually approved, the committee said it had been unable to establish the exact circumstances. The report, however, cited testimony by several witnesses that Mitchell, by then the director of the Nixon campaign, had reluctantly approved it, possibly with the knowledge of White House officials.

Within hours after the arrest of the Watergate burglars, a "massive cover-up" had begun and "eventually encompassed destruction and secretion of documents, obstruction of official investigations, subornation of perjury and offers of money and executive clemency to the Watergate defendants to secure silence."

The report noted that existence of a cover-up could not be "seriously disputed" in view of the guilty pleas by some of the participants.

While refraining from direct accusations, the report addressed the question of the motivations for payments made to the original Watergate break-in defendants: "None of those who authorized or participated in the making of those payments used their own money. To the contrary, they used campaign funds contributed by others who had no knowledge that their money was being employed to pay the legal fees of the Watergate defendants and to support their families. Also relevant is the clandestine nature of the payoffs, which were made with $100 bills and placed in 'drops' by an unseen intermediary using a code name."

Citing the White House tape transcripts, the report noted that "even the President recognized that the payoffs smacked of a cover-up."

Weicker charges abuses. In a separate personal report released June 29, Sen. Lowell P. Weicker (R, Conn.) charged that "every major substantive part of the Constitution was violated, abused and undermined during the Watergate period."

Emphasizing that his statement was based on the "known" facts of Watergate and related scandals gathered by the Ervin Committee and other investigative bodies—not on "new facts of scandal"—Weicker listed examples which he said illustrated how the White House had overstepped its constitutional and statutory authority: domestic intelligence plans "containing proposals that were specifically identified as illegal," the "enemies" list and misuse of the IRS, use of campaign funds for payoffs to the Watergate burglars, warrantless wiretaps of government officials and reporters and obstruction of House and Senate investigations.

Weicker said First Amendment guarantees had been subverted by intimidation of the press and issuance of false information by Administration spokesmen. "The President himself," Weicker said, "misled the press in news conferences and official statements, as to the investigation, its results, and the substance of evidence involving himself and the Watergate matter."

Weicker charges political use. Sen. Lowell P. Weicker Jr. (R, Conn.), a member of the Watergate Committee, had accused the Internal Revenue Service (IRS) April 8 of acting as a "public lending library" for White House efforts to aid political friends and harass political enemies.

Appearing at a joint hearing of Senate Judiciary Subcommittees on Constitutional Rights and Administrative Practice and Procedure, and the Foreign Relations Subcommittee on Surveillance, Weicker disclosed a collection of documents, gathered by the Watergate Committee, showing politically motivated tax audits, undercover White House investigations and military spying on civilians.

One 1969 IRS memo describing the creation of a special activists "study unit" advised that the unit's function of examining tax returns of "ideological, militant, subversive, radical or other" organizations must not become publicly known, since disclosure "might embarrass the Administration." The unit was abolished in August 1973 after, according to Weicker, assembling tax data on about 10,000 persons.

According to the documents, former presidential counsel John W. Dean 3rd and former White House and Treasury Department official John J. Caulfield—both involved in the Watergate cover-up—were central characters in political use of the IRS.

A 1971 set of Dean-Caulfield memos suggested that the Administration was interested in helping evanglist Billy Graham and actor John Wayne, both supporters of President Nixon, with their tax problems. One memo referred to a "back-door" copy of an audit on Graham and promised similar material on Wayne. Dean was later supplied with audit histories of several entertainment figures "whose economic condition is similar to that of John Wayne."

Another 1971 series of memos from Caufield to Dean outlined possible measures to conduct "discreet" audits on Emile DeAntonio, producer of "Millhouse: A White Comedy," a film satirizing Nixon, and on the film's distributors. Caulfield also referred to the release of derogatory Federal Bureau of Investigation data on DeAntonio.

Weicker also gave the committees a list of 54 undercover White House investigations by Anthony T. Ulasewicz, some of which had been disclosed earlier. Subjects ranged from possible "improper conduct" by Donald F. Nixon Jr., the President's nephew, "scandals" in the backgrounds of Democratic Sens. Edmund S. Muskie (Me.) and Hubert H. Humphrey (Minn.), to a check "on a comedian named Dixon who was doing imitations of the President."

Committee won access to IRS data—The IRS had agreed to give the Senate Watergate Committee tax returns and other politically sensitive materials from its files on President Nixon's friend Charles G. Rebozo and the President's brother F. Donald Nixon, the New York Times reported April 24.

The IRS decision, an abrupt reversal of its previously stated position, included an agreement to provide a wide variety of tax returns and other data deemed essential by the committee to its investigation of Rebozo's handling of the $100,000 cash presidential campaign contribution by billionaire industrialist Howard Hughes in 1969 and 1970, the Times reported.

The Times had reported April 21 that Terry Lenzner, assistant chief counsel to the Watergate panel, had circulated a memorandum to committee members that in effect charged the IRS with obstructing his investigation into the handling of the Hughes gift. Contrary to an agreement for full exchange of data made with IRS agents in January, Lenzner's memo said, the IRS had not been forthcoming and stated April 12 that the committee would receive no additional data, pending resolution of a disagreement over language in the agreement.

The IRS responded to the charges in Lenzner's memorandum April 21: "The IRS flatly denies that it has engaged in any cover-up . . . and asserts that it has been cooperating . . . to the fullest extent consistent with the disclosure limitations in the tax laws."

The latest exchange agreement between the IRS and the committee, Times sources said, contained a proviso limiting access to the data to Carmine Bellino, chief investigator for the full committee, and Richard Schultz, an assistant minority counsel. Neither Lenzner nor his direct aides was to receive direct access to the materials, although relevant findings were to be made available, the sources said.

Lenzner's investigation had been enlarged March 21 when Herbert W. Kalmbach, personal attorney to President Nixon, told the committee of an April 30, 1973 meeting he had with Rebozo, in which Rebozo had admitted distributing parts of the Hughes campaign gift to the President's brothers, F. Donald Nixon and Edward C. Nixon, the President's personal secretary Rose Mary Woods and "others." Rebozo sought his legal advice, Kalmbach reportedly testified, because the IRS was then investigating Rebozo's handling of the money.

In his memorandum, Lenzner had also charged that the IRS had used the White House as a go-between in its investigation of the Hughes gift. Before the IRS got in touch with him, Rebozo had already been informed by White House aide John D. Ehrlichman of the IRS's interest in the Hughes cash.

Impeachment panel releases data. The House Judiciary Committee July 16 released evidence collected in its impeachment inquiry concerning possible White House attempts to misuse the Internal Revenue Service for political gain.

The committee detailed repeated attempts by the White House, some successful, to gain confidential tax information on individuals from the IRS and to use its tax-return audits to hurt political enemies and protect friends of the President.

Among the evidence was testimony from both of the Nixon Administration's first two commissioners of Internal Revenue that they had offered their resignations in protest against what they considered improper White House pressures and actions. One of them, Randolph W. Thrower, did resign in January 1971 after he tried without success to see Nixon to warn him, as Thrower put it in

an affidavit, "that any suggestion of introduction of political influence into the IRS would be very damaging to him and his administration, as well as to the revenue system and the general public interest."

Thrower's successor, Johnnie Walters, testified that former White House counsel John W. Dean 3rd gave him a list in September 1972 of 490 supporters of the Democratic presidential nominee, Sen. George McGovern (D, S.D.), and asked the service to inspect their taxes. Walters said he advised Dean "that compliance with the request would be disastrous for the IRS and for the administration."

Walters said he also had intense pressure from Nixon aide John D. Ehrlichman in the summer of 1972 to create a tax problem for Lawrence F. O'Brien, then Democratic national chairman. O'Brien had been audited and his return closed, Walters said, but Ehrlichman continued to press for action, with some of the requests relayed through then-Treasury Secretary George P. Shultz. Walters said he told Ehrlichman over the telephone, with Shultz on an extension, that the IRS file on O'Brien's return was closed. Ehrlichman was said to have replied angrily, "I'm goddamn tired of your foot-dragging tactics." Walters said he then had told Shultz "that he could have my job any time he wanted it."

The committee included in its data Ehrlichman's statement at a closed hearing of the Senate Watergate committee, that IRS personnel "down in the woodwork" had "75 well-selected reasons why they shouldn't audit him [O'Brien], and they weren't having any of the same reasons with regard to Republicans at that time, and I thought there was a little unevenhandedness." "I wanted them to turn up something and send him to jail before the election," Ehrlichman told the Senate committee, "and unfortunately it didn't materialize."

The IRS did pass along to the White House a report requested in March 1970 by Clark Mollenhoff, then White House special counsel, on the taxes of Gerald Wallace, brother of Gov. George C. Wallace (D, Ala.). Mollenhoff's affidavit said he sought the report only after Nixon aide H. R. Haldeman assured him "the report was to be obtained at the request of the President." Mollenhoff delivered the report to Haldeman, he said, but later was accused by Haldeman, among others, of being the source of a "leak" of derogatory material from the report to columnist Jack Anderson.

Anderson's column, apparently based on the leaked report, appeared three weeks before the Alabama gubernatorial primary in 1970. Mollenhoff asserted in the affidavit that the leak came from "the highest White House level." (Anderson said he had been shown the report by the late Murray Chotiner, a long-time political adviser to Nixon.)

Confidential information from the IRS was obtained on several occasions by Dean, according to the evidence. In September 1971 Dean received data on an IRS audit of evangelist Billy Graham, a friend of Nixon's, which he relayed to Haldeman with a note, "Can we do anything to help?" Haldeman's answer was, "No, it's already covered." In October 1971 Dean obtained a copy of a tax audit of actor John Wayne, a supporter of Nixon. The evidence included Dean's testimony at a closed hearing of the Senate Watergate committee that Nixon requested that tax audits "be turned off on friends of his."

Other evidence indicated Nixon's desire to have the IRS harass left wing organizations. "Nearly 18 months ago, the President indicated a desire for IRS to move against leftist organizations taking advantage of tax shelters," White House aide Tom Huston wrote Haldeman in September 1970. Huston added he had pressed the IRS on the issue "to no avail."

Nixon's interest in pressing for probes of his political opponents was indicated in a transcript of a Sept. 15, 1972 White House tape. According to the text, Haldeman told the President that Dean was "moving ruthlessly on the investigation of McGovern people, Kennedy stuff, and all that too . . . and Dean's working the thing through IRS. . . ."

Dean had told the Senate Watergate committee that the conversation turned eventually to "use of the Internal Revenue Service to attack our enemies." Dean said

he cited the White House lack of "clout" at the IRS because of Democratic holdovers in the agency and "the President seemed somewhat annoyed and said that the Democratic administrations had used this tool well, and after the election we would get people in these agencies who would be responsive to White House requirements."

Dean told Nixon on March 13, 1973, according to another transcript, that "we have a couple of sources" at the IRS and "we can get right in and get what we need."

One of the sources was revealed in the committee's evidence to be Vernon D. Acree, assistant commissioner of Internal Revenue, who was promoted in April 1972 to be commissioner of customs.

Impeachment Probability Grows

Doar says evidence merits impeachment. John M. Doar, special counsel to the House Judiciary Committee, urged committee members July 19, 1974 to recommend President Nixon's impeachment. Such action was supported by Albert E. Jenner Jr., special Republican counsel to the committee.

Abandoning the neutrality that had characterized his staff's 10-week presentation of evidence, Doar presented to the panel five sets of proposed articles of impeachment and a 306-page summary of evidence, which he said buttressed his arguments.

The proposed articles of impeachment, 29 in all, were composed by both the members and staff of the committee. Essentially, the articles centered on four allegations against the President:

He obstructed justice by participating in the cover-up that followed the Watergate break-in.

He abused the powers of the presidency by invading the civil rights and privacy of U.S. citizens and by misusing or attempting to misuse agencies of the U.S. government.

His refusal to honor subpoenas by the

Judiciary Committee was contemptuous of Congress.

He committed fraud in connection with his income taxes and expenditure of public funds on his personal property.

The summary of evidence presented by Doar was intended to draw together the mountain of impeachment data into a cohesive argument that, in the view of the committee staff, "demonstrates various abuses of Presidential power." The document provided a detailed narrative of the Watergate case and information on the other alleged abuses of power.

"Circumstances strongly suggest," the summary said, "that President Nixon decided, shortly after learning of the Watergate break-in, on a plan to cover up the identities of high officials of the White House and the Committee for the Reelection of the President directly involved in the illegal operation." Until after the 1972 election, the summary added, "President Nixon's policy of containment—of 'cutting the loss'—worked . . . because two of the President's assistants, John Dean, counsel to the President, and Herbert Kalmbach, personal attorney to the President, assigned to carry out the President's policy, did their jobs well—with the full support of the power and authority of the office of President of the United States."

Contrary to Nixon's statement that on Sept. 15, 1972 he knew nothing of the case, the summary contended he had already done the following things: met with H.R. Haldeman, his chief of staff, and John N. Mitchell, his campaign manager, both of whom were "fully apprised of" White House connections to Watergate; arranged a misleading explanation for Mitchell's resignation; received from L. Patrick Gray 3rd, then acting FBI director, a warning about White House interference in the FBI's Watergate inquiry; "prevented" a personal appearance before the Watergate grand jury by Maurice H. Stans, his chief campaign fund raiser and former commerce secretary; and "made an untrue public statement about Dean's 'complete investigation' of the Watergate matter," when in fact Dean "acted to narrow and frustrate the FBI investigation"

and "conducted no independent investigation of his own."

The summary also reviewed Nixon's March 21, 1973 meeting with Dean, during which Dean detailed the payment of "hush money" to the convicted Watergate conspirators: "The President did not condemn the payments or the involvement of his closest aides. He did not direct that the activity be stopped. The President did not express any surprise or shock. He did not report it to the proper investigatory authorities." Subsequently, the summary added, the President repeatedly modified his accounts of the meeting.

"The 'report' that the President . . . requested Dean to make in March 1973 was one that was designed to mislead investigators and insulate the President from charges of concealment," the summary asserted.

When his associates lied or "stonewalled" to sustain the cover-up, the summary said, "the President condoned this conduct, approved it, directed it, rewarded it and, in some cases, advised witnesses on how to impede the investigators." Moreover, when the cover-up began to unravel in late March 1973, "there is clear and convincing evidence that the President took over in late March the active management of the cover-up," the Doar summary stated.

Other areas touched by the summary: wiretapping and other "illegal and improper" intelligence gathering activities; the burglary of Daniel Ellsberg's psychiatrist's office and the concealment of those activities; and improper use of the Internal Revenue Service.

Clandestine activities—The Judiciary Committee July 18 released a four-volume 2,090-page record of the evidence accumulated by its staff concerning clandestine activities sponsored by the White House. A 225-page rebuttal by the President's special counsel, James D. St. Clair, accompanied the publication of the evidence.

The evidence, much of which was already a part of the public record, specifically dealt with the operations of the "plumbers" investigative unit, wiretaps on 13 government officials and four newsmen, the White House-financed activities of political trickster Donald H. Segretti, activities of John J. Caulfield and Anthony T. Ulasewicz, who had made secret inquiries for the White House, and the stillborn domestic surveillance plan of 1970, which had called for the lifting of bars against certain illegal activities.

The mass of evidence suggested that clandestine White House activities originated because of national security concerns but later became overtly political operations. The documents also showed that Nixon and his top aides were aware in March and April 1973 that some of the activities of the White House "plumbers" investigative unit were illegal.

The evidence cited White House concern about leaks of national security information and the highly secret wiretap program that was instituted in 1969 to combat the leaks. In 1970, the evidence indicated, the President was ready to approve implementation of the domestic surveillance plan proposed by White House aide Tom Charles Huston. Nixon rescinded his approval at the last minute because of objections from FBI Director J. Edgar Hoover, who refused to countenance the illegalties of the plan.

In 1971, White House efforts against news leaks took the form of 17 wiretaps against government officials and newsmen, as well as the creation of the "plumbers." Part of the evidence released was Nixon's assessment of the wiretaps, which he made known to John W. Dean 3rd, his counsel, Feb. 28, 1973. "They never helped. Just gobs and gobs of material: gossip and bullshitting," Nixon said. The evidence pointed out that two of the taps remained in effect even after the two officials in question—unnamed in the report, but widely known to be former National Security Council advisers Morton Halperin and Anthony Lake—had left the Administration and become foreign policy advisers to one of the 1972 Democratic presidential hopefuls.

As for the "plumbers," one previously unreleased document showed that Nixon was warned March 21, 1973 of the possible illegality of the "plumbers" 1971 break-in at the office of Daniel Ellsberg's psychiatrist. "That's an illegal search and seizure that may be sufficient for at least a mistrial," Nixon was told by aide John D. Ehrlichman, who was apparently referring to the then-ongoing trial of Ellsberg.

St. Clair's defense of the President consisted of White House memorandums, including a hitherto unpublished 1973 affidavit by Kissinger, demonstrating Administration anxiety over leaks of classified information from 1969 through 1971. In addition, the defense volume reprinted many of the newspaper articles that supposedly prompted the President to authorize both the 17 wiretaps and the "plumbers."

Committee votes to recommend impeachment. The House Judiciary Committee voted July 30 to approve three articles of impeachment against President Nixon. They charged Nixon with obstruction of justice in connection with the Watergate scandal, abuse of presidential powers and attempting to impede the impeachment process by defying committee subpoenas for evidence.

The committee's final deliberations, which were nationally televised, began July 24 with a motion by Rep. Harold D. Donohue (Mass.), second ranking Democrat on the panel. "I move that the committee report to the House a resolution, together with articles, impeaching the President of the United States, Richard M. Nixon."

Nixon Admits 'Serious... Omission,' Then Resigns

The Watergate scandal finally caused the overthrow of the Nixon Administration in August 1974. President Nixon resigned after admitting, in effect, that he had obstructed justice in the Watergate affair.

Nixon surrenders Presidency. Richard Milhous Nixon, 61, resigned as president of the United States Aug. 9 after a week of dramatic developments. Vice President Gerald Rudolph Ford, 61, was sworn in as his successor. It was the first time in the history of the nation that its president had resigned.

The resignation, a dramatic conclusion to the effects of the Watergate scandal on the Nixon presidency, was announced Aug. 8, three days after Nixon released a statement and transcript of tape recordings admitting "a serious act of omission" in his previous accounts of the Watergate cover-up.

According to Nixon's statement, six days after the break-in at the Democratic Party's national headquarters in the Watergate building in Washington, D.C. June 17, 1972, he had ordered the Federal Bureau of Investigation's probe of the break-in halted. Furthermore, Nixon stated, he had kept this part of the record secret from investigating bodies, his own counsel and the public.

The admission destroyed what remained of Nixon's support in Congress against a tide of impeachment that was already swelling. The President's support had been eroding dangerously since the House Judiciary Committee had approved three articles of impeachment. Within 48 hours of Nixon's statement of complicity, the 10 committee members who had voted against impeachment reversed themselves and announced that they would vote for impeachment.

The development was accompanied by serious defections in the Republican Congressional leadership and acknowledgment from all sides that the vote for impeachment in the House was a foregone conclusion and conviction by the Senate certain.

This assessment was delivered to the President by the senior Republican leaders of the Congress. Shortly afterwards, Nixon made his final decision to resign. He announced his decision the evening of Aug. 8, to a television audience estimated at 110–130 million persons. In his 16-minute address, Nixon conceded he had made "some" wrong judgments. He said he was resigning because he no longer had "a strong enough political base in Congress" to carry out his duties of office.

Blocking of investigation admitted. The presidential statement and tape transcripts that triggered the intense pressure leading to Nixon's resignation August 9 had been released August 5. They effectively constituted a confession to obstruction of justice—the charge contained in the first article of impeachment voted by the House Judiciary Committee.

The transcripts Nixon released covered three meetings with H. R. Haldeman, then White House chief of staff, on June 23, 1972, six days after the Watergate break-in. Informed that the Federal Bureau of Investigation's (FBI) probe of the break-in was pointing to officials in his reelection campaign, Nixon instructed Haldeman to tell the FBI, "Don't go any further into this case period!"

While Nixon's earlier statements on the Watergate case attributed his concern over the FBI's investigations to national security problems and possible conflicts with the Central Intelligence Agency (CIA), the latest transcripts—and Nixon's own statement about them—finally indicated that political considerations had played a major role.

According to the transcripts, Nixon told Haldeman to base the curtailment of FBI activities on possible reopening of questions about the CIA's role in the abortive 1961 "Bay of Pigs" invasion of Cuba (some of the Watergate burglary conspirators had been involved in the CIA operation). Haldeman assured Nixon that the CIA ploy would give L. Patrick Gray, then acting FBI director, sufficient justification to drop the investigation of the "laundering" (through a Mexican lawyer and bank) of the campaign funds used to finance the Watergate operation.

Nixon then told Haldeman that Gray should be instructed—through CIA Director Richard Helms and Deputy Director Vernon A. Walters—to curtail the investigation.

In the written statement announcing release of the transcripts, Nixon referred to other transcripts released earlier (April 29–30), which he said then would "tell it all" concerning his role in Watergate and the cover-up.

But in early May, he continued, he had

begun a "preliminary review" of some of the 64 conversations subpoenaed by Watergate special prosecutor Leon Jaworski, including two from June 23, 1972. Nixon said he recognized that the tapes "presented potential problems," but he "did not inform my staff or my counsel of it, or those arguing my case, nor did I amend my submission to the Judiciary Committee. . . ." As a result, those arguing and judging his case were proceeding with "information that was incomplete and in some respects erroneous. This was a serious act of omission for which I take full responsibility and which I deeply regret."

Nixon reported that he and his counsel had reviewed and analyzed many of the tapes, a process which "made it clear that portions of the tapes of these June 23 conversations are at variance with certain of my previous statements."

These included, Nixon said, the statement of May 22, 1973, in which he recalled that he had been concerned that the FBI's investigation of Watergate might expose "unrelated covert activities" of the CIA or "sensitive national security matters" involving the "plumbers" unit. He thus ordered that the FBI "coordinate" its investigation with the CIA. The May 22 statement, he said, was based on his "recollection at the time"—some 11 months after the break in "plus documentary materials and relevant public testimony of those involved."

In his latest statement, however, Nixon acknowledged that the June 23 tapes showed he had discussed the "political aspects of the situation" at the time he gave the instructions, and that he was "aware of the advantages this course of action would have with respect to limiting possible public exposure of involvement by persons connected with the re-election committee."

Nixon said his review of additional tapes had not revealed other "major inconsistencies with what I have previously submitted," and that he had no reason to believe that there would be others.

Nixon acknowledged that a House vote of impeachment was "virtually a foregone conclusion."

Nixon also urged that "the evidence be looked at in its entirety, and the events be looked at in perspective." Whatever his mistakes in handling Watergate, Nixon continued, "the basic truth remains that when all the facts were brought to my attention I insisted on a full investigation and prosecution of those guilty." Nixon concluded that the full record "does not justify the extreme step of impeachment and removal of a President."

The roles of the tapes & the courts— Nixon's Aug. 5 statement said the three key transcripts had been made public partly as a result of the process of compliance with a July 24 Supreme Court decision. This reflected the central role played by that order in the events leading to his resignation.

In setting procedures for compliance with the order, U.S. District Court Judge John J. Sirica, who was to screen the tapes before transmitting them to the Watergate prosecution, had suggested that special presidential counsel James D. St. Clair personally review the tapes, along with Nixon.

According to news reports Aug. 5–6, St. Clair had first become aware of the incriminating material involving Nixon and the cover-up during this review and—threatening resignation—had insisted that the transcripts be made public and that Nixon let it be known that he had withheld evidence from his counsel.

White House Deputy Press Secretary Gerald L. Warren denied Aug. 6 that Nixon's decision to release the transcripts had been based on "any sort of ultimatum or anything like that" from St. Clair.

According to news reports Aug. 7–10, key roles in the prelude to resignation were played by White House chief of staff Alexander M. Haig Jr. and Rep. Charles E. Wiggins (R, Calif.), a spokesman for the Nixon defense in the House.

After learning the content of the tapes, Haig—along with St. Clair—reportedly sensed the inevitability of Nixon's fall. To get a reading on Congressional reaction to the evidence, Haig and St. Clair summoned Wiggins to the White House Aug. 2. Wiggins said later that he was stunned by the transcripts and the direct evidence that Nixon had ordered the cover-up. Wiggins told the Nixon aides that impeachment and conviction would no longer be in question and that Nixon should consider resigning. Haig and St. Clair reportedly agreed, setting the stage for convincing Nixon that further struggle against leaving office would be futile.

Top Nixon Aides Convicted

Four convicted of cover-up. Four key aides to former President Richard M. Nixon were found guilty by a federal jury in Washington Jan. 1, 1975 of conspiracy to obstruct justice in connection with the June 17, 1972 break-in at the Watergate headquarters of the Democratic National Committee. A fifth defendant was found not guilty.

The nine-woman, three-man jury was given final instructions by presiding Judge John J. Sirica Dec. 30, 1974 and deliberated about 15 hours before returning its verdict. The verdicts:

H.R. Haldeman, former chief of staff at the Nixon White House, was convicted of one count of conspiracy, one count of obstruction of justice and three counts of perjury with regard to his Senate Watergate Committee testimony concerning his and Nixon's knowledge of the cover-up.

John N. Mitchell, former attorney general and director of the Committee to Re-elect the President, was found guilty of one count of conspiracy, one count of obstruction of justice, two counts of making false declarations to the grand jury regarding covert intelligence-gathering operations against the Democrats and one count of perjury for having denied in testimony before the Senate Watergate Committee that he discussed destruction of documents at a meeting two days after the break-in.

John D. Ehrlichman, former domestic affairs adviser to Nixon, was found guilty of one count of conspiracy, one count of obstruction of justice and two counts of making false declarations to the grand jury when he denied being able to remember various facts about the break-in and the cover-up.

Robert C. Mardian, a former assistant attorney general and an attorney for the Nixon re-election committee, was found guilty of one count of conspiracy.

Kenneth W. Parkinson, a re-election committee attorney hired after the break-in to deal with Watergate-related litigation, was found not guilty of one count of conspiracy and one count of obstruction of justice.

The conspiracy charge against the defendants involved payment of $429,500 in hush money to the seven original Watergate break-in defendants, destruction of documents, offers of Presidential clemency and schemes to obstruct investigations and other functions of government agencies.

Charles W. Colson, special counsel to former President Nixon, and Gordon Strachan, an aide of Haldeman, were also named in the original cover-up indictment. Cover-up charges were dropped against Colson, however, when he pleaded guilty in connection with the Ellsberg burglary. Strachan's case was severed from the main trial to allow determination of whether the indictment against him was based on testimony he gave under immunity from prosecution.

Sirica Feb. 21 imposed prison sentences of 2-1/2 to 8 years each on Mitchell, Haldeman and Ehrlichman and of 10 months to 3 years on Mardian.

Inquiries, Reforms & Other Activities

Rockefeller Heads Investigation

Panel to probe CIA. President Gerald R. Ford Jan. 5, 1975 named Vice President Nelson A. Rockefeller to head an eight-member commission that was to investigate and report back within 90 days on allegations of illegal domestic spying by the Central Intelligence Agency (CIA). The New York Times had reported Dec. 22, 1974 that the CIA had conducted during the Nixon Administration a "massive, illegal domestic intelligence operation" against the antiwar movement and other dissident groups. (The National Security Act of 1947 prohibited the CIA from engaging in domestic intelligence activities.)

In a statement Jan. 4, Ford said he was naming a "blue ribbon" panel to "determine whether the CIA has exceeded its statutory authority, ... to determine whether existing safeguards are adequate to preclude agency activities that might go beyond its authority and to make appropriate recommendations." The commission, the President said, would have the benefit of the report on domestic spying by William Colby, director of the CIA.

Others named to the commission were: John T. Connor, chairman of Allied Chemical Corp. and secretary of commerce in the Johnson Administration; C. Douglas Dillon, managing director of Dillon, Read & Co., a New York City investment banking firm, and secretary of the Treasury in the Kennedy and Johnson Administrations; Erwin N. Griswold, an attorney and solicitor general in the Johnson and Kennedy Administrations; Lane Kirkland, secretary treasurer of the AFL-CIO; Gen. Lyman L. Lemnitzer (ret.), chairman of the Joint Chiefs of Staff in the Kennedy Administration and former supreme commander of the North Atlantic Treaty Organization (NATO); Ronald Reagan, who retired Jan. 6 after eight years as Republican governor of California; and Edgar F. Shannon Jr., who retired in 1974 after 15 years as president of the University of Virginia.

None of the commission members, a White House spokesman said, had former connections with the CIA. Rockefeller was the only member with a direct intelligence background. Since 1969, he had served on the President's Foreign Intelligence Advisory Board, a high-level civilian review board established by President Kennedy in the aftermath of the Bay of Pigs invasion. Rockefeller also had close connections to Secretary of State Henry A. Kissinger, whom the former New York governor had employed as a foreign policy adviser in the 1960s. Kissinger, who was reported to have been instrumental in Ford's decision to set up the blue ribbon commission, was, in his capacity as director of the National Security Council, chairman of the 40 Committee, which oversaw the CIA's covert operations.

Ron Nessen, White House press secretary, said Jan. 6 that all members of the panel had been checked and "would not have been picked if they had any connection with the CIA which would hamper them." He said Rockefeller had some knowledge of how the CIA operated.

Nessen said the Ford Administration would not stop CIA officials from testifying before Congressional committees planning to study charges of domestic spying.

Legislative Action

Privacy act passed. A bill to restrict federal collection and use of data on individuals was approved by the Senate Dec. 17, 1974 and by the House Dec. 18. President Ford signed the measure Jan. 1, 1975.

The Privacy Act of 1974 required the public disclosure by agencies of any computer data bank operation by them or collection of data on individuals. The individuals would have the right to inspect such files and correct misinformation.

Exchange of the data between agencies was barred without the individual's permission except for "routine" exchanges, such as for paycheck information. There was an exemption in the bill for data on individuals kept by federal law enforcement agencies.

The bill barred the sale or rental of mailing lists maintained by federal agencies and prohibited, beginning in 1975, state and local governments from requiring Social Security numbers as a condition for voting or registering a car or obtaining a driver's license. A special commission was to be established to study the problems of protection of individual privacy in this area.

Congressional Hearings

CIA chief answers domestic spying charges. William E. Colby, director of the

Central Intelligence Agency, told a Senate subcommittee Jan. 15, 1975 that his agency in the past had engaged in domestic intelligence gathering activities. However, he "flatly" denied that these activities amounted to "a massive, illegal domestic intelligence operation," as alleged in the New York Times of Dec. 22, 1974.

Colby's denial was contained in a report he made to the Intelligence Subcommittee of the Senate Appropriations Committee, one of four Congressional panels probing the charges by the Times.

In his report, a text of which was released to the press, Colby conceded that CIA agents had infiltrated dissident and antiwar political groups in the U.S., opened the mail of private citizens, tapped the telephone of U.S. residents and participated in a government counterintelligence program that led to the amassment of files on 10,000 U.S. citizens. Colby insisted that such "missteps" in the 27-year history of the CIA were "few and far between and were exceptions to the thrust of the agency's . . . primary mission," the collection and production of foreign intelligence.

Answering the assertion that the CIA had accumulated files on dissident groups in the U.S., Colby replied that in 1967, in connection with the investigation of the National Advisory Commission on Civil Disorders, the CIA had established a Counterintelligence Office to "look into the possibility of foreign links to American dissident elements." "Periodically, thereafter," he said, "various reports were drawn up on the foreign aspects of the antiwar, youth and similar movements and their possible links to American counterparts."

In the course of the program, the CIA sought "to obtain access to foreign circles" and "recruited or inserted about a dozen individuals into American dissident circles in order to establish their credentials for operations abroad," Colby reported. During this time, "some individuals submitted reports on the activities" of the dissidents. This information was reported to the FBI and "in the process . . . was also placed in CIA files," he said.

Beginning in 1970, Colby said, the agency participated in the Nixon Administration's interagency intelligence evaluation program, which was instituted after the so-called Huston plan was scrapped.

A review of this program in 1973, Colby added, resulted in orders limiting it to collection of data abroad and emphasizing that its targets were foreign connections to U.S. dissidents, not the dissidents themselves. In 1974, even more restrictive guidelines were issued, Colby said.

While this program was in operation, the report stated, "files were established on about 10,000 citizens." About two-thirds were begun because of FBI requests for information on activities of U.S. citizens abroad or by the filing of reports received from the FBI "for possible later use in connection with our [the CIA's] work abroad." The remaining third of the files, he said, "were opened on the basis of CIA foreign intelligence or counterintelligence known to be of interest to the FBI." Colby pointed out that in the "past several months" the files had been cleansed of data not justified by the agency's counterintelligence responsibilities, and that about 1,000 files had been removed from the active index.

Colby also reported that concurrent with the counterintelligence program, beginning in 1967, the CIA infiltrated 10 agents into dissident organizations operating in the Washington area. The purpose of this program, which he said ended in December 1968, was to gather information "relating to plans for demonstrations, pickets, protests or break-ins that might endanger CIA personnel, facilities and information."

"There have been lists developed at various times in the past, however, which do appear questionable under CIA's authority; for example, caused by an excessive effort to identify possible "'threats'" to the agency's security from dissident elements, or from a belief that such lists could identify later applicants or contacts who might be dangerous to the agency's security. They did not usually result from CIA collection efforts (although as I noted above, they sometimes did), but were compilations of names passed to us from other government agencies such as the FBI, some police forces, and several

Congressional committees or developed from news clippings, casual informants, etc. A number of these listings have been eliminated in the past three years, and the agency's current directives clearly require that no such listings be maintained."

Colby denied the allegation by the Times that at least one antiwar congressman had been placed under CIA surveillance. The CIA did have some files on congressmen, Colby admitted, but these fell into "categories" such as ex-employes, routine security clearance and "some whose names were included in reports received from other government agencies or developed in the course of our foreign intelligence operations."

As to the Times' charges regarding surreptitious break-ins by CIA agents, Colby responded that there had been three instances involving employes or ex-employes, whose loyalties were in doubt. A fourth attempted entry was unsuccessful, he added. Colby admitted that the CIA between 1951 and 1965 had "employed telephone taps" against 21 U.S. residents.

Each of the taps was initiated to check on leaks of classified information, and all but two of the individuals involved were directly connected with the CIA, Colby said. Two taps against private citizens approved by then-Attorney General Robert Kennedy were placed in 1963 to determine the sources of sensitive intelligence information they were thought to be receiving. In 1965, President Johnson issued an order requiring approval by the attorney general of all national security wiretaps, Colby said.

Colby also said the CIA had conducted "physical surveillance (followed)" in 1971 and 1972 against five U.S. citizens who were not CIA employes. "We had clear indications they were receiving classified information." He also cited an alleged plot in 1971 and 1972 to assassinate the vice president and kidnap the director of the CIA. In this case, Colby said, the CIA alerted the FBI and the Secret Service and carried out physical surveillance in two U.S. cities.

(The Washington Post reported Jan. 16 that it had obtained a private memorandum indicating that Colby had told the appropriations subcommittee that the

CIA's physical surveillance of five U.S. citizens involved, among others, Jack Anderson, the syndicated columnist; Michael Getler, a Post reporter, and Victor Marchetti, a former CIA employe, who wrote a book criticizing the agency.)

Finally, Colby conceded that the CIA between 1953 and 1973 had conducted "several programs to survey and open selected mail between the United States and two Communist countries." (Other published reports identified the countries as the Soviet Union and Communist China.)

Helms also denies CIA illegalities. Richard Helms, director of the CIA from 1966 to 1973, testified before the Senate Armed Services Subcommittee on Central Intelligence Jan. 16. Helms, whose testimony was behind closed doors, said in a prepared statement released to the press, "I am indignant at the irresponsible attacks made upon the true ends of the intelligence function."

Helms asserted that the "principal allegations" concerning domestic spying by the CIA remained unsupported and had been "undermined by contrary evidence in the press itself."

In the past it had been rare that U.S. citizens became involved with foreign intelligence operations, Helms said, but "in the late 1950s and early 1960s came the sudden and quite dramatic upsurge of extreme radicalism in this country and abroad. . . ." In response "to the express concern of the President," the CIA collaborated with the FBI to determine if this unrest was "inspired by, coordinated with, or funded by anti-American subversion mechanisms abroad." Helms, who provided no details, said that an investigation did show that the "agitation here did in fact have some overseas connections."

Helms also gave testimony before the Senate Foreign Relations Committee Jan. 22. Sen. Gale McGee (D, Wyo.), a committee member, quoted Helms as saying that if there had been CIA infiltration of U.S. dissident groups, it had occurred without his knowledge. McGee said questioning of Helms in the closed hearing mostly concerned testimony he had given before the committee in 1973 during confirmation hearings on his appointment as U.S. ambassador to Iran. At that time, Helms denied the CIA had engaged in domestic spying operations.

Senate votes CIA, FBI inquiry. The Senate Jan. 27 voted 82-4 to create a bipartisan, select committee to investigate alleged illegal spying on citizens and other abuses of power by the CIA, the FBI and other government intelligence and law enforcement agencies.

Under the terms of the resolution approving the investigation, an 11-member panel was authorized to investigate "the extent, if any, to which illegal, improper or unethical activities were engaged in by any agency or by any persons, acting either individually or in combination with others, in carrying out any intelligence or surveillance activities by or on behalf of any agency of the federal government." In addition to the CIA and the FBI, the special committee was to scrutinize the Defense Intelligence Agency (DIA), the National Security Agency (NSA), the Bureau of Intelligence and Research of the State Department, the intelligence arms of the Army, Navy and Air Force, and the Treasury Department's Bureau of Alcohol, Tobacco and Firearms.

Senate majority leader Mike Mansfield (D, Mont.) immediately named Frank Church (Ida.), Philip A. Hart (Mich.), Walter F. Mondale (Minn.), Walter Huddleston (Ky.), Robert B. Morgan (N.C.) and Gary W. Hart (Colo.) as the Democratic members of the committee. In anticipation of the panel's creation, Republican minority leader Sen. Hugh Scott (Pa.) Jan. 22 had named Sens. John G. Tower (Tex.), Barry Goldwater (Ariz.), Charles McC. Mathias (Md.), Richard Schweiker (Pa.) and Howard H. Baker (Tenn.) as the GOP members of the select committee.

Church was subsequently selected as chairman of the committee, and Tower was named vice chairman. The panel was given a budget of $750,000 and ordered to report within nine months.

Tighter wiretap curbs urged. A Senate study released Feb. 16 recommended tighter controls on national security wiretapping. The joint study, which was conducted by panels of the Judiciary Committee and Foreign Relations Committee, concluded that during the Nixon Administraion, the White House played a major and "unparalleled" role in initiating and maintaining wiretaps on 14 federal officials and three newsmen; that an attempt was made to hide the wiretaps and to deny their existence; and that some of the targets were followed as well as wiretapped.

The study cited testimony that members of Congress and members of their staffs were wiretapped. It found that agencies other than the Federal Bureau of Investigation had installed taps and said a presidential directive that the attorney general approve all warrantless wiretaps in advance had been ignored at times.

House creates inquiry panel. The House of Representatives, by 286–120 vote Feb. 19, 1975, created a select committee to investigate charges of "illegal or improper" intelligence activities by U.S. government agencies. Speaker Carl Albert (D, Okla.) named seven Democrats and three Republicans to the Select Committee on Intelligence and appointed Rep. Lucien Nedzi (D, Mich.), chairman of the Armed Services Intelligence Subcommittee, as its head.

The resolution setting up the committee authorized an inquiry into the activities of the following: National Security Council, the U.S. Intelligence Board, the President's Foreign Intelligence Advisory Board, Central Intelligence Agency (CIA), Defense Intelligence Agency, National Security Agency, the intelligence branches of the Army, Navy and Air Force, Intelligence and Research Bureau of the State Department, Federal Bureau of Investigation (FBI), Treasury Department, Justice Department, Energy Research and Development Agency, and "any other instrumentalities" of the federal government engaged in intelligence work in the U.S. and abroad.

The House July 17 replaced this Select Committee on Intelligence with a larger committee having the same authority. Disagreements within the original committee, it was reported, had hampered its work.

House Speaker Albert named Rep. Otis G. Pike (D, N.Y.) to replace Nedzi as committee chairman. Nedzi's credibility had been challenged as a result of disclosures that he had not acted on briefings of illegal CIA activities.

Data Collected on Congress Members & Others

FBI files on Congress members. FBI Director Clarence M. Kelley Jan. 21, 1975 confirmed various newspaper reports that the bureau kept files on members of Congress. However, he asserted that such information had not been actively sought by the FBI and was mostly the byproduct of unrelated FBI investigations.

Ron Nessen, White House press secretary, said Jan. 22 that the FBI had assured President Ford that it had not spied on members of Congress.

The Washington Post Jan. 18 had cited two former top officials of the FBI, who said the agency had compiled files containing information on the personal lives of members of Congress. Cartha D. DeLoach and Louis B. Nichols said the files contained data on "girl friends and drinking problems. . ., as well as other personal information," which DeLoach characterized as " 'junk,' " the Post said.

While the two former officials claimed that the information had been placed in the files after persons interviewed by the FBI on unrelated matters had volunteered it, the Post cited an informed source who said that J. Edgar Hoover, the late director of the bureau, had ordered derogatory material gathered on former Rep. William R. Anderson (D, Tenn.). Anderson had criticized Hoover for his statements about Philip and Daniel Berrigan, Catholic priests named by Hoover as having plotted to kidnap a high government official, later identified as Henry A. Kissinger, then director of the National Security Council.

In a written statement Jan. 21, Kelley said, "Such files exist because they relate to an investigation or a background check, correspondence with the member of Congress, or information not solicited by the FBI, but volunteered by the public." In the case of unsolicited allegations, Kelley said, the FBI investigated only when the charges fell under bureau jurisdiction.

(In a TV "conversation" Jan. 23, President Ford said that "under no circumstances" should the FBI spy on members of Congress or other U.S. citizens. "Mistakes were made going back to 1964 or 1965," Ford asserted, but "it has stopped now.")

FBI tapped and harassed King. The Washington Post reported Jan. 25, 1975 that President Johnson had ordered the FBI to electronicly bug and wiretap civil rights leaders during the 1964 Democratic national convention in Atlantic City, N.J. The source of its story, the Post said, was a Senate Watergate Committee memorandum summarizing a 1973 interview with Leo T. Clark, a former FBI agent, who was a key member of the team that carried out the surveillance.

According to the memorandum, wiretaps were installed in the hotel suite of Martin Luther King Jr., the late civil rights leader, and at an Atlantic City storefront used by civil rights groups. As a result of the wiretaps, the memo said, President Johnson obtained reports on the conversations of then Attorney General Robert F. Kennedy, members of Congress and other key convention delegates.

In the interview, Clark indicated that the stated purpose of the FBI operations was to gather intelligence on potential violence or disruptions. However, Clark acknowledged that Cartha D. DeLoach, assistant to the late FBI Director J. Edgar Hoover, ordered the surveillance kept secret from the Secret Service and the FBI's Newark N.J. office, which normally would have coordinated security at the convention.

Information from the operation, Clark said, was transmitted to President Johnson over a special telephone line that bypassed the White House switchboard. Clark also told the interviewers DeLoach had admitted that Kennedy, as the attorney general, had not been informed of the bugs. But DeLoach, Clark said, indicated Jóhnson was aware of them.

"'In a DeLoach conversation with the President, Clark heard mention of discussions concerning the seating of delegates or delegations, of vice presidential candidate possibilities, and the identities of congressmen and senators going in and out of King's quarters,' " the Post quoted the memo as saying.

The Post also obtained DeLoach's sworn testimony in 1973 before the Senate Watergate Committee. In the secret testimony DeLoach denied having had a direct line to Johnson or having spoken to him during the convention. Instead, DeLoach said FBI activities focused on one delegate suspected of connections with the Communist Party and on possible violence at the convention.

The New York Times reported March 9 that the FBI had tried to end King's criticism of the agency by mailing to his wife, Coretta King, a tape recording considered unsavory by some FBI agents. The recording, picked up by a "bug" put in a room of the Willard Hotel in Washington in 1963, was apparently of a party held by King and other officials of the Southern Christian Leadership Conference (SCLC), which King headed.

Mrs. King told the Times she remembered receiving in January 1965 "a tape that was rather curious, unlabeled." "As a matter of fact," she said, "Martin and I listened to the tape and we found much of it unintelligible. We concluded there was nothing in the tape to discredit him." She and her husband immediately "presumed" that the FBI had been the source of the tape, Mrs. King added.

One retired FBI agent, Arthur Murtagh, who was then attached to the bureau's Atlanta office, characterized the agency's activities against the late civil rights leader as second "only to the way they went after Jimmy Hoffa," former president of the Teamsters Union.

Other incidents of harassment, the Times said, included:

The bureau sought to disrupt a banquet in Atlanta honoring the awarding of the Nobel Peace Prize to King in 1964.

Two former FBI officers said a "monograph" on King's personal life was circulated among government officials during the Kennedy Administration.

When Kennedy learned of the "monograph," he ordered Hoover to retrieve every copy.

Murtagh and other former officials recounted the FBI practice of telephone calls—sometimes false fire alarms—to places where King was to speak and to King's associates to cause discord among them.

The Senate Select Committee on Intelligence said Nov. 18, 1975 that the mailing of the tape was part of a six-year FBI effort to discredit King. It said he had received a copy in November 1964, only 34 days before he was to accept the Nobel Peace Prize. An accompanying, unsigned note was reported to have read: "King, there is only one thing left for you to do. You know what it is. You have just 34 days in which to do (the exact number has been selected for a specific reason). It has definite practical significance. You are done. There is but one way out for you."

F. A. O. Schwarz 3rd, chief counsel to the committee, said that the panel's staff had established that the tape was produced with the aid of an electronic surveillance device placed by the FBI and that FBI officials had written the note. Moreover, in December 1964, the FBI mailed anonymously a second tape recording, possibly of the same incident, to King's wife, Coretta Scott King, Schwarz said.

Schwarz said staff investigators had discovered an FBI memo to Hoover from William Sullivan, then the bureau's chief of counterintelligence, recommending that the FBI discredit King by "knocking him off his pedestal." The FBI adopted the plan, Schwarz said.

Although the FBI instituted 16 separate wiretaps and bugged eight hotel rooms, Schwarz said, it never established that King was criminally suspect, a national security risk or an inciter of violence. Moreover, Hoover ordered other FBI officials to rewrite reports showing that King apparently was not a threat to the country.

Officials of the FBI acknowledged in testimony before the committee Nov. 19 that repeated attempts to discredit King and other targets of its counterintelligence program, Cointelpro, were legally unjustified. James B. Adams, assistant deputy director of the bureau, told the committee that the approximately 25 separate "actions" taken against King in the 1960s had "no statutory basis or justification."

FBI tapped black lawyer. In legal papers filed in the federal district court in Detroit, the FBI admitted monitoring 40 conversations of a black lawyer who was not under criminal investigation, Melvin Wulf, legal director of the American Civil Liberties Union (ACLU), said Feb. 4. The FBI filed the papers, Wulf said, in response to a civil suit by Abdeen M. Jabara, a Detroit attorney.

Jabara had charged the FBI with violating his constitutional rights of free speech and assembly by investigating him although it had no reason to believe he had engaged in criminal activity. The ACLU joined in the suit.

According to Wulf, the bureau's interest in Jabara stemmed from the fact that he represented a group of Arab students in the U.S.

Since 1972, the FBI papers said, Jabara had been monitored 40 times, during which he spoke to persons who were the targets of 13 separate surveillance operations by the bureau. No taps were placed on his home or office telephones, the papers said.

Levi confirms Hoover's secret files. J. Edgar Hoover kept secret files with derogatory information on presidents, congressmen and other prominent persons, Attorney General Edward H. Levi disclosed to a House subcommittee Feb. 27. His testimony—Levi's first as attorney general—also indicated that the FBI had been misused by at least three presidents for political purposes.

Hoover's files, which dated to 1920, contained 164 file folders and jackets, 48 of which concerned "public figures or prominent persons," Levi told the Judiciary Committee's Subcommittee on Civil Rights and Constitutional Rights. Included in the 48 files, Levi said, was information on "presidents, executive branch employes and 17 individuals who were members of Congress." (Two of the men named in the files were still in Congress, Levi added.) One document suggested that derogatory material on a congressman who had attacked Hoover "was improperly disseminated," Levi said without elaboration.

Levi described five instances of "misuse of the resources" of the FBI. He did not name the Presidents who allegedly misused the agency, but Deputy Attorney General Laurence H. Silberman supplied the names to newsman after the hearing.

Levi said one instance involved "a check of FBI files on the staff of a campaign opponent." According to Silberman, President Johnson made the request through an aide, Bill Moyers, about Sen. Barry Goldwater, the 1964 Republican candidate.

One president, Levi testified, "caused the FBI to gather intelligence relating to a political convention under circumstances that . . . could . . . have been suspected of being politically motivated." Silberman confirmed that it was Johnson and the incident was the bugging of the hotel suite of Martin Luther King Jr. at the 1964 Democratic national convention. Silberman said a similar incident had occurred in 1968. (The New York Times reported Feb. 28 that in 1968 the FBI had obtained phone records of members of the staff of Spiro T. Agnew, then Republican candidate for Vice President.)

In a "few instances," Levi testified, the FBI was ordered to report on "certain activities" of congressmen who opposed presidential policies. A Justice Department spokesman said that President Johnson on two occasions, President Nixon once and President Kennedy once had ordered data gathered on representatives and senators critical of their policies.

"In a very small number of instances . . . ," Levi said, "derogatory information legitimately obtained by the bureau was disseminated to other members of the executive branch to enable them to discredit their critics."

Levi said the FBI was used to conduct an investigation of another federal law enforcement agency. Justice Department officials said that President Johnson in 1967 asked the FBI to look into the involvement of the Treasury Department's Narcotics Bureau in the 1965 investigation of Robert G. (Bobby) Baker, a Johnson protege later convicted of income tax evasion. According to one Justice Department source, Johnson demanded to know if any of the persons involved were close to Robert Kennedy, then the attorney general.

In his subcommittee testimony, Levi urged that an executive order be issued restricting to a few officials the authority of the White House to ask the FBI for information. He said it was "inappropriate" for a president to ask the FBI for information on congressmen.

Levi and FBI Director Clarence M. Kelley, who also testified, said that present law and procedures did not allow the FBI to destroy the existing files on congressmen.

Colby admits CIA files on Rep. Abzug. CIA Director William E. Colby acknowledged March 5, 1975 that his agency had kept files on Rep. Bella S. Abzug (D, N.Y.) since 1953. The files, Colby said, contained copies of two letters Abzug had written on behalf of clients when she was a practicing attorney.

In testimony before House Government Operations Subcommittee on Government Information and Individual Rights, which was headed by Abzug, Colby conceded that Abzug was one of four past and current members of Congress on whom special counterintelligence files had been kept as part of the agency's operation against Vietnam War dissidents. While refusing to name the other three, Colby said the operation, terminated in March 1974, found there had been "no substantial foreign manipulation of or assistance to the antiwar movement."

Among the contents of the CIA's file on Abzug: copies of letters she wrote to the Soviet government in 1958 and 1960 on behalf of clients seeking to locate potential heirs in estate cases; data concerning her representation of a client in 1953 before the now-defunct House Committee on un-American Activities; details of her Paris meeting with the Provisional Revolutionary Government of South Vietnam in 1972; the names of lawyers on the mailing list of the American Peace Council and the minutes of a meeting of the Vietnam Mobilization Committee, once a leading antiwar group.

Agency opened mail to senators and Nixon. The Senate Select Committee on Intelligence disclosed Sept. 24, 1975 that the CIA, as part of a 20-year mail-intercept program, had opened and copied the mail of Richard M. Nixon as well as Sens. Edward M. Kennedy (D, Mass.) and Hubert H. Humphrey (D, Minn.).

According to committee chairman Sen. Frank Church (D, Ida.), CIA men at a New York post office worked from a "watch list" of at least 1,300 persons targeted for CIA surveillance. These CIA officers, who photographed letters of persons on the list, evidently strayed from the list and opened the mail of many prominent U.S. citizens and institutions that had not been targeted for surveillance, Church said. He added that he even found a letter he wrote to his mother-in-law in the CIA's files.

Besides his own letter and some correspondence to Nixon, Humphrey and Kennedy, Church said the CIA had opened mail to and from the late civil rights leader Martin Luther King Jr. and his wife, Coretta; John D. Rockefeller 4th; Arthur F. Burns, chairman of the Federal Reserve Board; Rep. Bella Abzug (D, N.Y.); the Rockefeller Foundation; the Ford Foundation and Harvard University. The incident involving Nixon, Church said, occurred in June 1968 when Nixon, who was then a leading candidate for the Republican presidential nomination, received a letter from an aide traveling in the Soviet Union.

The committee, operating in open session, heard testimony Sept. 23 from Tom Charles Huston, a former aide to Nixon, who in 1970 drafted a domestic intelligence plan that called for the lifting of "present restrictions" against the use of burglaries and mail openings by intelligence agents.

Huston testified that he and, to the best of his knowledge, Nixon were unaware that some of the illegal or improper domestic activities proposed in the Huston plan had been going on for years in the CIA and FBI. "If we had known all these tools were being used and still not getting results, it might have changed the whole approach," he testified.

Huston also said that there had never been any discussion in his presence, in the White House or in the interagency committee that drafted the Huston plan of the questionable constitutionality of the plan. "It was my opinion at the time" that Fourth Amendment prohibitions against search and seizure without judicial warrant "didn't apply to the President" in cases of national security.

Church commented during Huston's testimony that the episode clearly showed that U.S. intelligence agencies had operated as "independent fiefdoms" that told neither the President nor each other of their illicit operations.

The committee took testimony Sept. 24 from James Angleton, former chief of the CIA's counterintelligence section and the official in charge of the mail-intercept program from 1955 to 1973. Angleton acknowledged that the intercept program was illegal but he nevertheless defended it as vital to U.S. security. It was "inconceivable," Angleton said, that a secret intelligence arm of the government should have to comply with all the government's overt orders.

The intercepts of mail to and from Communist countries, particularly the Soviet Union, produced a number of items that were of such intelligence value, Angleton said, that it could only be assumed that the Soviet officials had so decided to communicate with agents and political sympathizers in the U.S. because they believed such communications would not be opened.

Asked by Church who had known of the intercept program, Angleton listed former CIA Director Richard Helms, Hoover and William C. Sullivan, former head of the FBI's domestic intelligence section.

Civilian Mail Checked

CIA mail-operation details. The Washington Post Jan. 10, 1975 reported details given by an unnamed former high-ranking intelligence officer, who said he had personally taken part in a CIA mail cover operation. Begun because the CIA was unable to obtain sufficient information from U.S. unions serving as conduits for agency funds to anti-communist trade unions in Europe in the 1950s, the ex-official said, the mail cover operation included interception of the mail of AFL-CIO president George Meany and two of Meany's senior international aides.

The Times Jan. 8 cited Melvin Crain, a political science professor at San Diego State University, who said that when he resigned his CIA post in 1959, the Post Office Department was covertly assisting the CIA in intercepting and copying the mail of U.S. citizens. CIA colleagues admitted the "mail tapping" was illegal and an unconstitutional violation of privacy, but justified it as necessary "to achieve our mission" of safeguarding U.S. security against the Soviet Union, Crain said. The alleged screening of letters—mostly correspondence from U.S. citizens to friends and relatives in the USSR—was started in the summer of 1958, the Times claimed.

William J. Cotter, the chief inspector of the U.S. Postal Service, told a House Judiciary Subcommittee March 18 that the CIA had ended an illegal mail-opening operation Feb. 15, 1973 after he told the agency to "get superior approval for this thing or discontinue it." He said he refused to extend the Feb. 15, 1973 deadline and the CIA suspended the program, which had dated from 1953.

Cotter had submitted to the Courts, Civil Liberties and Administration of Justice Subcommittee March 18 a Postal Service study showing that federal, state and local agencies had conducted more than 8,500 mail surveillances in the previous two years. The surveillance, known as mail cover, did not involve opening of mail, said Cotter, who explained that it entailed making a record of names and addresses from the outside of the envelope.

Cotter said opening of mail required a court order and added that with the exception of the CIA, the rule had not been violated. Four hundred thirty-one such orders were issued the previous year, he said.

Cotter, a CIA agent for 18 years, said the CIA's program had been initiated in 1953 as a "survey" of mail between the U.S. and the Soviet Union. At the time, postal officials understood it to be a simple mail cover operation for monitoring names of senders and addressees on envelopes. However, sometime around 1955, the CIA people "went one step further . . . without the concurrence of the postal people and surreptitiously appropriated some letters, opened some letters," Cotter testified. Unlike most mail covers, which postal employes conducted, Cotter said, employes of the CIA were authorized "to shuffle . . . and sort mail. . . . Obviously they . . . removed it from the premises, opened it, took pictures of it and got it back in the mainstream the next day."

Crain told the subcommittee March 21 about an agency briefing he attended in 1958, at which he was informed that the mail opening program was the result of a joint CIA, Federal Bureau of Investigation and Post Office operation.

CIA access to mail barred. Postmaster General Benjamin Franklin Bailar issued an order prohibiting the Central Intelligence Agency from having access "to any kind of mail in the custody of the Postal Service, whether by way of cooperative mail covers or otherwise," it was reported May 21. Bailar's March 5 letter notifying CIA Director William E. Colby of the restrictions had been prompted by the disclosures of the CIA mail interceptions.

In reply March 13, Colby said he shared Bailar's concern over protecting the integrity of the mails and said the CIA had "no intention of reinstituting" its mail-opening program.

In a separate development, the New York Times reported Aug. 4 that Justice Department lawyers had concluded that CIA employes had acted illegally when they opened and photographed mail in transit between the U.S. and Communist-bloc countries.

Suit filed in CIA mail openings. A class action damage suit was filed in federal district court in Providence, R.I. July 22 against 30 present and former officials of the Central Intelligence Agency, charging them with illegally opening mail. The suit, filed by the American Civil Liberties Union on behalf of Rodney Driver, a University of Rhode Island mathematics professor, and other Americans whose mail was opened, sought compensatory damages of $20,000 for each letter opened and $100,000 in punitive damages for each plaintiff.

Driver claimed that three letters he sent to the Soviet Union were opened and copied.

CIA mail opening operation detailed. Current and former officials of the Central Intelligence Agency, appearing before the Senate Select Committee on Intelligence Oct. 21, testified that they and "obviously everyone" else involved knew that an operation in which 215,000 pieces of mail were opened was illegal.

According to figures made available to the committee by the CIA, the covers of 2.7-million pieces of mail to and from the U.S.S.R. were photographed between 1953 and 1973 in the agency's New York mail surveillance program. The CIA opened and photographed the contents of 215,820 individual letters, the figures showed.

Testimony before the committee Oct. 21 revealed that two internal investigations of the New York operation, one in 1960 and the other in 1969, found the program to have produced little of intelligence value. Gordon Stewart, inspector general of the CIA in 1969, testified that his office was "quite surprised" to discover that the program was going on and recommended that it be transferred to the Federal Bureau of Investigation.

Stewart and two former staff members of the inspector general's office, John Glennon and Thomas Abernathy, said they had suspected the program was illegal. Moreover, Glennon remarked that "obviously everyone [in the CIA who was involved] realized it was illegal."

Richard Helms, who directed the CIA from 1966 to 1973, testified Oct. 22 that

he had known the operation was illegal. However, he added that he had assumed that Allen Dulles, the agency's director when the program was started in 1953, had "made his legal peace with it."

Helms said he was uncertain if Presidents Eisenhower and Kennedy had been informed of the operation, and he did not recall discussing it with President Nixon. He believed, however, that he had mentioned the intercept operation to President Johnson in 1967.

Prior to Helms' testimony, three former postmasters general appeared before the committee. J. Edward Day, postmaster general between 1961 and 1963, and Winston Blount, who held the position from 1969 to 1971, refused to concede that the openings had been illegal. John Gronouski, who headed the Post Office from 1963 to 1965, claimed that he knew nothing about the program and that he would have opposed it if he had.

Day recalled that he had been visited in 1961 by Dulles and Kermit Roosevelt, then a CIA official. When told by them that they had something "very secret" to discuss, Day said he replied, "Do I have to know about it?" Dulles and Roosevelt in turn responded that he did not, Day testified.

Blount said he was told of a secret project in which the Post Office was cooperating with the CIA. When he asked if he should seek advice about the project's legality, Blount testified, he was informed that the matter of legality had already been discussed with then Attorney General John Mitchell.

Mitchell, appearing before the committee under subpoena Oct. 24, denied that the CIA or FBI had told him they were secretly opening mail.

The New York times reported Oct. 25 that Mitchell and Helms had met in June 1970 and that Helms had referred to the intercept program in an aside from their main topic of discussion. (Helms had testified Oct. 23 that after speaking to Mitchell, he had met with Blount and said that Mitchell had "no problem" with the project.)

Cointelpro Action

FBI harassed Trotskyists. The FBI

made public over 3,000 pages of internal documents March 18 detailing agency efforts to harass the Socialist Workers Party, a splinter communist party loyal to the ideology of the Leon Trotsky, the Soviet revolutionary. (A civil suit filed under the amended Freedom of Information Act resulted in a federal court order compelling the FBI to release 3,138 pages of documents to the party and its youth affiliate, the Young Socialist Alliance.)

The documents showed that the party had been an object of FBI surveillance since 1944, as well as a target of the agency's counterintelligence program, Cointelpro, whose purpose was to disrupt party activities and harass party members and their families. According to the documents, Cointelpro was involved in 41 separate operations against the party between 1961 and 1971.

Among the activities described by the documents:

■The arrest and conviction record of the party's candidate for a New York City political office was sent anonymously to the New York Daily News, which later published the information in one of its columns.

■In 1963 an anonymous letter was sent to a black candidate for mayor of San Francisco, telling him of the presence of party members in his campaign staff.

■J. Edgar Hoover, director of the FBI until his death in 1972, personally approved dissemination of anonymous leaflets designed to cause dissension among various political factions and parties of the far left.

■An anonymous phone call alleged that a party-operated print shop was attempting to defraud the State of New York by creating bogus unemployment insurance claims for party members.

FBI threat against activist charged. The American Civil Liberties Union (ACLU) March 17 made public documents indicating that the Federal Bureau of Investigation (FBI) had fabricated a threatening letter to persuade a black civil rights worker to leave Mississippi in 1969. Within a month of receiving the letter, the civil rights worker, Muhammad Kenyatta, returned to Pennsylvania with his family.

The ACLU said it had obtained the documents in connection with a suit Kenyatta had filed against the FBI charging violations of his constitutional rights. They showed that Kenyatta, then known as Donald W. Jackson, had been a target of the FBI's counterintelligence program, Cointelpro.

The letter, purportedly written by a committee of Tougaloo (Miss.) College students, was actually prepared and sent by the FBI's office in Jackson, the documents showed. It warned Kenyatta that if he did not leave, "we shall consider contacting local authorities regarding some of your activities or take other measures available to us which would have a more direct effect and which would not be as cordial as this note."

A year before the letter was sent, the FBI documents showed, Kenyatta had been placed on the bureau's Cointelpro "agitation list." The FBI said Kenyatta had tried to organize black power groups and start racist publications.

The documents said that the Jackson office of the FBI, acting on a tip that Kenyatta had stolen a television set from the Tougaloo campus, encouraged college officials to file a complaint against Kenyatta. (Kenyatta said the charge was dropped after he agreed to pay a fine for disturbing the peace. He denied both charges.)

Levi reveals more FBI harassment. Attorney General Edward H. Levi revealed May 23 that the Federal Bureau of Investigation had conducted five previously undisclosed counter-intelligence programs from 1960 to 1971. Two of these programs—part of the FBI's anti-radical effort known collectively as Cointelpro— were designed to pit organized crime against the Communist Party USA and to disrupt the activities of unidentified Puerto Rican independence groups. Levi, who made the disclosures in a letter May 23 to House Judiciary Committee Chairman Peter W. Rodino Jr. (D, N.J.), did not provide details on the other three programs, which he said "were in the area of foreign intelligence and ... classified secret."

According to Levi, the program to turn organized crime against the Communist

Party was dubbed "Operation Hoodwink" and in operation between October 1966 and July 1968. It revolved around four bogus letters prepared and mailed by FBI agents, Levi said. The letters contained, among other things, accusations of unfair labor practices against one organized crime figure, as well as charges that organized crime had been behind the bombing of the Communist Party USA headquarters in New York City.

Asked about the purpose of Operation Hoodwink, a Justice Department spokesman said it was "just to have them sort of disrupt each other." To his knowledge, he said, it was not the FBI's intention for the groups to commit violent acts against each other.

The activities against the Puerto Rican independence groups, Levi stated, involved 37 separate actions between August 1960 and April 1970, including mailings by FBI agents to individuals and groups. Among the examples cited by Levi was a letter to two members of an independence group saying that the group leader and a member were having a "love affair." Another instance, involved the mailing of 300 copies of a flier alleging that an independence group had misused its funds.

FBI discloses disruptive tactics. The Federal Bureau of Investigation Aug. 15 made public hitherto secret documents describing counterintelligence tactics the agency used in the late 1960s against such organizations as the Ku Klux Klan, the Communist Party and the Black Panthers.

According to the documents, most of which concerned the Klan, the FBI infiltrated the Klan with 2,000 informants, fabricated news stories hostile to Klan leaders and mailed large numbers of anonymous postcards to Klan members in an effort to frighten them into resigning. At one point, the documents showed, informants held high positions in seven of the 14 Klan groups around the country. One state group was actually headed by an FBI informant.

Other documents released showed that FBI tactics against the American Communist Party had included anonymous mailings to Jewish members of the party, telling of anti-Semitism in the Soviet Union.

The FBI still used Cointelpro techniques for two and a half years after the program was supposed to have been officially terminated in April 1971, according to heretofore secret documents made public Oct. 5.

The documents, which were obtained in connection with a $27-million damage suit filed against the bureau by the Socialist Workers Party, said FBI agents visited 28 party members or associates between April 1971 and December 1973 to tell them of the FBI's knowledge of their affiliation and to seek further information. In addition, the documents revealed that FBI agents had telephoned members of the SWP or its youth affiliate, the Young Socialist Alliance, and used what the documents called a "jury-duty pretext" to gain information about their places of birth, employment, marital status and similar data.

Another document detailed how in 1965 the Cleveland field office of the bureau informed Cleveland school officials on "a strictly confidential basis" that one of the teachers in the Cleveland school system was married to an official of the Ohio SWP. "As a direct result" of the FBI's action, one document said, the teacher's contract was not renewed.

Actions described. Documents and testimony presented to the Senate Select Committee on Intelligence described various FBI actions in the Cointelpro program. Among the targets of FBI actions, according to the information given to the committee, were the Ku Klux Klan (KKK), the Vietnam Veterans Against the War (VVAW), the Black Panther Party, a University of Chicago professor, and Jane Fonda.

Testimony concerning the KKK was given Dec. 2 by a former FBI informer, Gary Rowe. He testified that the FBI had instructed him to have sexual relations with the wives of as many Klan members as possible, in order to obtain information and create discord. (An FBI official denied that such instructions had ever been given, although the bureau agent who had been Rowe's superior told the committee that Rowe "couldn't be an angel and be a good informant.")

Another former FBI informer, Mary Jo Cook, gave testimony before the committee Dec. 2 describing her work in infiltrating the Vietnam Veterans Against the War. She said that the FBI told her to gain the confidence of emotionally unstable members of the VVAW by acting as a "big sister" for them.

According to a story in the Dec. 3 Los Angeles Times, the Senate committee possessed documents revealing an attempt by the FBI to cripple the Black Panther Party, by aggravating a conflict existing between the Panther Party and another black militant organization called US. FBI field officers were told, in orders sent out by then FBI Director J. Edgar Hoover, "to submit imaginative and hard-hitting counter-intelligence measures" to the head office in a biweekly letter which "should also contain accomplishments obtained during the previous two-week period."

These orders were issued two months before the Jan. 17, 1969 murder of two BPP members, for which two members of the US Party were convicted. The Committee also had nine cartoons—some critical of the Panthers, and others of the US Party—which committee sources said the FBI had circulated in an attempt to embitter relations between the two groups.

A Dec. 15 story in The New York Times described two FBI memos (in the possession of the Senate committee) relating to an attempt to discredit film actress Jane Fonda. The first memo (written by an FBI agent in Los Angeles on June 17, 1970) requested permission from the head office to send a letter to the gossip columnist of Variety, the entertainment business newspaper. The letter would say that Jane Fonda, when attending a Black Panther rally on June 13, 1970, encouraged the audience to give money for the purchase of guns by the Panthers, and led the audience in a chant containing the words "we will kill Richard Nixon". (Miss Fonda stated that she has never helped raise money for guns, or said that she wanted to kill Nixon.) The second

memo contained Hoover's approval of the plan, on the condition that it could not be traced back to the FBI. However, the columnist to whom the letter was supposed to have been sent said that he had no memory of ever having received such a letter.

The FBI also used a letter in an endeavor to discredit a professor of the University of Chicago in 1968, according to FBI documents obtained by the Senate committee Dec. 18. The letter was about Richard Flacks, an assistant professor of sociology who had become somewhat well-known by his opposition to the war in Vietnam, his support of the Students for a Democratic Society, and his involvement in student demonstrations. The letter, which was signed by "a concerned alumnus," was sent to the trustees of the university, in the hope that drawing their attention to Flacks' activities might "discourage Flacks or even result in his ultimate removal from the University of Chicago." According to FBI records, the letter did not have any effect.

Policy on blacks. FBI documents released April 5, 1976, in response to a freedom-of-information suit, explained FBI aims in a Cointelpro operation directed specifically against black groups.

A letter dated Aug. 25, 1967, which FBI headquarters sent to field offices at the start of the program, said: "The purpose of this new counterintelligence endeavor is to expose, disrupt, misdirect, discredit or otherwise neutralize the activities of black nationalist, hate-type groups, their leadership, spokesmen, membership and supporters, and to counter their propensity for violence and civil disorder."

A telegram that followed the letter, named, among other black groups, the Student Nonviolent Coordinating Committee (SNCC) and the Southern Christian Leadership Conference as having "radical and violence-prone leaders, members and followers."

Continued Attacks on Agencies

Colby warns of jeopardy to CIA. In testimony before the House Defense Appropriations Subcommittee Feb. 20, 1975, CIA Director William Colby warned that "exaggerated" charges of improper conduct by his agency "had placed American intelligence in danger."

He testified in part:

"Mr. Chairman, these last two months have placed American intelligence in danger. The almost hysterical excitement that surrounds any news story mentioning CIA, or referring even to a perfectly legitimate activity of CIA, has raised the question whether secret intelligence operations can be conducted by the United States.

"A number of the intelligence services abroad with which CIA works have expressed concern over its situation and over the fate of the sensitive information they provide to us. A number of our individual agents abroad are deeply worried that their names might be revealed with resultant danger to their lives as well as their livelihoods.

"A number of Americans who have collaborated with CIA as a patriotic contribution to their country are deeply concerned that their reputations will be besmirched and their businesses ruined by sensational misrepresentation of this association. And our own employes are torn between the sensational allegations of CIA misdeeds and their own knowledge that they served their nation during critical times in the best way they know how."

Colby warned again April 7 that the CIA was being jeopardized by unjustified and sensational headlines.

Addressing the annual convention of American Newspaper Publishers Association in New Orleans, Colby said the CIA was proud of the U.S.' open society but that "this open society must be protected, and that intelligence, even secret intelligence, must play a part in that protection."

Because the CIA had become "the nation's number one sensational lead." Colby said, other intelligence agencies were "questioning our ability to keep their work for us secret." U.S. businesses that had aided the CIA were afraid their operations "abroad [will be] destroyed by a revelation of their patriotic assistance to the CIA," Colby said.

CIA officer resigns to defend agency—
David A. Phillips, 52, chief of Latin American operations for the Central Intelligence Agency (CIA), resigned effective May 9 to organize an association of former agency employes for the purpose of defending the organization against outside attack, it was reported March 22.

An open letter Phillips sent to 250 former agency officers said in part:

"As chief of Latin American operations, I have been deeply concerned about the decline of morale at Langley [CIA headquarters outside Washington] and abroad. Snowballing innuendo, egregious stories and charges and even honest concerns have presented us with the basic dilemma of issuing either a general statement which reassures few but preserves security or a comprehensive accounting which satisfies some but at the expense of operations and agents.

"Under the circumstances, there is little doubt that a thorough Congressional review is the best, if not only, solution even though some leakage of sensitive details on foreign operations seems almost inevitable . . . our capabilities abroad are being damaged. More of our agents and friends . . . are saying thanks but no thanks. Friendly liaison services are beginning to back away from us. The Marchettis and the Agees have the stage and only a few challenge them."

Victor Marchetti and Philip Agee, former CIA officers, wrote books critical of the CIA.

CIA monitored Socialist Workers. The Central Intelligence Agency monitored the activities of the Socialist Workers Party (SWP) from 1951 to 1974, according to documents the party made public July 13. The documents were obtained by the SWP in the course of a lawsuit seeking to stop surveillance of the party by the CIA and other government agencies.

A spokesman for the CIA said July 17 that it could "be assumed" that agents designated in the documents as "R-4, R-5, R-6 and R-7" had been working for the agency when they gathered information in 1969 and 1970 about the Young Socialist Alliance (YSA), the youth affiliate of the SWP. The spokesman indicated that the agents might have been part of Operation Chaos, a CIA operation to spy on antiwar and black activist groups around the nation between 1967 and 1973.

Other documents released by the party included memoranda, dated 1959 and 1961, dealing with YSA literature and a copy of the 1968 New York State election ballot listing the names of SWP candidates.

White House surveillance denied. Administration and CIA officials July 10 denied reports emanating from the House Select Committee on Intelligence, said to have been based on unreleased CIA documents, that the agency had maintained an operative on the staff of the Nixon White House whose function was to secretly provide the agency with information on activities there.

The New York Times July 9 had cited a memorandum prepared the previous day by A. Searle Field, the House committee's staff director, indicating the existtence of the classified CIA materials. The Times reported that an unidentified source close to the House investigation regarded the CIA materials as giving no evidence that President Nixon was aware of this "infiltration of the executive," as Field called it. In its article that day and in subsequent ones, the Times said the CIA documents were an unreleased portion of a 1973 study ordered by James R. Schlesinger, then the agency's director, parts of which had been made public July 8 by Director William E. Colby.

CBS television reported July 10 that the CIA document had been made available to it by Rep. Lucien N. Nedzi (D, Mich.), then chairman of the House Committee. CBS quoted Nedzi as saying "the issue" was whether the alleged placement of a CIA operative in the White House, or in other branches of the government, had been done "without the knowledge of the office in which the individuals were serving."

CIA Director Colby declared July 10 that the agency had "never done anything with respect to the White House that's not known to the White House" and that reports of infiltration were "outrageous nonsense." Ron Nessen, the presidential press secretary, said there "may be a handful" of CIA agents working at the White House but that their employment "shows up on the payroll . . . they're here quite openly."

The New York Times said Rep. Nedzi read a page of the CIA document July 11 which indicated the agency had "detailed" employes to the White House from time to time. However, the paper quoted Nedzi as saying he had heard "nothing" to support claims that a high-level CIA operative had been in the White House when Richard Nixon was in office. Nedzi specifically denied charges by L. Fletcher

Prouty, a former Defense Department intelligence officer, that Alexander P. Butterfield, a former Nixon aide in the White House, had been a CIA agent. Col. Prouty, once the Air Force's liaison with the CIA, had told reporters that Butterfield had been the agency's "contact man" in the White House and that Gen. Alexander M. Haig, former chief of staff for Nixon, had been the Army's "contact" with the agency. Prouty said his information came from E. Howard Hunt Jr., a former CIA agent convicted of participating in the Watergate break-in. He said "detailed" CIA personnel went to government jobs "with the knowledge of the department head" but that "if you run that through three or four generations of supervisors" the knowledge "disappeared."

The CIA issued a statement July 11 insisting that Butterfield had "never been an employe" of the agency and had "never been assigned to or worked for" it "in any capacity." It said that "detailing" employes was a "long-established and widespread practice in government."

Butterfield declared July 13 that while on Nixon's staff he "had no contact whatsoever with the CIA" and that he had "never met Howard Hunt in my life."

In a July 14 telephone interview with the Springfield (Mass.) Daily News, Prouty said: "They may have told me the wrong name to cover up the real informer." According to the New York Times, however, Prouty denied July 15 that he had made such a statement the previous day. Interviewed July 15 at Eglin Air Force Base in Florida by CBS television, Hunt said the report about Butterfield had been "an unfortunate invention on Mr. Prouty's part." Also interviewed by CBS that day, Prouty declared: "The name that they mentioned was Butterfield. The only name that I heard in the office was Butterfield."

Curbs on some FBI tactics to be set. Attorney General Edward H. Levi said Aug. 13 that he had tentatively approved Justice Department guidelines designed to curtail some of the Federal Bureau of Investigation's domestic intelligence operations. The proposed guidelines, which Levi outlined before the American Bar Association's annual convention in Montreal, were part of the results of a comprehensive review of FBI investigative practices ordered by the attorney general.

Among the details of the guidelines:

All FBI files containing unsolicited charges about individuals would have to be thrown out after 90 days if the charges could not be proved.

Electronic surveillance would be used in "full-scale investigations" only and would be subject to periodic review by the attorney general. (Levi did not define "full-scale.")

Infiltration of domestic groups would be prohibited except in cases when intrusions by FBI agents were intended to prevent violence.

The decades-old practice of conducting open-ended, unsupervised probes of domestic groups suspected of subversive activities would be ended.

The FBI would be barred from using informants as agents provocateurs, who incited others to commit criminal acts.

To end use of the FBI by the White House for political purposes, all White House orders would have to be in writing and signed by a high-level authority.

Rockefeller Panel Finds CIA 'Invasions' of Rights

Most agency activities termed legal. The Rockefeller Commission said in its final report, released June 10, 1975, that the Central Intelligence Agency had engaged in activities that were "plainly unlawful and constituted improper invasions upon the rights of Americans." The report also said, however, that a "great majority" of the CIA's domestic activities during its 28-year history had been in compliance with its statutory authority.

According to the panel, chaired by Vice President Nelson A. Rockefeller, the CIA illegally opened mail to and from the Soviet Union and other countries at various times between 1952 and 1974; established in violation of its charter a supersecret Special Operations Group that amassed 13,000 files, 7,200 of them on dissident U.S. citizens, and compiled a computerized index of 300,000 individual names and organizations; infiltrated domestic political groups; and undertook 32 wiretaps, an equal number of room buggings and 12 break-ins, as well as the investigation of the tax records of 16 persons.

In its 299-page report, submitted to President Ford June 6, the commission made 30 recommendations to insure against recurrence of illegal or improper activities. These included strengthened Congressional and executive oversight, internal reorganization of the agency and more precise definition of what the agency should or should not do.

Illegal mail surveillance confirmed—According to the commission, the mail interception operation had been begun in 1952 as a program for surveying mail to and from the Soviet Union that passed through a New York City postal facility. Designed to identify persons cooperating with Soviet intelligence and to determine Soviet mail censorship techniques, the interception program's "primary purpose" eventually became participation with the Federal Bureau of Investigation "in internal security functions."

During the year before the termination of the New York mail interception operation in 1973, more than half of 4.35 million pieces of mail intended for the Soviet Union were examined, 33,000 envelopes photographed and 8,700 letters opened, the report stated. Smaller mail intercepts were run in San Francisco in 1969-71, in Hawaii during 1954-55 and in New Orleans for a short period in 1957.

The commission, which noted that the intercept program was in contravention of postal regulations, revealed the existence of a 1962 memorandum indicating the agency was aware that the openings violated federal criminal laws barring obstruction or delay of the mails. Moreover, the intercept operation violated the 1947 National Security Act prohibition against CIA involvement in internal security matters, the commission said.

Operation Chaos—Another section of

the Rockefeller Commission's report concerned the Special Operations Group—later known as "Operation Chaos"—established in 1967 at the request of President Lyndon B. Johnson to "collect, coordinate, evaluate and report on the extent of foreign influence on domestic dissidence." Although the stated purpose of the group was to determine if U.S. dissidents had foreign contacts, the report said, "accumulation of considerable material on domestic dissidents and their activities" occurred. In the six years the operation existed, 13,000 files, 7,200 of them on U.S. citizens, were compiled, and the names of 300,000 persons and organizations found in the files were entered into an agency computer. From the information in these files, the report continued, the group prepared 3,500 memorandums for internal agency use, 3,000 memorandums for dissemination to the FBI and 37 memorandums that went to the White House and high level federal officials. The staff of Operation Chaos, "steadily enlarged in response to repeated presidential requests for more information," reached a maximum of 52 persons in 1971, the commission said.

Beginning in late 1969, Operation Chaos used a number of agents to collect information abroad on connections between U.S. dissidents and foreign groups. To insure proper " 'cover' " for its agents, the commission said, the CIA recruited persons from the dissident groups or sought others who were instructed to join the dissident groups. While these recruits were not generally told to collect domestic information on dissident groups, they nonetheless did so during the time they were developing ties with the dissidents. On three occasions, however, "an agent of the operation was specifically directed to collect domestic intelligence," the commission's report revealed.

"Some domestic activities of Operation Chaos" the report said, "exceeded the CIA's statutory authority. . . . More significantly the operation became a repository for large quantities of information on the domestic activities of American citizens . . . and much of it was not directly related to the question of the existence of foreign connections."

The report also criticized the isolation

of the group from supervision by the regular agency chain of command, a situation that made it possible, the report said, for the operation "to stray over the bounds of the agency's authority without the knowledge of senior officials." According to the commission, the operation was so isolated from the rest of the agency that James Angleton, head of the counterintelligence section, of which the operation was nominally a part, was never aware of the Special Operations Group or its successor, Operation Chaos. Testimony by Angleton and the head of Operation Chaos indicated that supervisory responsibility lay with Richard Helms, director of the CIA from 1966–73.

Other chapters of the commission's report dealt with the CIA Office of Security, which was in charge of protecting agency security and sources, besides conducting routine investigations of persons seeking affiliation with the CIA. "Investigation disclosed," the report said, "the domestic use of 32 wiretaps, the last in 1965; 32 instances of bugging, the last in 1968 and 12 break-ins, the last in 1971. None of these activities was conducted under judicial warrant, and only one with the approval of the attorney general." To determine whether 16 persons were security risks with foreign connections, the report said, the CIA obtained information from the Internal Revenue Service on the income tax records of these individuals. The CIA did not comply with existing statutory and regulatory procedures for obtaining such information, the report stated.

"The unauthorized entries described were illegal when they were conducted and would be illegal . . . today. Likewise, the review of individuals' tax returns . . . violated specific statutes and regulations prohibiting such conduct," the commission said. The commission added "that while some of the instances of electronic eavesdropping were proper when conducted, many were not."

The following are excerpts from the official summary of the report to President Ford by the Commission on Central Intelligence Activities Within the United States. It was made public June 10.

A. Individual Rights

The Bill of Rights in the Constitution protects individual liberties against encroachment by government. Many statutes and the common law also reflect this protection.

The First Amendment protects the freedoms of speech and of the press, the right of the people to assemble peaceably, and the right to petition the government for redress of grievances. It has been construed to protect freedom of peaceable political association. In addition, the Fourth Amendment declares:

The right of the people to be secure in their persons, houses, papers, and effects, against unreasonable searches and seizures, shall not be violated. . . .

In accordance with the objectives enunciated in these and other Constitutional amendments, the Supreme Court has outlined the following basic constitutional doctrines:

1. Any intrusive investigation of an American citizen by the government must have a sufficient basis to warrant the invasion caused by the particular investigative practices which are utilized;

2. Government monitoring of a citizen's political activities requires even greater justification;

3. The scope of any resulting intrusion on personal privacy must not exceed the degree reasonably believed necessary;

4. With certain exceptions, the scope of which are not sharply defined, these conditions must be met, at least for significant investigative intrusions, to the satisfaction of an uninvolved governmental body such as a court.

These constitutional standards give content to an accepted principle of our society—the right of each person to a high degree of individual privacy.

In recognition of this right, President Truman and the Congress—in enacting the law creating the CIA in 1947—included a clause providing that the CIA should have no police, subpoena, law-enforcement powers or internal security functions.

Since then, Congress has further outlined citizen rights in statutes limiting electronic surveillance and granting individuals access to certain information in government files, underscoring the general concern of Congress and the executive branch in this area. . . .

C. National Security

Individual liberties likewise depend on maintaining public order at home and in protecting the country against infiltration from abroad and armed attack. Ensuring domestic tranquility and providing for a common defense are not only Constitutional goals but necessary pre-conditions for a free, democratic system. The process of orderly and lawful change is the essence of democracy. Violent change, or forcing a change of government by the stealthy action of "enemies, foreign or domestic," is contrary to our Constitutional system.

The government has both the right and the obligation within Constitutional limits to use its available power to protect the people and their established form of government. Nevertheless, the mere invocation of the "national security" does not grant unlimited power to the government. The degree of the danger and the type of action contemplated to meet that danger require careful evaluation, to ensure that the danger is sufficient to justify the action and that fundamental rights are respected.

D. Resolving the Issues

Individual freedoms and privacy are fundamental in our society. Constitutional government must be maintained. An effective and efficient intelligence system is necessary; and to be effective, many of its activities must be conducted in secrecy.

Satisfying these objectives presents considerable opportunity for conflict. The vigorous pursuit of intelligence by certain methods can lead to invasions of individual rights. The preservation of the United States requires an effective intelligence capability, but the preservation of individual liberties within the United States requires limitations or restrictions on gatherings of intelligence. The drawing of reasonable lines—where legitimate intelligence needs end and erosion of Constitutional government begins—is difficult.

In seeking to draw such lines, we have been guided in the first instance by the commands of the Constitution as they have been interpreted by the Supreme Court, the laws as written by Congress, the values we believe are reflected in the democratic process, and the faith we have in a free society. We have also sought to be fully cognizant of the needs of national security, the requirements of a strong national defense against external aggression and internal subversion, and the duty of the government to protect its citizens.

In the final analysis, public safety and individual liberty sustain each other.

FINDINGS
AND CONCLUSIONS
Summary of Findings

A detailed analysis of the facts has convinced the commission that the great majority of the CIA's domestic activities comply with its statutory authority.

Nevertheless, over the 28 years of its history, the CIA has engaged in some activities that should be criticized and not permitted to happen again—both in light of the limits imposed on the Agency by law and as a matter of public policy.

Some of these activities were initiated or ordered by Presidents, either directly or indirectly.

Some of them fall within the doubtful area between responsibilities delegated to the CIA by Congress and the National Security Council on the one hand and activities specifically prohibited to the Agency on the other.

Some of them are plainly unlawful and constituted improper invasions upon the rights of Americans.

The agency's own recent actions, undertaken for the most part in 1973 and 1974, have gone far to terminate the activities upon which this investigation has focused. The recommendations of the commission are designed to clarify areas of doubt concerning the Agency's authority, to strengthen the Agency's structure, and to guard against recurrences of these improprieties.

The CIA's Role and Authority

The Central Intelligence Agency was established by the National Security Act of 1947 as the nation's first comprehensive peacetime foreign intelligence service. The objective was to provide the President with coordinated intelligence, which the country lacked prior to the attack on Pearl Harbor.

The director of central intelligence reports directly to the President. The CIA receives its policy direction and guidance from the National Security Council, composed of the President, the Vice President, and the Secretaries of State and Defense.

The statute directs the CIA to correlate, evaluate, and disseminate intelligence obtained from United States intelligence agencies, and to perform such other functions related to intelligence as the National Security Council directs. Recognizing that the CIA would be dealing with sensitive, secret materials, Congress made the director of central intelligence responsible for protecting intelligence sources and methods from unauthorized disclosure.

At the same time, Congress sought to assure the American public that it was not establishing a secret police which would threaten the civil liberties of Americans. It specifically forbade the CIA from exercising "police, subpoena, or law-enforcement powers or internal security functions." The CIA was not to replace the Federal Bureau of Investigation in conducting domestic activities to investigate crime or internal subversion.

Although Congress contemplated that the focus of the CIA would be on foreign intelligence, it understood that some of its activities would be conducted within the United States. The CIA necessarily maintains its headquarters here, procures logistical support, recruits and trains employees, tests equipment, and conducts other domestic activities in support of its foreign intelligence mission. It makes necessary investigations in the United States to maintain the security of its facilities and personnel.

Additionally, it has been understood from the beginning that the CIA is permitted to collect foreign intelligence—that is, information concerning foreign capabilities, intentions, and activities—from American citizens within this country by overt means.

Determining the legal propriety of domestic activities of the CIA requires the application of the law to the particular facts involved. This task involves consideration of more than the National Security Act and the directives of the National Security Council; constitutional and other statutory provisions also circumscribe the domestic activities of the CIA. Among the applicable constitutional provisions are the First Amendment, protecting freedom of speech, of the press, and of peaceable assembly; and the Fourth Amendment, prohibiting unreasonable searches and seizures. Among the statutory provisions are those which limit such activities as electronic eavesdropping and interception of the mails. . . .

Indices and Files on American Citizens

Findings

Biographical information is a major resource of an intelligence agency. The CIA maintains a number of files and indices that include biographical information on Americans.

As a part of its normal process of indexing names and information of foreign intelligence interest, the directorate of operations has indexed some 7 million names of all nationalities. An estimated 115,000 of these are believed to be American citizens.

Where a person is believed to be of possibly continuing intelligence interest, files to collect information as received are opened. An estimated 57,-000 out of a total of 750,000 such files concern American citizens. For the most part, the names of Americans appear in indices and files as actual or potential sources of information or assistance to the CIA. In addition to these files, files on some 7,200 American citizens, relating primarily to their domestic activities, were, as already stated, compiled within the Directorate of operations as part of Operation Chaos.

The directorate of administration maintains a number of files on persons who have been associated with the CIA. These files are maintained for security, personnel, training, medical and payroll purposes. Very few are maintained on persons unaware that they have a relationship with the CIA. However, the Office of Security maintained files on American citizens associated with dissident groups who were never affiliated with the agency because they were considered a threat to the physical security of agency facilities and employees. These files were also maintained, in part, for use in future security clearance determinations. Dissemination of security files is restricted to persons with an operational need for them.

The office of legislative counsel maintains files concerning its relationships with congressmen.

Conclusions

Although maintenance of most of the indices, files, and records of the Agency has been necessary and proper, the standards applied by the Agency at some points during its history have permitted the accumulation and indexing of materials not needed for legitimate intelligence or security purposes. Included in this category are many of the files related to Operation Chaos and the activities of the Office of Security concerning dissident groups.

Constant vigilance by the agency is essential to prevent the collection of information on United States citizens which is not needed for proper intelligence activities. The executive order recommended by the commission will ensure purging of nonessential or improper materials from agency files.

Intelligence Community's Activities & Misdeeds

FBI admits burglaries. Clarence M. Kelley, director of the Federal Bureau of Investigation, admitted July 14, 1975 that the agency had conducted a number of burglaries and break-ins since World War II in order to get "information relative to the security of the nation." Speaking at a news conference to mark the start of his third year in office, Kelley said the break-ins had continued beyond 1966, previously given as the year they had been terminated, but that he himself had not been asked to approve any while serving as FBI director.

He described the number of break-ins he knew about as "not many" and said he did "not note in these activities any gross abuse of authority." They were not, he said, "a corruption of the trust that was placed in us." Regarding the prospect of future FBI break-ins, Kelley added: "If ever anything of this type comes up and I can't foresee this need—but if ever it did come up and it became a matter of grave concern, a matter that is to be solved only through such activity, I would present it to the attorney general and would be guided by his opinion as to such activity."

In answer to another question, Kelley said the FBI would go on collating whatever material it received about the lives and habits of famous people, including members of Congress, because the "abuse" of such information was in its "publication" rather than its collection. He also defended the bureau's counterintelligence program, known as Cointelpro and abandoned in 1971, and said its purpose had been "to do something that would ultimately . . . benefit the nation."

The Washington Post July 16, citing an unnamed former FBI agent, said that until 1966 the agency had committed as many as 100 burglaries a year, mostly in "security cases" but also in ordinary criminal proceedings. The Post said the break-ins had been stopped by former Attorney General Ramsey Clark.

According to the New York Times July 22, FBI agents in 1959 entered the Washington, D.C. hotel room of a New York Post reporter at the request of J. Edgar Hoover, then agency director, who was concerned about an investigation of the bureau being conducted by the newsman. The Times said its source, who asked not to be identified, had come forward to discredit remarks made in his July 14 news conference by Kelley, who had asserted the break-ins had all been carried out for reasons either of foreign intelligence or national security. The paper quoted its source as declaring the purpose of the Washington break-in had been to find signs that the reporter "might have had a female in the room or was drinking heavily." However, the "fellow was clean as a whistle" and the agents didn't find "anything that was worthwhile."

According to data made public Sept. 25 by the Senate Select Committee on Intelligence, the FBI had committed at least 238 illegal break-ins against dissident U.S. groups and individuals.

Sen. Frank Church, chairman of the committee, said an FBI report showed 238 "entries" by FBI agents in connection with the investigation of 14 "domestic subversive targets" had been made between 1942 and 1968, and "numerous" but uncounted entries involving three other "domestic subversion targets" had been carried out between 1952 and 1966. (According to sources outside the committee, the New York Times reported Sept. 26, the FBI's statistics did not include break-ins involving espionage and organized crime investigations.)

The committee also made public a top-level bureau memorandum acknowledging the unlawful nature of such break-ins. The memorandum, dated July 19, 1966, was sent by Assistant FBI Director William C. Sullivan to Cartha D. DeLoach, a high-ranking aide to J. Edgar Hoover, then the bureau's director. It said:

"We do not obtain authorization for 'black bag' jobs outside the bureau. Such technique involves trespass and is clearly illegal; therefore, it would be impossible to obtain any legal sanction for it. Despite this, 'black bag' jobs have been used because they represent an invaluable technique in combatting subversive activities of a clandestine nature aimed directly at undermining and destroying our nation." (The break-ins were designated "black bag" jobs because of the small black bag often used to carry burglar's tools.)

Detailed memoranda giving approval for the burglaries were signed by Hoover or his long-time aide, the late Clyde Tolson, and placed in a safe in the office of the assistant director under a "Do Not File" procedure, the Sullivan memorandum said. At the same time, "in the field, the special agent in charge prepares an informal memorandum showing that he obtained bureau authority and this memorandum is filed in his safe until the next inspection by bureau inspectors, at which time it is destroyed."

Sen. Richard Schweiker (R, Pa.), a

member of the committee, said head-quarters memoranda signed by Hoover or Tolson were kept out of regular bureau files, which carried serial numbers and could not be destroyed without leaving a gap in the numbering.

The Sullivan memorandum ended with an order in Hoover's handwriting: "no more such techniques must be used. H."

SWP offices burglarized—Official FBI papers, released March 28, 1976, revealed that the FBI had burglarized the New York City offices of the Socialist Workers Party (SWP) at least 92 times between 1960 and 1966. The papers had been sought by the leftist party as evidence for its $27 million lawsuit against the FBI.

On most of the occasions, the FBI records showed, nothing had been taken from the SWP offices, but numerous papers had been photographed. The SWP papers photographed included cor-respondence, records of political contribu-tions, minutes of party meetings and notes on legal strategy of party members facing federal prosecution.

According to the March 29 New York Times, the FBI actions against the SWP were not included in the 238 break-ins pre-viously admitted by the FBI.

The Times quoted an unidentified FBI source as saying that agents who under-took the burglaries received substantial bonuses. The agents, if arrested, would have had to take personal responsibility for the burglary, without naming the bu-reau.

Peter Camejo, the SWP candidate for President, March 28 charged that New York City police had afforded the FBI agents protection while they carried out the burglaries. As evidence, he quoted from the released FBI records requests for authorizations for the burglaries say-ing: "Full security assured," and, "Se-curity set forth at the time of the original authorization remains the same."

FBI sources quoted in the March 29 Times story expressed doubt that the FBI would have informed the police in advance of burglaries.

Camejo took issue with FBI director Clarence M. Kelley's statement that the burglaries were undertaken for reasons of national security. He said the information obtained by the FBI had been used "to get SWP members fired from their jobs and to otherwise disrupt the legal political activities of the SWP."

The SWP March 29 named three other incidents that, it maintained, the New York police had not investigated thoroughly: bombings of SWP offices in 1973 and 1966, and the throwing of a live grenade at an office in 1969. According to the SWP, two persons were injured in the 1973 bombing.

FBI & IRS intelligence budgets. The re-constituted House Select Committee on Intelligence Aug. 7, 1975 obtained data on the intelligence expenditures of the FBI and Internal Revenue Service.

Eugene W. Walsh, assistant director of the FBI's administrative division, testified that the agency was spending $82.5 million a year on intelligence gathering and counterespionage. While he declined to offer a breakdown of how the bureau spent the money, he conceded that the funds had never been carefully audited by anyone outside the FBI.

Donald Alexander, director of the IRS, testified that his agency had spent $11.8 million in fiscal 1974 on intelligence gathering, mostly the pursuit of numerous tips about tax cheaters. He said he had found this operation to be generally ineffective and had scaled it down to $4.3 million a year.

GAO audit finds few FBI convictions. The Federal Bureau of Investigation's domestic intelligence operation produced few warnings of extremist or subversive activities and even fewer convictions, the General Accounting Office said in a report to Congress Sept. 24.

The GAO study, undertaken for the House Judiciary Subcommittee on Civil and Constitutional Rights, said that a survey of 676 FBI domestic intelligence investigations in 10 cities indicated that only 12 produced advance warning of ex-tremist or subversive activities. Of the 676 investigations, 16 were referred for prose-cution and four resulted in conviction.

FBI keeps list of security risks. The Federal Bureau of Investigation maintained a current list of U.S. residents it considered potential threats to national security, according to FBI documents released Oct. 22 by Rep. Robert W. Kastenmeier (D, Wis.), chairman of the Courts, Civil Liberties and Administration of Justice Subcommittee of the Judiciary Committee.

Among the documents made public was one from President Franklin Roosevelt to the late FBI director, J. Edgar Hoover, dated 1939, ordering the FBI to compile a "custodial detention" list of individuals with "Communistic, Fascist, Nazi and other nationalistic background" who were deemed national security risks.

Kastenmeier also released a memorandum from Clarence Kelley, current director of the FBI, stating that the detention list, renamed the "security index" in 1943, had been discontinued, as were "all plans for the apprehension of those listed," when Congress repealed the emergency detention provision of the Internal Security Act in 1971.

Kelley said that the FBI subsequently obtained Justice Department approval to establish a new list of suspected subversives. The new list was to be used by the bureau as an "administrative aid" in watching potential troublemakers during an emergency, "pending legal steps by the President to take further action." As of August, the new list contained the names of 1,294 persons, Kelley said.

The current index, Kelley said, "was reviewed continuously," with some names deleted and others added. Individuals were not included on the list solely because of their opposition to government policies or membership in allegedly subversive organizations, he said. To be placed on the list, Kelley explained, a person must have "exhibited a willingness or capacity of engaging in treason, rebellion, sedition, sabotage, espionage, assassination of government officials, terrorism, guerrilla warfare" or other acts threatening to disrupt operations of the government.

Kelley claimed that past indexes could not be reconstructed since no records had been kept of persons whose names had been entered or deleted. However, Kelley's latter statement was apparently superseded by a report in the New York Times Oct. 25 that the bureau had discovered "only within the last several days" an intact file containing most of the names of the 15,000 individuals once included on the defunct security index.

Senate committee says FBI offered political services. The staff of the Senate Select Committee on Intelligence issued a report Dec. 3, 1975 accusing the FBI of providing political services for Presidents from Roosevelt to Nixon.

According to the report, the FBI in 1940 ran "name checks" (checks of its files) and supplied reports on persons opposing the foreign policy of President Roosevelt. In 1949, an investigation by the FBI of the National Lawyers Guild was passed on to President Truman. And in 1956, when President Eisenhower asked for a report on racial tension from the FBI, the report contained information "not only of incidents of violence, but also on the activities of seven governors and congressmen in groups opposing integration, as well as the role of Communists in civil rights lobbying efforts and the N.A.A.C.P.'s [National Association for the Advancement of Colored People] plans to push legislation."

Under the Kennedy administration, the Senate committee report said, Attorney General Robert Kennedy authorized wiretaps on newsmen, as well as on government officials, two lobbyists, and a Congressional staff member.

President Johnson received information from the FBI on seven newsmen, on members of the staff of his 1964 presidential opponent, Barry Goldwater, and on persons opposing his foreign policy, according to the report.

President Nixon, according to the report, had the FBI carry out wiretaps of newsmen and White House officials.

The report left open in several cases the question of whether the activities described of the FBI had been motivated politically, or by a desire to preserve national security, or prevent violence.

Newspaper says FBI backed right-wing terrorists. A story in the Jan. 11, 1976

San Diego Union said that the FBI, had provided both weapons and explosives for, and had played a part in the formation of, a right-wing terrorist organization in California called the Secret Army Organization. Clarence M. Kelley, director of the bureau, acknowledged Jan. 11 that the FBI had maintained an informant within the group, but denied that it had supported any terrorist activities.

The San Diego Union story was based on testimony given before a California court in July 1972. A report prepared in June 1975 by the American Civil Liberties Union (ACLU) for the Senate Committee on Intelligence also purported to describe an illegitimate involvement of the FBI with the group.

The Secret Army Organization operated in San Diego in the early 1970s. Its activities were directed against anti-war protesters and dissidents, and allegedly involved burglaries of homes and offices, bombings, and kidnapping and assassination plots.

FBI support for the terrorist group was set forth in testimony given to a California court by Howard B. Godfrey, a former FBI informant. According to the Jan. 11 New York Times account of the testimony, Godfrey described his actions as follows: Under instructions from the FBI, he said, he helped found the group. He obtained between $10,000 and $20,000 worth of weapons and explosives from the bureau for use by the group. And on Jan. 6, 1972 he went along in the car from which a member of the group other than himself fired a pistol in an attempt to murder Peter Bohmer, a San Diego professor and radical.

According to sources on the Senate Intelligence committee Godfrey took possession of the pistol, and turned it over to the FBI agent to whom he reported, Steven Christiansen. The sources said that Christiansen concealed the gun for half a year while the San Diego police were looking for evidence on the affair.

The ACLU report quoted another FBI informant, John Rasperry, as saying that the FBI had told him to kill Bohmer, but he had not.

FBI rules on the use of informants, according to the New York Times Jan. 11

story, prohibited them from initiating a crime, but did permit them to lead and supply a violent group.

U.S. monitored cable traffic. The federal government, with the cooperation of three international telegraphic companies, secretly monitored overseas cable traffic for 28 years, according to a report released by the Senate Select Committee on Intelligence Nov. 6, 1975.

The committee made public its report on the secret monitoring program known as "Operation Shamrock" despite opposition from President Ford who said through a spokesman that committee disclosure of the classified operation might damage the U.S. intelligence effort. Moreover, the spokesman said, the President had avoided discussing the program publicly to avoid criticism of former officials "who acted in good faith during difficult times in the cold war period."

According to the committee's report, James Forrestal, secretary of defense in 1947, asked the three cable companies to voluntarily turn over to the government the message traffic of certain foreign intelligence targets. The companies—RCA Global Communications, ITT World Communications and Western Union International—were assured that if they cooperated they would suffer no adverse publicity nor face criminal liability as long as the Truman Administration was in office. Although the program apparently had the approval of Truman and his attorney general, Tom C. Clark, the report said, it continued after 1949 without the express consent of any President or attorney general. Operation Shamrock was terminated in May 1975 by Secretary of Defense James R. Schlesinger.

Until the early 1960s, the government received paper tapes of messages that went out over company cables and microfilm of messages transmitted by short wave. With the advent of computers, the companies began keeping copies of messages on magnetic tapes, which they turned over to the National Security Agency for analysis. The NSA in turn disseminated data to other agencies.

On the average, the report indicated, the NSA selected 150,000 messages a month for its analysts to review. Thousands were later distributed to other agencies.

Reform Plans

Pike panel offers reforms. In its final act before disbanding Feb. 11, the House Select Intelligence Committee Feb. 10, 1976 voted, 9–4, to submit a series of proposals for reforming the federal intelligence system.

The committee, chaired by Rep. Otis G. Pike (D, N.Y.), recommended, in addition to a permanent oversight committee, the following proposals:

■ That the General Accounting Office be authorized to make full audits of the intelligence agencies, without exemptions for classified matters.

■ That a foreign operations subcommittee be created within the National Security Council, the members of which would be required to make individual written reports to the President on the possible consequences of proposed covert operations.

■ That within 48 hours of presidential approval of any covert operation, a permanent House intelligence committee be given a detailed description of it by the director of central intelligence, as well as a written statement by the President that it was necessary to national security.

■ That assassinations and paramilitary operations be prohibited except in wartime.

■ That the 1947 National Security Act be amended to allow disclosure to Congressional committees of intelligence-related information, and that the intelligence committee or the House by vote could make public classified information.

■ That an inspector general for intelligence be created.

■ That the Defense Intelligence Agency be abolished, because it had failed in its task of coordinating military intelligence and often merely duplicated CIA efforts in an inferior way.

■ That the intelligence agencies be barred from employing U.S. citizens who worked for educational, religious or news organizations.

The committee report, still unreleased but extensively reported, was highly controversial. Apart from attacks by members of the administration, several committee members questioned its findings. Rep. Dale Milford (D, Tex.) said Feb. 3 that "over 50% of the charges and conclusions are not based on the committee record." Rep. Robert McClory (R, Ill.) the same day termed it "a diatribe against the CIA."

The committee staff director, A. Searle Field, however, said Feb. 3 that "almost every line is documented and footnoted."

Pike had charged on Feb. 2 that the administration was endeavoring to block release of the report because it made various officials, including Secretary of State Henry Kissinger, "look bad."

Intelligence structure revised. President Ford announced at a televised news conference Feb. 17 his plans for revision of the command structure of U.S. foreign intelligence operations and establishment of guidelines for such operations.

The President said he was acting because, "As Americans, we must not and will not tolerate actions by our government which will abridge the rights of our citizens. At the same time, we must maintain a strong effective intelligence capability . . . . I will not be a party to the dismantling of the CIA [Central Intelligence Agency] or other intelligence agencies."

"We must have a comprehensive intelligence capability," Ford emphasized.

The President proposed a three-part plan:

■ He was establishing by executive order a "new command structure for foreign intelligence." All policy direction would come from the National Security Council, consisting of the President, the Vice President and the secretaries of state and defense. Management of the policy would be conducted by a new committee that would be headed by the CIA director, George Bush.

A new independent oversight board

made up of private citizens would be established "to monitor the performance of our intelligence operations." The members of that board were former undersecretary of state Robert D. Murphy, 81, chairman; Washington lawyer Stephen Ailes, 63, a former secretary of the Army and currently president of the Association of American Railroads; and New York economist Leo Cherne, 63, a member of the existing President's Foreign Intelligence Board since 1973.

■ "A comprehensive set of public guidelines" was being issued "to improve the performance of the intelligence agencies and to restore public confidence in them." These were to "serve as legally binding charters for our intelligence activities." The charters were to "provide stringent protections for the rights of American citizens."

Ford said he would meet with Congressional leaders "to map out legislation to provide judicial safeguards against electronic surveillance and mail openings" and he would also "support legislation that would prohibit attempts on the lives of foreign leaders in peacetime."

■ "Special legislation to safeguard critical intelligence secrets" would be proposed to Congress. The legislation "would make it a crime for a government employe who has access to certain highly classified information to reveal that information improperly."

An executive order covering operation of the government's foreign intelligence activities was issued by the President Feb. 18, to be effective March 1. It proscribed, in general, spying on Americans or testing drugs on them, infiltrating domestic groups or intercepting mail for any other reason than counterespionage or security checks on government employes.

On covert operations abroad, the order stipulated that no federal employe "shall engage in, or conspire to engage in, political assassination."

Language in the other provisions also would permit the CIA: (a) to infiltrate within the U.S. organizations "composed primarily of non-United States persons . . . reasonably believed to be acting on behalf of a foreign power"; (b) to collect information within the U.S. on "corporations or other commercial organizations which constitutes foreign intelligence or counterintelligence"; (c) to gather domestic intelligence against U.S. citizens, corporations or resident aliens who were "reasonably believed to be acting on behalf of a foreign power or engaging in international terrorist or narcotics activities"; (d) to enter into arrangements with academic institutions for research and other services.

FBI gets test guidelines. The justice department March 10 issued provisional guidelines for the conduct of intelligence activities by the Federal Bureau of Investigation (FBI). Revelations before Congressional committees of FBI activities in its counter intelligence program (called Cointelpro and directed against domestic radical and antiwar groups from the mid 1950s to the early 1970s) had prompted the demand for guidelines.

Activities prohibited to FBI men under the guidelines included inciting to riot, illegal entry and the anonymous circulation of information intended to hold "an individual up to scorn, ridicule or disgrace."

FBI agents would be allowed, in certain circumstances, with authorization from FBI headquarters, to infiltrate groups, use electronic surveillance, and check (without opening) suspects' mail.

Under the guidelines, groups involved—or those which "will" become involved—in violence or illegality intended to overthrow the government or interfere with foreign governments or their representatives could be investigated. Also, investigations could be undertaken of groups which were "substantially impairing—for the purpose of influencing the United States Government policies or decisions"—federal or state governments or interstate commerce.

A provision in draft versions of the guidelines which would have allowed the FBI to take "preventive action" to forestall imminent violence was dropped from the guidelines because of Congressional opposition. Congressmen had voiced concern that the provision would open the way to a renewal of Cointelpro abuses.

Attorney General Edward H. Levi said March 10 that the dropped provision was "never intended" nor would it have had the effect of "an affirmation or legitimization of Cointelpro." It had been dropped in response to the opposition expressed concerning it, Levi said.

The guidelines also provided that requests for investigations from the White House would have to be made in writing, and state precisely what was to be investigated. In addition, there would have to be a statement "signed by the subject of the investigation acknowledging that he has consented to the investigation."

Some Congressmen objected that the guidelines would still allow the FBI too much leeway in choosing groups to investigate.

Some Cointelpro targets to be notified. Attorney General Edward H. Levi announced April 1 that he had formed a panel within the Justice Department to review FBI actions under its Cointelpro program and, in some cases, to notify individuals who had been Cointelpro targets.

Notification, Levi said, would be restricted to those individuals who had actually suffered injury as a result of improper FBI actions, and who were not already aware that they had been targets.

The attorney general March 30, in a letter to the attorney of columnist Joseph Kraft said that the FBI files on Kraft would be destroyed. The files contained the results of electronic and physical surveillance of Kraft in 1969. According to court and Congressional records, the FBI surveillance had been carried out at the request of then White House counsel John D. Ehrlichman, who sought to determine the source of leaks from the National Security Council.

Criminal data curbs urged. The National Advisory Commission on Criminal Justice Standards & Goals Nov. 5, 1973 had released a report that called on states to enact laws controlling dissemination of

data contained in computerized criminal information systems.

Citing the "substantial growth" in number and size of automated criminal file systems, the commission asserted there was a need to protect these files from invasion or injury. It recommended passage of state laws setting minimum standards for security and privacy.

"Dissemination of personal criminal justice information should be on a need and right to know basis within the government. There should be neither direct nor indirect dissemination of such information to non-governmental agencies or personnel," the commission said. However, the commission added, each person should have the right to review files relating to him, the only exception being investigative files.

In a related development, The Small Business Administration (SBA) and the Defense Investigative Service said Sept. 25 they were withdrawing their federal court suit to gain blanket access to computerized criminal files in Massachusetts.

The Massachusetts Criminal History Systems Board had denied both agencies access to its files, contending that neither met state requirements that the files be opened only to criminal justice agencies and agencies with statutory authority to use the files to conduct investigations.

Massachusetts Gov. Francis W. Sargent and four members of Congress had petitioned Attorney General Elliot Richardson Aug. 3 to suspend operation of the computerized criminal information system of the Federal Bureau of Investigation (FBI). The group charged that the FBI's criminal data program permitted dissemination of outdated and inaccurate criminal records, failed to prevent unauthorized access to the files, and did not allow individuals the right to review and correct errors in their files. (FBI Director Clarence M. Kelley said Nov. 20 he would welcome legislation placing strict controls over computerized criminal information systems to protect individual rights.)

In 1974 the Justice Department proposed new regulations to limit access to criminal information compiled by the FBI and state and local police agencies.

The regulations, published in the Federal Register Feb. 14, were intended as an interim measure until Congress could pass legislation restricting the use of criminal records. The Justice Department had offered a bill Feb. 2, and Sen. Sam J. Ervin Jr. (D, N.C.), chairman of the Judiciary Committee's Subcommittee on Constitutional Rights and a co-sponsor of the Justice Department measure, offered his own, somewhat stricter measure.

The Justice Department regulations, which would apply to federal law enforcement agencies as well as state or local police agencies receiving funds from the Law Enforcement Assistance Administration, were aimed at preventing government agencies and private groups from obtaining criminal information from police data banks for other than criminal justice purposes. State and local agencies would also have to seal arrest records of individuals not found guilty or whose cases were not disposed of in five years. Sealed records would be available only to law enforcement agencies for criminal justice purposes, to persons compiling statistics or to the individuals involved.

While the regulations contained no provisions for sealing FBI records, they restricted their dissemination to federal agencies authorized by statute or executive order to receive them.

The legislation offered by the Justice Department would go further in protecting individual rights than the interim regulations of Feb. 14. Under the proposed bill, an individual could review and correct information in his record, and bring lawsuits against persons who improperly disclosed his records.

Another provision would require sealing of arrest records seven years after release in felony cases and five years in misdemeanor cases, although seals could be broken after subsequent arrests for other crimes. Another section would bar police agencies from giving incomplete records to noncriminal justice agencies, and forbid disclosure of information for purposes of employment or credit unless specifically authorized by statute or executive order.

U.S. to keep track of habitual felons. President Ford told the convention of the International Association of Chiefs of Police in Washington Sept. 24, 1974 that the Justice Department had started a new program to keep track of habitual criminals.

Advocating "swift and prolonged punishment," Ford said the professional criminal had to be taken out "of circulation." Only by making crime "hazardous and costly" would others then be deterred from following careers of crime, he said.

In pursuit of this goal, Ford said, he had instructed the Justice Department to undertake in cooperation with state and local governments, a career criminal impact program to target and keep track of repeat offenders. He said the effort would be similar to the program in Washington, which kept track of major repeaters, insuring "that these cases receive the most urgent attention of the prosecutors."

Use of Tax Data

Access to tax returns curbed. President Ford Sept. 20, 1974 signed an executive order restricting White House access to income-tax returns. The President's decision was related to abuses charged to the Nixon Administration. "I think he's seen what happened in the past," Deputy Press Secretary John W. Hushen told reporters of the President's action, "and he wants to make sure it doesn't happen in the future, at least while he is in the White House."

The order specified that only the President could direct disclosure of any tax return to a member of the White House staff. To do so, the President personally would request in writing the desired returns and personally designate in writing the person authorized to see the return on the President's behalf.

The order was a companion piece to the Treasury Department's legislative proposal before Congress to curb access to tax returns by other federal agencies.

(The Treasury Department's legislative proposal, submitted Sept. 11, would limit access to income tax returns by government units other than the White House, but the Internal Revenue Service would be required to furnish "any return or return information" to the President if requested and White House employes could obtain access to such material with a signed personal request from the President.)

Another bill on the subject was being co-sponsored by Sen. Lowell P. Weicker (R, Conn.) and Rep. Jerry Litton (D, Mo.). They issued a joint statement Sept. 20 calling Ford's action "a first step" but asserting that "presidential accessibility to the confidential tax return of American citizens is better preserved by statute." An executive order, they said, could be "changed, revoked or disregarded."

IRS Commissioner Donald C. Alexander told a Senate Appropriations panel April 16, 1975 that in fiscal 1974 the IRS had made available to a dozen other federal agencies the tax returns of 8,210 individuals. The bulk of the returns, Alexander and other IRS officials testified, was given to the Justice Department and the Federal Bureau of Investigation.

The IRS officials said the agency had not usually checked on the legitimacy of requests by federal agencies. However, they stated that the IRS no longer provided tax returns of prospective Presidential appointees to the White House and instead was informing the President as to whether the individuals had outstanding tax obligations or were under IRS investigation. The officials conceded that present system for distribution of tax returns could result in abuses.

Five former commissioners of the Internal Revenue Service told a Senate Finance subcommittee April 28 that they favored some sort of Congressional action to limit disclosure of tax information to other federal agencies. In their testimony before the Subcommittee on the Administration of the Internal Revenue Code, four of the former officials warned against going too far, however, stating that an overly strict disclosure law would hamper prosecutions not involving tax laws.

Harold R. Tyler, deputy attorney general, who testified before the subcommittee April 21, also had cautioned against unduly restricting Justice Department attorneys in their prosecution of non-tax cases. Other Justice Department officials had expressed similar concerns, saying that narrowed access to tax information might have a disastrous impact on investigations and prosecutions involving white collar crime and corrupt politicians.

Misuse of IRS Charged

Suit alleges IRS political harassment. The New York Civil Liberties Union (NYCLU) filed a class-action civil rights suit in Washington March 25, 1975. It charged that the IRS had subjected over 11,000 people and organizations to special tax investigations "due to their political beliefs and activities." The suit was brought by Walter Teague 3rd, an antiwar activist, and the Indochina Solidarity Committee, an antiwar group.

An NYCLU spokesman indicated the suit was the first court test of the legality of the Special Service Staff (SSS), an IRS intelligence unit created in 1969 to gather tax data on political dissidents. The SSS was abolished in 1973 by Donald C. Alexander shortly after he became IRS commissioner.

Former Sen. Sam J. Ervin Jr. (D, N.C.) said in December 1974 in the introduction to a staff report of the Judiciary Constitutional Rights Subcommittee that the operations of the SSS represented "a dangerous abuse of the enormous powers Americans have given to the tax collection arm of government." Ervin found the SSS involved in political surveillance "unauthorized by law, unnecessary to the administration of tax laws, and in the very least, a waste of the taxpayers' money." "The purpose of the IRS is to enforce the tax laws, not . . . political orthodoxy," he said.

The Congressional Joint Committee on Internal Revenue Taxation published a report June 6 which said that five present or former members of Congress had been among the 11,458 individuals and organizations in the SSS' files.

In related IRS developments, the House Government Operations subcommittee investigating IRS activities disclosed June 20 the existence of a master list containing the names of persons and organizations under scrutiny by the tax service. The list included the mayor of Los

Angeles, a member of Congress, a former attorney general, a former ambassador to Great Britain, the American Legion and the American Civil Liberties Union. In testimony before the subcommittee that day, Commissioner Alexander reportedly took the view that the IRS had done nothing illegal but had merely broken its own internal rules. Chairman Benjamin S. Rosenthal (D, N.Y.) remarked: "I don't think you are sensitive to the problem we perceive of the invasion of civil rights and civil liberties in the U.S." Rep. Drinan added: "I see no feeling on the part of your people that you are embarrassed and horrified and going to put a stop to it." (Alexander had declared in a June 20 speech to the tax committee of the New York State Bar Association that "public confidence" in the IRS would be "seriously damaged" if it "becomes entangled in information gathering, confidential informants and fishing expeditions relating to persons who are merely suspected of committing nontax-related crimes.")

IRS undercover work. In testimony before a House Government Operations subcommittee July 8, 1975, IRS Commissioner Alexander said that an undercover IRS agent had been paid $54,961 over a year-and-a-half period during which he eavesdropped on conversations in bars in Miami and Fort Lauderdale, Florida and gathered allegations against 913 persons, none of which were substantiated.

The project, in which the agent attempted to draw out persons frequenting the bars and obtain from them evidence of financial irregularities, was known as Operation Sunshine. Also discussed before the subcommittee but not elaborated on in news accounts were two similar IRS activities in the Miami area, Operation W and Operation Rosebud. After testifying that he had learned of Operations W and Rosebud only the previous day, Commissioner Alexander remarked: "We don't need money, in my judgment, for such things as Operation Sunshine, Operation W and Operation Leprechaun."

A 28-page IRS report on Operation Leprechaun had been made public June 23 by the Congressional Joint Committee on Internal Revenue Taxation. According to the report, the project had involved a single IRS agent, John T. Harrison, who had obtained information on the sexual and drinking activities of 70 persons in the Miami area that "was of little or no value" in most cases. The New York Times June 25 said Operation Leprechaun, described in the IRS report as an isolated case, had been begun in 1972 and was ended in the current year only after newspaper reports appeared. The Times said Commissioner Alexander, named to his post in 1973, had denied knowledge of the project until the news accounts made it public.

The Times added that members of the House Government Operations subcommittee, who received the report June 24, criticized it for covering up more than it revealed. When asked for depositions and other materials relevant to the investigation, Commissioner Alexander said they were "tax-related" and that the service was forbidden by law to make them available to the subcommittee. Rep. Andrew Maguire (D, N.J.) charged that Alexander was using the term "tax-related" in the same way former President Richard M. Nixon "used 'national security'—to cover up anything he wanted covered up."

An item in the IRS report about which members of the subcommittee were especially curious was the theft of a filing cabinet belonging to a Republican candidate for Congress from the Miami area, but Alexander and his counsel said they were still investigating whether the theft, committed in November 1972, had been carried out as part of Operation Leprechaun. (The Washington Post June 25 said the cabinet was in IRS possession. The paper cited a Miami Herald report in March that said Nelson Vega, a Miami resident, had sworn to local police that he and Roberto Novoa, both IRS informants working for Harrison, had taken the cabinet.)

The IRS was also involved in a controversy over its alleged use of a female informant to gather information of the sex lives and drinking habits of prominent

Miami residents. The woman, Elsa Suarez, told reporters March 14 she was recruited in 1972 "to get dirt" on 30 Miami-area public officials, including three federal judges and Richard Gerstein, state attorney for Dade County. She claimed to have been offered $20,000 a year for life and a home abroad if she came up with information that would "get" Gerstein. "I never did sleep with anybody or get any good dirt during the three months I was on the job," she said. Her activities were part of Operation Leprechaun, she said.

Operation Leprechaun defended—E. J. Vitkus, assistant regional commissioner for the southeast IRS division, told a House Ways and Means subcommittee Dec. 2 that he considered expenditures for Operation Leprechaun, which gathered "sex and booze" information on 30 prominent Floridians, "money well spent."

Denying Leprechaun was inappropriate or improper, Vitkus said the operation was not unusual although it was larger than most. He said this was because it was in an area with numerous allegations of corruption and organized crime influence.

Halt in tax probes defended. IRS Commissioner Alexander Sept. 30, 1975 defended his decision in August to suspend largescale undercover investigations of trust accounts established in the Bahamas and on some Caribbean islands by U.S. citizens to avoid paying taxes.

Alexander said that as a result of his decision, some "former and a few present IRS employes," had begun a concerted effort to discredit him because they disagreed with his policies. These individuals, Alexander said, "have reacted by criticizing me personally, attempting to block efforts to uncover and eliminate inappropriate activities by IRS employes and informers, and by circulating scurrilous rumors about my personal character."

Published allegations in the weeks following the suspension of the investigations said that Alexander had halted an intelligence-gathering operation to protect businessmen, that he once arranged to meet a convicted swindler in connection

with a tax problem and that, as a lawyer before entering government service, he gave a client improper advice.

Much of the criticism directed at Alexander concerned his decision to curtail dissemination of information from two previously top-secret operations intended to identify U.S. citizens trying to evade income taxes by means of illegal overseas tax shelters. The first of the operations designed to penetrate the secrecy of these foreign trusts was begun in 1965. Dubbed "Operation Tradewinds," the operation was put together by an IRS agent who assembled network of confidential informants in the Bahamas to obtain information about secret U.S. investments, particularly those by organized crime.

In 1973, an informant in Miami obtained a list of 300 Americans with secret trust investments in the Castle Bank and Trust Co. Ltd. of the Bahamas. With the help of a woman who diverted the attention of a Castle official whose briefcase contained the list, the informant had photographed 450-pages of Castle Bank records.

The list became the basis for "Operation Haven," a nationwide investigation based in New York. According to IRS officials, Operation Haven resulted in recommendations for prosecutions in five criminal cases, in seven criminal cases still under investigation and in the processing of 63 civil cases with recommended taxes and penalties of $33 million.

However, when the IRS's investigative methods came under criticism earlier in 1975, Alexander ordered a halt to payments to informers, and Operation Tradewinds stopped. When the incident involving the photographing of the briefcase's contents came under investigation in August, Alexander halted dissemination of information already obtained through Operation Haven.

Senate Reports Score Abuses, Urge Reforms

Senate panel criticizes domestic spying. The Senate Select Committee on Intelligence reported April 28, 1976 that the FBI and other U.S. agencies had conducted investigations—often employing "illegal or improper" methods—of a vast number of Americans.

The committee urged that the activities of the intelligence agencies be governed by statutory rules, and offered 96 recommendations as a basis for legislation. The proposals—all dealing with domestic intelligence—were contained in the second volume of the committee's final report.

The domestic investigations, the report maintained, were sometimes justified on a "guilty until proven innocent" basis. It said that this resulted in the recording of intimate details of the lives of persons engaged merely in "legal and peaceful political activites."

The main proposals made by the committee were:

■ That domestic intelligence investigations be limited to cases in which there were specific grounds to believe that terrorist or hostile espionage activities had been committed or were about to be committed. Political views or activities, the committee stressed, would not be grounds for an investigation. Continuation of a preliminary investigation beyond 30 days, or of a full investigation beyond a year would require approval by the Attorney General or his designee.

■ That domestic intelligence investigations be conducted (with a few narrow exceptions) only by the FBI.

■ That judicial warrants be required for use of electronic surveillance, mail-opening or unauthorized entry.

The committee also called for closer supervision and review of the FBI by the attorney general, vigorous oversight of the FBI and other agencies by a permanent Senate Intelligence Committee, and an eight-year maximum term for the head of the FBI.

The report maintained that abuses by the intelligence agencies stemmed from the failure of the "constitutional system of checks and balances." The executive branch, Congress and the courts all shared blame for abdicating their responsibilities, the report said.

The report's documentation of domestic intelligence activities covered the following areas:

Size of U.S. intelligence operations—The report said that FBI headquarters alone had opened more than 500,000 domestic intelligence files, and that additional files had been developed at FBI field offices. In one year—1972—the FBI had opened 65,000 files, the report said, noting that these files usually contained information on more than one individual or group.

Nearly a quarter of a million letters were opened in the U.S. by the Central Intelligence Agency between 1953 and 1973, the report said. From their contents, the CIA compiled an index of nearly 1.5 million names.

Under a secret agreement with three U.S. telegraph companies, the panel found, the National Security Agency obtained millions of telegrams sent to, from or through the U.S. And, it said, the Army developed files on an estimated 100,000 citizens between the mid 1960s and 1971.

The IRS, between 1969 and 1973, created intelligence files on more than 11,000 individuals or groups and initiated tax investigations for political reasons, the report said. It also noted that an FBI list of persons to be interned in the event of a "national emergency" at one time numbered at least 26,000 persons.

Targets of the investigations—The report said that investigations had been conducted not only against individuals and political groups on the right and left but also against religious groups, establishment politicians, advocates of nonviolence and racial harmony and supporters of women's rights.

Specific targets named in the report included Dr. Martin Luther King Jr., the National Association for the Advancement of Colored People, the Socialist Workers Party, the John Birch Society, the Conservative American Christian Action Council, the late Adlai E. Stevenson, who was twice a Democratic nominee for president, and former Supreme Court Justice William O. Douglas. In 1970, the FBI had ordered investigations of every member of the Students for a Democratic Society, and of all black student groups "regardless of their past or present involvement in disorders," the report said.

Investigations had been continued for decades, the report found, even when no criminal acts were uncovered. Thus, the report noted, an investigation of the NAACP for possible connections with the Communist Party lasted for 25 years, even though an initial report determined that the organization had a "strong tendency" to avoid alignment with communist activities.

The report argued that the "guilty until proven innocent" theory had held sway in the case of an FBI investigation of an adviser to the Rev. Dr. King. In support of this contention, it quoted an FBI headquarters memo:

"The bureau does not agree with the expressed belief of the field office that _____ is not sympathetic to the [Communist] party cause. While there may not be any evidence that _____ is a Communist, neither is there any substantial evidence that _____ is anti-Communist."

Covert activity—The report detailed a number of activities—chiefly engaged in by the FBI under Cointelpro [the agency's counterintelligence program]—aimed at disrupting, discrediting or neutralizing groups and individuals. Some tactics employed by the FBI, the report said, were "indisputably degrading to a free society."

Among the FBI tactics noted in the report were:

■ Anonymously attacking a target's political views in an attempt to have his employer fire him.

■ Attempting to destroy marriages by mailing anonymous letters to the spouses of targets.

■ Falsely and anonymously naming as government informers members of groups known to be violent. Expulsion from the group or physical harm for the person so labeled could result from the action, the report observed.

■ Sending an anonymous letter to the captain of a Chicago street gang, intended to "intensify . . . animosity" between the gang and the Black Panther Party, and possibly provoke "retaliatory action."

The report stated that the FBI and the CIA, in collecting information, had often adopted "illegal and improper means." Both the FBI and the CIA had conducted warrantless break-ins the report said. In the 1960s, it said, hundreds of break-ins had been conducted, some to install microphones, others to steal documents.

The report noted also that government informants attached to violent groups sometimes themselves had to engage in violence. To illustrate this, the report cited the case of an FBI informer, placed in the Ku Klux Klan, who had participated in assaults on blacks.

Media & political uses of intelligence—Information gathered from intelligence investigations was used by the FBI in attempts to discredit target groups or individuals, the report said. FBI field offices, the report noted, were specifically asked to collect data on the "scurrilous and depraved nature of many of the characters, activities, habits and living conditions representative of New Left adherents" for prompt relay to the news media.

The report observed that the FBI also, through a relationship with the chairman of the board of a national magazine, had sought to influence articles relating to the FBI published in that magazine. One article, the report said, was "squelched," another was "postponed" and in the case of a third, publication was "forestalled."

Besides using the media to discredit particular targets, the report faulted the FBI for distorting data in its public statements in ways calculated to influence or justify government policy. The report cited two cases of this, both involving overstatement of communist influence. One case involved former director J. Edgar Hoover's congressional testimony on forces behind the civil rights movement; the other concerned the bureau's reports on Vietnam war demonstrators.

Responsibility for abuses—The report charged that senior officials in the executive branch, and particularly the attorney general, had "virtually abdicated their constitutional responsibility to oversee and set standards for intelligence activity." Congress also had often failed to exercise adequate oversight, the report said.

The report noted that oversight had

failed in some instances, however, because the intelligence agencies had concealed, or only partially disclosed, the activities in which they were engaged.

It charged that pressure exerted on the intelligence agencies by executive officials for results on specific problems was itself responsible for excesses and improprieties. The report quoted testimony given to the committee by senior intelligence officials, to the effect that the intelligence agencies had been concerned only with the "flap potential" that exposure of their activities might have. The illegality or unconstitutionality of the activities had never been suggested as a reason for not doing them, according to the testimony.

Cost—Besides the number of persons affected, another yardstick of the excesses of the domestic intelligence programs was their dollar cost, the report said. It observed that the FBI had budgeted $7 million in fiscal 1976 for domestic security informants, more than twice the amount allocated to informants on organized crime. For the same period, the FBI total budget for domestic security and counterintelligence programs totalled at least $80 million, the report said.

The FBI domestic security programs were also extremely wasteful, the report argued, when measured by their court successes. The FBI, the report said, launched over half a million investigations between 1960 and 1974 of persons or groups deemed "subversive." The investigations, the report said, were primarily justified on the basis of federal laws outlawing planning or advocating action to overthrow the government. Yet, the report noted, not a single prosecution had been brought under those laws since 1957.

The report also cited a General Accounting Office study of 17,528 FBI domestic intelligence investigations in 1974. Only 1.3% of the investigations, the report said, resulted in convictions.

The basic lesson to be drawn from the report, the committee held, was that the FBI should restrict its actions "to investigating conduct rather than ideas or associations." By doing so, the agency could avoid the "wasteful dispersion of resources" that had plagued its past investi-

tigation, the report said. More importantly, such a change in policy was necessary to safeguard "the constitutional rights of Americans," the report argued.

Senate staff reports detail FBI misdeeds. The staff of the Senate Select Intelligence Committee, in a number of follow-up studies to the committee's official report, added more particulars to the documentation of FBI abuses and excesses in the field of domestic intelligence.

Studies were issued on:

Persecution of Dr. King—The report on the FBI campaign against Dr. Martin Luther King, released May 5, charged that the FBI effort had been "marked by extreme personal vindictiveness," particularly by J. Edgar Hoover, then FBI director.

Hoover, the report noted, had as early as February 1962 jotted the remark, "King is no good," on a memo that had come to him. By May 1962, the FBI had included King on a list of persons to be interned in the event of a national emergency.

The FBI did not begin its investigation of alleged communist influence on King or his church organization, the Southern Christian Leadership Conference, until October 1962.

The report did not say whether former Attorney General Robert F. Kennedy had known of the FBI's persistent bugging of King's hotel rooms. No evidence had been found, the report said, to show that Kennedy had been "expressly informed." However, the report noted that a Dec. 15, 1966 FBI memo had stated that Kennedy in 1964 had received an 8-page account of King's activities based on wiretap material. The 1966 memo said that the report to Kennedy had been "couched in such a manner that it is obvious that a microphone was the source."

The FBI continued its anti-King posture even after the civil rights leader was assassinated, the report said. In April 1969, the agency's Atlanta bureau formulated a plan for "counterintelligence action" against King's widow, Coretta Scott King. However, the report said, Hoover decided against implementing the plan at that time.

Harassment of the Black Panther Party— A staff study, issued May 6, added detail to reports that the FBI had attempted to destroy the Panthers by bringing them into conflict with other violence-prone groups. In San Diego in 1969, the report said, this policy had taken the form of circulating derogatory cartoons of party members. Although the cartoons had been originated by the FBI, they purported to be the work of an organization called United Slaves, the report noted. (In January 1969, two Panthers had been killed in a fight with United Slave members.) The report said that the local FBI office claimed, in a memo dated Sept. 19, 1969, that "shootings, beatings, and a high degree of unrest continues [sic] to prevail in the ghetto area of southeast San Diego." The memo was quoted further:

"Although no specific counterintelligence action can be credited with contributing to this overall situation, it is felt that a substantial amount of the unrest is directly attributable to this program."

In Chicago, the report said, the FBI and the city police both had maintained paid informants in the Panther party and had pooled the information gained. The report quoted an FBI memo which said that this collaboration had been "crucial to police" in conducting a raid on Panther member Fred Hampton's apartment. Hampton was killed during the raid.

The report also detailed FBI attempts to exacerbate, by sending forged letters, a split that had developed between two Panther factions, one led by Huey P. Newton, the other by Eldridge Cleaver.

Electronic surveillance— The staff report on FBI bugging, issued May 9, asserted that members of Congress had been recorded on wiretaps that were used to provide information for Presidents Lyndon B. Johnson and Richard M. Nixon. The congressmen had not themselves been targets of the wiretaps, the report said, but they had come under surveillance when they met with foreign-government representatives who were targets.

The report also listed several instances of FBI wiretaps that possibly were politically motivated. Among them:

■ A Roosevelt-Administration wiretap on the Los Angeles Chamber of Commerce.

■ A Truman-era wiretap on a former White House aide. The report did not name the aide, but the May 10 Washington Post said "reliable sources" had identified him as Washington lawyer Thomas G. Corcoran.

■ Kennedy-Administration wiretaps that had been justified as pertaining to the investigation of a sugar lobby. The taps were removed after the Administration had won passage of a bill it had sought.

Electronic Surveillance

Kelley urges wider FBI authority. FBI Director Clarence M. Kelley said Sep. 21, 1974 that the FBI needed broader wiretapping authority to watch revolutionary bombers. With such increased freedom to wiretap, Kelley said, the FBI could effectively watch the groups that he said were responsible for many of the 2,000 bombings annually in the U.S.

Noting that civil libertarians might object to legislation widening FBI electronic surveillance powers, Kelley said the bombers presented a more serious threat to U.S. society than a new wiretapping law. "We are responsible people and are not going to cause people to needlessly lose their rights," he said.

Presidential power unchanged. The Supreme Court Oct. 15, 1974, by refusing to review, upheld Presidential wiretapping authority.

The court declined to hear a challenge to the President's right to authorize warrantless wiretaps to gather foreign intelligence. The court's refusal to hear the case, which involved the 1964 espionage conviction of Soviet national Igor A. Ivanov, did not signify its approval or disapproval of wiretapping, but had the effect of permitting federal agents to continue the practice. In upholding Ivanov's conviction, the Court of Appeals for the 3rd Circuit had ruled that the evidence obtained from the wiretap was admissible in court if the surveillance had been found to be reasonably related to the exercise of presidential power in the area of foreign affairs.

Three of court's justices, one short of the required number, voted to take jurisdiction. They were William O. Douglas, William J. Brennan Jr. and Potter Stewart. Justice Thurgood Marshall, who served as soliciter general for two years during which the case was pending, did not participate.

Wiretap ban upheld—The Supreme Court April 19, 1976 upheld, by declining to review, a decision on government wiretaps that raised several issues.

The action came on a suit brought by the Jewish Defense League (JDL) against former Attorney General John N. Mitchell and nine past or present employes of the Federal Bureau of Investigation for wiretaps on the JDL office in New York City in 1970 and 1971.

The U.S. Court of Appeals for the District of Columbia had ruled that the wiretaps were illegal because they had been installed without a court warrant. The appellate court had stated that warrantless wiretaps were legal only when directed against agents of foreign governments.

However, in its decision, the appellate court also had suggested that officials might escape paying damages for the illegal wiretaps. In its instructions to the U.S. District Court (where the case was remanded for final disposition of the damages question), the appellate court said that damages should be denied if the defendants had shown "a subjective good faith belief that it was constitutional to install warrantless wiretaps under the circumstances of this case, and that this belief was itself reasonable."

All the parties to the suit had sought Supreme Court review.

Baker scandal figure wins award. U.S. District Court Judge Charles R. Richey Jan. 10, 1975 ordered the Justice Department to pay damages of $903,232 to Fred B. Black Jr., whose 1964 conviction for income tax evasion was overturned by the Supreme Court in 1966 because the FBI illegally monitored his Washington hotel suite for more than three months in 1963. Black was retried in 1968 and acquitted.

Justice Department lawyers said it was the first time the government had been ordered to pay damages because of illegal surveillance.

Black, a former Washington lobbyist and business associate of Robert G. Baker, the former Senate Democratic secretary, claimed that dissemination of information gleaned from the microphone placed in the wall of his hotel room caused a loss of earnings of $843,232. Black was awarded $60,000 for loss of reputation.

Warrantless wiretapping curbed. The U.S. Circuit Court of Appeals for the District of Columbia ruled June 23, 1975 that the Executive Branch needed court approval before it could wiretap domestic organizations, even if the surveillance were for reasons of national security.

The decision involved a warrantless wiretap placed for 208 days in 1970 and 1971 on the New York City headquarters of the Jewish Defense League, a militant Zionist group whose anti-Soviet activities in the U.S. were creating diplomatic tension between the U.S. and U.S.S.R.

In arguing that the tap had been legal, the federal government had defended the surveillance on the grounds that it "was authorized by the President..., acting through the attorney general in the exercise of his authority relating to foreign affairs, and was deemed essential to protect this nation...against hostile acts of a foreign power and to obtain foreign intelligence information deemed essential to the security of the United States."

The appellate court rejected that reasoning, however, holding that then-Attorney General John N. Mitchell should have obtained court approval of the tap since it was being installed on a domestic organization that was neither an agent of nor acting in collaboration with a foreign government.

While the court did not address the issue of wiretaps on agents of foreign governments, it did state: "Indeed, our analysis would suggest that, absent exigent circumstances, no wiretapping in the area of foreign affairs should be exempt from prior judicial scrutiny, irrespective of the justification for the surveillance or the importance of the information sought."

Wiretaps decline. The number of wiretaps officially sanctioned by state and federal courts in 1974 was down 16% from the year before, the Administrative Office of the U.S. Courts said in its annual wiretapping and electronic surveillance report to Congress May 2, 1975. In the 24 jurisdictions in which officially permitted state and federal wiretaps were legal, 728 taps were authorized and 694 "bugs" installed, enabling agents to listen to more than 40,000 persons engaged in 590,000 conversations, the office reported.

Federal court-ordered wiretaps numbered 121 in 1974, down from 130 in 1973. State courts issued 607 wiretap orders, 127 fewer than the previous year. The report also indicated that no federal judge turned down a Justice Department request for a tap. On the state level, only two applications were denied, both in Connecticut.

The cost of federal wiretaps, which had been as high as $2.2 million in 1971, fell to $1.3 million in 1974. Expenditures on the state level were $4.2 million. Average state and federal costs rose to $8,087 per installation, up from $5,632 in 1973.

However, warrantless wiretapping by the federal government for purposes of national security rose sharply between 1972 and 1974, according to Justice Department statistics made public June 24. The figures, contained in a letter from Attorney General Edward H. Levi to Sen. Edward M. Kennedy (D, Mass.), showed that such wiretaps had averaged 108 for each year between 1969-1972 and then increased to an average of 156 a year during 1973-1974. In addition, Levi's letter said that microphone surveillances, installed without judicial warrant to intercept room conversations, had averaged 20 a year during 1969-1972, but jumped to an average of 41 a year in 1973 and 1974.

Levi in his letter, which Kennedy released without comment, defended national security wiretaps conducted without prior judicial approval. "Based on an examination of the relevant precedents," Levi said, "it is the position of the Justice Department that the executive may conduct electronic surveillance in the interests of national security and foreign intelligence and in the aid of his conduct of the nation's foreign affairs, without obtaining a judicial warrant."

(During Senate hearings on his nomination as attorney general, Levi Jan. 27 had upheld government wiretapping and surveillance in specific areas although he said protection was needed "against undue use.")

In a related development, the National Wiretap Commission released data June 23 showing that fewer than 2% of the violations of federal wiretapping laws uncovered by telephone company employes resulted in the arrest or federal prosecution of those responsible for the taps. The statistics, compiled for the commission by the Federal Bureau of Investigation and the various operating companies of American Telephone & Telegraph Corp., indicated that 1,457 wiretaps had been discovered on or near company instruments during the 7½-year period ended June 30, 1974. Federal arrests or prosecution followed in 27 of those cases, the commission said.

Illegal wiretaps revealed. The New York state police regularly conducted illegal wiretapping and bugging operations during Nelson Rockefeller's tenure as governor, Newsday reported Jan. 4, 1976.

Newsday also reported that current and former members of the state police had acknowledged that financial records of a police informants fund had been falsified to conceal purchases of tapping and bugging equipment that was not authorized in the state police budget. According to the newspaper, Rockefeller's office was informed of the falsified records by state auditors in 1969.

Hugh Morrow, a spokesman for Rockefeller, who served as governor from 1959 to 1973, said: "To the best of Nelson Rockefeller's knowledge, the state police never engaged in any illegal electronic surveillance. . . . If it happened, it was certainly without his knowledge." During his confirmation hearings for the vice presidency, Rockefeller had sworn that "all of these [taps and bugs had been] . . . done with appropriate authorizations by judges."

Two former state police investigators, however, told Newsday that they had tapped the home phone of William Kunstler, an attorney for radical causes, during 1969 without obtaining a court order.

Newsday's sources said illicit eavesdropping became a regular practice in the early 1960s when the Rockefeller administration set up two new units within the state police: the Special Investigations Unit (SIU) and the Special Services branch.

SIU was specifically established to intensify a state attack on organized crime. Reportedly, the unit made extensive use of legal and illegal taps and bugs.

The Special Services branch, Newsday had reported in November 1975, amassed extensive files of noncriminal intelligence data on political dissenters and public officials. It was also reported to have used illegal taps to collect information.

Nixon testifies on taps. In a court deposition released March 10, 1976, ex-President Richard M. Nixon testified under oath that he had ordered telephone wiretaps of 17 government officials and newsmen in 1969 to locate news leaks but that Secretary of State Henry Kissinger, then Nixon's national security adviser, had the responsibility for selecting those to be tapped. The responsibility for carrying out the program lay with then FBI Director J. Edgar Hoover, Nixon said.

The deposition, taken Jan. 15 at Nixon's San Clemente, Calif. house, was filed in U.S. district court in the District of Columbia in a damage suit brought by Morton H. Halperin, a former National Security Council aide and one of the 17 persons tapped. An account of Nixon's testimony had appeared in the New York Times Jan. 18.

In a deposition in the same lawsuit, filed Jan. 12, Kissinger had testified that Nixon had authorized a general program but specifically ordered electronic surveillance on Halperin "and certain others."

(The deposition disclosed Kissinger's practice of having his personal secretaries monitor business telephone calls from his White House office and make summaries of the conversations.)

In other testimony on the topic before the Senate Foreign Relations Committee in July 1973, Kissinger had said he "had no knowledge of when an individual tap was terminated and I was not involved in termination decisions."

In his deposition, Nixon said, "I, of course, did not select the names myself because I did not know [them]. I told Dr. Kissinger that he should inform Mr. Hoover of any names that he considered to be prime suspects." Nixon explained that this included those who had access to the leaked information and those who "had previous records about being loose in their talk."

"It was his [Kissinger's] responsibility not to control the program," Nixon testified, "but solely to furnish the information to Mr. Hoover."

Nixon further stated he had no recollection of Halperin's name "coming up" during the discussion in which the program was authorized.

In other points, Nixon said the final decision on removal of a tap was to be made by himself or Hoover; the material gathered in the taps was shifted from Kissinger to the White House because of the burden of work already on the National Security Council; "there was no political use and no private use" made of the material, "none was intended" and even if there were any misuse of the material it would be difficult to determine whether it was done in "good faith" or not, "whether their motivation was political or whether their motivation was basically the security of the nation."

In defending the program, Nixon said four previous administrations had engaged in such practices; he had been advised it was legal; a foreign policy mission might "take precedence" over an individual's right to privacy; "had we not been able to conduct our policy with some confidentiality, we could not have made the progress that we have made"; and leaked information on the secret U.S. bombing in neutral Cambodia "was directly responsible for the deaths of thousands of Americans because it required the discontinuance of a policy that saved American lives."

Haldeman deposition—Another deposition in the same court case, from former Nixon chief of staff H. R. Haldeman, was filed March 11.

In the 1974 impeachment hearings, it had been disclosed that Haldeman had learned from the Halperin tap that former Defense Secretary Clark M. Clifford was preparing an anti-Nixon article and had suggested a rebuttal.

Queried in the deposition about political use of information from a national security wiretap, Haldeman testified he found nothing improper in such practice and the question of legality had not occurred to him at the time.

Sons of H. L. Hunt acquitted of wiretapping charges. Nelson Bunker and W. Herbert Hunt were acquitted of wiretapping charges in U.S. District Court in Lubbock, Tex. Sept. 26, 1975. The men, sons of H. L. Hunt, the late oil billionaire, and themselves two of the nation's wealthiest men, had admitted hiring detectives to tap their employes but said they did not know at the time that it was against the law to do so.

The trial, which began Sept. 16 after it was transferred from Dallas because of advance publicity, stemmed from the phone tapping, in 1969, of employes of the H. L. H. Food Products Division of the Hunt Oil Company. The detectives, whom the Hunts admitted hiring to determine if any Hunt workers were pilfering funds from the company, were convicted in the case, which dated back to 1969. The Hunts said the pilfering involved a $50 million embezzlement scheme.

After the verdict was announced, the Hunts said they were fortunate to have had the financial means to hire the legal talent necessary to counter the government's case.

Other Developments

CIA aided Washington police. Maurice J. Cullinane, chief of police of Wash-

ington, released a report March 12, 1975 detailing surveillance of civil rights and antiwar groups in the District of Columbia. He also acknowledged that the District police had borrowed from the Central Intelligence Agency (CIA) five automobiles with drivers, seven portable radios and a radio receiver for monitoring major demonstrations in 1969 and 1970. The police maintained individual files on a number of local political activists, including Walter F. Fauntroy, the District's delegate to the House, the report said.

The CIA provided equipment for and training in electronic surveillance, surreptitious entry and lockpicking for Washington, D.C. area police, according to CIA documents reported in the Washington Star Jan. 11, 1976 and the Washington Post Jan. 13. The documents were obtained by the newspapers through requests under the Freedom of Information Act.

One of the documents set forth the reason for the CIA assistance as "the need [of the local police departments] to combat the tangible threats posed by radical terrorist groups within their jurisdiction." It also stated that "the initial request for the above training originated with senior officials of the Washington, D.C., Metropolitan Police Department." However, police officials contacted by the Washington Post said that the CIA had initiated the liaison.

Among the CIA-police activities described in the documents were:

■ Classes given by the CIA in 1967 for police officials of Washington, D.C. and Arlington and Fairfax, Va. on explosives, weaponry, and air and paramilitary operations.

■ The supplying by the CIA to the Washington, D.C. police of radio-equipped vehicles for use during an antiwar demonstration in 1969.

■ CIA classes for 1968–69 for 18 Washington, D.C. police officers on lockpicking, photo surveillance, and surreptitious entry.

■ Requests made to the CIA in 1971 by the Washington, D.C. police for "construction of an audio transmitting device ...identical to items previously supplied the requestor" and for training in telephone taps and disguise techniques.

■ The instruction to a CIA official to meet the former police chief of Fairfax County, William Durrer, in Puerto Rico and furnish him with a rental car paid for by the CIA.

CIA officials, in inter-office memoranda, maintained that the activities described were legal under the Omnibus Crime Control and Safe Streets Act of 1968, although the CIA charter barred it from taking part in domestic law enforcement. Extensive assistance to local police was apparently ended in 1973 because of the publicity generated by disclosures concerning it.

Chicago police kept dossiers. Undercover agents of the Chicago police department infiltrated local community and civil rights groups, and the department's intelligence division kept dossiers on Chicago businessmen, politicians and journalists, the Chicago Daily News reported March 21, 1975. A list of those on whom the police had kept files was obtained by the Daily News from attorneys for a black policeman's organization who had subpoenaed police files in connection with an antidiscrimination suit.

As a result of the disclosures, Cook County State's Attorney Bernard M. Carey, a Republican, ordered a grand jury investigation. Subpoenas were ordered served on James M. Rochford, the police superintendent, and three of his principal deputies by Carey, who said he had learned of police dossiers that had been kept on him and one of his assistants.

Chicago Mayor Richard J. Daley, a Democrat, issued a statement March 21 asserting that he opposed such infiltration practices and that he had been assured by police officials the program had been halted in November 1974.

The Daily News reported undercover police agents had been active in such groups as the Metropolitan Area Housing Alliance, a coalition of community action organizations; People United to Save Humanity (PUSH), which was headed by the Rev. Jesse L. Jackson; the Citizen's Action Program; the Organization for a Better Austin, a neighborhood improvement group, and the Alliance to End Repression, which was involved in cases of alleged police brutality.

One undercover agent, Marcus W. Salone, was so successful that he served as president of the Austin group for two years and led a demonstration in front of Carey's suburban home demanding more vigorous prosecution of slum landlords, Carey said.

Among those on whom the police kept files were Gaylord Freeman, chairman of the First National Bank, and Arthur Woods, chairman of Sears Roebuck & Co., who were reported to have contributed to civil rights groups and political opponents of Mayor Daley; Rev. Theodore Hesburgh, president of Notre Dame (Ind.) University; Gale Sayers, the former Chicago Bears football star; Barnabas Sears, a prominent Chicago lawyer, and State Sen. Richard Newhouse, who ran against Daley in the February 1975 Democratic mayoral primary.

The Chicago Daily News reported April 12 that an Army intelligence unit, working with Chicago police, aided the terrorist activities of a right-wing group that preyed on anti-Vietnam war groups from 1969 to 1971. The terrorists, "who were members of a now-defunct organization known as the Legion of Justice, beat, gassed and wreaked general havoc on members of groups opposed to the Vietnam war," the Daily News said. The paper asserted that Army's 113th Military Intelligence Group headquartered in suburban Evanston supplied the legion with tear gas, mace, and electronic equipment in addition to money.

Los Angeles police data guides. Los Angeles officials April 10, 1975 announced the publication of tentative guidelines designed to limit the collection of information on individuals and groups by the city's police department. Under the guidelines, political beliefs, sexual orientation, drinking habits and "ecological orientation" would no longer be grounds for the police's opening of a file on a person or group.

Samuel L. Williams, president of the police commission, noting that police collection of secret information had begun in the 1920s, stated that in the prior 18 months more than two million cards on 55,000 individuals had been destroyed. He added that data on 2,500 individuals and organizations had been retained.

Mistaken drug raids. Acting on uncorroborated tips, four federal drug agents April 23, 1973 had mistakenly raided the homes of two Collinsville, Ill. families.

Agents from the Office of Drug Abuse Law Enforcement (DALE), with 11 local narcotics officers, knocked down two doors to the apartment occupied by Mr. and Mrs. Herbert Giglotto. The couple was held at gunpoint, while the raiders, who did not identify themselves until the middle of the raid, ransacked drawers and closets, shattered pottery, and threw a television set on the floor. The Giglottos were physically abused and subjected to obscenities from the 15 agents, who were dressed in shabby, "undercover" clothing.

Later that evening a similar raid was carried out against the Collinsville family of Donald Askew.

In both instances the agents operated without authorization from superiors and without search or arrest warrants. No narcotics were uncovered and no arrests were made.

As a result of the raid, the four agents were suspended May 1; however, the Bureau of Narcotics and Dangerous Drugs (BNDD) acknowledged June 15 that the men had been later reinstated and they had taken part in other raids. At the time of the suspension, DALE director Myles J. Ambrose said: "People who use their badge to violate other peoples' constitutional rights are worse than criminals. I have absolutely no intention of whitewashing or absolving them." Ambrose said he had asked appropriate agencies to suspend the local agents who participated.

The Giglottos filed a $1 million damage suit against the federal government May 24, contending the agents had violated their 4th Amendment right to be free from unreasonable searches and seizures. The Askew family previously had announced they had filed a $100,000 suit against the federal government.

A federal grand jury began an inquiry into the raids in early May. The Justice Department's Civil Rights Division entered the case a month later, taking over responsibility for an investigation of the raids from the local DALE office in St. Louis. The Federal Bureau of Investigation entered the case June 18.

Both families complained of harassment after the raids. The Giglottos July 3 announced their intention to move away from downstate Illinois and start a new life. "We just can't take the harassment any more," Herbert Giglotto said.

In a related development, the brother-in-law of a convicted heroin smuggler received a $160,000 settlement June 9 for damage to his Massapequa, N.Y. home by federal drug agents looking for money supposedly hidden there by his brother-in-law.

John Comorti said he protested to agents that he did not have the $4 million they were seeking, but they dug holes in his yard, ripped aluminum siding from his house, ransacked his home's interior and punched holes in the interior walls.

In the Collinsville, Ill. case, however, a federal jury in Alton, Ill. April 2, 1974 acquitted 10 undercover agents involved of charges that they had conspired to deprive the victims of the raids of their civil rights. Subsequently, the Justice Department dropped all other charges stemming from the raids.

The agents built their trial defense on the argument that they had mistakenly raided six homes in three southeastern Illinois communities in the belief that the occupants were armed and dangerous drug dealers and users.

A New York Times survey, made public June 25, 1974, indicated that the Collinsville raids were not isolated incidents but two of numerous "mistaken, violent and often illegal" police raids that occurred across the nation over the past three years. The raids were undertaken by local, state, and federal narcotics officers, all in search of illicit drugs and their dealers.

The Times said that at least four deaths could be attributed to these erroneous raids. In one raid, a policeman was shot to death by a frightened woman whose apartment was broken into by undercover police in search of illegal drugs.

On April 24, 1972, Dirk Dickenson was surprised by an undercover raid on his isolated, northern California mountain cabin. The agents, who sought a "giant" drug-producing lab, arrived on foot and in a borrowed helicopter. Dickenson fled in terror and was fatally shot in the back. No lab was found.

The U.S. attorney in San Francisco later ruled the killing "justifiable homicide," although BNDD rules stipulated that fleeing suspects were not to be shot at.

Bell monitored calls to curb cheating. The Bell Telephone System secretly monitored millions of long-distance phone calls in six cities to curb electronic toll-call frauds, the St. Louis Post-Dispatch reported Feb. 2, 1975. The action, confirmed by company spokesmen, was conducted in St. Louis, New York, Detroit, Miami, Los Angeles and Newark, N.J. over a six-year period ending May 1, 1970. According to the newspaper, more than 30 million calls were monitored in the first four years of the program, which depended upon electronic detection of irregularity, or attempt to bypass toll-charge mechanism through illegal devices known as "blue boxes" or "black boxes" that could cut directly into switching equipment to complete free calls.

If the equipment detected indications of fraud, up to 90 seconds of the conversation were taped and the tapes sent to New York for analysis, according to the report. It said more than 1,500,000 calls were thus partly recorded in four years; fewer than 25,000 of those analyzed indicated fraud and fewer than 500 were confirmed as fraudulent.

The program was said to have been kept secret because of the potential damage by disclosure to the company's public image. In the report and in follow-up reports Feb. 3, William Mullane, press relations director for the American Telephone and Telegraph Co., confirmed the activity, which he said the company did not consider illegal. He said precautions had been taken to isolate the suspected tapes for study only by a small group of trained security personnel. The program was ended, he said, "because we found a better way" to detect use of illegal equipment.

Companies testify in privacy invasion probe. The Privacy Protection Study Commission held hearings Feb. 11-13, 1976 in New York City. Credit and other companies told commission members that records of clients were frequently turned over to government agencies without notification of the disclosure to the clients.

The commission was formed in June 1975 jointly by the executive and legislative branches to determine whether the Privacy Act of 1974 should be extended to nonfederal government and private firms. The act required federal agencies to notify individuals of information held by the agency concerning them, and prohibited the use of the information for other purposes.

Officials of American Express Co. said Feb. 11 that it routinely gave information on clients' credit card use in response to subpoenas of government agencies—the Justice Department, the Internal Revenue Service (IRS), the Immigration Service, and the Drug Enforcement Agency—and of private attorneys on divorce cases.

Rep. Edward Koch (D, N.Y.), a member of the commission, asked why clients were not informed by the company prior to compliance with the subpoenas. Gary Beller, assistant general counsel for American Express, answered, "I can see us getting involved in motions to quash subpoenas. This would add to the cost of our operations."

American Express, however, announced Feb. 13 that it would henceforth give clients prior notice of subpoenas of their records, except when such notice would hinder a felony investigation.

Among other companies that told the commission they gave the government information from their customers' files were American Telephone and Telegraph Co. (AT&T), Atlantic Richfield Co. (ARCO), American Airlines, and Sheraton Hotels.

An AT&T lawyer said Feb. 12 that in less that 25% of the cases where customers' records were subpoenaed were the customers notified before the subpoenas were complied with. He said that company policy was to afford prior notification, but that most cases fell into two "exceptional" categories: those where the Federal Bureau of Investigation, in requesting the records, cited national security, or those where it claimed that disclosure would impede a felony investigation.

AT&T also acknowledged that it did not require subpoenas when the FBI director, his assistant, or a Congressional committee pursuing a formal investigation personally requested records of long-distance calls.

The director of reservations for Sheraton hotels, Edward Prichard, said Feb. 13 that occupant information—sometimes including who was with the occupant—was supplied by phone if held by the central computer. He said only about 30% of reservations, however, were made through the computer, and information about other reservations had to be sought from the individual hotels.

Rep. Bella S. Abzug (D, N.Y.), who supported extension of the privacy act to private companies, said Feb. 12 that one credit bureau, in Nashua, N.H., had tried to make its clients pay a "ransom" for their credit files. She quoted from a letter she said was sent by the bureau to its clients the passage: "We have decided to give you a chance [by paying $7.50] to obtain sole possession of your complete file before it becomes part of a large computerized data bank, which may allow unlimited access by thousands of people."

Bank Secrecy Act upheld. The Supreme Court April 1, 1975 upheld the 1970 Bank Secrecy Act, which gave the government broad access to bank customer records.

Justice William H. Rehnquist, writing for the 6–3 majority, conceded that the authority conferred on the Treasury Department by the act "might well surprise or even shock those who lived in an earlier era . . . ," but he added that "the latter didn't live . . . to see the heavy utilization of our domestic banking system by the minions of organized crime. . . ."

Under regulations established by the Treasury Department, banks were required to record all customer checks and microfilm those over $100, keep records of depositors' identities and all loans over $5,000 except mortgages, and report domestic deposits or withdrawals larger than $10,000 and foreign financial transactions exceeding $5,000. The regulation of foreign transactions was aimed at preventing leakage of untaxed money to secret Swiss bank accounts.

Justices William O. Douglas, William J. Brennan Jr. and Thurgood Marshall dissented. All wrote separate opinions. Calling the Treasury regulations resulting from the act "a sledgehammer approach to a problem that only a delicate scalpel can manage," Douglas warned that a government agent could invade an individual's private life merely by scrutinizing the checks he wrote. Marshall conceded that law enforcement officials would be aided by the "dragnet requirements" of the act, but added, "Those who wrote our Constitution, however, recognized more important values."

Several California banks, which had challenged the act, argued that the domestic reporting requirement violated their rights against unreasonable searches and seizures—a contention rejected by the court majority, which quoted a 1950 court ruling that "neither incorporated nor unincorporated associations can plead an unqualified right to conduct their affairs in secret." The court avoided dealing with similar search and seizure claims by individual depositors, ruling they had failed to prove the reporting requirement would affect them.

Bank data held not private—The Supreme Court ruled, 7–2, April 21, 1976 that individuals could not challenge, on Fourth Amendment grounds, government subpoenas of their bank records. The court's ruling, written by Justice Lewis F. Powell, Jr., said that the "depositor takes the risk, in revealing his affairs to another [i.e., bank employes], that the information will be conveyed by that person to the government."

The ruling, which involved records that banks were obliged to keep under the Bank Secrecy Act of 1970, reinstated the conviction of a Georgia man on charges relating to the operation of an unregistered still.

The decision said that bank records were the property of the bank rather than of the customer. Thus the bank could challenge a government subpoena, but a customer could not. The bank would not have to inform customers of subpoenas of their records, the decision added.

Dissenting from the ruling were Justices William J. Brennan, Jr. and Thurgood Marshall, who reiterated their objections to the Bank Secrecy Act.

School records controversy. A section of the 1974 education law giving parents and students access to confidential school records aroused such opposition from college administrators and teachers that its sponsor, Sen. James L. Buckley (R, N.Y.) agreed to amend it.

Buckley and Sen. Claiborne Pell (D, R.I.), chairman of the Senate Education Subcommittee, said Dec. 4, 1974 that they would introduce amendments to a libraries bill before the House to limit provisions of the Family Educational Rights and Privacy Act, sponsored by Buckley and adopted as an amendment to the Elementary and Secondary Education Act of 1974. The law was signed by President Ford in August and it went into effect Nov. 19.

The so-called "Buckley Amendment" barred federal education aid to institutions or agencies that denied parents the right to inspect and challenge records about their children. This right shifted to the students when they became 18 or entered college.

The amendment was aimed primarily at elementary and secondary schools, and Buckley apparently overlooked its implications for colleges and universities. Campus officials warned in October and November that the law would cause legal and administrative difficulties because it allowed students to see confidential letters of recommendation submitted by teachers and financial statements submitted by parents.

The clarifying legislation was approved by both houses of Congress Dec. 19 and signed by the President Dec. 31.

The clarification barred disclosure to students of medical records, except through a physician chosen by the student. Parental financial records were not required to be disclosed, nor were confidential recommendations pertaining to school or employment applications if the data were received before 1975. A student could waive his right to see data received after Jan. 1, 1975, although he could request the names of these supplying confidential recommendations. The schools were barred from denying admission or benefits to students refusing waiver.

Index